THE
POEM IN
QUESTION

THE POEM IN QUESTION

Robert E. Bourdette, Jr.

University of New Orleans

Michael Cohen

Murray State University

Harcourt Brace Jovanovich, Inc.
New York · San Diego · Chicago · San Francisco · Atlanta
London · Sydney · Toronto

Requests for permission to make copies of any part of the work should
be mailed to: Permissions, Harcourt Brace Jovanovich, Publishers, 757 Third
Avenue, New York, N.Y. 10017.

Copyrights and acknowledgments will be found on pages 462–69, which
constitute a continuation of the copyright page.

ISBN: 0-15-570654-3
Library of Congress Catalog Card Number: 82-83355
Printed in the United States of America

for
Katharine Weston Cohen
and for
Helen, Bob, Sheryl
Dale, Matt, and Dan

Each increases the delight
of "flawed words and stubborn sounds."

PREFACE

Students first embarking on a study of poetry are often understandably baffled. What seems as if it ought to be a natural process of comprehension and enjoyment becomes one of intimidating difficulties. For such readers, *The Poem in Question* provides a practical method of inquiry for getting answers about the meaning of a poem. This approach to poetry begins by encouraging students to focus and refine their own questions about a poem by following them with the questions Who? When? Where? What? How? and Why?—questions that work as well for the reader of poetry as for the reporter, historian, or scientist. Each chapter of *The Poem in Question* provides practice in relating the questions raised by each line of a poem to one of these six organizing questions as a way of getting at the larger issue of what the poem means. The text is suitable for either a one-semester or full-year course in poetry, for introductory literature courses, or as a supplement to accompany a chronological anthology of poems. Because it is also a basic guide to reading poetry, the book can also be used independently.

The approach of *The Poem in Question* derives from certain fundamental assumptions about poetry. The first is that poetry is more like other forms of communication than unlike them. Poems resemble love letters, cries for help, words of advice, stories, jokes, conversations, speeches, philosophical essays, arguments, reveries, and reports of strange, wonderful, or horrible experiences. We make sense of poems in the same way that we make sense of these other things. What poetry shares with them—what makes it accessible to us and responsive to our questions—is its human origin.

This book also assumes that a poem is not an isolated artifact, but something that at every point touches individual experience and the world around. Poetry does not need special procedures to enable us to understand it; we measure it against our own lives—and our own lives are measured against poetry. A poem's integral connection with life—with science and art, with politics and sports, with gossip and philosophy—is emphasized in this book. To explore these connections, the reader proceeds from the lines on the page to the world itself, seeking information outside the poem. The questioning method in this book enables students to recognize when such investigation is essential and it provides clues about where to begin the search.

Each chapter incorporates these assumptions about poetry while exploring a single question (such as "Who is speaking?") and illustrates, through an extended reading of at least one poem and a variety of additional examples, the discoveries about a poem's meaning to which the question leads. The extensive exercises and the writing assignments in each chapter continue the focus on the chapter's particular question. Succeeding chapters are incremental, drawing on the poems of previous chapters and showing how they can be illuminated by new perspectives and questions. A final chapter specifically addresses the special questions raised in reading modern poetry.

The following features of *The Poem in Question* should be noted:
1. Each poem includes the date of publication and glosses of words, phrases, and allusions not readily found in a desk dictionary.
2. A section of poems for further reading is included, with no commentary and only minimal glossing.
3. Half the poems in the book were written in the twentieth century; the other half include the standard favorite selections from the past.
4. The text gives special attention to the problem of reading longer poems, with more than a dozen included in the discussions and exercises; in addition, the anthology section includes a generous selection of longer poems.
5. In addition to the two writing suggestions in each chapter, an appendix on writing about poetry offers guidelines, suggestions, and two complete sample essays, one a close reading ("To an Athlete Dying Young"), the other a documented research essay ("Ozymandias").
6. A glossary and a selective bibliography are included.

This book has acquired debts to our students, colleagues, friends and relations, that no acknowledgment can adequately word or repay. Since the idea for the book originated in classroom discussion, our students deserve our first and deepest gratitude. Our colleagues willingly and patiently listened to us, argued with us, found us poems and pointed out our errors. We thank most particularly Michael Bellamy, Stevan Dittman, Roy Helton, Richard Levin, Michael Mooney, Mary Wagoner, and James T. Watt. For their helpful comments and suggestions, we also thank the following reviewers of the manuscript: R. H. Deutsch, California State University, Northridge; Oliver H. Evans, Western Michigan University; Robert Foxworthy, Fullerton College; Frank E. Garratt, Jr., Tacoma Community College; B. J. Leggett, University of Tennessee, Knoxville; George S. Lensing, University of North Carolina, Chapel Hill; Joseph F. Trimmer, Ball State University; and Suzanne Wolkenfeld. David Earnest, Mary FitzGerald, John Gery, Mavis Goodheart, Don and Artie Hedrick, Richard LeMon, Gene and Louise Miller, Raeburn Miller, Branimir and Marilyn Rieger, Richard Steiger, Kip Steinkamp, Barry Wade, Richard Weaver, David Wilson, and Deb and Edith Wylder helped and encouraged us. Colin, Susan, and Freda Leakey, Bernard and Angela Levy, and the Honorable Paul and Nell Martin provided hospitality and cogent criticism while parts of this book were being written. Grants from Murray State University and the University of New Orleans Liberal Arts Research Fund aided in the research and typing expenses. For clerical help, our thanks to Matthew and Daniel Cohen, Jamie Helton, Eileen Long, and Suzanne Shelton Hill. At Harcourt Brace Jovanovich, Drake Bush and Joe Bennett first saw merit in this text and encouraged us in its development; our thanks to them, to Eben W. Ludlow, and especially to our editors, Paul Nockleby and Natalie Bowen.

Robert E. Bourdette, Jr.
Michael Cohen

CONTENTS

Contents

Contents

IV
HOW? 213

Contents

Contents

VI
POEMS FOR FURTHER READING 351

Contents

It is hard to talk about a poem,
for talking about poetry leads
you out in every direction. I do
not see the art of poetry as
separated from life.
　—*Louis Simpson*

That is the essence of science:
ask an impertinent question, and you
are on the way to the
pertinent answer.
　—*J. Bronowski*

One poem proves another and the whole. . . .
　—*Wallace Stevens*

PART

I

SOME IMPORTANT QUESTIONS

CHAPTER ONE

DOES A POEM HAVE MEANING?
CAN WE DISCOVER IT?

A poem, Robert Frost once said, begins in delight and ends in wisdom. But learning to read poems can too often be an experience that begins in irritation and ends in confusion. Part of the irritation is caused by poetry's seeming so unlike more familiar patterns of daily speech and writing. Poems often don't seem to make sense—they don't seem to have any meaning.

The appearance of poems *can* be strange and puzzling. They may contain unfamiliar words or, what may be more baffling, familiar words used in quite strange ways:

> Inside the veins there are navies setting forth
> —Robert Bly, from "Waking from Sleep"

Poems can serve up letters that do not seem, at first, to form words at all:

> l(a
>
> le
> af
> fa
>
> ll
>
> s)
> one
> l
>
> iness

> —E. E. Cummings, "l(a"

3

4

**Does a Poem Have Meaning?
Can We Discover It?**

They can contain strange patterns of lines on the page:

> Constantly risking absurdity
> > and death
> whenever he performs
> > above the heads
> > > of his audience

> —Lawrence Ferlinghetti, from
> "Constantly Risking Absurdity"

Sometimes they can seem complete nonsense:

> Toltex by Mixtex Mixtex by Aztex
> Aztex by Spanishtex Spanishtex by Mexitex
> by Mexitex   by Mexitex   by Texaco

> —Earle Birney, from "Irapuato"

Puzzlement at encountering such lines is further increased by people—poets and critics and teachers—who act as if such things were perfectly clear, who talk about the meanings of these poems without providing any clues about how they were derived. And when different, even contradictory, meanings are attached to the same poem by several of these critics or teachers, you may be left with the sense that there is no necessary connection between the poem and its alleged meaning. Does it mean anything? Does it mean everything?

Even if you are willing to grant that a poem has meaning, you may be hesitant about asking the questions that naturally occur in reading because such questions suggest that you have missed what others seem to understand. You may be irritated about the very need to ask questions because it seems poems ought to communicate what they mean without all the difficulties. Thus irritation gives way to confusion. Where is that delight and wisdom of a poem that Robert Frost described and how do you share in it?

The answer begins by taking your own questions *seriously*. This is what the scientist J. Bronowski was getting at in his book *The Ascent of Man* when he wrote, "Ask an impertinent question, and you are on the way to the pertinent answer." This is the best way to discover the apparent mysteries of science and the world, as well as poetry. A first impertinent—and important—question about poetry might well be, "Is there any reassurance that a poem *has* meaning?"

IS THERE MEANING?

As long as we are not talking about "poems" written by computers or by chimpanzees banging indiscriminately on typewriters, you can be sure that any poem you encounter was written by a person like yourself, that it was written at a particular time and place, and that it is written in language. All these things guarantee that the poem is about some human concerns—concerns which you can recognize and share. Given that human dimension—a speaker, a point in time, a surrounding landscape, a psychological context, a sense of voice and tone—those words, no matter how mysterious they may seem, fit into their places like pieces of a puzzle, revealing a design that connects with your interests and concerns and curiosities.

Poetry is much more like other kinds of human discourse—writing or talking or winking or shrugging—than it is unlike them. Poems are not laundry lists or love letters, but they are *like* laundry lists and love letters—and cries for help and diary entries and words of advice and stories and jokes and conversations and speeches and philosophic essays and arguments and reports of strange, wonderful, and horrible experiences. The meaning of poems is as various as the meaning of these human occurrences because meaning is not always something we can put into a paraphrase.

Some poems are more obviously like ordinary discourse than others:

ORDER IN THE STREETS
(from instructions printed on a child's toy,
Christmas 1968, as reported in the *New York Times*)

    1. 2. 3.
    Switch on.

    Jeep rushes
    to the scene
    of riot   5

    Jeep goes
    in all directions
    by mystery action.

    Jeep stops periodically
    to turn hood over   10

Does a Poem Have Meaning?
Can We Discover It?

machine gun appears
with realistic
shooting noise.

After putting down riot,
jeep goes   15
back to the headquarters.

1969
Donald Justice (b. 1925)

Such a poem is a direct piece of human communication—the imperfectly
translated directions for a toy. Imagine the following poem as a note taped to
a refrigerator door:

THIS IS JUST TO SAY

I have eaten
the plums
that were in
the icebox

and which   5
you were probably
saving
for breakfast

forgive me
they were delicious   10
so sweet
and so cold

1934
William Carlos Williams
(1883–1963)

In these poems the record of experience is very straightforward. Donald Justice
has arranged what he found printed on a toy jeep into a poem, and William
Carlos Williams reports a theft of some plums with direct language. When
John Keats made a poetic record of something that actually happened to him—

going out on a fine autumn day—it came out somewhat transformed. Here is the experience as he described it in a letter to a friend:

> How beautiful the season is now—How fine the air. A temperate sharpness about it. Really, without joking, chaste weather—Dian skies—I never lik'd stubble-fields so much as now—Aye better than the chilly green of the Spring. Somehow a stubble-plain looks warm—in the same way that some pictures look warm—This struck me so much in my Sunday's walk that I composed upon it.

(September 21, 1819)

And here is the poem he made of that experience:

TO AUTUMN

1

Season of mists and mellow fruitfulness,
   Close bosom-friend of the maturing sun;
Conspiring with him how to load and bless
   With fruit the vines that round the thatch-eves run;
To bend with apples the moss'd cottage-trees   5
   And fill all fruit with ripeness to the core;
     To swell the gourd, and plump the hazel shells
   With a sweet kernel; to set budding more,
And still more, later flowers for the bees,
Until they think warm days will never cease,   10
     For Summer has o'er-brimm'd their clammy cells.

2

Who hath not seen thee oft amid thy store?
   Sometimes whoever seeks abroad may find
Thee sitting careless on a granary floor,
   Thy hair soft-lifted by the winnowing wind;   15
Or on a half-reap'd furrow sound asleep,
   Drows'd with the fume of poppies, while thy hook
     Spares the next swath and all its twinéd flowers:
And sometimes like a gleaner thou dost keep
   Steady thy laden head across a brook;   20
   Or by a cyder-press, with patient look,
     Thou watchest the last oozings hour by hour.

8

**Does a Poem Have Meaning?
Can We Discover It?**

3

Where are the songs of Spring? Ay, where are they?
   Think not of them, thou hast thy music too,—
While barréd clouds bloom the soft-dying day,   25
   And touch the stubble-plains with rosy hue;
Then in a wailful choir the small gnats mourn
   Among the river sallows, borne aloft
      Or sinking as the light wind lives or dies;
And full-grown lambs loud bleat from hilly bourn;   30
   Hedge-crickets sing; and now with treble soft
   The red-breast whistles from a garden-croft;
      And gathering swallows twitter in the skies.

                                   1820
John Keats (1795–1821)

Poetry like this is a reaction to life, an attempt to convey to others the poet's thoughts, feelings, and attitudes. If it were not meant to convey some meaning, there would be little point in it. The human senses, feelings, and thought processes we share with poets are all guarantees that what they write can mean something to us.

But sometimes the poet seems to be translating events into another language—talking about one kind of experience as if it were another:

THE POISON TREE

I was angry with my friend,
I told my wrath, my wrath did end;
I was angry with my foe,
I told it not, my wrath did grow.

And I watered it in fears,   5
Night and morning with my tears;
And I sunned it with smiles
And with soft deceitful wiles.

And it grew both day and night,
Till it bore an apple bright;   10
And my foe beheld it shine,
And knew that it was mine.

And into my garden stole
When the night had veiled the pole:
In the morning glad I see   15
My foe outstretched beneath the tree.

1794
William Blake (1757–1827)

The second stanza begins "And I watered it in fears" (a STANZA is a group of lines forming one unit or division of a poem). When we read this line, we may realize that Blake (or his speaker) is talking about his anger, but he is now speaking of it as a tree. This kind of comparison or translation of one thing into another without the use of *like* or *as* is called METAPHOR, and it is basic to poetry. But metaphor is also one of the things that makes the reading of poetry difficult at times. Despite the metaphor, or rather *through* it, Blake is still talking about human experience. If he did not actually kill someone with concealed anger, he knew what it is to let anger poison a friendship (notice how natural it is to slip into metaphor in ordinary language: "to *poison* a friendship"). It is obvious that Blake is talking about real human concerns we can readily understand: what happens when we conceal anger instead of talking about it. But in many poems the metaphor or indirect ways of saying things can be much more difficult to understand. In such cases, we need to have confidence that a poem is ultimately understandable because it was written by a man or a woman, but we also need a method to get at its meaning. And that necessity leads to our next important question.

HOW CAN MEANING BE DISCOVERED?

Suppose that you are willing to give a poem the benefit of the doubt; you assume that it does have meaning or meanings. How are you to get at it? Is there a method to follow? Let us look at an example and see how we might proceed:

THE GARDEN

en robe de parade—Samain

Like a skein of loose silk blown against a wall,
She walks by the railing of a path in Kensington Gardens,

---

en robe de parade: dressed for a great occasion. Pound's use of the French poet Albert Samain's phrase is called an EPIGRAPH: a quotation at the beginning of a poem or other work that relates in some way to the subject of the poem.

And she is dying piece-meal
    of a sort of emotional anemia.

And round about there is a rabble   5
Of the filthy, sturdy, unkillable infants of the very poor.
They shall inherit the earth.

In her is the end of breeding.
Her boredom is exquisite and excessive.
She would like some one to speak to her,   10
And is almost afraid that I
    will commit that indiscretion.

                    1916

Ezra Pound (1885–1972)

    If you had trouble grasping this poem, it may have been because unfamiliar details puzzled you. At the same time, whatever familiar details you were able to recognize claimed your attention. Confronted with confusing details, you will naturally fasten on things that seem to make sense—to make this search for the familiar. But doing so carries a danger. If you make a pattern of meaning using only the recognizable details of a poem, you can easily misread. Making your own poem out of only part of the lines on the page can lead to frustration and complete misunderstanding.

    We can illustrate this problem, using "The Garden" as an example. Reader A is puzzled by the poem. Her eye catches the word "dying" in the third line. That at least is a recognizable idea and might be a clue to what the poem is about. Almost without realizing it, Reader A begins to overemphasize other words that somehow seem associated with the idea of dying: "anemia," "unkillable infants," "end of breeding," "boredom," "afraid" all leap out at her. Using these associated words as clues, she decides that the poem is about a woman who is dying of anemia, probably brought on by having too many children. The woman is obviously poor, she can't have any more children, and she is bored. Because she is dying, the woman in the poem is naturally afraid.

    Reader B is also puzzled by "The Garden," but he spots the familiar word "emotional," which looks like a good clue to the meaning of the poem. He reorganizes the poem around that word and others he associates with it: "loose silk," "gardens," "sturdy infants," "exquisite," "indiscretion." For him, the poem is about a woman, gowned elegantly in loose silk, who is walking in a garden. She is an emotional person, moved by all the sturdy infants around her. She is obviously in love with someone and is about to commit an indiscretion with her approaching lover.

    These two examples exaggerate misreadings of "The Garden," but they show a real danger. In each version significant details have been left out or ignored and others given too much importance. How do you learn to avoid these traps and to keep each possible meaning of the poem from taking over until you have looked at everything? If it is important to pay attention to the context of *all* the words and come up with an intelligent appreciation of what the poem might mean, then it is reasonable to ask exactly how you might proceed.

Questioning Line by Line

The comprehensive question "What does the poem mean?" is of little help because it is too broad and too unfocused. We need to ask the more specific questions that occur—very often subconsciously—as we read. We need to make these subconscious questions explicit. Look, for example, at the first line of Pound's poem:

> Like a skein of loose silk blown against a wall.

As we read this line for the first time, we don't know what this poem is going to be about, what the poet is up to, or why the poem is starting off with this odd comparison. Even if we glance through the poem, we may be in doubt as to the answers to all these reasonable questions. But this first line prompts a specific question: Who or what is "like a skein of loose silk blown against a wall"? And this specific question might be even further refined: Why does the poet use those particular words—"loose silk," "blown against a wall"?

By asking such questions, we become aware that the poet is making a very specific comparison, and we are ready to ask further questions about the significance of this SIMILE (a comparison using *like* or *as*). By asking these questions, we are better able to recognize answers when they appear and to actively look for more. If we didn't ask the questions, we would just be puzzled. Having asked them, we realize, as we read the second line of the poem, that at least one of our questions has been answered:

> Like a skein of loose silk blown against a wall,
> *She* walks by the railing of a path in Kensington Gardens.

This simple question "Who?" and its answer have taken us at least part way into the larger meaning of the poem. We now know that a "she" is being talked about and that this figure is being described in a peculiar way.

The simile which compares the "she" of line 2 to a "skein of loose silk blown against a wall" is one example of FIGURATIVE LANGUAGE; Blake's metaphor of a poison tree is another. In figurative language, comparisons are frequent. In LITERAL LANGUAGE, words are taken to be exactly what they mean. The sentence "He is a skunk," understood in its literal sense, means "He is

12

**Does a Poem Have Meaning?
Can We Discover It?**

that black-and-white furred animal that produces a stinking smell." Figurative language, on the other hand, involves the use of words in their connotative sense: the words make a comparison or analogy. The sentence "He is a skunk," understood in its figurative sense, means that "He is like a skunk because his actions are terrible; they stink!" In most poems, figurative and literal language occur together:

> *figurative:* [She is] Like a skein of loose silk blown against a wall.
> *literal:* She walks by the railing of a path in Kensington Gardens.

As we proceed into "The Garden," the details become more involved, and specific questions will be all the more useful. The name "Kensington Gardens" gives us an answer to questions we might have asked about the title of the poem—"What garden? Where?" We are now given a location for the events of the poem. Yet this reference to place prompts some other questions. Where is Kensington Gardens? Why does the poet refer to this place? Is this place significant?

The very first question we asked—Who or what is like a skein of loose silk blown against a wall?—was answered simply by moving to the next line of the poem. Many questions will be answered in just this way. Occasionally, however, we will have to go outside the poem for an answer. The question about Kensington Gardens is an example. The poem is called "The Garden," and a specific garden is named. But there is nothing further in the poem to gloss (explain) the reference to Kensington Gardens. For an answer to this particular question we need to go outside the poem—to a gazetteer, a map, atlas, or dictionary. But until we start asking explicit questions we won't be finding *any* answers inside or outside the poem.

Lines 3–4 give additional information about the "she" of the poem:

> And she is dying piece-meal
> of a sort of emotional anemia.

As we read the first line of the poem, we asked about the significance of the simile. Why does the poet compare her to "a skein of loose silk blown against a wall"? Why "*loose* silk"? Why "loose silk *blown against a wall*"? Would another simile do as well? Why not, for example, "sturdy burlap"? We are now prepared to ask a series of questions about the words of the simile and how they connect to the description of the "she" as "dying piece-meal / of a sort of emotional anemia."

The questioning process applied to the opening lines of Pound's "The Garden" may seem almost too simple. Your eye, no doubt, had already caught the word "she" in the second line even as you read the first; you may have known that Kensington Gardens is in London; you may have already begun to relate the simile to the rest of the poem. But slowing down the mental process enables us to see the steps by which we ask questions and find answers. We can then apply this process when the subject matter is much more complicated and difficult.

Finish reading "The Garden," asking questions line by line. Jot them down. Exercise O, at the end of the chapter, gives a line-by-line set of questions which you may wish to discuss and argue about after you have made your own list.

Organizing Questions

After listing your own questions or looking at the list of questions in Exercise O, you may be struck with some terrifying thoughts. Each line of a poem prompts many questions; a whole poem will generate a host of questions. How do you tackle them all? Which are the more important? How does each of them relate to the meaning of the whole poem? What we need is a way to group the questions so that we can move from individual lines to the meaning of the entire poem. What we need, in other words, is a scheme to organize our questions.

The meaning of a poem is its human dimension: poetry communicates experiences, feelings, and ideas through recognizable human elements—through speakers and settings and times. We may not immediately recognize exactly who is speaking or where or when, but we can ask questions about these things. And these questions will group and organize our other questions prompted by each line of the poem.

(1) Who is the speaker and of what importance is the speaker to what is being said in the poem?
(2) When do the poem's events occur? Is the time given—in clock time or seasons or ages of man? Is there a sequence or change of time in the poem?
(3) Where does the poem take place and how is that setting significant to the poem?

Many of the questions we asked about "The Garden" can be grouped under a general question about speaker. It isn't until the next to last line (11) that we discover all of the poem is being spoken to us by a narrator or speaker who is not only observing and describing the woman, but is directly involved:

> She would like some one to speak to her
> And is almost afraid that I
> will commit that indiscretion.

Who is this speaker? What is the speaker's attitude toward the woman? These questions give direction to the previous questions about why she is described in that peculiar way. The narrator's attitude is being revealed through the comparison of her to loose silk, the mention of emotional anemia, and so on. Asking who is speaking in this poem helps organize many of the line-by-line questions. In the next chapter we will return to "The Garden" and explore this first question further.

Asking questions provides a way into the mystery of poetry. "Learning the secret of flight from a bird was a good deal like learning the secret of magic from a magician," Orville Wright said. "After you once know the trick and know what to look for, you see things that you did not notice when you did not know exactly what to look for."

Asking questions is at least one of the tricks.

EXERCISES

A.   WAKING FROM SLEEP

Inside the veins there are navies setting forth,
Tiny explosions at the water lines,
And seagulls weaving in the wind of the salty blood.

It is the morning. The country has slept the whole winter.
Window seats were covered with fur skins, the yard was full   5
Of stiff dogs, and hands that clumsily held heavy books.

Now we wake, and rise from bed, and eat breakfast!—
Shouts rise from the harbor of the blood,
Mists, and masts rising, the knock of wooden tackle in the sunlight.

Now we sing, and do tiny dances on the kitchen floor.   10
Our whole body is like a harbor at dawn;
We know that our master has left us for the day.

1962
Robert Bly (b. 1926)

1. In the first line, how does Bly use both literal and figurative language? What is unusual about the first line of the poem?
2. How do the other lines help to explain this curious first line?
3. Where in the poem is there a metaphor that helps explain the meaning of line 1? Where is there a simile that extends the metaphor's comparison?
4. How does the title aid us in understanding the metaphors used in the poem?
5. How are the words "country" and "winter" in stanza 2 related to the poem's other comparisons?

B.   l(a

l(a

le
af
fa

ll   5

s)
one
l

iness

1958
E. E. Cummings (1895–1963)

1. None of the individual lines of this poem makes sense by itself. Line 5 might be the number 11, line 7 the word "one," and line 8 might be the number 1. Is this a poem about numbers?
2. Write the poem out, all on a single horizontal line. What does this rearrangement reveal?
3. How do the division of words and the vertical appearance of the poem as Cummings wrote it embody its meaning?
4. Why is the one line of the poem that is a recognizable word—"one"— isolated as it is?

C.   **CONSTANTLY RISKING ABSURDITY**

Constantly risking absurdity
                    and death
        whenever he performs
                    above the heads
                                of his audience   5
        the poet like an acrobat
                    climbs on rime
                        to a high wire of his own making
        and balancing on eyebeams
                            above a sea of faces   10
                paces his way
                    to the other side of day

16

**Does a Poem Have Meaning?
Can We Discover It?**

performing entrechats
          and sleight-of-foot tricks
and other high theatrics   15
          and all without mistaking
    any thing
          for what it may not be
  for he's the super realist
          who must perforce perceive   20
    taut truth
          before the taking of each stance or step
in his supposed advance
          toward the still higher perch
where Beauty stands and waits   25
      with gravity
          to start her death-defying leap
  And he
    a little charleychaplin man
          who may or may not catch   30
    her fair eternal form
          spreadeagled in the empty air
    of existence

                     1958
        Lawrence Ferlinghetti (b. 1919)

1. Only the first five lines of this poem were printed earlier in the chapter because the next few lines reveal something about the reason for the pattern of lines in the poem. How does the arrangement of lines support the central metaphor Ferlinghetti uses to describe the poet?
2. What are some of the precise phrases that link "acrobat" and "poet"?
3. Look at the phrase "balancing on eyebeams" (line 9). How does it describe what the poet does? How does this same phrase describe what the arrangement of lines on the page does?

D.   **IRAPUATO**

For reasons any
      brigadier
          could tell
  this is a favourite

---

entrechat: a difficult leap in ballet during which the dancer crosses the feet a number of times.

         nook   5
                  for massacre
      Toltex by Mixtex Mixtex by Aztex
      Aztex by Spanishtex Spanishtex by Mexitex
      by Mexitex   by Mexitex   by Texaco

      So any farmer can see how the strawberries   10
      are the biggest
                    and reddest
                         in the whole damn continent
      but why
                    when arranged   15
                        under the market flies
      do they look like small clotting hearts?

                                                   1955
                                    Earle Birney (b. 1904)

1. The usual spellings of the words in stanza 2 are Toltecs, Mixtecs, Aztecs, Spanish, and Mexicans. What syllables, as Birney alters these words, do these words have in common? How does this common element lead up to the one unaltered word in the passage—"Texaco"?
2. The first six lines of the poem make a statement. How do the next three lines illustrate that statement?
3. What is the relationship of the simile that Birney uses in the last line to the statement and illustration in the first nine lines?

E. In the directions printed on a child's toy, Donald Justice found a poem (p. 5). In the words that people write or say as ordinary prose, we can often recognize just such a pattern—a ready-made poem, in fact. For example, an Englishman, William Whewell, wrote a textbook, *An Elementary Treatise on Mechanics* (1819), in which this sentence appears:

   And hence no force, however great, can stretch a cord, however fine, into a horizontal line which is accurately straight.

Sometime later, at a dinner honoring Whewell, a friend of his asked the audience if anyone knew the author of the following poetic stanza:

         And hence no force, however great,
            Can stretch a cord, however fine,
            Into a horizontal line
         That shall be absolutely straight.

18

**Does a Poem Have Meaning?
Can We Discover It?**

The friend had found a poem in Whewell's prose by altering only the last clause of Whewell's original sentence. According to Martin Gardner, who tells this story in his column "Mathematical Puzzles" in *Scientific American* (September 1979, p. 28), Whewell was not much amused at the discovery, and when he brought out the next edition of his book, he altered the passage to avoid the accidental poem.

1. What, besides rhyme, gives Whewell's lines a pattern?
2. Why did the friend feel the need to alter the last phrase of the original sentence?
3. Look at printed material—everything from cereal boxes to newspapers— and try to find examples of accidental patterns of rhyme or rhythm or parallel phrases.

F. Here is a poem made out of ordinary, even very colloquial, conversation:

UNCLE IV SURVEYS HIS DOMAIN FROM HIS ROCKER OF A SUNDAY AFTERNOON AS AUNT DORY STARTS TO CHOP KINDLING

Mister Williams
lets youn me move
tother side the house

the woman
choppin woods
mite nigh the awkerdist thing
I seen

1969
Jonathan Williams (b. 1929)

1. What about this isolated piece of conversation makes it different from any other sentence—for example, "How are you, Mr. Williams, and what did you have for lunch today?"
2. What is it about these words and their arrangement that gives you a sense of the speaker and his world?

G. In this chapter, we saw how a poem—as in the Keats example—can grow out of actual experience. In the following example, Dorothy Wordsworth (1771–1855) wrote in her journal impressions of a walk in the English Lake District:

When we were in the woods beyond Gowbarrow Park we saw a few daffodils close to the water-side. We fancied that the lake had floated the seeds ashore, and that the little colony had so sprung up. But as we went along there were more and yet more; and at last, under the boughs of the trees, we saw that there was a long belt of them along the shore, about the breadth of a country turnpike road. I never saw daffodils so beautiful. They grew among the mossy stones about and about them; some rested their heads upon these stones as on a pillow for weariness; and the rest tossed and reeled and danced, and seemed as if they verily laughed with the wind that blew upon them over the lake; they looked so gay, ever glancing, ever changing. This wind blew directly over the lake to them. There was here and there a little knot, and a few stragglers a few yards higher up; but they were so few as not to disturb the simplicity, unity, and life of that one busy highway.

(April 15, 1802)

Her brother, William, turned that experience into a poem:

I WANDERED LONELY AS A CLOUD

I wandered lonely as a cloud
That floats on high o'er vales and hills,
When all at once I saw a crowd,
A host, of golden daffodils;
Beside the lake, beneath the trees,   5
Fluttering and dancing in the breeze.

Continuous as the stars that shine
And twinkle on the milky way,
They stretched in never-ending line
Along the margin of a bay: 10
Ten thousand saw I at a glance,
Tossing their heads in sprightly dance.

The waves beside them danced; but they
Out-did the sparkling waves in glee:
A poet could not but be gay,   15
In such a jocund company:
I gazed—and gazed—but little thought
What wealth the show to me had brought:

For oft, when on my couch I lie
In vacant or in pensive mood, 20
They flash upon that inward eye
Which is the bliss of solitude;
And then my heart with pleasure fills,
And dances with the daffodils.

1807
William Wordsworth (1770–1850)

1. What details of the actual experience are not included in the poem?
2. What details are in the poem that are not in the prose account?

H. METAPHORS

I'm a riddle in nine syllables,
An elephant, a ponderous house,
A melon strolling on two tendrils.
O red fruit, ivory, fine timbers!
This loaf's big with its yeasty rising. 5
Money's new-minted in this fat purse.
I'm a means, a stage, a cow in calf.
I've eaten a bag of green apples,
Boarded the train there's no getting off.

1960
Sylvia Plath (1932–1963)

1. We know from the title that the various things mentioned in the poem are
   metaphors. We also know from the first line that the poem is a riddle. So,
   two important questions are, "Why does the speaker apply these metaphors
   to herself?" and "What is the answer to the riddle?"
2. Read through the metaphors and make a list of the qualities they suggest.
   Pay special attention to the adjectives.
3. Note that the poem has nine lines and each line has nine syllables. What
   is the significance of the number 9 in the structure of the poem? How does
   this number reinforce the answer to the riddle?

I. THE HEAVY BEAR

"the withness of the body"—Whitehead

The heavy bear who goes with me,
A manifold honey to smear his face,

The Heavy Bear

Clumsy and lumbering here and there,
The central ton of every place,
The hungry beating brutish one   5
In love with candy, anger, and sleep,
Crazy factotum, dishevelling all,
Climbs the building, kicks the football,
Boxes his brother in the hate-ridden city.

Breathing at my side, that heavy animal,   10
That heavy bear who sleeps with me,
Howls in his sleep for a world of sugar,
A sweetness intimate as the water's clasp,
Howls in his sleep because the tight-rope
Trembles and shows the darkness beneath.   15
—The strutting show-off is terrified,
Dressed in his dress-suit, bulging his pants,
Trembles to think that his quivering meat
Must finally wince to nothing at all.

That inescapable animal walks with me,   20
Has followed me since the black womb held,
Moves where I move, distorting my gesture,
A caricature, a swollen shadow,
A stupid clown of the spirit's motive,
Perplexes and affronts with his own darkness,   25
The secret life of belly and bone,
Opaque, too near, my private, yet unknown,
Stretches to embrace the very dear
With whom I would walk without him near,
Touches her grossly, although a word   30
Would bare my heart and make me clear,
Stumbles, flounders, and strives to be fed
Dragging me with him in his mouthing care,
Amid the hundred million of his kind,
The scrimmage of appetite everywhere.   35

1938
Delmore Schwartz (1913–1966)

1. How does the *epigraph* of this poem focus attention on the fact that the
   words "the heavy bear" are being used metaphorically?

22

**Does a Poem Have Meaning?
Can We Discover It?**

2. Is the comparison aimed at things the speaker likes about the body or things he dislikes?
3. What different aspects of the comparison are emphasized in each stanza?

J. Besides metaphor and simile, figurative language includes other comparative devices. Two of these are PERSONIFICATION, the treatment of an inanimate object or quality as if it were alive or human (Lady Luck); and METONYMY, the representation of something by one of its parts ("Give us a hand!") or by something closely associated with it ("The Pentagon announced today . . ."). Find examples of metaphor, simile, personification, and metonymy in the following poem by Lord Byron; then read the next poem, in which Ogden Nash comments on the use of figurative language.

THE DESTRUCTION OF SENNACHERIB

1

The Assyrian came down like the wolf on the fold,
And his cohorts were gleaming in purple and gold;
And the sheen of their spears was like stars on the sea,
When the blue wave rolls nightly on deep Galilee.

2

Like the leaves of the forest when summer is green,   5
That host with their banners at sunset were seen:
Like the leaves of the forest when autumn hath blown,
That host on the morrow lay withered and strown.

3

For the Angel of Death spread his wings on the blast,
And breathed in the face of the foe as he passed;   10
And the eyes of the sleepers waxed deadly and chill,
And their hearts but once heaved, and forever grew still!

4

And there lay the steed with his nostril all wide,
But through it there rolled not the breath of his pride;
And the foam of his gasping lay white on the turf,   15
And cold as the spray of the rock-beating surf.

---

destruction of Sennacherib: an episode in Palestinian history detailed in 2 Chronicles 32.

5

And there lay the rider distorted and pale,
With the dew on his brow, and the rust on his mail:
And the tents were all silent, the banners alone,
The lances unlifted, the trumpet unblown.   20

6

And the widows of Ashur are loud in their wail,
And the idols are broke in the temple of Baal;
And the might of the Gentile, unsmote by the sword,
Hath melted like snow in the glance of the Lord!

1815

George Gordon, Lord Byron (1788–1824)

VERY LIKE A WHALE

One thing that literature would be greatly the better for
Would be a more restricted employment by authors of simile
    and metaphor.
Authors of all races, be they Greeks, Roman, Teutons or Celts,
Can't seem just to say that anything is the thing it is but have to
    go out of their way to say that it is like something else.
What does it mean when we are told   5
That the Assyrian came down like a wolf on the fold?
In the first place, George Gordon Byron had had enough
    experience
To know that it probably wasn't just one Assyrian, it was a lot of
    Assyrians.
However, as too many arguments are apt to induce apoplexy and
    thus hinder longevity,
We'll let it pass as one Assyrian for the sake of brevity.   10
Now then, this particular Assyrian, the one whose cohorts were
    gleaming in purple and gold,
Just what does the poet mean when he says he came down like a
    wolf on the fold?
In heaven and earth more than is dreamed of in our philosophy
    there are a great many things,

---

very like a whale: Nash's title is from *Hamlet* (III, ii), a scene in which Hamlet, pretending
madness in front of Polonius, compares the shape of a cloud to a whale.

**Does a Poem Have Meaning?
Can We Discover It?**

But I don't imagine that among them there is a wolf with purple
    and gold cohorts or purple and gold anythings.
No, no, Lord Byron, before I'll believe that this Assyrian was   15
    actually like a wolf I must have some kind of proof;
Did he run on all fours and did he have a hairy tail and a big
    red mouth and big white teeth and did he say Woof woof
    woof?
Frankly I think it very unlikely, and all you were entitled to say,
    at the very most,
Was that the Assyrian cohorts came down like a lot of Assyrian
    cohorts about to destroy the Hebrew host.
But that wasn't fancy enough for Lord Byron, oh dear me no, he
    had to invent a lot of figures of speech and then interpolate
    them,
With the result that whenever you mention Old Testament   20
    soldiers to people they say Oh yes, they're the ones that a lot
    of wolves dressed up in gold and purple ate them
That's the kind of thing that's being done all the time by poets,
    from Homer to Tennyson;
They're always comparing ladies to lilies and veal to venison.
How about the man who wrote,
Her little feet stole in and out like mice beneath her petticoat?
Wouldn't anybody but a poet think twice   25
Before stating that his girl's feet were mice?
Then they always say things like that after a winter storm
The snow is a white blanket. Oh it is, is it, all right then, you
    sleep under a six-inch blanket of snow and I'll sleep under a
    half-inch blanket of unpoetical blanket material and we'll see
    which one keeps warm,
And after that maybe you'll begin to comprehend dimly
What I mean by too much metaphor and simile.   30

1931
Ogden Nash (1902–1971)

1. What qualities of metaphor and simile is Nash humorously attacking?
2. What valuable functions of metaphor and simile as illustrated in the poems
   and discussion in this chapter might be used to counter Nash's comments
   on the excesses of these devices?

---

her little feet stole in and out like mice: a quotation from Sir John Suckling's "A Ballad Upon a
Wedding" (1646).

K. Another device of figurative language is the SYMBOL—a word or image that is meant literally but that also stands for something else, as the Cross symbolizes Christianity or the Star of David, Judaism. These are examples of a TRADITIONAL SYMBOL—a symbol with public associations, based on historical events or well-known writings such as the Bible. Blake uses the traditional symbol of the lamb in the following poem:

THE LAMB

Little Lamb, who made thee?
Dost thou know who made thee,
Gave thee life and bid thee feed
By the stream and o'er the mead—
Gave thee clothing of delight,   5
Softest clothing, woolly bright,
Gave thee such a tender voice,
Making all the vales rejoice?
   Little lamb, who made thee,
   Dost thou know who made thee?   10

   Little lamb, I'll tell thee,
   Little lamb, I'll tell thee!
He is called by thy name,
For he calls himself a Lamb;
He is meek and he is mild,   15
He became a little child:
I a child, and thou a lamb,
We are called by his name.
   Little lamb, God bless thee,
   Little lamb, God bless thee!   20

1789
William Blake (1757–1827)

1. Whom does the lamb represent?
2. What qualities of the lamb make it an apt symbol?
3. What do we learn about the speaker in this poem?

   Blake published "The Lamb" in *Songs of Innocence* (1789). In 1794, he published *Songs of Innocence and of Experience, Showing the Two Contrary States of the Human Soul*, in which he paired poems about innocence and experience. Here is the poem he paired with "The Lamb":

Does a Poem Have Meaning?
Can We Discover It?

THE TYGER

Tyger, Tyger, burning bright,
In the forests of the night;
What immortal hand or eye
Could frame thy fearful symmetry?

In what distant deeps or skies   5
Burnt the fire of thine eyes!
On what wings dare he aspire?
What the hand, dare seize the fire?

And what shoulder, & what art,
Could twist the sinews of thy heart?   10
And when thy heart began to beat,
What dread hand? & what dread feet?

What the hammer? what the chain,
In what furnace was thy brain?
What the anvil? what dread grasp,   15
Dare its deadly terrors clasp?

When the stars threw down their spears
And water'd heaven with their tears:
Did he smile his work to see?
Did he who made the Lamb make thee?   20

Tyger, Tyger burning bright,
In the forests of the night:
What immortal hand or eye,
Dare frame thy fearful symmetry?

1794
William Blake (1757–1827)

1. The traditional symbol of the lamb in the first poem is opposed here to a
   CREATED SYMBOL—one without traditional associations. What qualities does
   the tiger have? How does Blake contrast the tiger's qualities with those of
   the lamb?
2. Look at the kinds of questions asked in each poem. How do they differ?
   The questions in "The Lamb" are answered. Why are those of "The Tyger" left unanswered?

L. Because poems so often involve the use of figurative language, readers sometimes assume that *all* poetry is figurative and that every word of a poem means something else than its literal meaning. But as we saw in William Carlos Williams' "This Is Just to Say" (p. 6), it is important to take the words of a poem literally just as far as possible before attempting any figurative reading. Williams' poem contains no metaphors or similes. The following poem, while radically different in mood and subject from Williams', also illustrates how useful it is, in understanding a poem, to establish the literal sense:

LOOSE WOMAN

Someone who well knew how she'd toss her chin
　　Passing the firehouse oglers, at their taunt,
　　Let it be flung up higher than she'd want,
Just held fast by a little hinge of skin.
Two boys come from the river kicked a thatch　　　　　5
　　Of underbrush and stopped. One wrecked a pair
　　Of sneakers blundering into her hair
And that day made a different sort of catch.

Her next-best talent, setting tongues to buzz,
　　Lasts longer than her best. It still occurs　　　　　10
　　To wonder had she been our fault or hers
And had she loved him. Who the bastard was,
Though long they asked and notebooked round about
　　And turned up not a few who would have known
　　That white inch where her neck met shoulderbone,　　15
Was one thing more we never did find out.

　　　　　　　　　　　　　　　　　1969
　　　　　　　　　　　X. J. Kennedy (b. 1929)

1. What does "it" refer to in line 3? What is "just held fast by a little hinge of skin" in line 4?
2. If we take literally the phrase "blundering into her hair" in line 7, what "different sort of catch" have the two boys made?
3. The word "loose" in the phrase "loose woman" usually is a metaphor—it doesn't mean literally *loose* as in "not fastened," but "immoral." Kennedy uses the phrase in its literal sense also. How?

M.   ## LOVELIEST OF TREES

Loveliest of trees, the cherry now
Is hung with bloom along the bough,
And stands about the woodland ride
Wearing white for Eastertide.

Now, of my threescore years and ten,   5
Twenty will not come again,
And take from seventy springs a score,
It only leaves me fifty more.

And since to look at things in bloom
Fifty springs are little room,   10
About the woodlands I will go
To see the cherry hung with snow.

1896
A. E. Housman (1859–1936)

1. What season and time are described in stanza 1?
2. How many years is "threescore years and ten"? How old is the speaker of the poem?
3. What is the relationship between the speaker's age and the statement that he is going "about the woodlands . . . to see the cherry hung with snow"?
4. What other lines or phrases provide a context for the use of the word "snow" in the last line?
5. In what ways is the word "snow" metaphoric? In what ways literal?

N.   ## NEXT TO OF COURSE GOD AMERICA I

"next to of course god america i
love you land of the pilgrims' and so forth oh
say can you see by the dawn's early my
country 'tis of centuries come and go
and are no more what of it we should worry   5
in every language even deafanddumb
thy sons acclaim your glorious name by gorry
by jingo by gee by gosh by gum
why talk of beauty what could be more beautiful than these heroic happy dead   10

who rushed like lions to the roaring slaughter
they did not stop to think they died instead
then shall the voice of liberty be mute?"

He spoke. And drank rapidly a glass of water.

1926

E. E. Cummings (1894–1962)

1. All but the last line of the poem are in quotation marks. How are the lines inside the quotation marks different from that line outside the quotation marks?
2. Look for phrases and fragments in this poem that may be familiar to you. What do the following fragments have in common?

"land of the pilgrims"

"by the dawn's early"

"my / country 'tis of"

"these heroic happy dead"

"voice of liberty"

3. What do the choice of phrases and the way they are run together inside the quotation marks indicate about the speaker?
4. Is the last line spoken by the speaker of the previous lines? What is the purpose of this final line?

O. Here are some questions to ask as you read Ezra Pound's "The Garden." Some of them may already have occurred to you:

line 1:   (a) Who/What is like "a skein of loose silk blown against a wall"?
      (b) Why is that person or thing like that?
      (c) Why are the words "loose," "silk," "blown" and "against a wall" all part of the comparison?
line 2:   "She walks by the railing of a path in Kensington Gardens"
      (a) Where is Kensington Gardens?
      (b) Is this place essential to the poem or could she be walking anywhere?
      (c) If the setting is important, why is it significant that she is walking there?
line 3:   "And she is dying piece-meal"
      (a) What is she dying of?

(b) Why is she described as dying "piece-meal," that is, slowly or bit by bit?

line 4: "Of a sort of emotional anemia"

    (a) What does "emotional" anemia (as opposed to the more familiar physical anemia) mean?

    (b) How can someone die of *emotional* anemia?

    (c) Why "sort of"? Why isn't Pound more exact here?

line 5: "And round about there is a rabble"

    (a) Why does the poem suddenly start talking about something else—"a rabble"?

    (b) What is/Who are the "rabble"?

    (c) Why this particular word—"rabble"?

    (d) What is the effect of seeing her in the midst of this rabble?

line 6: "Of the filthy, sturdy, unkillable infants of the very poor"

    (a) Why are the "rabble"—the "filthy, sturdy, unkillable infants"—described with these words?

    (b) Why is it important that these children be "infants of the very poor"?

line 7: "They shall inherit the earth"

    (a) Why are these infants said to be going to "inherit the earth"?

    (b) What does that statement have to do with what the reader knows about "her"?

line 8: "In her is the end of breeding"

    (a) What does the word "breeding" mean here?

    (b) Why is the "end" of breeding said to be "in her"?

line 9: "Her boredom is exquisite and excessive"

    (a) Why is she bored?

    (b) Why is her boredom described as "exquisite"? Why "excessive"?

line 10: "She would like some one to speak to her,"

    (a) Why does she want some one to speak to her?

    (b) She wants some one to speak to her rather than wanting to speak to some one. Why?

line 11: "And is almost afraid that I"

    (a) Why is she *almost* afraid?

    (b) What causes her fear in the first place?

    (c) Who is the "I" in the poem?

line 12: "will commit that indiscretion."

    (a) What is the indiscretion that she is almost afraid the "I" of the poem will commit?

line 1, again: Now that you have read through the poem and have asked some questions line by line, what answers help explain the precision of Pound's simile in line 1?

WRITING SUGGESTIONS_____

1. Choose a short poem from Poems for Further Reading. As an experiment to see what kinds of questions each line generates, cover the whole poem and then uncover one line at a time. Jot down the questions that occur to you and then the answers to these questions as you find them. After you have done this, reread the poem. In a brief essay, explain which organizing question—who, when, where—provides the best entry into the meaning of the poem and why. Illustrate with examples drawn from the poem.
2. Describe one of your own experiences, avoiding the use of metaphors and similes; then, like Syliva Plath in "Metaphors" (p. 20), list a series of metaphors that capture the essence of that experience.

PART

II

WHO? WHEN? WHERE?

CHAPTER TWO

WHO?

When Sherlock Holmes first meets his partner, Dr. John Watson, he astonishes Watson by seeming to know all sorts of things about him—that he is a doctor, that he has recently been in Afghanistan, and that he has been injured. Holmes discovers these things about Watson, not by having a secret source of information, but by noticing details of dress, complexion, and behavior. When we ask who is speaking in a poem, we can proceed in much the same way that the great detective did, looking at all the details and their context, putting together information about the identity and the attitude of the speaker. Such investigation is especially important in those poems where the human element is brought forward—where a speaker addresses us directly as "I."

Ezra Pound's "The Garden" (p. 9) is such a first-person poem; in the last two lines, the poem's speaker refers to himself for the first time:

> She would like some one to speak to her,
> And is almost afraid that *I*
>   will commit that indiscretion.

Who is this "I"? We already have many questions about the other lines of the poem, and most of them are about the woman: Why is she "like a skein of loose silk?" Why does she embody the "end of breeding"? Why is she surrounded by the "infants of the very poor"? When we get to those last lines, we are suddenly aware that there are *two* people involved—the woman and the speaker who is observing her. These observations do not exist in a vacuum; they come from a speaker and reveal his own attitudes. Had a description of the woman been given by another observer or by the woman herself, it would have been different.

What is the speaker's attitude about this woman? Does he approve of her or like her? He compares her to "a skein of loose silk blown against a wall," and characterizes her as dying of "emotional anemia," as excessively bored,

35

and as representing "the end of breeding." Why doesn't the speaker approve? Presumably it is because of what the woman is like. But what can we say about what she's like from his description?

He says that in her is the end of breeding. This might mean the *end result* of breeding in the sense of training in good manners and social behavior, or it might mean that she is the *last* of her particular breed, in the different sense of her line of descent. Notice also that the speaker says the woman is surrounded by the sturdy, unkillable infants of the very poor. Our process of reading the poem has to include investigating particular words (like *breeding*) and their contexts (*the end of breeding*) but we must also set one piece of information against another, compare one line with another continually. The infants are *unkillable*, while she is *dying*; there is an opposition here. They are children of the *very poor*, while in her is the end of breeding, and she is like *silk*, an expensive cloth. Here there seems to be another opposition, and we are justified in concluding that the woman is not only well bred, but probably rich. The speaker's attitude is revealed as a preference for the poor, or at least a conviction that the poor are stronger, *sturdier*, and without the "emotional anemia" of the woman.

Her emotional anemia is connected with her excessive boredom. The speaker concludes that she would like someone to speak to her, perhaps to relieve the boredom, but "she is almost afraid that I / will commit that indiscretion." Why should it be an indiscretion for the speaker to speak to her? Is it, perhaps, because he has allied himself with the rabble of the children of the very poor, or because he is obviously of a lower social or economic class that she might consider it an indiscretion?

Without answering *every* question about "The Garden," these comments should make it apparent that concentrating on the first-person speaker and his attitudes helps us to focus other questions and to start getting some answers to them. We have asked who the speaker is, and we have begun to identify him as a person with certain attitudes about class.

At this point, it seems reasonable to ask whether Ezra Pound is telling us some of his own attitudes about class, "breeding," and the rich in "The Garden." In other words, wherever we have said "the speaker" in the previous discussion, could we have said "Ezra Pound" instead? There is nothing in the poem that indicates that the speaker is anyone other than the poet speaking in his own voice, but to better answer this question, we have to go outside the poem—to Pound's other poems, to his prose comments, to his biography. In these we can find attitudes similar to those of the speaker in "The Garden." We are thus probably justified in concluding that the speaker is the poet.

But we would not be justified in concluding that the speaker and the poet are always identical. Poems can be autobiographical, telling of real experiences that the poet has had, but they can also contain invented characters and speakers. The poet can have a speaker whose attitude is disagreeable or evil, just as a novelist, a playwright, or a movie writer can put speeches in the mouth of a villain that the author does not agree with at all. Poetry is a form of fiction like these others. It is important to remember this fictional quality of poetry because even when poets are describing their own real experiences, they may change them slightly, or alter their own role in them, to fit the needs of the poem. As the poet Jon Stallworthy wrote in "A True Confession":

> For poets are liars. Their lives
> scan less than their smooth
> confessions. But now and then our lies
> betray us into truth.

THE POET AS "I"—THE AUTOBIOGRAPHICAL SPEAKER

All poems are autobiographical in the sense that they reflect, however transformed, the poet's experiences, interests, concerns; but occasionally we have good reason to believe that the poet's own life is the subject of the poem:

TEN DEFINITIONS OF LIFETIME

1

Slush, my brother said, it's
slush—the first word
I ever knew I was learning. Ankle-deep,
I shivered with cold
understanding.   5

2

Scout's Honor: it was another boy scout
who betrayed me—one way of finding out
what honor means.

3

At graduation, bold with endings,
I kissed her at last.   10
Twelve years, she said,
erasing the difference
between delay and loss.

4

When the bomb dissolved Hiroshima
every man in my company   15
got bombed on PX
patriotism.

5

I told the bosun:
a ship defines the ocean.
He said: horse   20
shit.

6

The many words for love
come easily; we would not learn the sounds
of separation.

7

In that single moment   25
I wanted to be immortal.
She whispered: a man who was immortal
would be as ugly
as a plastic flower.

8

All I learned in grad school   30
was the meaning of humility;
all I have ever forgotten
is what I learned in grad school.

9

Universe
ity: those who can, teach;   35
those who cannot
are the servants of teachers.

PX: post exchange. **bosun:** a Navy noncommissioned officer.

10

The poet is the unacknowledged
lexicographer of mankind.

1975

Philip Appleman (b. 1926)

What are the "ten definitions," and how do they define a lifetime? Appleman does not give a detailed picture of his life here, but he does offer brief
glimpses of important and emotionally charged moments throughout his life—
as a boy (stanzas 1 and 2), as a serviceman during the war (4 and 5), as a young
lover and later a maturer one (3, 6, and 7), as a university student and teacher
(8 and 9), and as a poet (10). Notice that the word *definition* means not only
"meaning or significance" but also "that which divides two areas or periods."
Such a play on words uses two or more meanings of a word at the same time
and is called a PUN.

These brief glimpses of a life are self-sufficient because they awaken associations within us. They do not define a lifetime in the sense of telling everything about who Appleman is and what he has done, but in a very short space
they do define things that are very important: what his memory calls up when
he thinks back over his life. But does this mean we can count on the literal
truth of all of these episodes actually having happened to Appleman? Suppose,
for example, that Appleman did not really learn about betrayal first from a Boy
Scout (stanza 2). We can be sure that he learned about it from someone, at
some time, as all of us do. Making his betrayer a Boy Scout enables the poet
to play a little with the word *honor*. Such a difference between what might be
expected—in this case honorable conduct from a Boy Scout—and what actually occurs—betrayal—is called IRONY OF SITUATION (another kind of irony is
defined on p. 75). Appleman may be sacrificing a minor literal truth in making his betrayer a Boy Scout, but he gets a greater poetic truth in exchange.

There is another such exchange in one of the most famous short autobiographical poems in the language, a poem by John Milton usually given the
title "On His Blindness":

WHEN I CONSIDER HOW MY LIGHT IS SPENT

When I consider how my light is spent,
   Ere half my days in this dark world and wide,

The poet . . . mankind: Appleman changes the sentence that ends the Romantic poet Shelley's
Defense of Poetry (1840): "Poets are the unacknowledged legislators of the world." A lexicographer
is a dictionary-maker, a writer of definitions.

And that one talent which is death to hide
Lodged with me useless, though my soul more bent
To serve therewith my Maker, and present   5
    My true account, lest He returning chide;
    "Doth God exact day-labor, light denied?"
I fondly ask. But Patience, to prevent
That murmur, soon replies, "God doth not need
    Either man's work or His own gifts. Who best   10
    Bear His mild yoke, they serve Him best. His state
Is kingly: thousands at His bidding speed,
    And post o'er land and ocean without rest;
    They also serve who only stand and wait."

1673
John Milton (1608–1674)

What the speaker is saying about himself may not at first be clear because of the complicated SYNTAX, or arrangement of words within the sentences. The entire first seven and a half lines consist of a single grammatical unit. There is no break or full pause in the meaning until we get to the middle of the eighth line and yet even that long sentence unit is compressed. The words that have been left out—an ELLIPSIS—can be filled in and a few words like *ere* and *therewith* modernized to fill out these lines:

> When I consider how my light is spent before half my days in this dark world and wide (are spent), and (when I consider that) this one talent which is death to hide (is) lodged with me useless, though my soul (is) more bent to serve my Maker (with it) and present my true account, lest he chide (me when he returns); "Does God exact day-labor (even when) light (is) denied?" I fondly ask.

If we look up the word *fondly* we will discover that the meaning it had at the time Milton wrote the poem was *foolishly*. Since poems often make a virtue of compression, a reader needs to be prepared to do this sort of rearrangement and expansion of syntax. Notice that in the rest of the poem there are short grammatical units, very few rearrangements of normal word order, and practically no ellipses.

---

one talent which is death to hide: Matthew 25: 14–30 describes a master who gave three servants *talents* (coins in use in the Middle East during Christ's lifetime) in different amounts: five, two, and one. Those servants who received the five and two talents invested and multiplied them, while the servant with only one buried his in anticipation of his master's wrath should he lose it. For this his one talent was taken from him and he was "cast into outer darkness."

When I Consider How
My Light Is Spent

Even if we did not know that this poem was written by John Milton, or that he was also the author of the religious poem *Paradise Lost*, we could still learn a great deal about the author from the kinds of images he uses and what he says about himself explicitly. For example, he uses the Bible in both direct and indirect reference—directly in referring to the parable of the talents and indirectly in his reference to his age. He says that his light is *spent*—that he has gone blind—before half his days in this world are over. The Bible measures the usual span of a man's life as threescore and ten years, or seventy years—note Housman's use of this phrase in "Loveliest of Trees." We can infer then that the speaker in Milton's poem is about thirty-five. Why doesn't he say this directly? Milton's complaint in the first eight lines seems to depend on the fact that he has half his life left in which to use his "talent," that he is more willing than ever, but that now it is merely "lodged" with him, useless.

Much of the first half of the poem depends on our knowing the parable of the talents and seeing its appropriateness here. Such a reference, to biblical, literary, historical or mythological events or persons is called an ALLUSION, and its usefulness depends on our knowing what the author is alluding to. The speaker is a man who believes that one should justify his existence on earth—that he should use his abilities, for Milton takes advantage of this sense of the word *talent* as well as the sense of a sum of money. And once we have come to this point in the poem, to Milton's allusion to the biblical coins known as *talents*, we can see some consistency in his use of the word *spent* in the first line; he could have written, after all, that his light was *gone*, or *extinguished*, or used any number of other ways of saying he had gone blind. "Spent" creates an IMAGE or word-picture that is consistent with the use of "talents" in the sense of coins.

From the poem we can infer that the speaker is a man with the conviction that God-given gifts must be justified by their use, and with a religious faith strong and deep enough to help him over great personal crises. These inferences are confirmed when we look beyond the poem to Milton's biography. Because Milton was not only a poet, but a man who regarded poetry as his profession and spent years in preparation and study for it, we might naturally expect his deep disappointment at those times when he felt blindness a great obstacle to practicing his art. He was a Puritan, and one willing to assert and defend his convictions even when it was dangerous to do so, both before and after the English Civil War in the seventeenth century. His religious faith not only solaced him in personal crises, but led him to want to write an ambitious poem about the events described in the Book of Genesis and about the eventual redemption of man by Christ. Since Milton had always intended to use his poetic gifts in this way—in praise of God—his complaints here are especially poignant.

THE POET AS NOVELIST—THE FICTIONAL SPEAKER

> If you really want to hear about it, the first thing you'll probably want to
> know is where I was born, and what my lousy childhood was like, and
> how my parents were occupied and all before they had me, and all that
> David Copperfield kind of crap, but I don't feel like going into it, if you
> want to know the truth. In the first place, that stuff bores me, and in the
> second place, my parents would have about two hemorrhages apiece if I
> told anything pretty personal about them.
>
> —J. D. Salinger, *The Catcher in the Rye*

When we pick up J. D. Salinger's novel and start reading, we soon realize
that the "I" who addresses us is a fictional character, not Salinger himself but
a narrator whose name is Holden Caulfield, and who, as you might have guessed
from the tone and vocabulary of even this short opening paragraph, is a teen-
aged boy. Thousands of novels, like *The Catcher in the Rye* (1951) and Dick-
ens' *David Copperfield* (1850), which Holden mentions, are written as if spoken or narrated by an "I" who is not the novelist. Such a fictional speaker is
sometimes called a PERSONA—the word means *mask* literally, and indeed the
writer does hide behind a kind of mask or disguise when using a persona.

Poets also use personas, wanting for various reasons to create speakers different from themselves. One reason might be mystery: the poem becomes a
puzzle and the reader tries to guess who its speaker is. One of the oldest kinds
of poetry, the riddle, employs the device of a persona that invites the reader to
guess its identity. Plath's "Metaphors" (p. 20) is a modern first-person riddle
of this sort.

Still another reason for using a persona is a sense of fun or novelty in
looking at the world from someone or some*thing* else's point of view. This
playfulness comes through in Peter Wild's poem on wolves:

AN APOLOGY FOR WOLVES

1

They have always
vilified us,
sensing our stealth
and their lack of it.

Apology: In addition to meaning *expression of regret*, the word also means *defense* or *justification*.

An Apology for Wolves

and moved by the first impulse   5
of their dim minds,
throw stones, beat shields,
catch us in their iron sights . . .

as if we wanted their women
or would steal their Gods . . .   10

2

it is true, we've been caught
on occasions with the remnants
of petticoats still in our mouths,
or sporting a red cap, just for a lark.

but we've got a bad press   15
which capitalizes on such exceptions:
a grandmother or two
coughed up now and then,

and doesn't consider
our loss of face   20
when driven into the suburbs
by a long winter and heavy snows.

3

actually, it's just a simple lack
of understanding—on their part,
a myopia common   25
to all muscular animals . . .

we mean no harm
but must pursue
that fine exhilaration
instinctively ours: 30

flaming tails in bushes
and leaves slipping along our backs.

1968
Peter Wild (b. 1940)

Perspective is everything. In Wild's poem the identity of the speaker means a different—and non-human—view of the world.

Another reason for choosing a fictional speaker is the poet's wish to tell a story from an especially revealing point of view. J. D. Salinger had Holden Caulfield tell his own story in *The Catcher in the Rye* because the teen-ager's language and perceptions best revealed the turmoil of the character. A poet often makes the same kind of choice, as in the poem that follows. Notice, while you read it, how curiosity about the "I" of the poem leads to a search for clues, to a comparison of the information given in different lines of the poem, and, finally, to a discovery about the identity of the speaker:

THE TRUTH

When I was four my father went to Scotland.
They *said* he went to Scotland.

When I woke up I think I thought that I was dreaming—
I was so little then that I thought dreams
Are in the room with you, like the cinema.   5
That's why you don't dream when it's still light—
They pull the shades down when it is, so you can sleep.
I thought that then, but that's not right.
Really it's in your head.

And it was light then—light at *night*.   10
I heard Stalky bark outside.
But really it was Mother crying—
She coughed so hard she cried.
She kept shaking Sister,
She shook her and shook her.   15
I thought Sister had had her nightmare.
But he wasn't barking, he had died.
There was dirt all over Sister.
It was all streaks, like mud. I cried.
She didn't, but she was older.   20
            I thought she didn't
Because she was older, I thought Stalky had just gone.
I got *everything* wrong.
I didn't get one single thing right.
It seems to me that I'd have thought   25

The Truth

It didn't happen, like a dream,
Except that it was light. At night.
They burnt our house down, they burnt down London.
Next day my mother cried all day, and after that
She said to me when she would come to see me: 30
"Your father has gone away to Scotland.
He will be back after the war."

The war then was different from the war now.
The war now is *nothing*.

I used to live in London till they burnt it.   35
What was it like? It was just like here.
No, that's the truth.
My mother would come here, some, but she would cry.
She said to Miss Elise, "He's not himself";
She said, "Don't you love me any more at all?"   40
I was *my*self.
Finally she wouldn't come at all.
She never said one thing my father said, or Sister.
Sometimes she did,
Sometimes she was the same, but that was when I dreamed it.   45
I could tell I was dreaming, she was just the same.

That Christmas she bought me a toy dog.

I asked her what was its name, and when she didn't know
I asked her over, and when she didn't know
I said, "You're not my mother, you're not my mother.   50
She *hasn't* gone to Scotland, she is dead!"
And she said, "Yes, he's dead, he's dead!"
And cried and cried; she *was* my mother,
She put her arms around me and we cried.

1945
Randall Jarrell (1914–1965)

Once again, our first question is "Who is speaking?" The way the speaker talks about himself in the first lines—"When I was four . . . I was so little then"—may tempt us to think he is much older now, looking back on things that happened in his early childhood, during World War II. Then we note the simplicity of the speaker's language throughout:

That's why you don't dream when it's still light—
They pull the shades down when it is, so you can sleep.
I thought that then, but that's not right.
Really it's in your head.

This simplicity of phrasing suggests that the child is not *very* much older, and as we proceed through the poem there are other indications that he is still very young—his thinking that London was burnt completely down, and the fact that the war is still going on (lines 33–34). We realize fairly quickly that, though he talks about having been "so little" then, he is not very much older now. This helps make sense of what looks like jumpy, confused thoughts and descriptions. The fascination of the poem comes from this choice of narrator— the way these happenings look to a very small child. One of the consequences of this choice of narrator is that the child speaker doesn't say everything an adult would—his perceptions of what happened are limited and so is his account of them. We must infer what has happened and what is happening as he gives us only partial information.

"It was light then," he says, "light at *night*"—why? What was going on? He says he heard the dog barking, then that the sound was really his mother crying—then that she coughed so hard she cried (wasn't the cough the sound that seemed to be the dog?). Each perception is stated as if true, but then changed by the next one to something closer to what must be the truth of the matter. The confusion of the child is mirrored in these consecutive and contradictory perceptions. The order mirrors his confusion also: his references jump from the sister back to the dog (16–17) and back to the sister (18). As he tries to find a reason for each perception, he tells us the first, erroneous one, then immediately corrects it. He thought it was his sister crying, but really it was his mother. Then he says his sister didn't cry because she was older. Then he says he *thought* this, which suggests that it wasn't true—although he doesn't say what *was* really true. Finally he just sums it up by saying he got everything wrong. We have to keep coming back to the poem's title: we have to realize that he is trying to get at the truth, that he is in effect taking us along with his thoughts, from the first mistaken perception of things, to the realization that he was mistaken, to some further correction of what actually happened.

Up to this point our interest has centered on the boy, his account of what happened, and his attempts to get at the truth of it. But then the mother enters again in lines 29–32. The boy has been sent away someplace where his mother comes to see him occasionally. While visiting, she tells him that his father has gone away to Scotland and will be back after the war. But we know from the first two lines of the poem that the boy knows otherwise:

When I was four my father went to Scotland.
They *said* he went to Scotland.

Gradually, we infer that the father is dead. The mother denies the truth, which the child tries desperately to get at. The next lines (33–36) are not about the mother. She has said that the father will be back after the war, and the next lines are about the war:

> The war then was different from the war now.
> The war now is *nothing.*
> I used to live in London till they burnt it.
> What was it like? It was just like here.

This passage is a clue to where the boy is now—presumably away from London and its raids.

After these intervening lines, we come back to the mother and her visits to the boy. He gives us three details about her behavior: she cries, she comments to Miss Elise that the boy is not himself, and she asks "Don't you love me any more at all?" Whatever *his* behavior to prompt the remark (he doesn't tell us about it), he doesn't answer the question, but in the next line addresses her *previous* comment and says "*I* was *my*self." The implication from the way he emphasizes the words is that *she* was not *her*self. And in the next lines this thought is continued: only in his dreams is she the same. He has no trouble, however, distinguishing his dreams from his waking moments, when his mother never talks about what his father or sister said.

Our questions about when all this is occurring are helped by line 47, which gives us the time of the last lines of the poem as Christmas:

> That Christmas she bought me a toy dog.
>
> I asked her what was its name, and when she didn't know
> I asked her over, and when she didn't know
> I said, "You're not my mother, you're not my mother.
> She *hasn't* gone to Scotland, she is dead!"

What prompts his outburst? Why does he say what he does, combining both parents? The toy dog to which the mother refuses to give a name seems to be the trigger. Why should this be so affecting? If we go back to the boy's account of the original episode, we recall the real dog, Stalky, and the boy realizes *and says* that the dog died during the burning of the London house. He does not say that the sister is dead, let alone the father, even though his thoughts make a fairly clear equation between the dog's situation and the sister's:

> She kept shaking Sister,
> She shook her and shook her.
> I thought Sister had had her nightmare.
> But he wasn't barking, he had died.
> There was dirt all over Sister
> It was all streaks, like mud. I cried.
> She didn't, but she was older.

> I thought she didn't
> Because she was older, I thought Stalky had just gone.
> I got *everything* wrong.

He has no trouble making the observation about the dog, but he does not do the same with either the sister or the father. In his outburst, he cries out against the change in his mother, and she instantly realizes what he is really saying. When she at last speaks the truth, then they are able to confront it and sorrow over it together:

> And she said, "Yes, he's dead, he's dead!"
> And cried and cried: she *was* my mother,
> She put her arms around me and we cried.

If we asked why the poet chose to tell the story through the child instead of giving a third-person account—or the mother's, say—we now may be able to see why. The way we have looked at the events of the poem is very analytical—very far from how compactly and powerfully they are told in the poem. It is precisely because he has chosen this narrator that Jarrell can get this effect; the amazing clarity with which the child sees and copes with tragic realities, yet can't quite cope with them, is shown to us from the *inside*. First-person accounts tend to put emphasis on the people and what they're like rather than on the happenings they describe—that's one reason for using this form, called a DRAMATIC MONOLOGUE: a poem spoken by a single fictional persona, revealing character or a special view of experience. In "The Truth," the form gives us a unique double view: the child's view of himself, in his own words, and also what is actually happening, which he may not be wholly equipped to understand, but which we can infer from what he tells us.

THE POET AS DRAMATIST—SPEAKERS AND LISTENERS

Another method poets have of masking their own voices is to stage a little play. In such a poem we are likely to get several speakers talking—dialogue, in other words. In the following example, we have just such a dialogue:

UP-HILL

> Does the road wind up-hill all the way?
> Yes, to the very end.
> Will the day's journey take the whole long day?
> From morn to night, my friend.

Up-Hill

But is there for the night a resting-place?   5
 A roof for when the slow dark hours begin.
May not the darkness hide it from my face?
 You cannot miss that inn.

Shall I meet other wayfarers at night?
 Those who have gone before.   10
Then must I knock, or call when just in sight?
 They will not keep you standing at that door.

Shall I find comfort, travel-sore and weak?
 Of labour you shall find the sum.
Will there be beds for me and all who seek?   15
 Yea, beds for all who come.

1862

Christina Rossetti (1830–1894)

When we ask our first question about speaker in this poem, at least a partial answer is readily found. The poem is a dialogue in which one speaker asks questions and another answers. But before long, we realize that the subject matter and the tone of the speakers differ markedly. (TONE is the poet's or speaker's attitude—sarcastic, serious, playful—as revealed in speech by intonation and pitch, in poetry by choice of words.) The first speaker—the questioner—asks a straightforward series of questions about a journey: how long it will take, what the road is like, and what kind of a resting-place awaits the traveler at the road's end. If we heard only this one voice, there would be no clue that the poem concerned more than a journey. But from the beginning the tone of the replies given by the second speaker suggests more meaning. The finality and emphasis of "the *very* end," "when the *slow dark hours* begin," "You cannot miss *that* inn" make us gradually aware that while the first speaker may be talking merely about a journey, the second is discussing graver issues: life and death, in fact. Our attention to speakers and their differences leads us to the conclusion that every reference by the first speaker to a journey is used by the second to apply to life and death: the road is life; the day is a lifetime; the inn, roof, and bed of the "resting-place" are the grave; and so on. A story or description in which every item represents something else in a parallel or equivalent story is called an ALLEGORY. "Up-Hill" contains such an allegory: each item referring to a journey also refers to something along the road of life.

 More than one speaker gives us more than one point of view—the possibility for disagreement, conflict, drama. The questions "Who is speaking?" and "Who is being spoken to?" become keys to many poems, but we still need inference to flesh out these dialogues, to stage the little plays these kinds of poems really are. Sometimes the dialogue is really a monologue with one speaker and one listener who does not speak. Read the following poem, inferring what you can about the speaker and the person spoken to. (The accent marks indicate which syllables Hopkins wants stressed.)

SPRING AND FALL:
To a Young Child

Márgarét, áre you gríeving
Over Goldengrove unleaving?
Leáves, líke the things of man, you
With your fresh thoughts care for, can you?
Ah! ás the heart grows older   5
It will come to such sights colder
By and by, nor spare a sigh
Though worlds of wanwood leafmeal lie;
And yet you *will* weep and know why.
Now no matter, child, the name: 10
Sórrow's spríngs áre the same.
Nor mouth had, no nor mind, expressed
What heart heard of, ghost guessed:
It ís the blight man was born for,
It is Margaret you mourn for.   15

composed 1880   1918
Gerard Manley Hopkins (1844–1889)

The language in this poem may offer obstacles at first. For example, Hopkins uses *ghost* in its literal, but now somewhat unusual, sense of *soul* or *spirit*. A good dictionary will point out this sense of the word but it will not directly tell us the meanings of words Hopkins constructs to suit his purposes. *Unleaving* (line 2) is a compressed way of saying *losing its leaves*. *Goldengrove*, which Hopkins capitalizes, at once names the autumn woods and describes its color, or perhaps more accurately, names the woods *by* describing its color. Although Hopkins' inventions seem unusual, the parts of his compounds are perfectly acceptable English words, even if not the most common today, and he does not try to change their meanings in combination. The word *wanwood*, for instance, is composed of *wan* (which can mean either pale or dark) and *wood*— it seems as if it were put together deliberately to contrast with *Goldengrove*. *Leafmeal* is the most interesting of the poet's compounds. *Meal* is something ground up or *milled*, and the floor of the woods is carpeted with something that could be called leafmeal, but the word also has an analogy in *piecemeal* (piece by piece), so that the word also helps describe how the forest floor got that way, as the trees shed, leaf by leaf, their brown autumn foliage. Hopkins is not doing anything secret or unfathomable here—he is using words already in the language and putting them together in a new combination, but it takes only a knowledge of English words—helped out with a good dictionary and sympathetic attention to the poem—to see his purpose.

But our starting question in this chapter was "Who is speaking?" This poem doesn't give us direct information about its speaker; in fact, the words "I" or "me" aren't used, though we know who is being spoken *to*—even know her name from the first line, and the fact that she is a young girl from the subtitle. But what can we infer about the speaker? The poem is subtitled "To a Young Child"—can we conclude that the speaker is *not* young? He or she assures the girl that "as the heart grows older / It will come to such sights colder / By and by. . . ." This suggests that the speaker talks from experience and is thus older. And notice the title. What is the relationship between the two seasons and the two people? between their attitudes and the seasons? With these questions we have come from concern with the speaker to wider questions about the subject of the poem. But our appreciation of it must start with the realization that it is a little dramatic scene which starts with the young girl and an older speaker walking through leaf-strewn autumn woods. The girl expresses sorrow at the leaves' fall; the older voice replies.

With all poems, but especially first-person ones, we can profit from remembering their human origins. Whether the poem features a solitary voice speaking to us, a speaker talking to a listener, or two or more voices in dialogue or conversation, we will be helped into the poem by this attention to who is speaking. We must remember that whether describing experiences or inventing characters who speak in their own voices, the poet is always writing a conscious piece of fiction. Poets are not newspaper reporters held to circumstantial truth about what happened. The truth they aim at has to do not with exactly what happened, but with what can be learned and conveyed about human thought and feeling.

EXERCISES

A. WESTERN WIND

> Western wind, when wilt thou blow,
>   The small rain down can rain?
> Christ, if my love were in my arms
>   And I in my bed again!

composed about 1300

Anonymous

1. What can be inferred about the speaker from the information in the poem?
2. What is it, according to each line of the poem, that the speaker wants?
3. What is the relationship between lines 1 and 2 and between lines 3 and 4?
4. Copy out the poem with the pairs of lines reversed, so that the lines are 3-4-1-2. What has changed and what is now missing?

B.   **NOT MARBLE NOR THE GILDED MONUMENTS**

Not marble nor the gilded monuments
Of princes shall outlive this powerful rhyme;
But you shall shine more bright in these conténts
Than unswept stone, besmeared with sluttish time.
When wasteful war shall statues overturn,   5
And broils root out the work of masonry,
Nor Mars his sword nor war's quick fire shall burn
The living record of your memory.
'Gainst death and all oblivious enmity
Shall you pace forth; your praise shall still find room   10
Even in the eyes of all posterity
That wear this world out to the ending doom.
   So, till the judgment that yourself arise,
   You will live in this, and dwell in lovers' eyes.

1609
William Shakespeare (1564–1616)

1. Who is being spoken to in the poem?
2. The poem seems to be mostly about the person spoken to; what do we learn about the speaker here?
3. What does "this" refer to in the last line? Compare it to line 2. How can "this" cause the person addressed to live and "dwell in lovers' eyes"?

C.   **NAMING OF PARTS**

Today we have naming of parts. Yesterday,
We had daily cleaning. And tomorrow morning,
We shall have what to do after firing. But today,
Today we have naming of parts. Japonica
Glistens like coral in all of the neighboring gardens,   5
   And today we have naming of parts.

Mars his sword: Mars' sword; Mars is the god of war. **ending doom:** the last judgment mentioned in the next line.

Naming of Parts

This is the lower sling swivel. And this
Is the upper sling swivel, whose use you will see,
When you are given your slings. And this is the piling swivel,
Which in your case you have not got. The branches   10
Hold in the gardens their silent, eloquent gestures,
     Which in our case we have not got.

This is the safety-catch, which is always released
With an easy flick of the thumb. And please do not let me
See anyone using his finger. You can do it quite easy   15
If you have any strength in your thumb. The blossoms
Are fragile and motionless, never letting anyone see
     Any of them using their finger.

And this you can see is the bolt. The purpose of this
Is to open the breech, as you see. We can slide it   20
Rapidly backwards and forwards: we call this
Easing the spring. And rapidly backwards and forwards
The early bees are assaulting and fumbling the flowers:
     They call it easing the Spring.

They call it easing the Spring: it is perfectly easy   25
If you have any strength in your thumb: like the bolt,
And the breech, and the cocking-piece, and the point
   of balance.
Which in our case we have not got; and the almond-blossom
Silent in all of the gardens and the bees going backwards
   and forwards,
     For today we have naming of parts.   30

                                 1946

Henry Reed (b. 1914)

1. Read the poem through several times. Remember our first interest in this chapter—who is speaking. Inferences can be made about the speaker or speakers in a poem from such things as subject or tone. What is the subject here? Is there more than one? The title is "Naming of Parts," and a number of parts do get named: sling swivels, piling swivels, a safety-catch, bolt, breech, and so on. What are these parts of? On the other hand Japonica, branches, blossoms, and bees seem to be parts of something quite different. What contrast is Reed making?

2. Can you notice anything familiar about the *tone* of the speaker when the swivels, bolts, and breeches are being talked about: "Today we will do this . . . here is the such-and-such . . . its purpose is to do thus-and-so."? (You may have heard that tone in this chapter.)

3. What change of tone occurs when the subject changes in each stanza from swivels, bolts, and breeches to Japonica, blossoms, and bees? Notice also the change from "Which in *your* case *you* have not got" (line 10) to "Which in *our* case *we* have not got" (12).

4. What is the dramatic situation in the poem—what sort of speaker and what sort of listener(s)? Do not forget to notice the date of the poem's publication, as this may be helpful.

5. What change occurs at the last sentence of each stanza? Is there a different speaker there? Is the last sentence of each stanza spoken at all, or is it merely thought? Could these sentences be the unspoken thoughts of the same person who speaks the first lines of each stanza, or are they the words of someone else?

6. Notice that within the shifts of subject and tone Reed has made the same phrases apply in two different senses: "naming of parts . . . which in your/our case you/we have not got . . . rapidly backwards and forwards . . . easing the spring/Spring . . . point of balance." What is Reed comparing and contrasting in this poem?

D. In recent decades a number of American poets have written poems which candidly reveal a great deal about themselves, and their work has come to be known as CONFESSIONAL POETRY. For a taste of the sort of poems the confessional poets write, read the following poems in this book: Sylvia Plath, "Tulips"; Adrienne Rich, "From a Survivor"; W. D. Snodgrass, "April Inventory"; Theodore Roethke, "My Papa's Waltz." You should be aware in reading these poems that although they are autobiographical, they do not necessarily tell the whole truth and nothing but the truth. Here is what a critic has said about the fidelity with which these poets reveal themselves:

> A true confessional poet places few barriers, if any, between the self and direct expression of that self, however painful that expression may prove. That is how he differs from all nonconfessional poets such as Eliot and Pound, writers who valued privacy and sought expression through the adoption of *personae* (Eliot's Prufrock, Pound's Mauberly). . . . This is not to say that confessional poems are wild, unchecked emotional outbursts. Few are. . . . While a confessional poem is one which mythologizes the poet's personal life, it has its elements of fancy like any other. It does not constitute, certainly, a mere recitation of fact for fact's sake; nor should the "facts" recited be mistaken for literal truth. . . . Therefore, we should not be at all surprised to find imaginary brothers, sisters, dream girls, dream lovers, in poetry of the most matter-of-fact kind. Indeed, Mrs. Sexton has spoken of writing, on occasion, a "disguised" poem, in which the pain of loss of one loved object is shifted to a fictitious one.
>
> —Robert Phillips, *The Confessional Poets*

ALL MY PRETTY ONES

> All my pretty ones?
> Did you say all? O hell-kite! All?
> What! all my pretty chickens and their dam
> At one fell swoop? . . .
> I cannot but remember such things were,
> That were most precious to me.
> —*Macbeth*

Father, this year's jinx rides us apart
where you followed our mother to her cold slumber,
a second shock boiling its stone to your heart,
leaving me here to shuffle and disencumber
you from the residence you could not afford: 5
a gold key, your half of a woollen mill,
twenty suits from Dunne's, an English Ford,
the love and legal verbiage of another will,
boxes of pictures of people I do not know.
I touch their cardboard faces. They must go.   10

But the eyes, as thick as wood in this album,
hold me. I stop here, where a small boy
waits in a ruffled dress for someone to come . . .
for this soldier who holds his bugle like a toy
or for this velvet lady who cannot smile.   15
Is this your father's father, this commodore
in a mailman suit? My father, time meanwhile
has made it unimportant who you are looking for.
I'll never know what these faces are all about.
I lock them into their book and throw them out.   20

This is the yellow scrapbook that you began
the year I was born; as crackling now and wrinkly
as tobacco leaves: clippings where Hoover outran
the Democrats, wiggling his dry finger at me
and Prohibition; news where the *Hindenburg* went   25
down and recent years where you went flush

All my pretty ones: from Shakespeare's *Macbeth* (IV, iii, 215–18); Macduff is lamenting the loss of his wife and children, murdered by Macbeth. **Hoover outran / the Democrats:** an allusion to the election of 1928. **Hindenburg:** a German dirigible that was destroyed by fire as it landed in New Jersey in 1936.

on war. This year, solvent but sick, you meant
to marry that pretty widow in a one-month rush.
But before you had that second chance, I cried
on your fat shoulder. Three days later you died.   30

These are the snapshots of marriage, stopped in places.
Side by side at the rail toward Nassau now;
here, with the winner's cup at the speedboat races,
here, in tails at the Cotillion, you take a bow,
here, by our kennel of dogs with their pink eyes,   35
running like show-bred pigs in their chain-link pen;
here, at the horseshow where my sister wins a prize;
and here, standing like a duke among groups of men.
Now I fold you down, my drunkard, my navigator,
my first lost keeper, to love or look at later.   40

I hold a five-year diary that my mother kept
for three years, telling all she does not say
of your alcoholic tendency. You overslept,
she writes. My God, father, each Christmas Day
with your blood, will I drink down your glass   45
of wine? The diary of your hurly-burly years
goes to my shelf to wait for my age to pass.
Only in this hoarded span will love persevere.
Whether you are pretty or not, I outlive you,
bend down my strange face to yours and forgive you.   50

1962
Anne Sexton (1928–1975)

1. Phillips says that confessional poems are not "wild, unchecked emotional
   outbursts." What evidences of control do you find in Sexton's poem?
2. What details might *not* be factual reports?
3. What of the speaker's attitude and emotions do we learn?
4. How has she distanced herself from the experiences described?

E. Robert Browning indicates the dramatic nature of the following poem by
   calling it a SOLILOQUY—a speech of an actor talking as if to himself but so
   the audience can hear. He also gives us the location or setting of the
   poem—a cloister, that is, a monastery or convent. And if we can learn
   about the speaker from tone as well as what is said, what do we begin to
   learn about this speaker when he starts with a growl?

Nassau: resort town in the Bahamas.

SOLILOQUY OF THE SPANISH CLOISTER

1

Gr-r-r--there go, my heart's abhorrence!
    Water your damned flower-pots, do!
If hate killed men, Brother Lawrence,
    God's blood, would not mine kill you!
What? your myrtle-bush wants trimming?   5
    Oh, that rose has prior claims—
Needs its leaden vase filled brimming?
    Hell dry you up with its flames!

2

At the meal we sit together;
    Salve tibi! I must hear   10
Wise talk of the kind of weather,
    Sort of season, time of year:
Not a plenteous cork-crop: scarcely
    Dare we hope oak-galls, I doubt;
What's the Latin name for "parsley"?   15
    What's the Greek name for Swine's Snout?

3

Whew! We'll have our platter burnished,
    Laid with care on our own shelf!
With a fire-new spoon we're furnished,
    And a goblet for ourself,   20
Rinsed like something sacrificial
    Ere 'tis fit to touch our chaps—
Marked with L. for our initial!
    (He-he! There his lily snaps!)

4

Saint, forsooth! While brown Dolores   25
    Squats outside the Convent bank
With Sanchicha, telling stories,
    Steeping tresses in the tank,
Blue-black, lustrous, thick like horsehairs,
    —Can't I see his dead eye glow,   30

---

salve tibi: hail to thee. **oak-galls:** swellings on oak trees, useful for tanning.

Bright as 'twere a Barbary corsair's?
  (That is, if he'd let it show!)

5

When he finishes refection,
  Knife and fork he never lays
Cross-wise, to my recollection,   35
  As do I, in Jesu's praise.
I the Trinity illustrate,
  Drinking watered orange-pulp—
In three sips the Arian frustrate;
  While he drains his at one gulp.   40

6

Oh, those melons? If he's able
  We're to have a feast! so nice!
One goes to the Abbot's table,
  All of us get each a slice.
How go on your flowers? None double?   45
  Not one fruit-sort can you spy?
Strange!—And I, too, at such trouble,
  Keep them close-nipped on the sly!

7

There's a great text in Galatians,
  Once you trip on it, entails   50
Twenty-nine distinct damnations,
  One sure, if another fails:
If I trip him just a-dying,
  Sure of heaven as sure can be,
Spin him round and send him flying   55
  Off to hell, a Manichee?

8

Or, my scrofulous French novel
  On grey paper with blunt type!

Barbary corsair: pirate on the African coast. **Arian:** a follower of Arius, a third-century heretic. **Galatians:** St. Paul's epistle to the Galatians. **Manichee:** a follower of the third-century Persian dualist Manes; by extension, any believer in dualism, which would be considered a heresy.

Simply glance at it, you grovel
    Hand and foot in Belial's gripe: 60
If I double down its pages
    At the woeful sixteenth print,
When he gathers his greengages,
    Ope a sieve and slip it in't?

9

Or, there's Satan!—one might venture   65
    Pledge one's soul to him, yet leave
Such a flaw in the indenture
    As he'd miss till, past retrieve,
Blasted lay that rose-acacia
    We're so proud of! *Hy, Zy, Hine* . . .   70
'St, there's Vespers! *Plena gratia*
    Ave, Virgo, Gr-r-r--you swine!

1842

Robert Browning (1812–1889)

1. Does the speaker ever name himself? How does his admission of hate for Brother Lawrence in stanza 1 affect our interpretation of what he says in the rest of the poem?
2. What does Brother Lawrence do in the cloister (stanzas 1, 2, 6)? Does this have anything to do with the speaker's hate? What exactly does the speaker find detestable about Brother Lawrence? What, for instance, seems to disturb him about the other monk in stanzas 3 and 5?
3. Do we learn more about Brother Lawrence or more about the speaker from this poem? Look at stanza 4, for example—whose lust is demonstrated by this stanza? And what about stanza 8—who *owns* the "scrofulous French novel"?
4. Notice that some lines are in italics—especially in stanza 2. How are these lines different from the rest of the soliloquy? Is it, for example, Brother Lawrence talking, or the speaker's own words (as opposed to his thoughts)?
5. What kinds of things has the speaker already done to indulge his hatred (look especially at the ends of stanzas 3 and 6)? What do these acts tell us about his character?
6. What would the speaker like to do to indulge his hatred for Brother Lawrence? Look particularly at the last three stanzas.

Belial: one of the names for Satan. **hy, zy, hine:** not clear—this may be an imitation of the bells for vespers (evening service) or perhaps the humming of a vespers hymn? **plena gratia ave, Virgo:** hail, Virgin, full of grace.

7. The speaker makes several references to scripture and to religious doctrine in stanzas 5 and 7. Quite aside from the traits of character we looked at in the last two questions, what do these references say about his "Christianity"?

WRITING SUGGESTIONS_____

1. One interpretation of "Western Wind" (p. 51) might suggest that the speaker of the poem has been abandoned by his or her lover. In an essay, support or refute that interpretation by using specific details from the poem.
2. A special case of the poet as novelist is the poet as historical novelist— writing a poem about a figure from the past and making the historical figure speak in the first person. Read the following poems in Poems for Further Reading, and select one for this exercise: John Hollander's "Hobbes, 1651" and Robert Lowell's "After the Surprising Conversions." Consult a good encyclopedia, *The Dictionary of National Biography, The Dictionary of American Biography,* or other reference works containing biographical articles, or individual biographies of the historical figures in these poems. Then write a short essay pointing out the specific features of the subject's life or personality that the poem highlights. Explain what the poem has added to your understanding of or sympathy for the character.

CHAPTER THREE

WHEN?

One of the things that makes us human is being aware of time—aware of clocks ticking, months passing, the past receding, and the future overtaking us. As a character says in Thornton Wilder's play *Our Town:*

> It goes so fast. We don't have time to look at one another. I didn't *realize.* So *all* that was going on and we never noticed! . . . Do any human beings ever realize life while they live it?—every, every minute?

Since this sense of time is so much a part of the human experience, it is no surprise to find the subject of time a recurring one in poetry. Even when the subject matter of the poem doesn't seem to be directly concerned with time, signals about time—suggestions about *when* the events, feelings, or ideas in the poem are happening—constitute essential elements of meaning. "When?" is thus an important question to ask of a poem, but we can get different kinds of answers. Time in poems can be indicated by clock or calendar references— that is, time of day, season of the year, period in a person's life—and by verb tenses.

CLOCKS AND CALENDARS

References to a time of day, a season, or a particular time of life are integral parts of several of the poems we have looked at in earlier chapters. A poet may refer to a specific time of day, as Robert Bly does in "Waking from Sleep":

> Inside the veins there are navies setting forth,
> Tiny explosions at the water lines,
> And seagulls weaving in the wind of the salty blood.
>
> It is the morning.

A poet may refer to a specific season, as John Keats does in "To Autumn":

> Season of mists and mellow fruitfulness,
>   Close bosom friend of the maturing sun.
> Conspiring with him how to load and bless
>   With fruit the vines that round the thatch-eves run.

Housman refers to spring in "Loveliest of Trees":

> Loveliest of trees, the cherry now
> Is hung with bloom along the bough,
> And stands about the woodland ride
> Wearing white for Eastertide.

A poet may refer to a specific time of life, as Randall Jarrell refers to childhood in "The Truth":

> I was so little then that I thought dreams
> Are in the room with you, like the cinema,
> That's why you don't dream when it's still light—
> They pull the shades down when it is, so you can sleep.

In each of these poems time is significant, since the time referred to affects the poem's language, imagery, and thus its meaning. For the reader, these references to time provide a context for lines or passages that otherwise might be difficult. Reread Robert Bly's "Waking from Sleep" (p. 14), in which many of the phrases and lines, out of context, seem to be talking either about a seaside scene or a countryside in winter:

> "There are navies setting forth"
> "Tiny explosions at the water lines"
> "Seagulls weaving in the wind"
> "The country has slept the whole winter"
> "Window seats were covered with fur skins, the yard was full
> Of stiff dogs, and hands that clumsily held heavy books."

These lines, especially the last three, are complicated; however, they do have the context of a specific time and occasion—morning, and waking from sleep. We can use this context to interpret the meaning of the more difficult lines. "Navies setting forth," "tiny explosions at the water lines," "seagulls weaving in the wind," are all comparisons to the activity of waking up and getting the blood circulating again. Morning is compared to things beginning—to "navies setting forth"—and it is contrasted to sleep and those things likened to sleep. The "country" that has "slept the whole winter" is the body, and the apparently difficult lines in that passage are further comparisons to the body in sleep:

> Window seats were covered with fur skins, the yard was full
> Of stiff dogs, and hands that clumsily held heavy books.

Morning has arrived, and sleep is the "master" that has left us for the day.

Bly has used the seasonal reference to winter as a comparison to the body in sleep. We have already seen the importance of such seasonal references in "Loveliest of Trees," with its springtime setting. In "Spring and Fall: To a Young Child," Hopkins uses literal seasons—spring and fall—to suggest comparisons between youth and age, innocence and wisdom. Here is a further example of seasonal reference as an essential part of a poem:

OCTOBER SPRING

> When crisp catalpa leaves
> come tumbling down the frosty morning air
> like tarpaulins for tulips,
> it's spring again in little college towns,
> October snipping at our brave beginnings,   5
> the new year pruned away to nine lean months
> of three-day weeks and fifty-
> minute hours. This new year lights
> no dogwood, no magnolia to find us
> limping through our shrunken moments or   10
> calling courage from our stubborn past,
> the long pilgrimage of algae,
> sponges, reptiles, flowers,
> men. No robins linger
> in the haze of this late spring   15
> to whistle, in our fifty-minute hours,
> the miracles to come: birds
> of brighter plumage, richer songs,
> flowers in the subtler shades, men and women
> walking together in peace.   20

---

catalpa leaves: the catalpa tree has large, heart-shaped leaves that appear late in the spring and are shed early in the fall.

> But the big catalpa leaves
> float crippled down the slanting sun,
> brown nourishment to our long
> hope, and we are clinging to
> our thinning years because brown leaves   25
> are clumsy promises: because it's
> spring again.

1975

Philip Appleman (b. 1926)

The title refers to two times, two different seasons. This pairing is a PARA-DOX, a statement or idea that is seemingly self-contradictory, yet true. How can this paradox be true? How can October be spring? How can spring be October? Answering these questions supplies the necessary context for understanding the various images and statements in the poem.

The first three lines establish the *time* of the poem:

> When crisp catalpa leaves
> come tumbling down the frosty morning air
> like tarpaulins for tulips.

The time is October, but in the next line Appleman introduces the paradox by stating: "It's spring again in little college towns." The reference to setting, to "little college towns," helps resolve the paradox. The season is fall; the month, October; Appleman, however, wants us to see that the beginning of one kind of year—the school year—is comparable to the beginning of another kind of year—the seasonal year. Thus, October becomes spring. He carries out this paradox and comparison in many of the lines that follow:

"October snipping at our brave beginnings"
"The new year pruned away to nine lean months"
"No magnolia to find us / limping through our shrunken moments"
"The haze of this late spring"
"brown nourishment"

In the final lines of the poem Appleman suggests further implications of the paradox:

> we are clinging to
> our thinning years because brown leaves
> are clumsy promises: because it's
> spring again.

The words "thinning years" echo the earlier lines (4–8) that describe the college term, "The new year pruned away to nine lean months," while expanding their implications. The literal season, autumn, reminds the speaker of the fact that time of life is passing—"our *thinning* years." But, paradoxically, the "brown leaves" of October are not a threat, but a promise of a new beginning. The beginning of the autumn season is part of a process that includes us:

> the long pilgrimage of algae,
> sponges, reptiles, flowers,
> men.

Instead of spring birds to whistle in the season, the brown leaves of October are "clumsy promises" of:

> the miracles to come: birds
> of brighter plumage, richer songs,
> flowers in subtler shades, men and women
> walking together in peace.

TIME AND TENSE

One of the most useful indications of time in a poem is the poet's use of *verb tenses*. Tense expresses distinctions of time, and the use of a specific tense— past, present, future—not only indicates the time of the poem, but involves certain nuances and subtle indications of meaning. In addition, the *change* of tense within a poem signals important shifts from one event to another, from one state of mind to a different one, from one idea to another.

In Randall Jarrell's "The Truth" (p. 44), attention to verb tenses aids the reader in answering some essential questions about meaning. Jarrell's poem begins:

> When I was four my father went to Scotland.
> They *said* he went to Scotland.

The speaker's use of the past tense—"was," "went," and "said,"—alerts the reader to essential information about speaker and meaning. The speaker is still young, but since he is telling about the past, when he was four, we realize that he is now, however, slightly older. The boy makes a distinction in tense, between then and now. He says:

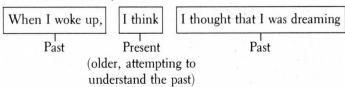

In another passage the boy says:

> I thought that then, but that's not right.
> Really it's in your head.

Here again, the verb tenses make a distinction between the speaker's past knowledge and his present, perhaps wiser, understanding of that past.

Time Past and Present

In poems with speakers, this use of past tense can remind the reader to watch for distinctions between the description of the past and the speaker's present understanding of that past.

MY PAPA'S WALTZ

The whiskey on your breath
Could make a small boy dizzy;
But I hung on like death:
Such waltzing was not easy.

We romped until the pans   5
Slid from the kitchen shelf;
My mother's countenance
Could not unfrown itself.

The hand that held my wrist
Was battered on one knuckle;   10
At every step you missed
My right ear scraped a buckle.

You beat time on my head
With a palm caked hard by dirt,
Then waltzed me off to bed   15
Still clinging to your shirt.

1948
Theodore Roethke (1908–1963)

For all its simplicity of vocabulary, "My Papa's Waltz" raises some interesting questions about meaning and tone. For instance, is the boy frightened of his father? How does the mother actually feel about what is going on? Is the father being cruel to his son? By considering both the speaker (as we did in the previous chapter) and the use of tense in the poem, the reader is better able to come up with at least some tentative answers to these and other questions.

Line 2 of the poem identifies the speaker as a "small boy," but the speaker is telling this incident in the past tense. There are no definite clues as to exactly how much later the speaker is recalling the waltz scene, but it is long enough for the speaker to look back and describe himself as a small boy at the time. Through his DICTION in the poem—his vocabulary and choice of words— Roethke shows both the simplicity of the child's viewpoint and the later, more complex feelings of the speaker:

> My mother's countenance
> Could not unfrown itself.

The word "countenance" stands out from the simpler words of the poem and is not a likely word for a small boy to use. It is the best clue in the poem to the older voice, first indicated by the speaker's use of the past tense. The boy was certainly aware of his mother's disapproval of his father's wild, slightly drunken dance about the kitchen; yet the older voice says "her countenance could not unfrown itself," suggesting perhaps that the speaker now realizes that the mother wasn't quite as angry as her countenance showed. The incident, for the boy, was a mixture of excitement ("We romped until the pans . . ."), some fear ("I hung on like death"), some pain ("my right ear scraped a buckle"), and some mixed feelings about his parents' behavior.

If the poem were in the present tense, the view of things would be limited by the child's age. Past tense, here, gives us the benefit of the older speaker's reflection. This more mature perception balances the elements of excitement, fear, pain, and confusion that the boy felt, with the enjoyment of that moment, which is allowed to predominate: "we *romped*"; [you] *waltzed* me off to bed."

Roethke's use of the past tense in "My Papa's Waltz" lets us make some general observations about the use of past tense in a poem. A poem set in the past tense with a speaker will usually show its past incidents, experiences, or feelings as they are seen through the speaker's *present* awareness or understanding. The reader needs to be alert to this distinction between past and present because the language the speaker uses to describe that past reveals a present attitude toward it. We can try out this generalization on the following poem:

FERN HILL

Now as I was young and easy under the apple boughs
About the lilting house and happy as the grass was green,

When?

The night above the dingle starry,
    Time let me hail and climb
    Golden in the heydays of his eyes,   5
And honoured among wagons I was prince of the apple towns
And once below a time I lordly had the trees and leaves
    Trail with daisies and barley
    Down the rivers of the windfall light.

And as I was green and carefree, famous among the barns   10
About the happy yard and singing as the farm was home,
    In the sun that is young once only,
      Time let me play and be
    Golden in the mercy of his means,
And green and golden I was huntsman and herdsman, the calves   15
Sang to my horn, the foxes on the hills barked clear and cold,
    And the sabbath rang slowly
    In the pebbles of the holy streams.

All the sun long it was running, it was lovely, the hay
Fields high as the house, the tunes from the chimneys, it was air   20
    And playing, lovely and watery
      And fire green as grass.
    And nightly under the simple stars
As I rode to sleep the owls were bearing the farm away,
All the moon long I heard, blessed among stables, the night-jars   25
    Flying with the ricks, and the horses
    Flashing into the dark.

And then to awake and the farm, like a wanderer white
With the dew, come back, the cock on his shoulder: it was all
    Shining, it was Adam and maiden,   30
    The sky gathered again
    And the sun grew round that very day.
So it must have been after the birth of the simple light
In the first, spinning place, the spellbound horses walking warm
    Out of the whinnying green stable   35
    On to the fields of praise.

---

dingle: a small wooded valley. **night-jars:** nocturnal birds like goatsuckers, whippoorwills, or night-hawks. **ricks:** piles of hay.

And honoured among foxes and pheasants by the gay house,
Under the new made clouds and happy as the heart was long,
   In the sun born over and over,
     I ran my heedless ways.   40
   My wishes raced through the house high hay
And nothing I cared, at my sky blue trades, that time allows
In all his tuneful turnings so few and such morning songs
   Before the children green and golden
     Follow him out of grace,   45

Nothing I cared, in the lamb white days, that time would take me
Up to the swallow thronged loft by the shadow of my hand,
   In the moon that is always rising,
     Nor that riding to sleep
   I should hear him fly with the high fields   50
And wake to the farm forever fled from the childless land.
Oh as I was young and easy in the mercy of his means,
   Time held me green and dying
   Though I sang in my chains like the sea.

1946

Dylan Thomas (1914–1953)

For all its complexity, "Fern Hill," in its first lines, gives us three clues that will provide answers about the language of the poem: the presence of a speaker, the use of past tense, and the speaker's attitude about the past he is describing:

> Now as *I was young and easy* under the apple boughs
> About the *lilting* house and *happy* as the grass was green.

Like "The Truth," and "My Papa's Waltz," this poem has a speaker *in the present* recalling the *past*. These first lines further tell us *when* these events take place ("Now as I was *young*"), and what the speaker's attitude is toward them (*easy, lilting, happy*). Time and attitude could change—in many poems they do—and the reader should be ready for such changes, but in "Fern Hill" the mood set in the opening lines is continued throughout the poem:

> "And *honoured* among wagons I was *prince* of the apple towns"

> "And as I was *green* and *carefree, famous* among the barns"

> "*honoured* among foxes"

> "my *sky blue* trades"

> "*lamb white* days"

This way of describing the past reveals both the boy's joy as it happened and an older, nostalgic feeling for those experiences. What does the older voice know or feel that his younger self didn't? For one thing, the older voice is intensely aware of time:

"Time let me hail and climb"

"Once below a time"

"Time let me play and be / Golden in the mercy of his means."

Perhaps the fullest statement of this juxtaposition of childhood joy and later awareness of time, between the past and the speaker's present awareness, is in the fifth stanza (lines 37–45). Both states of mind are represented in this stanza. For the child, time has no meaning: "The sun [is] born over and over." At his "sky blue trades," innocent and carefree play, he is "happy as the heart was long." But the speaker, looking back at that world, describes his younger self as "heedless," not because the child was irresponsible, but because he was heedless of time. The child instinctively thought that time was endless; it is the older voice in the poem that recognizes and laments the fact that time "allows so few and such morning songs."

The distinction between the two selves in the poem, indicated by the speaker's use of past tense, also explains one of the reasons for Thomas's intentionally rich and elaborate language. Through this language, Thomas conveys the child's timeless sense of wonder at the world, and the complex, allusive references to time reveal the speaker's present knowledge (though his younger self didn't realize it) that

Time held me green and dying
Though I sang in my chains like the sea.

Tense Shifts and Time Shifts

So far, we have been concerned with the consistent use of past tense. When there is a speaker, past tense implies present tense—the speaker's present, backward look. But other poems contain explicit tense shifts and less subtle contrasts between past and present:

BELLS FOR JOHN WHITESIDE'S DAUGHTER

There was such speed in her little body,
And such lightness in her footfall,
It is no wonder her brown study
Astonishes us all.

Her wars were bruited in our high window.   5
We looked among orchard trees and beyond
Where she took arms against her shadow,
Or harried unto the pond

The lazy geese, like a snow cloud
Dripping their snow on the green grass,   10
Tricking and stopping, sleepy and proud,
Who cried in goose, Alas,

For the tireless heart within the little
Lady with rod that made them rise
From their noon apple-dreams and scuttle   15
Goose-fashion under the skies!

But now go the bells, and we are ready,
In one house we are sternly stopped
To say we are vexed at her brown study,
Lying so primly propped.   20

1924
John Crowe Ransom (1888–1974)

In the first stanza there is an explicit contrast of times, a shift from the past to the present tense:

> There *was* such speed in her little body
> And such lightness in her footfall,
> It *is* no wonder her brown study
> *Astonishes* us all.

Ransom uses this contrast between past and present tense to organize the entire poem. Noting this contrast helps answer some of the questions that the poem encourages. Why exactly is the speaker talking about John Whiteside's daughter, and exactly what is he telling us about her? Why does the speaker emphasize her speed and lightness? Why should her "brown study" (deep thoughtfulness, daydreaming) astonish? The repetition of "brown study" is a clue that this phrase is very important to the meaning of the poem.

We can begin by noting, first of all, how the contrast of tenses organizes the poem:

---

bruited: reported.

When?

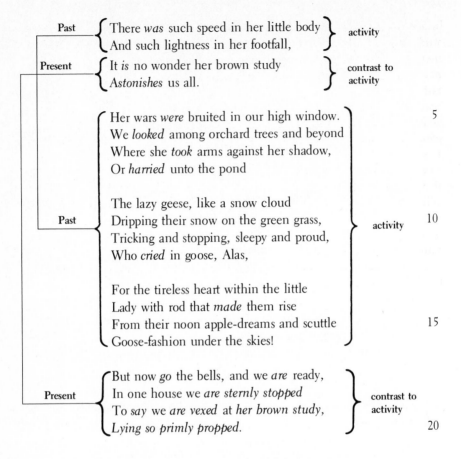

Past { There *was* such speed in her little body
And such lightness in her footfall, } activity

Present { It *is* no wonder her brown study
Astonishes us all. } contrast to activity

Her wars *were* bruited in our high window.   5
We *looked* among orchard trees and beyond
Where she *took* arms against her shadow,
Or *harried* unto the pond

Past { The lazy geese, like a snow cloud
Dripping their snow on the green grass,   10
Tricking and stopping, sleepy and proud,
Who *cried* in goose, Alas, } activity

For the tireless heart within the little
Lady with rod that *made* them rise
From their noon apple-dreams and scuttle   15
Goose-fashion under the skies!

Present { But now *go* the bells, and we *are* ready,
In one house we *are sternly stopped*
To *say* we *are vexed* at *her brown study*,
Lying so primly propped. } contrast to activity   20

The contrast between past and present involves some other contrasts. In lines 1–2 of the first stanza, the girl's "speed" and "lightness" (a past condition) are described, and these qualities are developed in stanzas 2–4, also set in the past tense. Her energetic activity is again referred to in the phrase "the tireless heart" (line 13). By contrast, lines 3–4 of stanza 1, set in the present tense, suggest a surprising change from her earlier speed and lightness: "her brown study / Astonishes us all."

One of the important questions about meaning in this poem involves the phrase "brown study." How will attention to the contrast of tenses in this poem help explain why Ransom has used this phrase? "Brown study" occurs in the stanza that is concerned with the present (stanza 1, lines 3–4), and it is repeated in the last stanza, also in the present. This suggests a contrast:

Past	*Present*
speed, lightness	brown study

In addition, the girl's "brown study" comes as a sudden and astonishing surprise to the speaker because it is such an unusual change from her earlier energetic, even pesky, activity. Thus, "brown study" must imply an astonishing *lack* of activity. Further contrasts and comparisons give more evidence. In the past, the girl harried the geese, "Who cried in goose, Alas, / For the tireless heart within the little / Lady" Now, in the present, the girl by her "brown study" and "Lying so primly propped," vexes the speaker. In the past it was the geese who cried, "Alas, / For the tireless heart within the little / Lady." Now, it is the speaker who is saying "we are vexed"; suggesting that "we" are also now crying "Alas, for the tireless heart." Why is this contrast implied? The title of the poem gives a further clue to the answer: "Bells [that is, funeral bells, tolling bells] for John Whiteside's Daughter." Ransom's careful use of contrast between past and present, between the girl's speed and lightness (then) and her "Lying [now] so primly propped," lets him suggest rather than bluntly announce the girl's death and its effect.

Here is another, humorous, example of how time shifts in poems provide a contrast between *then* and *now:*

ON THE VANITY OF EARTHLY GREATNESS

The tusks that clashed in mighty brawls
Of mastodons, are billiard balls.

The sword of Charlemagne the Just
Is ferric oxide, known as rust.

The grizzly bear whose potent hug   5
Was feared by all, is now a rug.

Great Caesar's bust is on the shelf,
And I don't feel very well myself.

1936
Arthur Guiterman (1871–1943)

Such time shifts provide a way of organizing the units of a poem. In the preceding poem, for instance, Guiterman contrasts past and present in each pair of lines.

Tense and time changes can also signal changed attitudes, circumstances, or fortunes:

THEY FLEE FROM ME

They flee from me that sometime did me seek,
With naked foot stalking in my chamber.
I have seen them gentle, tame, and meek
That now are wild and do not remember
That sometime they put themselves in danger   5
To take bread at my hand, and now they range
Busily seeking with a continual change.

Thankéd be Fortune, it hath been otherwise
Twenty times better, but once in special:
In thin array, after a pleasant guise,   10
When her loose gown from her shoulders did fall
And she me caught in her arms long and small;
Therewith all sweetly did me kiss,
And softly said, "Dear heart, how like you this?"

It was no dream; I lay broad waking.   15
But all is turnéd through my gentleness
Into a strange fashion of forsaking;
And I have leave to go, of her goodness,
And she also to use newfangleness.
But since that I so kindely am servéd,   20
I would fain know what she hath deservéd.

composed about 1535   1557
Sir Thomas Wyatt (1503–1542)

There are possible difficulties here of syntax, unfamiliar words, and poten-
tially baffling imagery. Attention to the homely details of tense and time shifts,
however, can go a long way to aid the reader through past and present:

Present	*Past*
They flee from me	that sometime did me seek
	I have seen them, gentle, tame, and meek
That now are wild and do not remember	
	That sometime they put themselves in danger
	To take bread at my hand
And now they range / Busily seeking	

guise: manner or appearance; Wyatt may be playing on two other meanings of the word—masque
or dance, and deceptive appearance. **small:** slender. **kindely:** in a way natural to human beings
and here, more specifically, to women. The word also puns on the sense of being kind. **fain:**
eagerly.

What is the speaker's purpose in making this contrast? If we compare the details in the phrases set in the present with those in the past, we see another contrast. All the images associated with the *present* are negative: *flee; wild; range, busily seeking.* The contrasting images describe the *past* more positively: *seek; gentle, tame, and meek; take bread at my hand.* This tone is borne out in the transition from the first to the second stanza. At the end of stanza 1, the speaker says: "Now they range / Busily seeking with a continual change." The second stanza begins:

> Thankéd be Fortune, it hath been otherwise
> Twenty times better, but once in special.

Then we get a specific scene set in the past:

> In thin array, after a pleasant guise,
> When her loose gown from her shoulders did fall
> And she me caught in her arms long and small;
> Therewith all sweetly did me kiss,
> And softly said, "Dear heart, how like you this?"

This reminiscence of the narrator answers one of the questions raised by the first stanza: Who are they who used to seek out the speaker? Some of the imagery in stanza 1 seemed to suggest animals—"stalking in my chamber," "wild," "take bread at my hand," "range,"—but now in stanza 2 we discover, partly through the contrast, that those who were "gentle, tame, and meek," are women and, as stanza 2 suggests, one woman in particular. In this second stanza we get the speaker's most intense expression of how good the past was when "they" (women; a woman) used to seek him out.

The third stanza makes another shift: "It was no dream, I lay broad waking." The speaker is in the present, speaking of that wonderful past. "But all *is* turnéd." With the present-tense verb, we are back in the present with all its negative associations and events:

> But all is turnéd through my gentleness,
> Into a strange fashion of forsaking;
> And I have leave to go, of her goodness,
> And she also to use newfangleness.
> But since that I so kindely am servéd,
> I would fain know what she hath deservéd.

When the speaker says he is served "so kindely" he is using VERBAL IRONY—words which convey a meaning opposite to their literal sense. It is not kind—that is, gentle, good, and helpful—of the woman to have treated the speaker in this way, although the pun on the word suggests that it *is* "kindely"—in the sense of *like womankind*—to have done so.

Looking at tense does not answer every question about the poem, but it does establish a context for exploring the poem's structure, the speaker's situation, and the tone with which he reports these events.

The Present as Process

The use of present tense in a poem, like the speaker's use of past tense or the use of contrasting tenses, also provides the reader with some clues about the poet's intentions. In "Spring and Fall: To a Young Child," the speaker begins,

> Margaret, are you grieving
> Over Goldengrove unleaving?

By using the present tense, the poet gives the situation immediacy; we are involved in the events in the very process of their occurring. We hear the conversation with Margaret as it happens. As the poet Elizabeth Bishop says, "The use of the present tense helps to convey this sense of the mind in action," ("An Interview with Elizabeth Bishop," *Shenandoah*, Winter, 1966).

In a poem set exclusively in the present tense, the explicit contrast of tenses and their implications that we have been considering so far are absent. The reader must find other clues to the organization and development of the poem. Bishop's statement provides such a clue. Since the poet, by using the present tense, is giving a sense of the mind in action, the reader must be prepared for a succession of ideas and, thus, for change in the poem as it progresses. The idea stated in the first line may change by the last line of the poem; the mood or feeling established at the beginning may alter—slightly or radically—by the end.

Reread John Milton's "When I Consider How My Light Is Spent" (p. 39), which uses the present tense to convey the mind in action. The first phrase of the poem, "When I *consider* how my light *is* spent," puts the experience into the present tense. The first two lines involve us in the present and unfolding concerns of the speaker's mind:

> When I consider how my light is spent,
> Ere half my days in this dark world and wide . . .

But more than this is on the speaker's mind. The anguish that his "light is spent" before half his life span is over is intensified by another awareness:

> *And* that one talent which is death to hide
> Lodg'd with me useless . . .

The "And" here indicates a further development in the poem. Not only is the speaker blind, but the blindness is made all the more painful by the realization that, as a result, his talent is useless. These two facts—the blindness and the uselessness of his talent—are made even more frustrating because he is eager to serve:

> my soul [is] more bent
> To serve therewith my Maker, and present
> My true account.

By using present tense, Milton is able to show the speaker's mind in the process of thinking. He is blind, his talent is apparently useless, yet he wants to serve; he wants to be able to present his true account. In the face of these developing and conflicting states of mind, the speaker asks the critical question:

> "Doth God exact day-labor, light denied?"

Then comes a major change in the poem. The word "But" signals the beginning of an answer:

> But Patience, to prevent
> That murmur, soon replies, "God doth not need
> Either man's work or His own gifts.

We can note still further changes in the development of the poem. The anguished question "Doth God exact day-labor, light denied?" becomes, in line 9, a "murmur," and the intense burden of blindness that the speaker describes in the first eight lines is now a "mild yoke."

By using present tense, Milton is able to show the speaker's state of mind as it moves from one realization to another. The speaker begins by considering his burden and the pain it causes, since it prevents him from serving God as he imagines he ought. He comes to understand in a new and changed way what God expects and what service really means: "They also serve who only stand and wait." Even though the poem has been in the present tense throughout, it has moved from describing one state of mind to its opposite—from despair to comfort.

Even though a present-tense poem may describe an actual scene or happening, it may still be more concerned with a process of mind and how outward events affect a sequence of thoughts. The following poem, "Dover Beach," illustrates this point, moving somehow from its calm, even romantic, opening to its pessimistic close. Although we can see that there indeed has been a change, we need to know how, and at what points, the poem changes as it progresses. This brings us back to the importance of tense and the shifts in mood or feeling that may occur in a present-tense poem.

DOVER BEACH

The sea is calm tonight.
The tide is full, the moon lies fair
Upon the straits; on the French coast the light
Gleams and is gone; the cliffs of England stand
Glimmering and vast, out in the tranquil bay.   5
Come to the window, sweet is the night-air!
Only, from the long line of spray
Where the sea meets the moon-blanched land,
Listen! you hear the grating roar
Of pebbles which the waves draw back, and fling,   10
At their return, up the high strand,
Begin, and cease, and then again begin,
With tremulous cadence slow, and bring
The eternal note of sadness in.

Sophocles long ago   15
Heard it on the Aegean, and it brought
Into his mind the turbid ebb and flow
Of human misery; we
Find also in the sound a thought,
Hearing it by this distant northern sea.   20

The Sea of Faith
Was once, too, at the full, and round earth's shore
Lay like the folds of a bright girdle furled.
But now I only hear
Its melancholy, long, withdrawing roar,   25
Retreating, to the breath
Of the night-wind, down the vast edges drear
And naked shingles of the world.

Ah, love, let us be true
To one another! For the world, which seems   30
To lie before us like a world of dreams,
So various, so beautiful, so new,
Hath really neither joy, nor love, nor light,
Nor certitude, nor peace, nor help for pain;
And we are here as on a darkling plain   35

Swept with confused alarms of struggle and flight,
Where ignorant armies clash by night.

                                        1867
                    Matthew Arnold (1822–1888)

If we look for external action in the poem—that is, a sequence of outward events—we find there are really only two: the speaker is at a window looking out at the sea (lines 1–5), and then he speaks to someone else in the room (6). Everything else in the poem is an inward event as the mind of the speaker moves through a series of associations that lead him from the calm description at the beginning to the despairing words at the end.

The speaker begins with a description of the sea and the night and the appearance of things. He then speaks to the other person in the room, inviting that person to share in this tranquil scene. Up to this point in the poem, the speaker has been emphasizing the *appearance* of things ("The sea is calm," "The tide is full," "The moon lies fair," and so on); at line 7, there is a definite change. The speaker now describes *sound:*

> Only, from the long line of spray
> Where the sea meets the moon-blanched land,
> *Listen! You hear the grating roar*
> *Of pebbles.*

The word "Only" signals a change much as the word "But" did in "When I Consider How My Light Is Spent." This is not just a transition from the visible to the audible; there is also a contrast between pleasant appearance and unpleasant sound: "The tranquil bay" becomes "the grating roar." This begins a train of associations that we follow as the poem develops.

Recall that the appearance of things is still the same, but the sound that the speaker now hears brings to his mind "the eternal note of sadness." Why "*eternal*"? When such a question occurs, it is useful to look around in the nearby lines to see if there is some explanation. Earlier, Arnold has partly prepared the reader for the word "eternal":

> you hear the grating roar
> Of pebbles which the waves draw back, and fling,
> At their return, up the high strand,
> *Begin, and cease, and then again begin . . .*

This last phrase suggests an *eternal* repetition of the waves against the shore.

In the second stanza, there is a further development of this idea of the "eternal note of sadness." We can PARAPHRASE this stanza (restate it in our own words) as follows:

The sound I am hearing, the speaker says, was also heard by Sophocles, the Greek playwright, a long time ago. This sound brought into Sophocles' mind a comparison between that sound and the "ebb and flow of human misery."

This sound has an "eternal note of sadness" for the speaker, since long ago Sophocles heard it and made a sad comparison, and *now* the speaker hears that same sound and finds

> also in the sound a thought,
> Hearing it by this distant northern sea.

What is the particular thought that the sound of the sea brings into the speaker's mind? Before we attempt to answer that question, let's review how the train of associations in the speaker's mind has developed so far. Such a train of associations is often called STREAM OF CONSCIOUSNESS.

The speaker began with the sight of the sea and the tranquil, peaceful appearance of things. He then hears the "grating roar" of the sea, which, for him at least, is in sharp contrast to its appearance. This sound recalls Sophocles' comparison of the waves to the "ebb and flow of human misery." Now by this distant northern sea (distant in time and space from Sophocles' world), the speaker hears this same sound. It makes him think of something that also creates sadness, the ebbing of the "Sea of Faith."

Two associations come together in stanza 3:

> The Sea of Faith
> Was once, too, at the full, and round earth's shore
> Lay like the folds of a bright girdle furled.
> But now I only hear
> Its melancholy, long, withdrawing roar.

The first lines of this passage are highly compressed. If we expand their syntax, they might read something like this: "The Sea of Faith was once, too, at the full (tide) like the real full tide I am looking at; this Sea of Faith, like the actual full tide, also (once) lay round earth's shores furled like the folds of a bright girdle (that is, a protective band)." The speaker connects the actual sea he is looking at to the Sea of Faith, a metaphorical sea of uniform belief in religion and other social institutions that once protected the speaker's world. The real sea out there is at full tide. Yet underneath its appearance is "the grating roar," the sound of the high tide beginning to withdraw. The speaker associates this sound with the ebbing of the Sea of Faith, "retreating" with "its melancholy, long, withdrawing roar." The word "roar" applied to the metaphoric "Sea of Faith" links to the earlier "grating roar" of the actual sea.

At this point, there is a further development. The speaker is concerned with the ebbing of the Sea of Faith. Now he turns to the other person:

> Ah, love, let us be true
> To one another.

The speaker has begun by asking the lover to share the beauty of the scene, and has ended with a recognition that in a world where the Sea of Faith no longer protects, it is desperately necessary for the lovers to be true to one another, to be faithful, since there is nothing else. The world that the speaker first described in the opening lines is really an illusion:

> For the world, which *seems*
> To lie before us like a land of dreams,
> So various, so beautiful, so new,
> Hath *really* neither joy, nor love, nor light,
> Nor certitude, nor peace, nor help for pain.

The poem ends with a final comparison:

> And we are here *as* on a darkling plain
> Swept with confused alarms of struggle and flight,
> Where ignorant armies clash by night.

It is important to remember that these last lines are one more association in the speaker's mind. The change that has occurred in the poem has not been in the external scene; the two people of the poem are still in the room looking out at the tranquil, moonlit scene. Neither has time changed in the poem. The only time that has passed is exactly as much time as it has taken the speaker to say the words. What has changed has been the speaker's mood. The chain of associations has led him from the opening phrases where he says "Sweet is the night-air," to the final image of the two lovers on "a darkling plain," protected, if at all, from the "confused alarms" of existence only by being "true to one another."

To sum up, distinctions of tense, like questions about speaker, provide another starting point from which to find answers about the meaning of a poem. Attention to references to a specific season or time of day, to a time of year, to a time in the speaker's life can help explain the language or images of a poem that are related to these indications of time. A speaker's use of past tense can alert the reader to note distinctions between the past and the speaker's present attitude toward the past. The use of contrasting or changing tenses in a poem provides organizational clues. Attention to these contrasts or changes in tense helps the reader to identify the specific time referred to in any given stanza or line. Finally, the use of present tense reminds us that the poem is a process in which things can change. The reader, then, can be alert for changes in feelings, ideas, or experience as the poem progresses.

EXERCISES

A.   **THE GROUNDHOG**

In June, amid the golden fields,
I saw a groundhog lying dead.
Dead lay he; my senses shook,
And mind outshot our naked frailty.
There lowly in the vigorous summer   5
His form began its senseless change,
And made my senses waver dim
Seeing nature ferocious in him.
Inspecting close his maggots' might
And seething cauldron of his being,   10
Half with loathing, half with a strange love,
I poked him with an angry stick.
The fever arose, became a frame
And Vigour circumscribed the skies,
Immense energy in the sun,   15
And through my frame a sunless trembling.
My stick had done nor good nor harm.
Then stood I silent in the day
Watching the object, as before;
And kept my reverence for knowledge   20
Trying for control, to be still,
To quell the passion of the blood;
Until I had bent down on my knees
Praying for joy in the sight of decay.
And so I left; and I returned   25
In Autumn strict of eye, to see
The sap gone out of the groundhog,
But the bony sodden hulk remained.
But the year had lost its meaning,
And in intellectual chains   30
I lost both love and loathing,

The Groundhog

Mured up in the wall of wisdom.
Another summer took the fields again
Massive and burning, full of life,
But when I chanced upon the spot   35
There was only a little hair left,
And bones bleaching in the sunlight
Beautiful as architecture;
I watched them like a geometer,
And cut a walking stick from a birch.   40
It has been three years, now.
There is no sign of the groundhog.
I stood there in the whirling summer,
My hand capped a withered heart,
And thought of China and of Greece,   45
Of Alexander in his tent;
Of Montaigne in his tower,
Of Saint Theresa in her wild lament.

1936
Richard Eberhart (b. 1904)

1. Begin by underscoring the tenses in this poem and the other references to time. Why is "June" (line 1) an important part of the poem, especially to lines 1–25?
2. When is the speaker of the poem actually speaking?
3. How does the shift to autumn (line 26) affect the language and imagery of the lines that follow?
4. The poem goes through several changes of seasons and the passing of the years. How do these changes also mark changes in the speaker's attitude?
5. The references to Alexander, Montaigne, and Saint Theresa require some explanatory footnotes. However, what does the emphasis on tense and time and change in the poem suggest about the meaning of the last four lines even without further information?

Alexander in his tent: Alexander the Great (356–323 B.C.). Alexander, the great conquerer, fell ill of a fever and died in his tent at the age of 33. **Montaigne in his tower:** Montaigne (1533–1592), the French philosopher and essayist, abruptly retired to his library tower in 1571. His essays sketch out a pattern of indifference to death, then skepticism, and finally a recognition of the individual's inability to know anything with certainty. **Saint Theresa in her wild lament:** St. Theresa of Avila (1515–1582), Spanish mystic and writer. In her autobiography she describes episodes of despair and of religious ecstasy.

B.

THE SOOTE SEASON

The soote season, that bud and bloom forth brings,
With green hath clad the hill and eke the vale;
The nightingale with feathers new she sings;
The turtle to her make hath told her tale,
Summer is come, for every spray now springs;   5
The hart hath hung his old head on the pale;
The buck in brake his winter coat he flings,
The fishes float with new repaired scale;
The adder all her slough away she slings,
The swift swallow pursueth the flies small;   10
The busy bee her honey now she mings,
Winter is worn, that was the flowers' bale.
And thus I see among these pleasant things,
Each care decays, and yet my sorrow springs.

1557

Henry Howard, Earl of Surrey (1517–1547)

TO THE VIRGINS, TO MAKE MUCH OF TIME

Gather ye rosebuds while ye may,
  Old time is still a-flying;
And this same flower that smiles today
  Tomorrow will be dying.

The glorious lamp of heaven, the sun,   5
  The higher he's a-getting,
The sooner will his race be run,
  And nearer he's to setting.

That age is best which is the first,
  When youth and blood are warmer;   10
But being spent, the worse, and worst
  Times still succeed the former.

---

soote: sweet. **eke:** also. **turtle:** turtledove. **make:** mate. **brake:** thicket. **mings:** remembers. **bale:** harm.

Then be not coy, but use your time,
    And while ye may, go marry;
For, having lost but once your prime,   15
    You may forever tarry.

1648
Robert Herrick (1591–1674)

NOTHING GOLD CAN STAY

Nature's first green is gold,
Her hardest hue to hold.
Her early leaf's a flower;
But only so an hour.
Then leaf subsides to leaf.   5
So Eden sank to grief,
So dawn goes down to day.
Nothing gold can stay.

1923
Robert Frost (1874–1963)

ZENITH: WALKER CREEK

The woodcock now spends his evenings more quietly.
The robin sings less urgently, more chirpy.
Grass which sprang up for a while as though
it meant to reach the stars each afternoon
has moderated its ambitions a little.   5
The fields have settled down to heavy feeding and breeding.
Marsh, its winter khaki conquered,
has greened itself into equator color,
swaying taller and taller with the tides' tickling.
"Nature's first green is gold." Her second   10
is opaque as billiard tables. Now she plays her game,
less urgency in the dawns, less melodrama.
The pheasant's declaration rings out half as often;
the minnows flutter calmly in their pools,

having learned at last that their prey cannot escape.   15
The shade is deeper, more desirable.
Dogs trot in preference to running,
spend more of daylight sprawling and panting.
The pedalling bicyclists shift to lower gears,
the bay blooms with looser and larger sails.   20
Our sun has given of its best in waxing:
it teeters above our heads as nearly
as the earth's escapism will permit,
toppling with some reluctance after noon
toward the west to keep us on the boil   25
till the anger of flies and the hunger of mosquitoes
drive us from sun to shade, from shade to the shelter
of screens, where, after fall of darkness, we drown
our senses in sunburn, poison ivy, gin.
These long days are all the promise we are given.   30

1977
Peter Davison (b. 1928)

1. In each poem, what season is being described, and to what—if anything—is each season being compared or contrasted?
2. In "The Soote Season," what quality of the season does the speaker emphasize? What is achieved by Surrey's holding off the entrance of the speaker until the last two lines of the poem? What relationship does the speaker see between himself and the season?
3. To whom is Herrick's poem addressed? What do the rosebuds (stanza 1), the sun (stanza 2), and "that age" (stanza 3) have in common? Why are these details part of the speaker's argument?
4. In Frost's poem, "Nothing Gold Can Stay," what two parts of the single season are being described? What do the two parts correspond to in the comparison to day? in the comparison to Eden? How does Frost relate the season to all of human and natural events?
5. What two seasons are being contrasted in Davison's "Zenith: Walker Creek"? Who is the speaker including when he uses the word "we"? How is that "we" affected by the season being described? Compare Davison's final line, "These long days are all the promise we are given," to Appleman's phrase in "October Spring" (p. 63), "because brown leaves are clumsy promises." What is meant by "promise(s)" in each poem, and what is the link between promise and season?

C. THE DEATH OF THE BALL TURRET GUNNER

From my mother's sleep I fell into the State,
And I hunched in its belly till my wet fur froze.
Six miles from earth, loosed from its dream of life,
I woke to black flak and the nightmare fighters.
When I died they washed me out of the turret with a hose.

1945
Randall Jarrell (1914–1965)

1. The use of past tense in poems involving speakers usually gives a later and
   fuller perspective on past events. Compare, for instance, "The Truth"
   (p. 44), "My Papa's Waltz" (p. 66), and "Fern Hill" (p. 67). How does
   Jarrell make dramatic use of this device?
2. What is the later and fuller perspective here, and how does it explain some
   of the metaphors in the poem—"my mother's sleep," "the State," "wet
   fur," "dream of life," "nightmare fighters"?

D. TO AN ATHLETE DYING YOUNG

The time you won your town the race
We chaired you through the market-place;
Man and boy stood cheering by,
And home we brought you shoulder-high.

Today, the road all runners come,   5
Shoulder-high we bring you home,
And set you at your threshold down,
Townsman of a stiller town.

Smart lad, to slip betimes away
From fields where glory does not stay   10
And early though the laurel grows
It withers quicker than the rose.

Eyes the shady night has shut
Cannot see the record cut,
And silence sounds no worse than cheers   15
After earth has stopped the ears:

When?

Now you will not swell the rout
Of lads that wore their honors out,
Runners whom renown outran
And the name died before the man.   20

So set, before its echoes fade,
The fleet foot on the sill of shade,
And hold to the low lintel up
The still-defended challenge-cup.

And round that early-laureled head   25
Will flock to gaze the strengthless dead,
And find unwithered on its curls
The garland briefer than a girl's.

1896
A. E. Housman (1859–1936)

1. Go through the poem, identifying the time indicated by tense in each
   stanza. What movement in time can be seen in the use of tenses?
2. What happened between the time of stanza 1 and the time of stanza 2?
3. Though the tense is different in each of the first two stanzas and the situation is dramatically different, Housman constructs a likeness between the
   two situations by using some of the same words and phrases. How does
   this likeness in vocabulary support the argument of the succeeding stanzas?

E.   **ODE TO A NIGHTINGALE**

1

My heart aches, and a drowsy numbness pains
    My sense, as though of hemlock I had drunk,
Or emptied some dull opiate to the drains
    One minute past, and Lethe-wards had sunk:
'Tis not through envy of thy happy lot,   5
    But being too happy in thine happiness—
        That thou, light-wingéd Dryad of the trees,
            In some melodious plot

ODE: a long, usually serious poem with an involved stanzaic pattern, though there is no conventionally fixed form. **hemlock:** a poisonous plant used as a powerful narcotic. **drains:** dregs. **Lethe-
wards:** toward Lethe, the river in classical mythology whose waters cause forgetfulness. **dryad:** a
tree-nymph.

Ode to a Nightingale

Of beechen green, and shadows numberless,
   Singest of summer in full-throated ease.   10

2

O, for a draught of vintage! that hath been
   Cooled a long age in the deep-delvéd earth,
Tasting of Flora and the country green,
   Dance, and Provençal song, and sunburnt mirth!
O for a beaker full of the warm South,   15
   Full of the true, the blushful Hippocrene,
      With beaded bubbles winking at the brim,
         And purple-stainéd mouth;
That I might drink, and leave the world unseen,
   And with thee fade away into the forest dim: 20

3

Fade far away, dissolve, and quite forget
   What thou among the leaves hast never known,
The weariness, the fever, and the fret
   Here, where men sit and hear each other groan;
Where palsy shakes a few, sad, last gray hairs,   25
   Where youth grows pale, and specter-thin, and dies;
      Where but to think is to be full of sorrow
         And leaden-eyed despairs,
Where Beauty cannot keep her lustrous eyes,
   Or new Love pine at them beyond tomorrow.   30

4

Away! away! for I will fly to thee,
   Not charioted by Bacchus and his pards,
But on the viewless wings of Poesy,
   Though the dull brain perplexes and retards:
Already with thee! tender is the night,   35
   And haply the Queen-Moon is on her throne,
      Clustered around by all her starry Fays;
         But here there is no light,

Flora: The Roman goddess of flowering plants. **Provençal:** of Provence, the region in France where the poetry of the troubadours flourished in the middle ages. **Hippocrene:** the spring on Mt. Helicon in Greece whose waters were said to inspire poetry. **Bacchus:** the god of wine. **pards:** leopards. **viewless:** invisible. **fays:** elves having magical powers.

When?

Save what from heaven is with the breezes blown
   Through verdurous glooms and winding mossy ways.   40

5

I cannot see what flowers are at my feet,
   Nor what soft incense hangs upon the boughs,
But, in embalmèd darkness, guess each sweet
   Wherewith the seasonable month endows
The grass, the thicket, and the fruit tree wild;   45
   White hawthorn, and the pastoral eglantine;
     Fast fading violets covered up in leaves;
      And mid-May's eldest child,
   The coming musk-rose, full of dewy wine,
    The murmurous haunt of flies on summer eves.   50

6

Darkling I listen; and for many a time
   I have been half in love with easeful Death,
Called him soft names in many a musèd rhyme,
   To take into the air my quiet breath;
Now more than ever seems it rich to die,   55
   To cease upon the midnight with no pain,
     While thou art pouring forth thy soul abroad
      In such an ecstasy!
   Still wouldst thou sing, and I have ears in vain—
    To thy high requiem become a sod.   60

7

Thou wast not born for death, immortal Bird!
   No hungry generations tread thee down;
The voice I hear this passing night was heard
   In ancient days by emperor and clown:
Perhaps the selfsame song that found a path   65
   Through the sad heart of Ruth, when, sick for home,
     She stood in tears amid the alien corn;
      The same that ofttimes hath
   Charmed magic casements, opening on the foam
    Of perilous seas, in faery lands forlorn.   70

---

darkling: in the dark. **Ruth:** the biblical figure who left her native land (see the Book of Ruth).

8

Forlorn! the very word is like a bell
  To toll me back from thee to my sole self!
Adieu! the fancy cannot cheat so well
  As she is famed to do, deceiving elf.
Adieu! adieu! thy plaintive anthem fades   75
  Past the near meadows, over the still stream,
    Up the hill side; and now 'tis buried deep
    In the next valley-glades:
  Was it a vision, or a waking dream?
  Fled is that music:—Do I wake or sleep?

1819
John Keats (1795–1821)

1. Like Wyatt's "They Flee from Me" (p. 74), Keats's "Ode to a Nightingale" may present difficulties to the reader—difficulties that involve syntax, vocabulary, and allusions to classical and poetic mythology. But the recognition that this is a poem spoken in the present tense by a speaker who is calling attention to his state of mind can take the reader through many of the apparent difficulties. Careful attention to the beginning of the poem will pay off. Who is being addressed in stanza 1—that is, who is the "thy," "thine," and "thou"? The allusion to "light-wingéd dryad" might be confusing without a footnote or other explanatory reference, but what is the context for this allusion?
2. What is the speaker's initial state of mind in stanza 1, and what is its cause? (check lines 1; 6–7)
3. What qualities of the nightingale does the speaker stress in stanza 1? (check lines 5–6; 10)
4. The phrase "My heart aches," the happiness that the speaker attributes to the nightingale, and the reference to the "full-throated ease" of the nightingale all set up a train of associations that is developed in stanza 2. What are those strands of associations linking stanzas 1 and 2? What does the speaker desire?
5. The speaker's mental associations are continued in stanza 3. What contrast is being made between the speaker's world and the nightingale's? What does the nightingale represent to the speaker at this point in the poem?
6. This "escape" series of associations is continued in stanzas 4, 5, and 6. What mode of escape is emphasized in line 33? How is this imaginative world described in stanza 5? What is the logical end of "escape" as described in stanza 6?

---

fancy: the poet's imagination.

7. What thought in stanza 6 brings the speaker back to the immediate world?
8. What quality of the nightingale is seen as an enduring one in stanza 7, and how does this emphasis connect to the speaker's earlier thoughts? How does the allusion to Ruth link to the speaker's situation?
9. What word links stanzas 7 and 8? What does that word and its association bring the speaker back to? What is the speaker's state of mind at the end of the poem?

WRITING SUGGESTIONS _____

1. In the following passage, Richard Eberhart describes the incidents that gave rise to "The Groundhog":

> Jack had thrown a shot groundhog onto a board above ground, flat to the open sun. I surveyed the corpse just now, keeping well out of the wind. The animal had lost all its form, all that we call grace and trimness; it was a seething mass of maggots; the shock of the sea-like motion and swirl of these was at first so great as to give the illusion of the viscera pulsing and moving. One looks at one's face in the glass, and wonders on the eternal question of consciousness. There was intense life, though no longer the groundhog's, in the rotting carcass; but it takes calm reason to stave off revulsion at decay. I think we must come to love the reality of decay, symbol again of the very forces of life. Life is the animating principle, and we are nothing but its nurslings.
>
> —quoted in Joel H. Roache, *Richard Eberhart:*
> *The Progress of an American Poet*

Eberhart says, "It takes calm reason to stave off revulsion at decay." In an essay, explain how his use of time in the poem, both structurally and figuratively, achieves this state of "calm reason."

2. The poet's or speaker's perspective on experience—point of view and distance in time from which the experience is viewed—is often indicated by verb tenses. Using "The Death of the Ball Turret Gunner" (p. 87), "Those Were the Days" (p. 418), "Ex-Basketball Player" (p. 422), or "I Have Not Lingered in European Monasteries" (p. 423), explain how that perspective works in the poem. Be specific in using examples of tense and tense changes.

CHAPTER FOUR

WHERE?

In "Dover Beach," Matthew Arnold describes the effect of a specific place on the consciousness. Such interplay between places and the people who visit or inhabit them is a constant of the human experience. Here, for example, the American writer Edward Abbey (b. 1927) describes his reaction to a natural scene:

> In deep stillness, in a somber solemn light, these beings stand, these fins of sandstone hollowed out by time, the juniper trees so shaggy, tough and beautiful, the dead or dying pinyon pines, the little shrubs of rabbit-brush and blackbrush, the dried-up stalks of asters and sunflowers gone to seed, the black-rooted silver-blue sage. How difficult to imagine this place without a human presence; how necessary. I am almost prepared to believe that this sweet virginal primitive land will be grateful for my departure and the absence of the tourists, will breathe metaphorically a sigh of relief—like a whisper of wind—when we are all and finally gone and the place and its creations can return to their ancient procedures unobserved and undisturbed by the busy, anxious, brooding consciousness of man.
> —*Desert Solitaire: A Season in the Wilderness*

A look back over the poems discussed so far confirms the importance of place in poetry. For example, much of the point of "October Spring" depends on the fact that Appleman is talking about a college town, where the school year begins in autumn. The location in an autumn forest is also important to Hopkins' "Spring and Fall." We cannot really make sense of Reed's "Naming of Parts" or Browning's "Soliloquy of the Spanish Cloister" without realizing that Reed's poem is set in an army training room of some sort and Browning's takes place in a monastery.

How important is place in Pound's "The Garden" (p. 9)? Could the setting—Kensington Gardens—as easily have been Central Park or Golden Gate Park or some other public place? It is true that there are many public places where one might have seen a rich woman surrounded by a "rabble / of the filthy, sturdy, unkillable infants of the very poor." But Pound does not make a point of the woman's *wealth* exactly, though he does emphasize that the children are those of the *very poor*. What he does say about the woman is that "In her is the end of breeding"—in other words, rather than wealth, what we have here is a matter of *class*. Class divorced from economic considerations—class having to do with birth and breeding—is more a European than an American phenomenon. In that sense we can say that the location of this poem *is* important. It fits Kensington Gardens in London where it would not fit Central Park because the speaker views this European phenomenon—the juxtaposition of classes as the woman is surrounded by this "rabble"—and he reacts to it. In fact he is part of the juxtaposition, because the woman is almost afraid he will commit the indiscretion of speaking to her. In other words the poem is at least partly about the speaker's reaction to this Old World class difference, and therefore it needs an Old World setting.

Asking questions about place, location, or setting can give us different kinds of information about a poem. Asking "Where?" may help explain why certain descriptions occur: the poet is describing things that can be seen at that location. Such a question may lead to answers about the poet's use of particular language, images, and comparisons. Finally, it may help us discover how place creates or changes an attitude in the speaker of the poem.

PLACE AND DESCRIPTION

Sometimes the poet tells us the location in the poem's title. We need to recall that setting in order to understand specific lines or descriptions:

MUSÉE DES BEAUX ARTS

About suffering they were never wrong,
The Old Masters: how well they understood
Its human position; how it takes place
While someone else is eating or opening a window or just walking
    dully along;
How, when the aged are reverently, passionately waiting   5
For the miraculous birth, there always must be
Children who did not specially want it to happen, skating
On a pond at the edge of the wood:

Musée des Beaux Arts

They never forgot
That even the dreadful martyrdom must run its course   10
Anyhow in a corner, some untidy spot
Where the dogs go on with their doggy life and the torturer's horse
Scratches its innocent behind on a tree.

In Brueghel's *Icarus* for instance: how everything turns away
Quite leisurely from the disaster; the ploughman may   15
Have heard the splash, the forsaken cry,
But for him it was not an important failure; the sun shone
As it had to on the white legs disappearing into the green
Water; and the expensive delicate ship that must have seen
Something amazing, a boy falling out of the sky,   20
Had somewhere to get to and sailed calmly on.

1940
W. H. Auden (1907–1973)

Here there is no personal voice, no first-person speaker we can ask about, and
the poem is not specific about time, either. There is merely a voice making the
opening assertion: "About suffering they were never wrong, / The Old Masters." Where does this idea about the Old Masters come from? One thing we
know is that the poem is taking place at the Musée des Beaux Arts or is somehow connected with this place. The title means Museum of Fine Arts, but
what does this location have to do with the opening statements about suffering
and the Old Masters? To see how location is important, we must pursue some
line-by-line questions.

The speaker asserts that the Old Masters were never wrong about suffering.
Whom exactly does he mean, and what did they have to say about suffering?
These are reasonable questions, and the poem will answer the second one if
we read on to the next clauses:

how well they understood
Its human position; how it takes place
While someone else is eating or opening a window or just walking
dully along.

What the Old Masters understood about suffering was its *human position*, which
is that suffering takes place while other people are doing ordinary things like
eating or opening windows. But who are the Old Masters? Check your dictionary and you will find that the phrase means the great European painters of
the sixteenth and seventeenth centuries. In the second stanza Auden makes
reference to a specific Old Master: Pieter Brueghel (c. 1525–1569), and to a

specific painting: Brueghel's *Landscape with the Fall of Icarus*. At this point you may say, "How can I understand this poem? I've never seen this painting; I have no idea what it looks like." It is true that seeing the painting is a great help in reading Auden's poem. But a careful look at the second stanza will reveal that Auden has described the painting for us in some detail, and especially that feature of it about which he has said the Old Masters were never wrong—the human position of suffering. We do need to know that Icarus is the figure in Greek mythology who flew too near the sun with wings made of wax, which melted, so that he fell into the Aegean Sea.

If you look at a reproduction of *Icarus* in an art book, you will see that the landscape and ploughman are prominent in the foreground, while the legs disappearing into the water are small and unobtrusive in one corner of the canvas. But Auden also tells us something of the relation between the picture's elements: everything is leisurely turning away from the disaster, he says; it is not important to the ploughman even though he may have heard the splash or cry, and the ship goes sailing on even though it must have seen the boy falling.

But what about the rest of the first stanza? How does location provide a context for these somewhat puzzling lines:

> How, when the aged are reverently, passionately waiting
> For the miraculous birth, there always must be
> Children who did not specially want it to happen, skating
> On a pond at the edge of the wood:
> They never forgot
> That even the dreadful martyrdom must run its course
> Anyhow in a corner, some untidy spot
> Where the dogs go on with their doggy life and the torturer's horse
> Scratches its innocent behind on a tree.

Who are the aged here? What miraculous birth? What children? Why don't they want it to happen, especially? What dreadful martyrdom? Who is the torturer? If we keep in mind what we already know about the poem, we can at least begin to answer these questions. We know the location—a museum—and we know Auden describes one particular painting in the second stanza. It is reasonable to suppose that these details also refer to paintings. If we conclude that these are descriptions of paintings, then we can infer some things about them, even though we have never been to the museum where Brueghel's *Icarus* hangs. The miraculous birth seems likely to be the birth of Christ—the miraculous birth about which paintings have been done for almost a thousand years. There are many possibilities for the "dreadful martyrdom"—the Massacre of the Innocents, the Crucifixion of Christ, or some mythological terror. But it doesn't really matter what the particular martyrdom is for Auden's stanza to make sense to us. There is a martyrdom going on—suffering—while the world goes right on with its business:

the dogs go on with their doggy life and the torturer's horse
Scratches its innocent behind on a tree.

Although place can be important in helping us to see what is going on in
a poem and why certain things are included, sometimes we are not directly
told the location of the poem:

EPIC

I have lived in important places, times
When great events were decided: who owned
That half a rood of rock, a no-man's land
Surrounded by our pitchfork-armed claims.
I heard the Duffys shouting 'Damn your soul'   5
And old McCabe stripped to the waist, seen
Step the plot defying blue cast-steel—
'Here is the march along these iron stones.'
That was the year of the Munich bother. Which
Was most important? I inclined   10
To lose my faith in Ballyrush and Gortin
Till Homer's ghost came whispering to my mind.
He said: I made the Iliad from such
A local row. Gods make their own importance.

1951
Patrick Kavanagh (1905–1967)

"I have lived in important places"—what places is this poem about? The
names—Duffy, McCabe, and the poet's, Kavanagh—may give a hint. If they
aren't enough, there are the additional proper names Ballyrush and Gortin. If
necessary, we can look them up in a place-name dictionary or gazetteer. At
this point we will know the poem is about Ireland, but that doesn't explain
everything at once.

The first two lines seem clear enough until we get to:

who owned
That half a rood of rock, a no-man's land
Surrounded by our pitchfork-armed claims.

---

row: quarrel, fight (in this sense, rhymes with "cow").

The definition of rood—a measure of land equal to a quarter of an acre—may be more puzzling than helpful. How can resolving the question of who owned an eighth of an acre of rock be the deciding of a great event?

> I heard the Duffys shouting 'Damn your soul'
> And old McCabe stripped to the waist, seen
> Step the plot defying blue cast-steel—
> 'Here is the march along these iron stones.'
> That was the year of the Munich bother.

The last line can be a help—it's a reference to a recognizable place, but what was the "Munich bother" and what year did it take place? An almanac or an encyclopedia will contain the information that Britain signed a very controversial peace agreement with the Germans at Munich in 1938—an agreement which did not succeed in averting war.

"Which was most important?" Kavanagh asks; the choice is between "the Munich bother" and the events he has mentioned concerning the Duffys and McCabe. The answer seems clear: "the Munich bother" was an event of worldwide importance; it was hoped it would prevent war, but it did not. The other events can have been of importance only in Ireland, or perhaps an even more limited locale—half a rood of rock. Yet Kavanagh calls the world event a "bother"—as if it were some harmless but annoying thing. We can see that the poem is working by contrasts, and the contrasts are represented by place: worldwide events on the one hand, represented by Munich; a local quarrel on the other, in a small part of Ireland. Why has Kavanagh set up these contrasts? The last lines of the poem answer this question:

> I inclined
> To lose my faith in Ballyrush and Gortin
> Till Homer's ghost came whispering to my mind.
> He said: I made the Iliad from such
> A local row. Gods make their own importance.

Homer was the greatest of classical poets and the *Iliad* one of the two long poems for which he is known. The *Iliad* is an EPIC, a long narrative poem describing heroic actions and characters. The *Iliad* tells the story of the Trojan war—a long struggle between a group of Greeks and the inhabitants of the city of Troy in Asia Minor. Homer's ghost whispers to Kavanagh that he "made the Iliad from such / A local row." We don't usually think of the Trojan war as a *local* quarrel, because it is so important in Greek literature. But this is precisely Homer's and Kavanagh's point: it was probably a rather small-time affair, involving a few hundred people at most. The poem works by these contrasts of places: Munich and Ireland, important and unimportant, Troy and Ireland. But with the last contrast we see that the seemingly unimportant and the important can change places—not only gods make their own importance; poets do too. Homer made the Trojan war important, and his ghost implies that Kavanagh can do the same with Ballyrush and Gortin and *his* local rows.

PLACE AND IMAGERY

How poets see places governs the language used to describe those places. This does not mean merely that if the poets enjoy a woodland scene, they will necessarily use words like *beautiful* and *lovely*, as, for example, Housman does in "Loveliest of Trees." How a poet sees a place governs the kinds of *comparisons* made and therefore the imagery of the poem: its metaphors, its similes, and often even the whole structure of the poem:

COMPOSED UPON WESTMINSTER BRIDGE, SEPTEMBER 3, 1802

Earth has not anything to show more fair;
Dull would he be of soul who could pass by
A sight so touching in its majesty:
This city now doth, like a garment, wear
The beauty of the morning; silent, bare,   5
Ships, towers, domes, theaters, and temples lie
Open unto the fields, and to the sky;
All bright and glittering in the smokeless air.
Never did sun more beautifully steep
In his first splendor, valley, rock, or hill;   10
Ne'er saw I, never felt, a calm so deep!
The river glideth at his own sweet will;
Dear God! the very houses seem asleep;
And all that mighty heart is lying still!

1802
William Wordsworth (1770–1850)

Notice the location of the poem. Westminster Bridge spans the Thames river in London, near the Houses of Parliament, Big Ben, and Westminster Abbey. If you are already familiar with some of Wordsworth's poetry, you may be surprised to find him writing about the city instead of his usual, more rural, subjects. But as he tells us in lines 9–10, no rural scene—valley, rock, or hill—could have been more beautifully lit by the sun than is this scene at this moment. But it isn't just the scene's beauty that has struck him. The reader needs to be aware of the place—London—and what Wordsworth implies it was ordinarily like to see how the language and imagery convey the impression this view makes.

The first three lines do not seem to assert anything directly about what the poet is seeing. He says first of all that Earth doesn't have anything more fair to show (than *this*, we fill in); then, that a person would be "dull of soul" if he could pass by a sight so touching in its majesty. With this third line we do have something said directly about the sight: it has *majesty*. Majesty is an attribute of people; it is a human property. Are any other human properties asserted of the scene? Look, for example, at the next two lines, which say that the city wears the beauty of the morning like a garment. The city is personified. Is the city the only personification in the poem? In the last three lines the river is said to have a *will*, and the houses to seem asleep; again, these are human properties, or at least the properties of living things, while neither the river nor the houses are actually alive. Why does Wordsworth use this figure of speech and compare the inanimate parts of the scene to living things? Let us bear in mind that he is talking about London, and return to our line-by-line reading of the poem.

In lines 4 and 5, the city wears the beauty of the morning like a garment. But in the next two lines, the ships, towers, domes, theatres, and temples that make up the city are *bare*. This seems a *paradox*. The fact that the two words *wear* and *bare* are rhyme words emphasizes this paradoxical quality: in wearing the beauty of the morning the city seems most bare. But remember that it is London, a big city, which Wordsworth is describing, and look at the next line: "All bright and glittering in the smokeless air." Why does he call attention to the fact that the air is *smokeless?* What must the air usually be like? If we have never been to London (and no one now alive can have been there in 1802 anyway!) we can at least imagine what the city must ordinarily have looked like, covered with a blanket of smoke. And now we can begin to appreciate why Wordsworth was struck with the extraordinary sight of the city this particular morning.

Wordsworth goes on to say that the ships, towers, domes, theatres, and temples, bare of their usual smoke, now lie open to the fields and the sky. Ordinarily they would not; they would be separated from the fields and sky by their smoke cover. And now, once again, look at lines 9–10:

> Never did sun more beautifully steep
> In his first splendor, valley, rock, or hill;

Wordsworth very carefully connects the city with the natural scene around it: the fields, the sky, valley, rock and hill. Ordinarily we would be led to expect certain qualities of the country and their opposites of the city:

Chicago

Country	City
smokeless	smoky
quiet	busy
bright	grimy

But Wordsworth's point is that as he has come upon the city, at this early hour, it has all the qualities we would expect of the country.

Here are two American place poems, examples in which setting and the poet's sense of it determine the imagery and figures of speech. The first is a comic poem about Boston snobbery:

BOSTON

I come from the city of Boston,
The home of the bean and the cod,
Where the Cabots speak only to Lowells,
And Lowells speak only to God.

1880
Samuel C. Bushnell (1852–1930)

CHICAGO

Hog Butcher for the World,
    Tool Maker, Stacker of Wheat,
    Player with Railroads and the Nation's Freight Handler;
    Stormy, husky, brawling,
    City of the Big Shoulders: 5
They tell me you are wicked and I believe them, for I have seen
    your painted women under the gas lamps luring the farm boys.
And they tell me you are crooked and I answer: Yes, it is true I have
    seen the gunman kill and go free to kill again.
And they tell me you are brutal and my reply is: On the face of
    women and children I have seen the marks of wanton hunger.
And having answered so I turn once more to those who sneer at this
    my city, and I give them back the sneer and say to them:
Come and show me another city with lifted head singing so proud to
    be alive and coarse and strong and cunning.   10

Flinging magnetic curses amid the toil of piling job on job, here is a
    tall bold slugger set vivid against the little soft cities;
Fierce as a dog with tongue lapping for action, cunning as a savage
    pitted against the wilderness,
        Bareheaded,
        Shoveling,
        Wrecking,   15
        Planning,
        Building, breaking, rebuilding,
Under the smoke, dust all over his mouth, laughing with white
    teeth.
Under the terrible burden of destiny laughing as a young man
    laughs.
Laughing even as an ignorant fighter laughs who has never lost
    a battle.   20
Bragging and laughing that under his wrist is the pulse, and under
    his ribs the heart of the people,
            Laughing!
Laughing the stormy, husky, brawling laughter of Youth, half naked,
    sweating, proud to be Hog Butcher, Tool Maker, Stacker of
    Wheat, Player with Railroads and Freight Handler to the
    Nation.

1916
Carl Sandburg (1878–1967)

    Bushnell succinctly captures place by mentioning features associated with
Boston (baked beans, codfish) and by skewering its social structure in the last
two lines. Sandburg personifies Chicago as Wordsworth did London. But the
personifications differ. Wordsworth's city is a calm, sleeping, majestic presence. Sandburg's is a young giant, anything but calm or asleep. What are the
characteristics of this personified city? Notice not only what qualities Sandburg
gives to Chicago but the language; many of the descriptive words are present
participles giving a sense of present action: *brawling, flinging, shoveling, wrecking, laughing.*

    Sandburg glorifies those very aspects of the city Wordsworth is glad to see
absent. Chicago's liveliness, its dust and smoke and noise and activity are all
attractive features for Sandburg. Where Wordsworth is struck by how much his
city resembles the surrounding countryside, Sandburg chooses to praise what
makes Chicago so essentially a big town: the industries, the railroads, the
wrecking and building, the commerce.

PLACE AND ATTITUDE

In the poems we have looked at so far in this chapter, a certain place at a certain time prompted the observation at the heart of the poem: that the great Renaissance painters were right in their depiction of suffering; that an out-of-the-way place can be just as important as any other; that one city can fit beautifully into the surrounding countryside and another can be impressive for qualities people often find objectionable, like dust and smoke. But the relationship between place and poem can be subtler than this. A place can not only affect the poet's thinking, but shape it, change it, and determine the organization of the poem.

In the following example by Wordsworth's friend Samuel Taylor Coleridge, we can see setting affecting the poet and the poem in these ways. The occasion for the poem was a visit by Coleridge's close friends, Charles and Mary Lamb. Coleridge had looked forward to walks with them among the natural scenes he loved, but on the morning of their arrival he injured his foot seriously enough to prevent his walking during their stay. On the evening the poem was written, Charles and Mary had gone for a walk while Coleridge remained sitting in a bower of lime trees near his cottage.

THIS LIME-TREE BOWER MY PRISON

Well, they are gone, and here must I remain,
This lime-tree bower my prison! I have lost
Beauties and feelings, such as would have been
Most sweet remembrance even when age
Had dimm'd mine eyes to blindness! They, meanwhile,   5
Friends, whom I never more may meet again,
On springy heath, along the hill-top edge,
Wander in gladness, and wind down, perchance,
To that still roaring dell, of which I told;
The roaring dell, o'erwooded, narrow, deep,   10
And only speckled by the mid-day sun;
Where its slim trunk the ash from rock to rock
Flings arching like a bridge;—that branchless ash,
Unsunn'd and damp, whose few poor yellow leaves
Ne'er tremble in the gale, yet tremble still,   15
Fann'd by the water-fall! and there my friends
Behold the dark green file of long lank weeds,
That all at once (a most fantastic sight!)

Still nod and drip beneath the dripping edge
Of the blue clay-stone.

           Now, my friends emerge   20
Beneath the wide wide Heaven—and view again
The many-steepled tract magnificent
Of hilly fields and meadows, and the sea,
With some fair bark, perhaps, whose sails light up
The slip of smooth clear blue betwixt two Isles   25
Of purple shadow! Yes! they wander on
In gladness all; but thou, methinks, most glad,
My gentle-hearted Charles! for thou hast pined
And hunger'd after Nature, many a year,
In the great City pent, winning thy way   30
With sad yet patient soul, through evil and pain
And strange calamity! Ah! slowly sink
Behind the western ridge, thou glorious Sun!
Shine in the slant beams of the sinking orb,
Ye purple heath flowers! richlier burn, ye clouds!   35
Live in the yellow light, ye distant groves!
And kindle, thou blue Ocean! So my friend
Struck with deep joy may stand, as I have stood,
Silent with swimming sense; yea, gazing round
On the wide landscape, gaze till all doth seem   40
Less gross than bodily; and of such hues
As veil the Almighty Spirit, when yet he makes
Spirits perceive his presence.

           A delight
Come sudden on my heart, and I am glad
As I myself were there! Nor in this bower,   45
This little lime-tree bower, have I not mark'd
Much that has sooth'd me. Pale beneath the blaze
Hung the transparent foliage; and I watch'd
Some broad and sunny leaf, and lov'd to see
The shadow of the leaf and stem above   50
Dappling its sunshine! And that walnut-tree
Was richly ting'd, and a deep radiance lay
Full on the ancient ivy, which usurps
Those fronting elms, and now, with blackest mass

Makes their dark branches gleam a lighter hue   55
Through the late twilight: and though now the bat
Wheels silent by, and not a swallow twitters,
Yet still the solitary humble-bee
Sings in the bean-flower! Henceforth I shall know
That Nature ne'er deserts the wise and pure;   60
No plot so narrow, be but Nature there,
No waste so vacant, but may well employ
Each faculty of sense, and keep the heart
Awake to Love and Beauty! and sometimes
'Tis well to be bereft of promis'd good,   65
That we may lift the soul, and contemplate
With lively joy the joys we cannot share.
My gentle-hearted Charles! when the last rook
Beat its straight path along the dusky air
Homewards, I blest it! deeming its black wing   70
(Now a dim speck, now vanishing in light)
Had cross'd the mighty Orb's dilated glory,
While thou stood'st gazing; or, when all was still,
Flew creeking o'er thy head, and had a charm
For thee, my gentle-hearted Charles, to whom   75
No sound is dissonant which tells of Life.

1800
Samuel Taylor Coleridge (1772–1834)

How can attention to place help in the reading of this poem? It can help if we are aware, at each point in this moderately long poem, what place Coleridge is describing at that point and what his attitude about the place is. As we go through the poem, we should also bear in mind that we have a first-person speaker in a present-tense poem, and be alert for the process and change that can occur in such poems.

The place where we begin is the lime-tree bower, and Coleridge tells us how he thinks of it at the poem's beginning—it is his prison. Why does he think it so?

> I have lost
> Beauties and feelings, such as would have been
> Most sweet to my remembrance

He is forced to remain there while his friends go, losing sights he might have seen with them and feelings he might have shared. These, he imagines (lines 5–8):

> They, meanwhile,
> Friends, whom I never more may meet again,
> On springy heath, along the hill-top edge,
> Wander. . . .

The place being described has shifted as Coleridge begins to imagine and describe the sights his friends are seeing: the heath, hill-top, roaring dell, ash trees, and waterfall.

He speaks of his friends wandering "in gladness" through these sights; he knows they must be enjoying them, and we must infer that he would wish to. Then there is a break and a new stanza (20–21):

> Now, my friends emerge
> Beneath the wide wide Heaven.

And again he describes particular sights he imagines they are seeing now—the "many-steepled track magnificent / Of hilly fields and meadows, and the sea." And his vicarious pleasure in these scenes, felt through his friends, has not changed: "they wander on / In gladness all." Coleridge says that Charles is probably the most pleased by these scenes, since he has been pent up in the city.

Up to this point the poet has been describing his own situation and what he imagines to be his friends'; now (32–35) he addresses the natural scene directly in an APOSTROPHE, words spoken to an absent person or to an inanimate object:

> Ah! slowly sink
> Behind the western ridge, thou glorious sun!
> Shine in the slant beams of the sinking orb,
> Ye purple heath-flowers!

Coleridge not only imagines the scene, but he speaks to it. Why?

> So my friend
> Struck with deep joy may stand, as I have stood,
> Silent with swimming sense.

He invokes those aspects of nature his friend is looking at so that they may be even more beautiful and so that Charles may enjoy the sight as he has done.

Then comes the last stanza of the poem:

> A delight
> Comes sudden on my heart, and I am glad
> As I myself were there! Nor in this bower,
> This little lime-tree bower, have I not marked
> Much that has soothed me.

If we look carefully at this last stanza and ask our two questions—what *place* is Coleridge describing and what *attitude* is he expressing about place?—we see that he is again describing the lime-tree bower, but that his original attitude about it has changed. He no longer sees it as a prison. Suddenly he feels heartened, and he recalls that the beauties of this very lime-tree bower have pleased and soothed him, as the sights his friends are now seeing have done. This return to the bower, the place we started from, is a shift of place only in a sense, because Coleridge now talks about Nature as a continuity, a larger place which unites him and his friends, rather than separating them (59–64):

> Henceforth I shall know
> That Nature ne'er deserts the wise and pure,
> No plot so narrow, be but Nature there,
> No waste so vacant, but may well employ
> Each faculty of sense, and keep the heart
> Awake to love and beauty.

Finally, when Coleridge sees the last rook of the evening flying, he blesses it, because he imagines that his friends saw it pass the sun or heard it fly overhead. The rook, then, becomes a symbol of unification.

Place, then, not only gives the poem a setting, but both creates and resolves the conflicts within it. It creates the conflict by imprisoning Coleridge and separating him from his friends. It resolves the conflict by showing him how it is a part of nature, which unifies them all.

The Wordsworth and Coleridge poems suggest that the ROMANTIC poets—the English poets writing at the beginning of the nineteenth century, including Wordsworth, Coleridge, Byron, Keats, and Shelley—often wrote of the power of a particular place to affect the feelings and to inspire the senses. But interest in place is by no means limited to a single era or tradition in poetry, and there are many modern poems of place. The following example extends the idea of place as a shaping force in the poem itself, taking it even further than Coleridge had done:

CORSONS INLET

I went for a walk over the dunes again this morning
to the sea,
then turned right along
   the surf

           rounded a naked headland   5
           and returned

  along the inlet shore:

it was muggy sunny, the wind from the sea steady and high,
crisp in the running sand,
    some breakthroughs of sun   10
  but after a bit

continuous overcast:

the walk liberating, I was released from forms,
from the perpendiculars,
    straight lines, blocks, boxes, binds   15
of thought
into the hues, shadings, rises, flowing bends and blends
      of sight:
           I allow myself eddies of meaning:
yield to a direction of significance   20
running
like a stream through the geography of my work:
  you can find
in my sayings
           swerves of action   25
           like the inlet's cutting edge:
        there are dunes of motion,
organizations of grass, white sandy paths of remembrance
in the overall wandering of mirroring mind:

but Overall is beyond me: is the sum of these events   30
I cannot draw, the ledger I cannot keep, the accounting
beyond the account:

in nature there are few sharp lines; there are areas of
primrose
    more or less dispersed;   35
disorderly orders of bayberry; between the rows
of dunes,
irregular swamps of reeds,
though not reeds alone, but grass, bayberry, yarrow, all . . .
predominantly reeds: 40

I have reached no conclusions, have erected no boundaries,
shutting out and shutting in, separating inside

Corsons Inlet

from outside: I have
drawn no lines:
as   45

manifold events of sand
change the dune's shape that will not be the same shape
tomorrow,

so I am willing to go along, to accept
the becoming   50
thought, to stake off no beginnings or ends, establish
        no walls:

by transitions the land falls from grassy dunes to creek
to undercreek: but there are no lines, though
        change in that transition is clear   55
        as any sharpness: but "sharpness" spread out,
allowed to occur over a wider range
than mental lines can keep:

the moon was full last night: today, low tide was low:
black shoals of mussels exposed to the risk   60
of air
and, earlier, of sun,
waved in and out with the waterline, waterline inexact,
caught always in the event of change:
        a young mottled gull stood free on the shoals   65
        and ate
to vomiting: another gull, squawking possession, cracked a crab,
picked out the entrails, swallowed the soft-shelled legs, a ruddy
turnstone running in to snatch leftover bits:

risk is full: every living thing in   70
siege: the demand is life, to keep life: the small
white blacklegged egret, how beautiful, quietly stalks and spears
        the shallows, darts to shore
                to stab—what? I couldn't
        see against the black mudflats—a frightened   75
        fiddler crab?

Where?

<pre>
        the news to my left over the dunes and
reeds and bayberry clumps was
        fall: thousands of tree swallows
        gathering for flight: 80
        an order held
        in constant change: a congregation
rich with entropy: nevertheless, separable, noticeable
        as one event,
                not chaos: preparations for   85
flight from winter,
cheet, cheet, cheet, cheet, wings rifling the green clumps,
beaks
at the bayberries
        a perception full of wind, flight, curve,   90
        sound:
        the possibility of rule as the sum of rulelessness:
the "field" of action
with moving, incalculable center:

in the smaller view, order tight with shape: 95
blue tiny flowers on a leafless weed: carapace of crab:
snail shell:
        pulsations of order
        in the bellies of minnows: orders swallowed,
broken down, transferred through membranes   100
to strengthen larger orders: but in the large view, no
lines or changeless shapes: the working in and out, together
        and against, of millions of events: this,
                so that I make
                no form of   105
                formlessness:

orders as summaries, as outcomes of actions override
or in some way result, not predictably (seeing me gain
the top of a dune,
the swallows   110
could take flight—some other fields of bayberry
        could enter fall
        berryless) and there is serenity:
</pre>

> no arranged terror: no forcing of image, plan,
> or thought: 115
> no propaganda, no humbling of reality to precept:
>
> terror pervades but is not arranged, all possibilities
> of escape open: no route shut, except in
>   the sudden loss of all routes:
>
>   I see narrow orders, limited tightness, but will   120
> not run to that easy victory:
>   still around the looser, wider forces work:
>   I will try
>   to fasten into order enlarging grasps of disorder, widening
> scope, but enjoying the freedom that   125
> Scope eludes my grasp, that there is no finality of vision,
> that I have perceived nothing completely,
>   that tomorrow a new walk is a new walk.

1965

A. R. Ammons (b. 1926)

Like many longer poems, this one may seem confusing upon first reading. Let us begin with what we know. The title gives us a specific *place*, and many closely observed details in the poem come from a walk in this place—the inlet.

Other lines in the poem are less concrete, more abstract; some of these are the author's thoughts about himself ("I have reached no conclusions") while others seem to be judgments whose origin is not quite so clear ("in nature there are few sharp lines," "risk is full: every living thing in / siege: the demand is life, to keep life"). Even a casual reading gives us the idea that the seaside walk affects the speaker's thoughts. But this is not a very precise description of the poem's content or what happens in it. How are the speaker's thoughts affected? Why should the place have such an effect? How does the poem show the effect of place?

The first dozen lines describe the walk the poet has taken. They create no problem. But then Ammons moves from describing the shore, the wind, the sun on the sand to describing something else (lines 13–18):

> the walk liberating, I was released from forms,
> from the perpendiculars
>   straight lines, blocks, boxes, binds
> of thought
> into the hues, shadings, rises, flowing bends and blends
>   of sight.

The transition is from details of external nature to a description of the mind, freed from "binds of thought." But there is more here than an account of the usual refreshment one might expect from leaving one's work to take a brisk walk outside. The key is in Ammons' description of the way he has been thinking: "the perpendiculars / straight lines, blocks, boxes, binds / of thought." Ammons describes his thoughts as artificial, boxlike, angular, constricting and geometric. But he allows his thoughts to be affected by the natural scene, which is the opposite of geometric and is composed of "hues, shadings, rises, flowing bends and blends" (19–29):

>   I allow myself eddies of meaning:
> yield to a direction of significance
> running
> like a stream through the geography of my work:
>   you can find
> in my sayings
>   swerves of action
>   like the inlet's cutting edge:
>   there are dunes of motion,
> organizations of grass, white sandy paths of remembrance
> in the overall wandering of mirroring mind.

Why does Ammons write lines of such various length, and begin some at a left margin, some farther to the right, some more than a dozen spaces in? The lines themselves explain why: they represent visually the eddies, swerves, and wanderings of the inlet and of the poet's reflecting mind. Ammons allows the walk to release his mind from constricting ways of thinking; then he lets his mind mirror what he sees around him in the inlet, forming new ways of thinking which reflect the surrounding scene. The poem's shape also reflects the surrounding scene and the poet's thinking.

The balance of the poem concerns this reflection of the scene by Ammons' thoughts; although it cannot be simplified, it involves, for example, holding back from arriving at conclusions, refraining from creating boundaries, and avoiding making artificial divisions or categories (41–48). Most significant, perhaps, is that Ammons refrains from making even this process an overall rule (30–32):

>   but Overall is beyond me: is the sum of these events
>   I cannot draw, the ledger I cannot keep, the accounting
>   beyond the account.

These lines prepare the way for Ammons' application of the sands' drift to his own mental state in lines 41–52, and both passages prepare the way for the poem's ending:

I will try
   to fasten into order enlarging grasps of disorder, widening
scope, but enjoying the freedom that
Scope eludes my grasp, that there is no finality of vision,
that I have perceived nothing completely,
   that tomorrow a new walk is a new walk.

The inlet has freed Ammons' thinking from its constricted and geometric boundaries and forms, but part of its lesson has been that even this lesson may change, may be different tomorrow, and the important thing is to be alert to that. "Tomorrow a new walk is a new walk" would be merely redundant, a tautology, without all that goes before it; with the rest of the poem it becomes another way of saying what Henry David Thoreau (1817–1862) says at the end of *Walden*:

   Only that day dawns to which we are awake. There
   is more day to dawn. The sun is but a morning star.

Ammons particularizes this effect of nature, its eternal newness.
   The shaping impulse of the poem comes from *place* in "Corsons Inlet." It is not a general effect of nature, but what can be learned and felt on a particular walk along the inlet, in which specific observations of sand, grass, wind, water and birds are internalized and seen to be of use to the mind. The place is a key to the workings of the poet's mind and to the process of the poem.

EXERCISES

A.

"VALE" FROM CARTHAGE
(*Spring 1944*)

I, now at Carthage. He, shot dead at Rome.
Shipmates last May. "And what if one of us,"
I asked last May, in fun, in gentleness,
"Wears doom, like dungarees, and doesn't know?"
He laughed, *"Not see Times Square again?"* The foam,   5
Feathering across that deck a year ago,
Swept those five words—like seeds—beyond the seas
   Into his future. There they grew like trees;
    And as he passed them there next spring, they laid
    Upon his road of fire their sudden shade.   10
Though he had always scraped his mess-kit pure
And scrubbed redeemingly his barracks floor,

Where?

Though all his buttons glowed their ritual-hymn
Like cloudless moons to intercede for him,
No furlough fluttered from the sky. He will   15
Not see Times Square—he will not see—he will
Not see Times
                change; at Carthage (while my friend,
Living those words at Rome, screamed in the end)
I saw an ancient Roman's tomb and read   20
"*Vale*" in stone. Here two wars mix their dead:
    Roman, my shipmate's dream walks hand in hand
    With yours tonight ("New York again" and "Rome"),
    Like widowed sisters bearing water home
    On tired heads through hot Tunisian sand   25
    In good cool urns, and says, "I understand."
Roman, you'll see your Forum Square no more;
What's left but this to say of any war?

1948
Peter Viereck (b. 1916)

1. What contrasts of place are made in the poem? (Look especially at lines 1, 5, 20, and 27.) The ancient city of Carthage (near modern Tunis) was destroyed by the Romans in 146 B.C. Carthage and Rome had been enemies warring for years. What is the connection between Carthage and Rome in this poem?
2. What does Times Square represent in line 5? What does it come to represent in lines 16, 17, and 18?
3. The speaker sees a Roman's tomb in Carthage with the word "Vale"—farewell—inscribed on it. How does he connect this with his friend's death? What is the importance of *place* and *time* in this connection?
4. How does attention to specific places and times in the poem help the speaker make a more universal statement at the end of the poem?

B.   **SHILOH**
A Requiem (April 1862)

Skimming lightly, wheeling still,
    The swallows fly low
Over the field in clouded days,
    The forest-field of Shiloh—
Over the field where April rain   5

Solaced the parched one stretched in pain
Through the pause of night
That followed the Sunday fight
   Around the church of Shiloh—
The church so lone, the log-built one,   10
That echoed to many a parting groan
     And natural prayer
   Of dying foemen mingled there—
Foemen at morn, but friends at eve—
   Fame or country least their care: 15
(What like a bullet can undeceive!)
   But now they lie low,
While over them the swallows skim,
  And all is hushed at Shiloh.

                   1866

Herman Melville (1819–1891)

1. A place is very often important because of what happened there at a particular time (Munich in 1938, for example). What time and place signals
   does Melville give to indicate why Shiloh is important?
2. Shiloh, in Tennessee, was the site of an especially bloody Civil War battle
   in April, 1862. What details about time and place does Melville emphasize?
3. What is the significance of the following details in the poem: the battlefield
   includes a church and the battle was fought on a Sunday (lines 8–9); the
   foes become friends after their death-wounds (14–15); the battle isn't anything like a church service, but there are many "natural prayers" said at
   Shiloh (10–12). What is the tone created by this choice of details?

C.   **TO ALTHEA, FROM PRISON**

When Love with unconfinéd wings
Hovers within my gates,
And my divine Althea brings
To whisper at the grates;
When I lie tangled in her hair   5
And fettered to her eye,
The gods that wanton in the air
Know no such liberty.

Where?

When flowing cups run swiftly round,
With no allaying Thames,   10
Our careless heads with roses bound,
Our hearts with loyal flames;
When thirsty grief in wine we steep,
When healths and draughts go free,
Fishes, that tipple in the deep,   15
Know no such liberty.

When, like committed linnets, I
With shriller throat shall sing
The sweetness, mercy, majesty,
And glories of my King;   20
When I shall voice aloud how good
He is, how great should be,
Enlargéd winds, that curl the flood,
Know no such liberty.

Stone walls do not a prison make,   25
Nor iron bars a cage;
Minds innocent and quiet take
That for an hermitage.
If I have freedom in my love,
And in my soul am free,   30
Angels alone, that soar above,
Enjoy such liberty.

                              1649
            Richard Lovelace (1618–1657)

1. How does the speaker's present location govern his choice of language in
   describing his relationship to Althea, to his friends, and to his king? What
   contrast does he make at the end of each stanza?
2. What specific examples does the speaker develop to prove the generalization that "Stone walls do not a prison make, / Nor iron bars a cage"?

---

no allaying Thames: no water (from the Thames) was used to dilute the wine. **committed linnets:**
caged birds. **glories of my King:** the speaker is in prison because he is a defender of Charles I
during the English Civil Wars and their aftermath, 1642–1660.

D. **NIGHTHAWKS***

The place is the corner of Empty and Bleak,
The time is night's most desolate hour,
The scene is Al's Coffee Cup or the Hamburger Tower
The persons in this drama do not speak.

We who peer through that curve of plate glass   5
Count three nighthawks seated there—patrons of life:
The counterman will be with you in a jiff,
The thick white mugs were never meant for demitasse.

The single man whose hunched back we see
Once put a gun to his head in Russian roulette,   10
Whirled the chamber, pulled the trigger, won the bet,
And now lives out his x years' guarantee.

And facing us, the two central characters
Have finished their coffee, and have lit
A contemplative cigarette;   15
His hand lies close, but not touching hers.

Not long ago together in a darkened room,
Mouth burned mouth, flesh beat and ground
On ravaged flesh, and yet they found
No local habitation and no name.   20

Oh, are we not lucky to be none of these!
We can look on with complacent eye:
Our satisfactions satisfy,
Our pleasures, our pleasures please.

                                    1971
                        Samuel Yellen (b. 1906)

1. Yellen identifies the place as "the corner of Empty and Bleak." How is this characterization of place developed in the poem? How is the place at once both particular and general?

---

* Yellen's poem is a direct response to a painting of this title by the American artist Edward Hopper (1882–1967).

2. Line 20 is an allusion to a speech by one of Shakespeare's characters, Duke
Theseus, in A *Midsummer Night's Dream:*

> The poet's eye, in a fine frenzy rolling,
> Doth glance from heaven to earth, from earth to heaven;
> And as imagination bodies forth
> The forms of things unknown, the poet's pen
> Turns them to shapes, and gives to airy nothing
> A local habitation and a name.

> (V, i, 12–17)

What is the connection between "the two central characters," who have
been unable to find a local habitation and a name, and the generalized
location of the poem, "the corner of Empty and Bleak"?

3. What is the answer to the rhetorical question the speaker asks in line 21?

E.   ## ELEGIAC STANZAS

Suggested by a Picture of Peele Castle, in a Storm,
Painted by Sir George Beaumont

I was thy neighbor once, thou rugged Pile!
Four summer weeks I dwelt in sight of thee:
I saw thee every day; and all the while
Thy Form was sleeping on a glassy sea.

So pure the sky, so quiet was the air!   5
So like, so very like, was day to day!
Whene'er I looked, thy Image still was there;
It trembled, but it never passed away.

How perfect was the calm! it seemed no sleep;
No mood, which season takes away, or brings: 10
I could have fancied that the mighty Deep
Was even the gentlest of all gentle Things.

Ah! then, if mine had been the Painter's hand,
To express what then I saw; and add the gleam,

---

elegiac stanzas: an ELEGY is usually a poem written to commemorate someone who is dead, though
in the sixteenth and seventeenth centuries it can mean other kinds of poems. Wordsworth's poem
elegizes his brother John, who was drowned in 1805—John is the person mentioned in line 42:
"Him, whom I deplore."

Elegiac Stanzas

The light that never was, on sea or land,   15
The consecration, and the Poet's dream;

I would have planted thee, thou hoary Pile
Amid a world how different from this!
Beside a sea that could not cease to smile;
On tranquil land, beneath a sky of bliss.   20

Thou shouldst have seemed a treasure house divine
Of peaceful years; a chronicle of heaven—
Of all the sunbeams that did ever shine
The very sweetest had to thee been given.

A picture had it been of lasting ease,   25
Elysian quiet, without toil or strife;
No motion but the moving tide, a breeze,
Or merely silent Nature's breathing life.

Such, in the fond illusion of my heart,
Such Picture would I at that time have made,   30
And seen the soul of truth in every part,
A steadfast peace that might not be betrayed.

So once it would have been—'tis so no more;
I have submitted to a new control:
A power is gone, which nothing can restore;   35
A deep distress hath humanized my Soul.

Not for a moment could I now behold
A smiling sea, and be what I have been:
The feeling of my loss will ne'er be old;
This, which I know, I speak with mind serene.   40

Then, Beaumont, Friend! who would have been the Friend,
If he had lived, of him whom I deplore,
This work of thine I blame not, but commend;
This sea in anger, and that dismal shore.

O 'tis a passionate Work!—yet wise and well,   45
Well chosen is the spirit that is here;

That Hulk which labors in the deadly swell,
This rueful sky, this pageantry of fear!

And this huge Castle, standing here sublime,
I love to see the look with which it braves,   50
Cased in the unfeeling armor of old time,
The lightning, the fierce wind, and trampling waves.

Farewell, farewell the heart that lives alone,
Housed in a dream, at distance from the Kind!
Such happiness, wherever it be known,   55
Is to be pitied; for 'tis surely blind.

But welcome fortitude, and patient cheer,
And frequent sights of what is to be borne!
Such sights, or worse, as are before me here—
Not without hope we suffer and we mourn.   60

1807
William Wordsworth (1770–1850)

1. How did Wordsworth see this place—Peele Castle—in the past? How does
   he see it now? How do these ways of seeing place reflect contrasting states
   of mind?
2. How does Beaumont's picture as described by Wordsworth relate to these
   contrasting states of mind?

F. STOPPING BY WOODS ON A SNOWY EVENING

Whose woods these are I think I know.
His house is in the village, though;
He will not see me stopping here
To watch his woods fill up with snow.

My little horse must think it queer   5
To stop without a farmhouse near
Between the woods and frozen lake
The darkest evening of the year.

He gives his harness bells a shake
To ask if there is some mistake.   10

The only other sound's the sweep
Of easy wind and downy flake.

The woods are lovely, dark and deep,
But I have promises to keep,
And miles to go before I sleep,   15
And miles to go before I sleep.

1923
Robert Frost (1874–1963)

1. What is the effect of place on the speaker?
2. What other views besides those of the speaker toward this place are stated
   or implied in the poem?
3. What conflict does the speaker have about this place?

G.   **MERRITT PARKWAY**

        As if it were
forever that they move, that we
        keep moving—

            Under a wan sky where
            as the lights went on a star   5
                pierced the haze and now
            follows steadily
                        a constant
            above our six lanes
            the dreamlike continuum . . .   10

And the people—ourselves!
        the humans from inside the
        cars, apparent
        only at gasoline stops
                        unsure,   15
            eyeing each other
            drink coffee hastily at the
            slot machines and hurry
        back to the cars
            vanish   20
            into them forever, to
            keep moving—

Houses now and then beyond the
sealed road, the trees / trees, bushes
passing by, passing   25
    the cars that
      keep moving ahead of
us, past us, pressing behind us
             and
        over left, those that come   30
      toward us shining too brightly
moving relentlessly

      in six lanes, gliding
      north and south, speeding with
      a slurred sound—   35

               1958
         Denise Levertov (b. 1923)

1. The place is identified in the title as the Merritt Parkway—a highway between Connecticut and New York. What qualities of people and cars trav-
   eling along a highway does Levertov concentrate on?
2. What is travel on the parkway being implicitly compared to?
3. What do the different line lengths and indentations represent in the poem?

H.   **COULD BE**

Could be Hastings Street,
Or Lenox Avenue.
Could be 18th & Vine
And still be true.

Could be 5th & Mound,   5
Could be Rampart:
When you pawned my watch
You pawned my heart.

Could be you love me,
Could be that you don't.   10
Might be that you'll come back,
Like as not you won't.

Hastings Street is weary,
Also Lenox Avenue.
Any place is dreary   15
Without my watch and you.

1948

Langston Hughes (1902–1967)

1. The speaker here insists place is *not* important—for the reasons given in the last two lines. But what effect does Hughes gain by using all these street names?
2. Does it detract from the sincerity of the speaker that he seems just as concerned about the loss of his watch as of his girl, or is this a convincing touch?

WRITING SUGGESTIONS_____

1. In an essay, compare and contrast Edward Abbey's description of the desert (p. 93) with the following poem. How is the sense of place similar and/or different in each?

DESERT PLACES

Snow falling and night falling fast, oh, fast
In a field I looked into going past,
And the ground almost covered smooth in snow,
But a few weeds and stubble showing last.

The woods around it have it—it is theirs.   5
All animals are smothered in their lairs.
I am too absent-spirited to count;
The loneliness includes me unawares.

And lonely as it is, that loneliness
Will be more lonely ere it will be less—   10
A blanker whiteness of benighted snow
With no expression, nothing to express.

They cannot scare me with their empty spaces
Between stars—on stars where no human race is.

I have it in me so much nearer home   15
To scare myself with my own desert places.

1936
Robert Frost (1874–1963)

2. Write an essay in which you compare or contrast Wordsworth's sense of place in "Elegiac Stanzas" (p. 118) with Thomas's in "Fern Hill" (p. 67). Consider the similarities or differences in the physical description used, the effect of time on the description, and the emotional associations of the place.

CHAPTER FIVE

PUTTING QUESTIONS TOGETHER: WHO AND WHEN AND WHERE?

The previous three chapters have discussed questions about speaker, time, and place separately, and the ways these questions help lead into the meaning of poems. Although each question is important by itself, it is often more meaningful when it is related to the others. As soon as we ask a question about the speaker in a poem, we are also involved in asking when the speaker is talking or what time is being described; similarly, questions about speaker and time often involve setting. This chapter brings together these questions in a detailed reading of one poem, showing the interrelatedness of speaker, time, and place. The exercises that follow provide an opportunity to practice putting these questions together in reading a series of challenging poems.

The following poem is one that might have been used as an example in any of the three previous chapters. There is a speaker, a definite time sequence that needs to be sorted out, and a setting. Identifying any one of these elements will help you better understand the imagery of the poem, yet it is the *combination* of speaker, time, and place that best explains the imagery and, hence, the meaning of the poem. Before reading the discussion that follows the poem, read the poem itself and jot down questions and tentative answers. In that way, you will be better able to respond to or argue with the analysis of the poem.

THE LIFEGUARD

In a stable of boats I lie still,
From all sleeping children hidden.
The leap of a fish from its shadow
Makes the whole lake instantly tremble.
With my foot on the water, I feel   5
The moon outside

Take on the utmost of its power.
I rise and go out through the boats.
I set my broad sole upon silver,
On the skin of the sky, on the moonlight,   10
Stepping outward from earth onto water
In quest of the miracle

This village of children believed
That I could perform as I dived
For one who had sunk from my sight.   15
I saw his cropped haircut go under.
I leapt, and my steep body flashed
Once, in the sun.

Dark drew all the light from my eyes.
Like a man who explores his death   20
By the pull of his slow-moving shoulders,
I hung head down in the cold,
Wide-eyed, contained, and alone
Among the weeds,

And my fingertips turned into stone   25
From clutching immovable blackness.
Time after time I leapt upward
Exploding in breath, and fell back
From the change in the children's faces
At my defeat.   30

Beneath them, I swam to the boathouse
With only my life in my arms
To wait for the lake to shine back

The Lifeguard

At the risen moon with such power
That my steps on the light of the ripples 35
Might be sustained.

Beneath me is nothing but brightness
Like the ghost of a snowfield in summer.
As I move toward the center of the lake,
Which is also the center of the moon, 40
I am thinking of how I may be
The savior of one

Who has already died in my care.
The dark trees fade from around me.
The moon's dust hovers together. 45
I call softly out, and the child's
Voice answers through blinding water.
Patiently, slowly,

He rises, dilating to break
The surface of stone with his forehead. 50
He is one I do not remember
Having ever seen in his life.
The ground I stand on is trembling
Upon his smile.

I wash the black mud from my hands. 55
On a light given off by the grave,
I kneel in the quick of the moon
At the heart of a distant forest
And hold in my arms a child
Of water, water, water. 60

1961
James Dickey (b. 1923)

The question "Who is speaking?" leads us to pick up hints or indications
that the speaker is a lifeguard. These come from the title, the references to
children, to swimming, and to a boathouse. The *setting* is a "village of children," and this image is explained by the references to the lake, boathouse,
lifeguard, and so on, which define the setting as a children's camp. Within
this larger setting are some specific locations. At one point, the lifeguard is in
a boathouse (line 31)—he also calls it more figuratively "a stable of boats"—

with the moonlight outside. In stanza 2, this particular locale seems to change from inside to outside (8–12):

> I rise and go out through the boats.
> I set my broad sole upon silver,
> On the skin of the sky, on the moonlight,
> Stepping from earth onto water
> In quest of the miracle. . . .

Time in the poem is indicated by both tense and imagery. The events of stanzas 1, 2, and 7–10 take place in the *present* on a moonlit night. In stanzas 3 through 5, time changes to the *past:* The lifeguard is

> In quest of the miracle
>
> This village of children *believed*
> That I could perform as I *dived*
> For one who had *sunk* from my sight.
> I *saw* his cropped haircut go under.
> I leapt, and my steep body *flashed*
> Once, in the *sun*.

Location also changes in this flashback, from the moonlit scene within the boathouse described in the first two stanzas to this sunlit scene.

Attention to these various indications of speaker, time, and place can certainly aid the reader in understanding the experience described in the poem. Yet because Dickey confronts us with paradoxical, seemingly unbelievable statements and images, it is easy to forget that such statements and images start with the real human situation we have already begun to learn about.

One of the first of these puzzling images occurs in lines 9–11:

> I set my broad sole upon silver,
> On the skin of the sky, on the moonlight,
> Stepping outward from earth onto water.

This unexpected language—"broad sole *upon* silver," "*on* the skin of the sky," "from earth *onto* water"—is just the first instance of some unusual details in the poem. In lines 41–43, for example, the lifeguard says:

> I am thinking of how I may be
> The savior of one
> Who has already died in my care.

The child, according to the lifeguard, has died in his care, but a few lines later he says:

The Lifeguard

> I call softly out, and the child's
> Voice answers through blinding water.
> Patiently, slowly,
>
> He [the child] rises, dilating to break
> The surface of stone with his forehead.

There are other paradoxes in the poem. The lifeguard says he has moved "toward the center of the lake" (39), but he also describes this same place as "the ground I stand on . . ." (53). Earlier in the day, the lifeguard "saw [the child's] cropped haircut go under" (16), but later he says, "He is one I do not remember / Having ever seen in his life" (51–52). All of these paradoxes pose questions that have to be resolved if we are to understand what the poem means. How can the lifeguard be the savior of one who has already died? If the child is dead, how can he answer? If the child has indeed drowned, how can he "patiently, slowly" rise? If the lifeguard is in the center of the lake, how can he be standing on ground?

In any poem, we have to be careful about substituting our own assumptions for the poet's actual language. Such care is all the more important in a poem like "The Lifeguard" where there seem to be so many contradictions. Confronted with these apparent contradictions of logic and sense, we may be tempted to "rewrite" the language so that it fits our expectations. For instance, when the lifeguard says "As I move toward the center of the lake," it is tempting to ignore the context of the surrounding lines and invent a realistic boat or visualize the lifeguard swimming there. If the lifeguard says he is standing on the ground, it is again tempting to forget context and to place the lifeguard on solid, dirt ground.

We can begin to resolve these paradoxes and difficulties by considering the relation of speaker, time, and place to the imagery of the poem. The lifeguard is speaking in the present tense with a flashback to past tense. This past event—the failure to save the child earlier in the day—preys on the lifeguard. His state of mind generates the imagery; remembering his state of mind explains the imagery.

As the poem begins, the lifeguard is in the boathouse. Why is he there? He says that he is "from all sleeping children hidden" (2). Why has he hidden from the children? This question is answered in lines 28–32:

> [I] fell back
> From the change in the children's faces
> At my defeat.
>
> Beneath them, I swam to the boathouse
> With only my life in my arms.

The lifeguard has failed to save the child from drowning; therefore, he is hiding from the children who expected him to succeed.

There is another reason why the lifeguard is in the boathouse at night (33–36). The lifeguard swam to the boathouse

> To wait for the lake to shine back
> At the risen moon with such power
> That my steps on the light of the ripples
> Might be sustained.

This image is surprising and, at first glance, illogical. Why does the lifeguard want the lake to reflect the light of the moon? We need to visualize this image—a scene in which the bright moonlight is being reflected on the surface of the lake. The lifeguard wants the lake to shine back at the moon so *that* his steps on the light of the ripples (of the water) might be sustained (supported). In other words, he wants to be able to walk on water. Certainly, this visual image, and what the lifeguard makes of it, is an involved one. But Dickey has prepared us for the logic of the image. Remember that the lifeguard's wish for the lake to reflect the moon results from his experiences earlier in the day. The beginning of the poem—set in the present tense at night—is the very situation he has hoped for. The moon is now shining on the water. He begins to do what he thinks is made possible by the appearance of the lake:

> I set my broad sole *upon* silver,
> *On* the skin of the sky, *on* the moonlight,
> Stepping outward from earth *onto* water. . . .

These words—particularly the prepositions "on" and "onto"—are unusual enough in their context that it is natural to unconsciously substitute the more logical words "in" and "into." People, even lifeguards, do not ordinarily walk on water, or think they can.

But now we can begin to see, especially after reading the first six stanzas carefully, that Dickey has exactly chosen his language to reflect not only the actions of the lifeguard, but his feelings. The lifeguard, having failed to save the child earlier in the day, is now "in quest of the miracle." This miraculous image, with its allusion to Christ walking on the water (see Matthew 14: 25; Mark 6: 48; John 6: 19), helps explain the intensity of the lifeguard's quest.

The impulse may be to make this image more logical than it is meant—to put the lifeguard in a boat or understand him to be swimming. In lines 39–42, however, the lifeguard says:

> As I *move* toward the center of the lake,
> Which is also at the center of the moon,
> I am *thinking* of how I may be
> The savior of one . . .

The Lifeguard

The way the lifeguard moves to the center of the lake is less important than what he is *thinking*, and his thinking is illustrated by the images of the poem.

Further puzzles are presented by the last stanza:

> I wash the black mud from my hands.
> On a light given off by the grave
> I kneel in the quick of the moon
> At the heart of a distant forest
> And hold in my arms, a child
> Of water, water, water.

As soon as we try to answer the question of *where* the lifeguard is at this moment, we can see the complications. Once again, the preposition "On" is a highly significant clue. If we put these words into ordinary sentence order, they would read:

> I kneel on a light given off by the grave [of the boy, which is] in the quick of the moon [which is] at the heart of a distant forest.

The passage suggests that the lifeguard is kneeling *on* the water, "in the quick of the moon." "Quick" here means the core or center and it also means the living part of something. This phrase is explained by an earlier reference (39–40):

> As I move toward the center of the lake
> Which is also the center of the moon . . .

The "quick of the moon" is described as being at the "heart of a distant forest." The last phrase can also give difficulties unless we pay attention to Dickey's precise use of language. The temptation is to read the lines as meaning that the lifeguard is in the heart of a forest on land, but the lifeguard says, "The dark trees fade from around me" (44). That is, the trees encircling the lake recede as the lifeguard moves toward the lake's center. But we still have him kneeling *on* the lake, which we recognize as a literal impossibility. The image of the moon shining on the water suggests solidity on which the lifeguard can walk to try to "save" the child and on which he can kneel. In the daytime, the lake was dark:

> Dark drew all the light from my eyes (19)

> And my fingertips turned into stone
> From clutching immovable blackness. (25–26)

But now the "miracle" occurs. The "moon's dust hovers together"; the child answers the lifeguard's call and breaks the surface of stone. This image of the surface of stone has been prepared for by several previous images—those in lines 25–26 just quoted, in the idea that the lake is a grave, and through the suggestion of a resurrection first hinted at in lines 3–4 in the leap of a fish from the darkness of the lake:

> The leap of a fish from its shadow
> Makes the whole lake instantly tremble.

Through this image, Dickey suggests that for the lifeguard there are things alive in the lake, living things that can leap from the darkness of the lake. The lake instantly trembles, reflecting the moon.

When the child "answers" the lifeguard's call and rises to the surface, the lifeguard says (51–52):

> He is one I do not remember
> Having ever seen in his life.

Since the lifeguard has seen the child earlier, this suggests that this is not the real child come to life again or even the dead child floating to the surface. The lifeguard continues:

> The ground I stand on is trembling
> Upon his smile.

The imagined child smiles and the fact that the lifeguard is able to imagine him smiling is a sign that the lifeguard has found forgiveness. In the final lines, he is at last able to "wash the black mud" from his hands—a connection to the earlier image, "And my fingertips turned into stone / From clutching immovable blackness" (25–26). At the same time, the lifeguard recognizes that the real child is indeed dead—that the recovery of the child has been imagined, though a miracle of self-forgiveness has occurred:

> And I hold in my arms a child
> Of water, water, water.

James Dickey's "The Lifeguard" is an illustration of the usefulness of the combination of evidence of speaker, time, and place. There are important clues in the change in verb tenses and in the way the speaker creates images from his experience. The meaning of the poem is carried by these images which derive from the lifeguard's inner feelings, the time sequence, and the particular setting.

EXERCISES

A. Read the following poem, a pastoral lyric. In a PASTORAL, a poet uses the persona of a rustic or country person, and the poem usually has shepherds or shepherdesses as characters and an idyllic rural landscape as setting; a LYRIC is a poem expressing personal emotion rather than telling a story or narrative.

THE PASSIONATE SHEPHERD TO HIS LOVE

Come live with me and be my love,
And we will all the pleasures prove
That valleys, groves, hills and fields,
Woods, or steepy mountain yields.

And we will sit upon the rocks,   5
Seeing the shepherds feed their flocks,
By shallow rivers to whose falls
Melodious birds sing madrigals.

And I will make thee beds of roses
And a thousand fragrant posies,   10
A cap of flowers, and a kirtle
Embroidered all with leaves of myrtle;

A gown made of the finest wool
Which from our pretty lambs we pull;
Fair linéd slippers for the cold,   15
With buckles of the purest gold;

A belt of straw and ivy buds,
With coral clasps and amber studs;
And if these pleasures may thee move,
Come live with me, and be my love.   20

The shepherds' swains shall dance and sing
For thy delight each May morning;
If these delights thy mind may move,
Then live with me and be my love.

1599
Christopher Marlowe (1564–1593)

1. How does the speaker describe the time he is inviting his love to share? How does he characterize the setting? Many poets have written "replies" to this poem. Here is one such reply:

THE NYMPH'S REPLY TO THE SHEPHERD

If all the world and love were young,
And truth in every shepherd's tongue,
These pretty pleasures might me move
To live with thee and be thy love.

Time drives the flocks from field to fold   5
When rivers rage and rocks grow cold,
And Philomel becometh dumb;
The rest complains of cares to come.

The flowers do fade, and wanton fields
To wayward winter reckoning yields;   10
A honey tongue, a heart of gall,
Is fancy's spring, but sorrow's fall.

Thy gowns, thy shoes, thy beds of roses,
Thy cap, thy kirtle, and thy posies
Soon break, soon wither, soon forgotten—   15
In folly ripe, in reason rotten.

Thy belt of straw and ivy buds,
Thy coral clasps and amber studs,
All these in me no means can move
To come to thee and be thy love.   20

But could youth last and love still breed,
Had joys no date nor age no need
Then these delights my mind might move
To live with thee and be thy love.

1600
Sir Walter Ralegh (1552–1618)

2. Who is the speaker in Ralegh's poem?
3. What attitude is implied by this speaker in lines 1–2? What does the nymph suggest about the speaker in Marlowe's poem?

4. In Marlowe's poem, the shepherd's reference to time and season is in lines 21–22. How does the nymph, the speaker of Ralegh's poem, reinterpret the shepherd's reference to time and season?
5. The shepherd describes an ideal landscape to tempt the nymph. What contrasts does she describe to explain why she won't join him?
6. In Ralegh's poem, what does the nymph mean by using seasonal references in line 12, "fancy's *spring*, but sorrow's *fall*"? What play on words is involved here?
7. What does the speaker in Ralegh's poem imply by the last stanza? Would she like to join the shepherd?

B.   **TALKING IN BED**

Talking in bed ought to be easiest,
Lying together there goes back so far,
An emblem of two people being honest.

Yet more and more time passes silently.
Outside, the wind's incomplete unrest   5
Builds and disperses clouds about the sky,

And dark towns heap upon the horizon.
None of this cares for us. Nothing shows why
At this unique distance from isolation

It becomes still more difficult to find   10
Words at once true and kind,
Or not untrue and not unkind.

                           1964
                   Philip Larkin (b. 1922)

1. Who is the speaker? What situation is the speaker describing?
2. What does the speaker mean by the phrase "an emblem of two people being honest"? How does this phrase relate to the specific situation described in the rest of the poem?
3. What is the paradox in the speaker's phrase "at this unique distance from isolation"?
4. How does the imagery in lines 5–7 emphasize the situation in the poem?
5. How is the passing of time important in the poem?
6. What effect is achieved by the use of present tense in the poem? What different effect would be created by putting all the verbs in the past tense?

C.   **THE SUN RISING**

                Busy old-fool, unruly sun,
                    Why dost thou thus
        Through windows, and through curtains call on us?
        Must to thy motions lovers' seasons run?
                    Saucy pedantic wretch, go chide   5
                    Late school boys, and sour prentices,
                Go tell court-huntsmen that the King will ride,
                Call country ants to harvest offices;
        Love, all alike, no season knows, nor clime,
        Nor hours, days, months, which are the rags of time.   10

                Thy beams, so reverend and strong
                    Why shouldst thou think?
        I could eclipse and cloud them with a wink,
        But that I would not lose her sight so long:
                    If her eyes have not blinded thine,   15
                    Look, and tomorrow late, tell me
                Whether both the Indias of spice and mine
                Be where thou left'st them, or lie here with me.
        Ask for those Kings whom thou saw'st yesterday,
        And thou shalt hear: all here in one bed lay.   20

                She's all states, and all princes, I,
                    Nothing else is.
        Princes do but play us; compared to this,
        All honor's mimic; all wealth alchemy.
                    Thou, sun, art half as happy as we,   25
                    In that the world's contracted thus;
                Thine age asks ease, and since thy duties be
                To warm the world, that's done in warming us.
        Shine here to us, and thou art everywhere;
        This bed thy center is, these walls, thy sphere.   30

                                    1633
                        John Donne (1572–1631)

1. Who is speaking and how does the situation affect the speaker's attitude
   toward the time of day?

---

prentices: apprentices. **offices:** duties. **clime:** climate.

2. What does the speaker say about love and time at the end of the first stanza? What does the speaker call the sun? What does this have to do with the way time is characterized?
3. How does the question asked in line 4 get answered in stanza 2?
4. What places are being compared in stanzas 2 and 3? What does this comparison have to do with the sun and with love?

D.   **MY LAST DUCHESS**
                          Ferrara

That's my last Duchess painted on the wall,
Looking as if she were alive. I call
That piece a wonder, now: Fra Pandolf's hands
Worked busily a day, and there she stands.
Will't please you sit and look at her? I said   5
"Fra Pandolf" by design, for never read
Strangers like you that pictured countenance,
The depth and passion of its earnest glance,
But to myself they turned (since none puts by
The curtain I have drawn for you, but I)   10
And seemed as they would ask me, if they durst,
How such a glance came there; so, not the first
Are you to turn and ask thus. Sir, 'twas not
Her husband's presence only, called that spot
Of joy into the Duchess' cheek: perhaps   15
Fra Pandolf chanced to say "Her mantle laps
Over my lady's wrist too much," or "Paint
Must never hope to reproduce the faint
Half-flush that dies along her throat": such stuff
Was courtesy, she thought, and cause enough   20
For calling up that spot of joy. She had
A heart—how shall I say?—too soon made glad,
Too easily impressed; she liked whate'er
She looked on, and her looks went everywhere.
Sir, 'twas all one! My favor at her breast,   25
The dropping of the daylight in the West,

Ferrara: a province in northern Italy, famous as a center of art and culture during the RENAIS-
SANCE—a period of great artistic and literary development that began in Italy about the middle of
the fifteenth century (1450) and spread to northern Europe and England during the following
century. **Fra Pandolf; Claus of Innsbruck:** Browning's inventions, both imaginary artists.

The bough of cherries some officious fool
Broke in the orchard for her, the white mule
She rode with round the terrace—all and each
Would draw from her alike the approving speech,   30
Or blush, at least. She thanked men—good! but thanked
Somehow—I know not how—as if she ranked
My gift of a nine-hundred-years-old name
With anybody's gift. Who'd stoop to blame
This sort of trifling? Even had you skill   35
In speech—which I have not—to make your will
Quite clear to such an one, and say, "Just this
Or that in you disgusts me; here you miss,
Or there exceed the mark"—and if she let
Herself be lessoned so, nor plainly set   40
Her wits to yours, forsooth, and made excuse,
—E'en then would be some stooping; and I choose
Never to stoop. Oh sir, she smiled, no doubt,
Whene'er I passed her; but who passed without
Much the same smile? This grew; I gave commands;   45
Then all smiles stopped together. There she stands
As if alive. Will't please you rise? We'll meet
The company below, then. I repeat,
The Count your master's known munificence
Is ample warrant that no just pretense   50
Of mine for dowry will be disallowed;
Though his fair daughter's self, as I avowed
At starting, is my object. Nay, we'll go
Together down, sir. Notice Neptune, though,
Taming a sea-horse, thought a rarity,   55
Which Claus of Innsbruck cast in bronze for me!

1842
Robert Browning (1812–1889)

1. Who is the *listener* in this poem; that is, who is hearing the Duke's revealing monologue? What implied questions or reactions on the part of
   this listener does the Duke respond to? What do the listener's reactions
   and the Duke's responses reveal about the situation and the Duke's personality?
2. What is the setting of the Duke's monologue? How is this setting made
   more specific through the choice of details? What nuances of the Duke's
   actions and personality does Browning bring out by these details?

3. What is the actual chronology of events as described in the poem, and how does Browning organize these chronological events?

E.   WRITTEN AFTER SWIMMING FROM SESTOS TO ABYDOS

1

If, in the month of dark December,
　　Leander, who was nightly wont
(What maid will not the tale remember?)
　　To cross thy stream, broad Hellespont!

2

If, when the wintry tempest roared,　　　　　　　　　　5
　　He sped to Hero, nothing loath,
And thus of old thy current poured,
　　Fair Venus! how I pity both!

3

For *me*, degenerate modern wretch,
　　Though in the genial month of May,　　　　　　　　　10
My dripping limbs I faintly stretch.
　　And think I've done a feat today.

4

But since he crossed the rapid tide,
　　According to the doubtful story,
To woo—and—Lord knows what beside,　　　　　　　　15
　　And swam for Love, as I for Glory;

5

'Twere hard to say who fared the best:
　　Sad mortals! thus the gods still plague you!
He lost his labor, I my jest;
　　For he was drowned, and I've the ague.　　　　　　　20

1812
George Gordon, Lord Byron (1788–1824)

Sestos, in Asia Minor, and **Abydos,** in Greece, are on either side of the **Hellespont,** the strait which narrows into the present-day city of Istanbul. According to legend, Leander, a young Greek, used to swim across the strait to visit his beloved Hero, a priestess of Aphrodite (Venus), until he drowned one stormy night. **ague:** a fever with chills; a cold.

1. Why has the speaker repeated Leander's feat?
2. What contrasts are enumerated between Leander's situation and time and the speaker's?
3. What is the speaker's attitude toward what he has done, and what is the tone of the poem?

F.   **JOURNEY OF THE MAGI**

"A cold coming we had of it,
Just the worst time of the year
For a journey, and such a long journey:
The ways deep and the weather sharp,
The very dead of winter."   5
And the camels galled, sore-footed, refractory,
Lying down in the melting snow.
There were times we regretted
The summer palaces on slopes, the terraces,
And the silken girls bringing sherbet.   10
Then the camel men cursing and grumbling
And running away, and wanting their liquor and women,
And the night-fires going out, and the lack of shelters,
And the cities hostile and the towns unfriendly
And the villages dirty and charging high prices: 15
A hard time we had of it.
At the end we preferred to travel all night,
Sleeping in snatches,
With the voices singing in our ears, saying
That this was all folly.   20

Then at dawn we came down to a temperate valley,
Wet, below the snow line, smelling of vegetation;
With a running stream and a water mill beating the darkness,
And three trees on the low sky,
And an old white horse galloped away in the meadow.   25
Then we came to a tavern with vine-leaves over the lintel,
Six hands at an open door dicing for pieces of silver,

Magi: the wise men mentioned in Matthew 2:1. **"A cold coming. . . ."**: Eliot took the first five lines, with slight changes, from a 1622 Christmas sermon by Lancelot Andrewes, an Anglican bishop.

And feet kicking the empty wineskins.
But there was no information, and so we continued
And arrived at evening, not a moment too soon   30
Finding the place; it was (you may say) satisfactory.

All this was a long time ago, I remember,
And I would do it again, but set down
This set down
This: were we led all that way for   35
Birth or Death? There was a Birth, certainly.
We had evidence and no doubt. I had seen birth and death,
But had thought they were different; this Birth was
Hard and bitter agony for us, like Death, our death.
We returned to our places, these Kingdoms,   40
But no longer at ease here, in the old dispensation,
With an alien people clutching their gods.
I should be glad of another death.

1927

T. S. Eliot (1888–1965)

1. When is the speaker recounting the events of the poem?
2. How does the speaker feel about the palaces left behind in the first stanza
   of the poem? How does he feel about them in the last stanza, after returning?
3. What do the details in stanza 2 forecast? Does the speaker know they foretell the future? What does Eliot accomplish by using a speaker with a
   limited point of view?

G.   SAILING TO BYZANTIUM

1

That is no country for old men. The young
In one another's arms, birds in the trees
—Those dying generations—at their song,
The salmon-falls, the mackerel-crowded seas,
Fish, flesh, or fowl, commend all summer long   5
Whatever is begotten, born, and dies.
Caught in that sensual music all neglect
Monuments of unaging intellect.

2

An aged man is but a paltry thing,
A tattered coat upon a stick, unless   10
Soul clap its hands and sing, and louder sing
For every tatter in its mortal dress,
Nor is there singing school but studying
Monuments of its own magnificence;
And therefore I have sailed the seas and come   15
To the holy city of Byzantium.

3

O sages standing in God's holy fire
As in the gold mosaic of a wall,
Come from the holy fire, perne in a gyre,
And be the singing-masters of my soul.   20
Consume my heart away; sick with desire
And fastened to a dying animal
It knows not what it is; and gather me
Into the artifice of eternity.

4

Once out of nature I shall never take   25
My bodily form from any natural thing,
But such a form as Grecian goldsmiths make
Of hammered gold and gold enamelling
To keep a drowsy Emperor awake;
Or set upon a golden bough to sing   30
To lords and ladies of Byzantium
Of what is past, or passing, or to come.

1927
William Butler Yeats (1865–1939)

The first line of the poem poses some important questions:

(1) Who is the speaker?
(2) What *place* ("country") is the speaker referring to?
(3) Why does the speaker say "*That* is no country for old men" rather than
    "*This* . . ."?

---

perne in a gyre: roughly, to spiral downward through time in a cycle of history.

These are basic questions. Everything else in the poem contributes to answers to these questions and these questions are answered—directly or indirectly—in the lines that follow.

Stanza 1

1. Line 1 refers to two different times—two different stages of life—"old men" and "the young." How does the rest of the stanza continue to develop this contrast?
2. Compare the line "Time held me green and dying" from Dylan Thomas's "Fern Hill" with Yeats's phrase "Those dying generations." How are the two similar or dissimilar? What paradox does Yeats suggest by the two words?
3. Who, according to the speaker, is "caught in that sensual music"? What lines in stanza 1 help explain the word "sensual"?
4. What two things are contrasted in lines 7–8? How is this contrast associated with the earlier references to "old men" and "the young"?

Stanza 2

1. How do lines 9–12 help further identify the speaker of the poem?
2. Stanza 1 contains at least two contrasts: "old men" / "the young" and "sensual music" / "monuments of unaging intellect." What associated contrasts are made in stanza 2?
3. Throughout the poem, Yeats refers to music and singing. What statements in stanza 1 are recalled by these lines:

> unless
> Soul clap its hands and sing, and louder sing
> For every tatter in its mortal dress.

4. Syntax is important to the meaning of the poem. What does "its" refer to in lines 10–14?
5. What place is identified in lines 15–16? Why does the speaker say he has traveled there? What has been implied so far about Byzantium and the place mentioned at the beginning of the poem?

Stanza 3

1. What does the speaker ask for in stanza 3?
2. What is "the dying animal" and to what is this "dying animal" contrasted?
3. How does the phrase "artifice of eternity" help explain what Byzantium represents? What phrases in the earlier stanzas compare to "artifice of eternity"?

<u>Stanza 4</u>

1. What does the phrase "Once out of nature" imply about the speaker's *present* situation?
2. What in the poem explains why the speaker says that "I shall never take / My bodily form from any natural thing"?
3. The following set of lines is similar in phrasing:

> "Whatever is begotten, born, and dies" (6)

> "Of what is past, or passing, or to come" (32)

What contrasts does this similarity highlight?

H.   **TULIPS**

The tulips are too excitable, it is winter here.
Look how white everything is, how quiet, how snowed in.
I am learning peacefulness, lying by myself quietly
As the light lies on these white walls, this bed, these hands.
I am nobody; I have nothing to do with explosions.   5
I have given my name and my day-clothes up to the nurses
And my history to the anesthetist and my body to surgeons.

They have propped my head between the pillows and the sheet-
    cuff
Like an eye between two white lids that will not shut.
Stupid pupil, it has to take everything in.   10
The nurses pass and pass, they are no trouble,
They pass the way gulls pass inland in their white caps,
Doing things with their hands, one just the same as another,
So it is impossible to tell how many there are.

My body is a pebble to them, they tend it as water   15
Tends to the pebbles it must run over, smoothing them gently.
They bring me numbness in their bright needles, they bring me
    sleep.
Now I have lost myself I am sick of baggage—
My patent-leather overnight case like a black pillbox,
My husband and child smiling out of the family photo;   20
Their smiles catch onto my skin, little smiling hooks.

I have let things slip, a thirty-year-old cargo boat
Stubbornly hanging on to my name and address.
They have swabbed me clear of my loving associations.
Scared and bare on the green plastic-pillowed trolley,   25
I watched my tea-set, my bureaus of linen, my books
Sink out of sight, and the water went over my head.
I am a nun now, I have never been so pure.

I didn't want any flowers, I only wanted
To lie with my hands turned up and be utterly empty.   30
How free it is, you have no idea how free—
The peacefulness is so big it dazes you,
And it asks nothing, a name tag, a few trinkets.
It is what the dead close on, finally; I imagine them
Shutting their mouths on it, like a Communion tablet.   35

The tulips are too red in the first place, they hurt me.
Even through the gift paper I could hear them breathe
Lightly, through their white swaddlings, like an awful baby.
Their redness talks to my wound, it corresponds.
They are subtle: they seem to float, though they weigh me
    down,   40
Upsetting me with their sudden tongues and their color,
A dozen red lead sinkers round my neck.

Nobody watched me before, now I am watched.
The tulips turn to me, and the window behind me,
Where once a day, the light slowly widens and slowly thins,   45
And I see myself, flat, ridiculous, a cut-paper shadow
Between the eye of the sun and the eyes of the tulips,
And I have no face, I have wanted to efface myself.
The vivid tulips eat my oxygen.

Before they came the air was calm enough,   50
Coming and going, breath by breath, without any fuss.
Then the tulips filled it up like a loud noise.
Now the air snags and eddies round them the way a river
Snags and eddies round a sunken rust-red engine.
They concentrate my attention, that was happy   55
Playing and resting without committing itself.

The walls, also, seem to be warming themselves.
The tulips should be behind bars like dangerous animals;
They are opening like the mouth of some great African cat,
And I am aware of my heart: it opens and closes   60
Its bowl of red blooms out of sheer love of me.
The water I taste is warm and salt, like the sea,
And comes from a country far away as health.

1962

Sylvia Plath (1932–1963)

1. What specific references in the poem indicate who the speaker is?
2. The speaker's opening words in "Tulips" indicate an attitude, a contrast, and a suggestion of place:

   The tulips are too excitable, it is winter here.
   Look how white everything is, how quiet, how snowed-in.

   The words "winter," "white," "snowed-in," suggest a season. Is the speaker using these words literally, to name a season, or is she using these words metaphorically? What information for this question do lines 6–7 supply?
3. The speaker says, "The tulips are too excitable." How is this attitude toward the tulips developed in the poem? What comparisons are made between the tulips and other things?
4. Tense is important in this poem. What distinctions of time are made in stanza 4 (lines 22–28) and what do these distinctions tell about the speaker?
5. In the last line of stanza 4, the words "I am a nun now" tell us about the speaker. From the evidence in the poem, are we to take the words literally or figuratively?
6. What change in the speaker's state of mind is suggested by the final lines of the poem (58–63)? What does "The water I taste is warm and salt" suggest? What is the meaning of "country" (63)? How does it compare to Yeats's use of the word in the first lines of "Sailing to Byzantium"?
7. On page 54, a critic is quoted as saying that the so-called confessional poet "places few barriers, if any, between [his or her] self and direct expression of that self, however painful that expression may prove. . . . This is not to say that confessional poems are wild, unchecked emotional outbursts." What does Plath do with both language and the way she handles the speaker to control the poem?

I. Look ahead to the first poem discussed in the following chapter, Wilfred Owen's "Futility," and answer the following questions about it.

1. What inferences can you make from the first line about speaker, listener(s), and the person referred to as "him"?
2. What information do subsequent lines give about the reason for the speaker's directions in line 1?
3. What contrast in time appears in the first two lines?
4. This contrast in time also involves what contrast in place?
5. What is implied by the word "even" in line 4?
6. What can you infer from lines 4 and 5 about the person referred to as "him"?
7. What effect of the sun is talked about in the first two lines of stanza 2? Why has the attention shifted from the sun's effect on "him"?
8. The phrase "clays of a cold star" is a periphrasis for "earth." PERIPHRASIS is the use of a longer word or phrase in place of a shorter or plainer expression. What does the use of this periphrasis allow Owen to suggest about the relationship between the man and the earth? What repetitions in lines 2 and 9 reinforce this connection?
9. Why does the "kind old sun" of line 7 become "fatuous sunbeams" in line 13? What in the preceding lines, 10–12, explains this changed characterization of the sun?
10. What is the significance of France in the poem? What hint is provided by the date of the poem?

WRITING SUGGESTIONS

1. Write an essay comparing Philip Larkin's "Talking in Bed" with Matthew Arnold's "Dover Beach" (p. 78). What parallels and contrasts are there in the use of imagery to convey the speaker's isolation and the sense of time and place? What does the speaker identify as the isolating force in each poem?
2. After reading Sylvia Plath's "Tulips," write an essay in which you explain how the imagery of the poem emerges from the interrelationship of speaker, time, and place.

PART

III

WHAT?

CHAPTER SIX

WHAT HAPPENED? EVENTS BEHIND THE POEM

No poem is written in a vacuum. Poets necessarily record their own experiences and their own world in writing a poem. The language used, the assumptions made, the cultural values implied or rejected, the topical events referred to—all of these reflect that changing world behind the poem.

Certainly, at least one mark of a poem's enduring excellence is its ability to escape those indications of the time and place when it was written and to speak directly to our experiences here and now. This communication of universal feelings and ideas enables a poem to remain vibrant, relevant, and effective despite drastic differences between the world when the poem was written and the reader's world.

And yet, there is another side to a poem's universality. It is, paradoxically, just those time-bound details of language, beliefs, and historical events that give a poem its power, its distinctiveness, its bite. The ideas or feelings that have universal appeal are grounded in, to use Shakespeare's phrase, "a local habitation and a name," and the vividness of those details helps prove whatever universal truths are in the poem.

"A LOCAL HABITATION AND A NAME"

We have seen in earlier chapters that we can ask a great many questions as we read with the assurance that answers can be found within the text of the poem. Yet in many poems we come up against puzzling details—details that are not directly explained within the poem. The word "France" in the following poem is such a puzzle:

FUTILITY

Move him into the sun—
Gently its touch awoke him once,
At home, whispering of fields unsown.
Always it woke him, even in France,
Until this morning and this snow.   5
If anything might rouse him now
The kind old sun will know.

Think how it wakes the seeds—
Woke, once, the clays of a cold star.
Are limbs, so dear-achieved, are sides,   10
Full-nerved—still warm—too hard to stir?
Was it for this the clay grew tall?
—O what made fatuous sunbeams toil
To break earth's sleep at all?

1918
Wilfred Owen (1893–1918)

In this poem, questions of *who, when,* and *where* lead to some valid inferences about the speaker, the general situation, and the relative significance of place. These questions, however, keep coming back to the word "France": Why is the speaker there? Why the contrast between "home" and France? Without this precise reference to a place, it would be justifiable to conclude that the poem is simply an outburst against the futility of life—anyone's life— in the face of inevitable death—anyone's death. But since there is this emphatic reference—"*even* in France"—another question must be asked: What is the significance of France in this poem?

What happened in France for Owen to make the reference to it so emphatic? The date of the poem provides one clue—1918. This is the time of the First World War. Its dreadful casualties—almost nine million men died during the course of the war—will explain the intensity, bitterness, and pathos of Owen's second stanza. And finding out about Owen's own experience in the war will enrich the poem even more.

"Futility" was written in June, 1918 and published the same month in the English magazine *The Nation*. During World War I (1914–1918), Wilfred Owen fought on the Western Front in France, starting in January, 1917. As Paul Fussell wrote in *The Great War and Modern Memory*, what Owen "encountered at the front was far worse than even a poet's imagination could have conceived. From then on [the middle of January, 1917] in the less than two years left to him, the emotions that dominated were horror, outrage, and pity:

horror at what he saw at the front; outrage at the inability of the civilian world—especially the church—to understand what was going on; pity for the poor, dumb, helpless, good-looking boys victimized by it all."

This horror, outrage, and pity is expressed in a letter Owen wrote to his mother on February 4, 1917:

> I suppose I can endure cold, and fatigue, and the face-to-face death, as well as another: but extra for me there is the universal pervasion of *Ugliness*. Hideous landscapes, vile noises, foul language and nothing but foul . . . everything unnatural, broken, blasted; the distortion of the dead, whose unburiable bodies sit outside the dug-outs all day, all night, the most execrable sights on earth. In poetry we call them the most glorious. But to sit with them all day, all night . . . and a week later to come back and find them still sitting there, in motionless groups, THAT is what saps the "soldierly spirit."
>
> —Owen and Bell, *Wilfred Owen: Collected Letters*

Owen became ill, but returned to the front (in France) in August, 1918. He was killed on November 4, 1918, just a week before the armistice was signed on November 11. Owen's experiences in the war explain exactly the significance and intense feeling that lie behind the single word "France" in a way no gloss or footnote could ever do.

The following poem tells us clearly enough what event is behind it—the loss of the *Titanic*—but why is this event given such profound significance?

THE CONVERGENCE OF THE TWAIN

(Lines on the loss of the "Titanic")

1

In a solitude of the sea
Deep from human vanity,
And the Pride of Life that planned her, stilly couches she.

2

Steel chambers, late the pyres
Of her salamandrine fires,   5
Cold currents thrid, and turn to rhythmic tidal lyres.

---

twain: two (forces). **stilly:** in stillness. **salamandrine:** bright red. The salamander was supposed to be able to live in fire, according to legend. **thrid:** thread.

What Happened?

3

Over the mirrors meant
To glass the opulent
The sea-worm crawls—grotesque, slimed, dumb, indifferent.

4

Jewels in joy designed   10
To ravish the sensuous mind
Lie lightless, all their sparkles bleared and black and blind.

5

Dim moon-eyed fishes near
Gaze at the gilded gear
And query: "What does this vaingloriousness down here?"   15

6

Well: while was fashioning
This creature of cleaving wing,
The Immanent Will that stirs and urges everything

7

Prepared a sinister mate
For her—so gaily great—   20
A Shape of Ice, for the time far and dissociate.

8

And as the smart ship grew
In stature, grace, and hue,
In shadowy silent distance grew the Iceberg too.

9

Alien they seemed to be: 25
No mortal eye could see
The intimate welding of their later history,

10

Or sign that they were bent
By paths coincident
On being anon twin halves of one august event,   30

Immanent Will: force or fate.

11

Till the Spinner of the Years
Said "Now!" And each one hears,
And consummation comes, and jars two hemispheres.

1912

Thomas Hardy (1840–1928)

Knowing that the *Titanic* was a passenger liner that sank in 1912 does not explain why Hardy gives it such significance. Why does he call the ship and iceberg "twin halves of one august event"?

In 1912, the *Titanic* was the largest passenger ship afloat. The name itself conjured up an object of prodigious size and power, like one of the Titans of Greek mythology. Because of the superior technology and design that went into its construction, the liner was advertised as absolutely unsinkable. On her very first voyage between Southampton, England, and New York City, the *Titanic* was crammed with passengers, many of whom were rich, powerful, and famous. When an iceberg gashed the hull of the supposedly unsinkable ship, over 1500 of the 2224 passengers and crew lost their lives. After the terrible disaster, much publicity was given to the question that one of the passengers asked as she boarded the ship: "Is this ship really unsinkable?" A deckhand is said to have replied, "Yes, lady, God himself could not sink this ship."

Hardy's poem speaks about universal concerns such as pride and vanity, fate and coincidence, man and nature, yet it gains its power because it is linked to this particular, single event—the apparently incredible sinking of an unsinkable ship. For Hardy's world at the turn of the century, the *Titanic* could easily represent mankind's unlimited power over nature and the exuberant confidence in the achievements of modern technology as yet unquestioned by the destruction of two world wars. Thus, the sinking of such a ship under such conditions could profoundly jar confidence in those achievements. In the words of one of the survivors of the disaster, John B. Thayer, the sinking of the *Titanic* woke the world with a start:

> There was peace, and the world had an even tenor to its ways. True enough, from time to time there were events—catastrophes—like the Johnstown Flood, the San Francisco Earthquake, or floods in China—which stirred the sleeping world, but not enough to keep it from resuming its slumber. It seems to me that the disaster about to occur was the event, which not only made the world rub its eyes and awake, but woke it with a start, keeping it moving at a rapidly accelerating pace ever since, with less and less peace, satisfaction and happiness. . . . To my mind the world of today awoke April 15, 1912.
>
> —quoted in Wade, *The Titanic: End of a Dream*

Spinner of the Years: another of Hardy's terms for fate.

A poem like "The Convergence of the Twain," prompted by topical events, is called an OCCASIONAL POEM—any poem written in response to a single event, such as a coronation. Such poems very often lose their importance or interest after the moment of the single incident or event has passed. But some occasional poems manage to outlast their limited, immediate context and, like Hardy's poem, convey some enduring insights into human experience. The following poem is another example:

THE CHARGE OF THE LIGHT BRIGADE

1

Half a league, half a league,
    Half a league onward,
All in the valley of Death
    Rode the six hundred.
"Forward, the Light Brigade!   5
Charge for the guns!" he said:
Into the valley of Death
    Rode the six hundred.

2

"Forward, the Light Brigade!"
Was there a man dismay'd?   10
Not tho' the soldier knew
    Some one had blunder'd:
Theirs not to make reply,
Theirs not to reason why,
Theirs but to do and die: 15
Into the valley of Death
    Rode the six hundred.

3

Cannon to right of them,
Cannon to left of them,
Cannon in front of them   20
    Volley'd and thunder'd;
Storm'd at with shot and shell,
Boldly they rode and well,
Into the jaws of Death,

---

light brigade: a brigade armed with light artillery. **league:** a measure of distance equal to about three miles.

Into the mouth of Hell   25
  Rode the six hundred.

4

Flash'd all their sabres bare,
Flash'd as they turn'd in air
Sab'ring the gunners there,
Charging an army, while   30
  All the world wonder'd:
Plunged in the battery-smoke
Right thro' the line they broke;
Cossack and Russian
Reel'd from the sabre-stroke   35
  Shatter'd and sunder'd.
Then they rode back, but not,
  Not the six hundred.

5

Cannon to right of them,
Cannon to left of them,   40
Cannon behind them
  Volley'd and thunder'd;
Storm'd at with shot and shell,
While horse and hero fell,
They that had fought so well   45
Came thro' the jaws of Death,
Back from the mouth of Hell,
All that was left of them,
Left of six hundred.

6

When can their glory fade?   50
O the wild charge they made!
  All the world wonder'd.
Honour the charge they made!
Honour the Light Brigade,
  Noble six hundred!   55

1854
Alfred, Lord Tennyson (1809–1892)

---

cossack: a member of a group of frontiersmen of southern Russia organized as cavalry in the Czarist army.

Tennyson's poem has outlived everybody with first-hand knowledge of the specific occasion that prompted it. Many people have heard the phrase "Theirs not to reason why, / Theirs but to do and die" (often misquoted as "do *or* die"—which certainly changes the meaning!) without knowing the original context. Tennyson's phrase *does* have an enduring quality as a description of soldiers in war; the specific event, however, gives the lines substance.

"The Charge of the Light Brigade" commemorates an incident in the Crimean War, a conflict between Russia and England. On October 25, 1854, a division of English cavalry was ordered to charge the Russians through a valley lined with Russian artillery. Some 700 horsemen charged down the valley; 195 returned. As the London *Times* said in an editorial three weeks later, "some hideous blunder" had occurred. Tennyson adapts this phrase in line 12: "Some one had blunder'd." The blunder amounted to this: The English commander-in-chief had sent word by Captain Lewis Nolan that Lord Lucan, who was commanding the English cavalry, was to recapture the Russian artillery on the heights. The man in command of the Light Brigade misunderstood, assuming that he was ordered to charge straight down the valley toward the Russian artillery at the far end. In an account of that charge, an historian describes the dimensions of the mistake:

> The crucial moment had arrived. Nolan threw back his head, and, "in a most disrespectful and significant manner," flung out his arm and, with a furious gesture, pointed, not to the Causeway Heights and the redoubts with the captured British guns, but to the end of the North Valley, where the Russian cavalry routed by the Heavy Brigade were now established with their guns in front of them. "There, my lord, is your enemy, there are your guns," he said, and with those words and that gesture the doom of the Light Brigade was sealed.

The account goes on to describe the fatal charge itself:

> The gallop became head-long, the troopers cheering and yelling; their blood was up, and they were on fire to get at the enemy. Hell for leather, with whistling bullets and crashing shells taking their toll every moment, cheers changing to death cries, horses falling with a scream, the first line of the Light Brigade—17th Lancers and 13th Light Dragoons—raced down the valley to the guns. Close behind them came the second line. Lord George Paget, remembering Lord Cardigan's stern admonition, "Your best support, mind, your best support," had increased the pace of his regiment, the 4th Light Dragoons, and caught up the 11th Hussars. The 8th Hussars, sternly kept in hand by their commanding officer, Colonel Shewell, advanced at a steady trot, and refused to increase their pace. The second

line therefore consisted of the 4th Light Dragoons and the 11th Hussars, with the 8th Hussars to the right rear.

As they, too, plunged into the inferno of fire, and as batteries and massed riflemen on each flank began to tear gaps in their ranks and trooper after trooper came crashing to the ground, they had a new and horrible difficulty to face. The ground was strewn with casualties of the first line— not only dead men and dead horses, but horses and men not yet dead, able to crawl, to scream, to writhe. They had perpetually to avoid riding over men they knew, while riderless horses, some unhurt, some horribly injured, tried to force their way into the ranks. Troop horses in battle, as long as they feel the hand of their rider and his weight on their backs, are, even when wounded, singularly free from fear. When Lord George Paget's charger was hit, he was astonished to find the horse showed no sign of panic. But, once deprived of his rider, the troop horse becomes crazed with terror. He does not gallop out of the action and seek safety; trained to range himself in line, he seeks the companionship of other horses, and, mad with fear, eyeballs protruding, he attempts to attach himself to some leader or to force himself into the ranks of the nearest squadrons. Lord George, riding in advance of the second line, found himself actually in danger. The poor brutes made dashes at him, trying to gallop with him. At one moment he was riding in the midst of seven riderless horses, who cringed and pushed against him as round shot and bullets came by, covering him with blood from their wounds, and so nearly unhorsing him that he was forced to use his sword to free himself.

And all the time, through the cheers, the groans, the ping of bullets whizzing through the air, the whirr and crash of shells, the earth-shaking thunder of galloping horses' hooves, when men were not merely falling one by one but being swept away in groups, words of command rang out as on the parade ground, "Close in to your centre. Back the right flank! Keep up, Private Smith. Left squadron, keep back. Look to your dressing." Until at last, as the ranks grew thinner and thinner, only one command was heard: "Close in! Close in! Close in to the centre! Close in! Close in!"

—Cecil Woodham-Smith, *The Reason Why*

FOLLOWING UP THE CLUES: WHAT HABITATIONS? WHAT NAMES?

The clues to the context of such occasional poems are often less direct than in either "The Convergence of the Twain" or "The Charge of the Light Brigade." In the following poem, the clues are the date in the title coupled with the allusions within the poem itself:

EASTER, 1968

Now we have buried the face we never knew.
Now we have silenced the voice we never heard,
Now he is dead we look on him with awe . . .
Dead king, dear martyr, and anointed Word.
Where thousands followed, each must go home   5
Into his secret heart and learn the pain,
Stand there on rock and, utterly alone,
Come to terms with this burning suffering man;
Torn by his hunger from our fat and greed,
And bitten by his thirst from careless sloth,   10
Must wake, inflamed, to answer for his blood
With the slow-moving inexorable truth
That we can earn even a moment's balm
Only with acts of caring, and fierce calm.

Head of an African, vital and young,   15
The full lips fervent as an open rose,
The high-domed forehead full of light and strong—
Look on this man again. The blood still flows.
Listen once more to the impassioned voice
Till we are lifted on his golden throat   20
And trumpet-call of agony and choice
Out of our hesitating shame and doubt.
Remember how he prayed before the task.
Remember how he walked, eyes bright and still,
Unarmed, his bronze face shining like a mask,   25
Through stones and curses, hatred hard as hail,
Now we have silenced the voice we never heard,
Break open, heart, and listen to his word.

1968
May Sarton (b. 1912)

Like its title, "Easter, 1968" is made up of two parts. The first stanza, coupled with the reference to Easter in the title, seems to be talking about the death and burial of Christ—"Dead king, dear martyr, and anointed Word" (line 4). However, the surprising transition from the first to the second stanza emphasizes that something else is being talked about—"Head of an African, vital and young" (15). The explanation for this transition is the title: *this* Easter poem is concerned with specific events in April, 1968.

Martin Luther King, Jr., the influential black leader and Nobel Prize winner for Peace, was assassinated in Memphis, Tennessee, on April 4, 1968, just before Easter. Thus, Sarton's poem emerges from the impact of King's sudden death and uses expressions (note "dead king") that are allusions to King's life and times: "impassioned voice" (19), "trumpet call of agony and choice" (21), "Remember how he prayed before the task" (23). This last phrase also provides a link between stanzas 1 and 2 because it echoes the episode in the Gospels where Christ prays in the Garden of Gethsemane shortly before he is betrayed into the hands of the Romans (see Matthew 26: 36–40; Mark 14: 32–36; Luke 22: 39–46).

On April 3, 1968, the day before he was assassinated, King spoke to a group in Memphis, where he had come to participate in a strike organized by the Sanitation Workers Union, mostly black, to protest their unjust treatment. This speech, described by Coretta King in a biography of her husband, illuminates Sarton's phrases such as "Remember how he prayed before the task" (23):

> The mantle of prophecy seemed to descend upon Martin. He told the people that his plane from Atlanta had been delayed that morning because "Dr. Martin Luther King is aboard," and there was a search for a possible bomb. He told of how, when he got to Memphis, there were threats and rumors of an attack on him.
>
> Then, Martin added, "I don't know what will happen now. We've got some difficult days ahead. But it really doesn't matter to me now. Because I've been to the mountain-top. I won't mind."
>
> "Like anybody else, I would like to live a long life. Longevity has its place. But I'm not concerned about that now. I just want to do God's will. And He's allowed me to go up to the mountain. And I've looked over, and I've seen the Promised Land."
>
> "I may not get there with you, but I want you to know tonight that we as a people will get to the Promised Land."
>
> "So I'm happy tonight. I'm not worried about anything. I'm not fearing any man. Mine eyes have seen the glory of the coming of the Lord. . . ."
>
> So intense was the audience's emotional response to Martin's words, so high was his own exaltation responding to their excitement, the action and reaction of one to the other, that he was overcome; he broke off there. I believe he intended to finish the quotation—"His truth is marching on." But he could not.
>
> —*My Life with Martin Luther King, Jr.*

Because so many of the events of King's life were reported in print and on television, Sarton could assume that her immediate audience would recognize her allusions and their context. On August 28, 1963, for instance, King spoke to tens of thousands of people who had converged on Washington, D.C., to dramatize the need for legislation that would completely integrate the black citizen into American society. Coretta King further describes his impassioned voice and "the trumpet-call of agony and choice" that so moved the crowds in Washington that day:

He started out with the written speech, delivering it with great eloquence. His main contention was that, "Instead of honoring her sacred obligations, America has given the Negro a bad check. We are here today to redeem that check, and we will not accept the idea that there is no money in the Bank of Justice." When he got to the rhythmic part of demanding freedom *now*, and wanting jobs *now*, the crowd caught the timing and shouted *now* in a cadence. Their response lifted Martin in a surge of emotion to new heights of inspiration. Abandoning his written speech, forgetting time, he spoke from his heart, his voice soaring magnificently out over the great crowd and over to all the world. It seemed to all of us there that day that his words flowed from some higher place, through Martin, to the weary people before him. Yea—Heaven itself opened up and we all seemed transformed.

He said, "I say to you today even though we face the difficulties of today and tomorrow, I still have a dream. It is a dream that is deeply rooted in the American dream. I have a dream that one day this nation will rise up, live out the true meaning of its creed: We hold these truths to be self-evident, that all men are created equal.

"I have a dream that one day on the red hills of Georgia the sons of former slaves and the sons of former slaveowners will be able to sit down together at the table of brotherhood. I have a dream that one day even the state of Mississippi, a state sweltering with the heat of oppression, will be transformed into an oasis of freedom and justice.

"I have a dream that one day every valley shall be exalted, every hill and mountain shall be made low. The rough places will be made plain and the crooked places will be made straight. This is the faith that I go back to the South with. With this faith we will be able to hew out of the mountains of despair the stone of hope. With this faith we will be able to work together, to pray together, to struggle together, to go to jail together, to stand up for freedom together, knowing we will be free one day.

"This will be the day when all of God's children will be able to sing with new meaning, 'Let freedom ring.' So let freedom ring from the prodigious hilltops of New Hampshire; let freedom ring from the mighty mountains of New York. But not only that. Let freedom ring from Stone Mountain of Georgia. Let freedom ring from every hill and molehill of Mississippi, from every mountainside.

"When we allow freedom to ring from every town and every hamlet, from every state and every city, we will be able to speed up that day when all of God's children, black men and white men, Jews and Gentiles, Protestants and Catholics, will be able to join hands and sing in the words of the old Negro spiritual, 'Free at last! Free at last! Great God A-mighty, we are free at last!' "

As Martin ended, there was the awed silence that is the greatest tribute an orator can be paid. And then a tremendous crash of sound as two hundred and fifty thousand people shouted ecstatic accord with his words. The feeling that they had of oneness and unity was complete. They kept on shouting in one thunderous voice, and for that brief moment the Kingdom of God seemed to have come on earth.

—*My Life with Martin Luther King, Jr.*

The poems in this chapter are rooted in historical events. They are like the ends of threads leading back into the maze of history. By following where they lead, we can discover what people thought and how they responded to the events of their own time. Here are three further examples. Note the kinds of clues that indicate a specific historical context. Note especially proper names of people and places and the dates of the poems. Consider the extent to which the poems are at once time-bound and universal.

PLATO TOLD

plato told

him:he couldn't
believe it(jesus

told him;he
wouldn't believe   5
it)lao

tsze
certainly told
him,and general
(yes   10

mam)
sherman;
and even

Lao-tsze: the Chinese philosopher who originated the philosophy of Taoism. **Sherman:** William Tecumseh Sherman, a Union general in the American Civil War (1861–1865) who said, "War is Hell!"

What Happened?

(believe it
or   15

not)you
told him:i told
him;we told him
(he didn't believe it,no

sir)it took   20
a nipponized bit of
the old sixth

avenue
el;in the top of his head:to tell

him   25

1944
E. E. Cummings (1894–1963)

WOODSTOCK

I came upon a child of God
He was walking along the road
And I asked him where are you going
And this he told me
I'm going on down to Yasgur's farm   5
I'm going to join in a rock'n'roll band
I'm going to camp out on the land
And try an' get my soul free
   We are stardust
   We are golden   10
   And we've got to get ourselves
   Back to the garden

Then can I walk beside you
I have come here to lose the smog

---

nipponized . . . el: In the 1930s, the United States sold scrap metal from the elevated railways in New York City to Japan (Nippon). This metal was made into weapons and ammunition that were later used by Japan against the United States in World War II.

And I feel to be a cog in something turning   15
Well maybe it is just the time of year
Or maybe it's the time of man
I don't know who I am
But life is for learning
   We are stardust   20
   We are golden
   And we've got to get ourselves
   Back to the garden

By the time we got to Woodstock
We were half a million strong   25
And everywhere there was song and celebration
And I dreamed I saw the bombers
Riding shotgun in the sky
And they were turning into butterflies
Above our nation   30
   We are stardust
   We are golden
   And we've got to get ourselves
   Back to the garden

1969
Joni Mitchell (b. 1943)

What was "Woodstock"? Date? Occasion? Where was "Yasgur's farm"? Why does Mitchell's song connect Woodstock and Yasgur's farm to the idea that "We've got to get ourselves / Back to the garden"? What related historical events were going on in the 1960s? To what do these lines refer: "And I dreamed I saw the bombers / Riding shotgun in the sky / And they were turning into butterflies"? What allusions and references in the poem connect time-bound details and universal concerns?

Here is a third poem that talks about a specific historical event:

KENT STATE, MAY 4, 1970

Ran out of tear gas and became panicky,
poor inept kids, and therefore they poured lead
into the other kids and shot them dead,
and now myself and the whole country
are weeping. It's not a matter of degree,   5

not less not more than the Indo-Chinese slaughtered,
it is the same; but mostly folk are shattered
by home truths (as I know who lost my boy).

I am not willing to go on this week
with business as usual, this month this year   10
let cars slow down and stop and builders break
off building and close up the theater.
You see, the children that we massacre
are our own children. Call the soldiers back.

1970

Paul Goodman (1911–1972)

Notice that Goodman assumes we know the reason the students were ral-
lying and protesting: the Vietnam war, which Goodman compares to these
killings:

It's not a matter of degree
not less not more than the Indo-Chinese slaughtered,
it is the same.

Given this comparison, which situation does "Call the soldiers back" apply to?
Confrontations with protesters? The war? Both?

Knowing that a poem may refer to one or more actual events can alert us
to the evidence that connects the poem to its historical context. We need to be
ready to ask "What happened?" and to follow up that question by further exploration if necessary. Sources for further exploration are suggested in the Appendix, Writing about Poems, and in the Selected Bibliography at the end of
this book. Above all, we need to see the poem as part of its world. It is an
essential part that—like a biography, a television newscast, a history book, a
situation comedy, a newspaper story, or a diary—can give us insight into the
human condition of another time—and our own.

EXERCISES_____

A.   **THE SOLDIER**

If I should die, think only this of me;
    That there's some corner of a foreign field
That is for ever England. There shall be

In that rich earth a richer dust concealed;
A dust whom England bore, shaped, made aware,   5
  Gave, once, her flowers to love, her ways to roam,
A body of England's, breathing English air,
  Washed by the rivers, blest by suns of home.

And think, this heart, all evil shed away,
  A pulse in the eternal mind, no less   10
    Gives somewhere back the thoughts by England given;
Her sights and sounds; dreams happy as her day;
  And laughter, learnt of friends; and gentleness,
    In hearts at peace, under an English heaven.

1914
Rupert Brooke (1887–1915)

World War I was declared on August 4, 1914. "The Soldier" was one
of Rupert Brooke's "1914" sonnets and was published in December, 1914,
in the magazine *New Numbers*. Timothy Rogers has described the situation and attitudes that shaped these sonnets:

> The first tentative jottings of four of the "1914" sonnets were
> made in a small field-notebook. Interspersed among them are notes
> from military lectures—'Every officer should be easily found', 'Ger-
> man explosive shells carry further back than forward', 'keep *strict* dis-
> cipline'—and personal memoranda—'Thompson, Officers Mess,
> doesn't make his bed up', 'Wanted: 1 curtain . . . table . . . chairs.'
> It is well that the beginnings of these idealistic sonnets would be thus
> preserved among tokens of a more practical concern. At the same
> time they are poems, not of war, but of preparation for war (Brooke's
> first title for "The Soldier" was "The Recruit"). . . . [Brooke] cap-
> tured the thoughts and feelings of the moment and gave eloquent
> expression to them. 'Rupert expressed us *all*,' said Henry James [the
> novelist (1843–1916)] 'at the highest tide of our actuality.' But the
> moment was to pass: the simple rhetoric became outmoded, the atti-
> tude of mind suspect.
>
> —*Rupert Brooke: A Reappraisal and Selection*

1. Why would "The Recruit" have been a good title for "The Soldier"?
2. Compare Brooke's poem to Wilfred Owen's "Futility" (p. 152) and to the
following two poems:

DULCE ET DECORUM EST

Bent double, like old beggars under sacks,
Knock-kneed, coughing like hags, we cursed through sludge,
Till on the haunting flares we turned our backs
And towards our distant rest began to trudge.
Men marched asleep. Many had lost their boots   5
But limped on, blood-shod. All went lame; all blind;
Drunk with fatigue; deaf even to the hoots
Of tired, outstripped Five-Nines that dropped behind.

Gas! Gas! Quick, boys!—An ecstasy of fumbling,
Fitting the clumsy helmets just in time;   10
But someone still was yelling out and stumbling
And flound'ring like a man in fire or lime.—
Dim, through the misty panes and thick green light,
As under a green sea, I saw him drowning.

In all my dreams, before my helpless sight,   15
He plunges at me, guttering, choking, drowning.

If in some smothering dreams you too could pace
Behind the wagon that we flung him in,
And watch the white eyes writhing in his face,
His hanging face, like a devil's sick of sin;   20
If you could hear, at every jolt, the blood
Come gargling from the froth-corrupted lungs,
Obscene as cancer, bitter as the cud
Of vile, incurable sores on innocent tongues,—
My friend, you would not tell with such high zest   25
To children ardent for some desperate glory,
The old Lie: Dulce et decorum est
Pro patria mori.

                                                  1920
                              Wilfred Owen (1893–1918)

Dulce et decorum est / Pro patria mori: from the Latin poet Horace (65–8 B.C.)—"It is sweet and fitting to die for one's country" (*Odes* III: 2). **five-nines:** exploding shells containing poison gas.

BREAK OF DAY IN THE TRENCHES

The darkness crumbles away—
It is the same old druid Time as ever.
Only a live thing leaps my hand—
A queer sardonic rat—
As I pull the parapet's poppy   5
To stick behind my ear.
Droll rat, they would shoot you if they knew
Your cosmopolitan sympathies.
Now you have touched this English hand
You will do the same to a German—   10
Soon, no doubt, if it be your pleasure
To cross the sleeping green between.
It seems you inwardly grin as you pass
Strong eyes, fine limbs, haughty athletes
Less chanced than you for life,   15
Bonds to the whims of murder,
Sprawled in the bowels of the earth,
The torn fields of France.
What do you see in our eyes
At the shrieking iron and flame   20
Hurled through still heavens?
What quaver—what heart aghast?
Poppies whose roots are in man's veins
Drop, and are ever dropping;
But mine in my ear is safe,   25
Just a little white with the dust.

composed 1916–18   1922
Isaac Rosenberg (1890–1918)

3. How does "The Soldier" differ in attitude from Owen's "Futility," from "Dulce et Decorum Est," and from "Break of Day in the Trenches"?
4. At the outset of the war, Wilfred Owen also felt that the war represented a "new crusade and modern knightliness." What had changed between 1914 and 1918?

B. "Kent State, May 4, 1970" is one poem that came out of the United States' involvement in the war in Vietnam, specifically the Cambodian invasion. Here are two further poems that emerged from that experience.

What details of the poems are clues to the historical context? What attitudes about the historical events are explicit or implicit in the poems?

VOICE FROM DANANG

After we had burned on the water a while,
amid the chopper-borne
shouts, flares, and thrashing rope ladders,
we put into quiet, dark rooms.

I couldn't touch you through my walls—   5
my nails screeled into chines.
Why had they bored lights in me like that?

You must have known we were set on sand.
It scratched in our ears
like blood leaking in crystals from my veins.   10
We waited under a noisy sky.

I have been watching my body fall apart—
toes and eyes like loose bearings,
my torch-light prick chases its batteries.

They lift us, number us, lift us, shelve us.   15
Have your ribs jackstrawed?
Once they tipped me up on concrete, my parts
thundered into my skull.

This will go on and on until we get back.
We are cool, invoiced cargo.   20
I last saw you shouting at a fly on a blue ceiling.

Danang: A city in South Vietnam that was a major supply depot for the American forces and that was also a major embarkation point for transporting the American dead back to the United States.
screeled into chines: Redshaw comments on these words: " 'Screeled' may be considered an onomatopoeic, portmanteau word with great justice. I did not, however, just make the word up, but remembered it in and from the speech of the lobstermen and fishermen in Marblehead (Massachusetts). . . . The word then described, pejoratively, I think, a way of hauling in a line, a lobster trap, a net. I use it to describe the sound and feel of fingernails (grown long in death) testing the confines of a body bag and/or metal box."

If there was confusion then, there is none now.
I had thought that a bag or box
could not keep me in, but this is plainly a cove—
white trees, black sand, waves, sun.   25

1973
Thomas Dillon Redshaw (b. 1944)

A POEM ABOUT POEMS ABOUT VIETNAM

The spotlights had you covered (thunder
in the wings). In the combat zones
and in the Circle, darkness. Under
the muzzles of the microphones
you opened fire, and a phalanx   5
of loudspeakers shook on the wall;
but all your cartridges were blanks
when you were at the Albert Hall.

Lord George Byron cared for Greece,
Auden and Cornford cared for Spain,   10
confronted bullets and disease
to make their poems' meaning plain;
but you—by what right did you wear
suffering like a service medal,
numbing the nerve that they laid bare,   15
when you were at the Albert Hall?

The poets of another time—
Owen with a rifle-butt
between his paper and the slime,
Donne quitting Her pillow to cut   20
a quill—knew that in love and war
dispatches from the front are all.

Circle: The Dress Circle in Albert Hall, the concert hall in London where a highly publicized reading of poems opposing U.S. involvement in Vietnam was held in 1965. **Byron:** The poet Byron, who died in 1824 in Greece, where he was involved in the cause of Greek independence. **Auden and Cornford:** W. H. Auden and John Cornford, English poets who went to Spain in 1937 to aid revolutionary groups fighting against Francisco Franco. **Owen:** Wilfred Owen; **Donne:** John Donne.

We believe them, they were there,
when you were at the Albert Hall.

Poet, they whisper in their sleep   25
louder from underground than all
the mikes that hung upon your lips
when you were at the Albert Hall.

                                        1969
                        Jon Stallworthy (b. 1935)

C.   **POLO GROUNDS**

Time is of the essence. This is a highly skilled
And beautiful mystery. Three or four seconds only
From the time that Riggs connects till he reaches first,
And in those seconds Jurges goes to his right,
Comes up with the ball, tosses to Witek at second   5
In time for the out—a double play.

(Red Barber crescendo. Crowd noises, obbligato;
Scattered staccatos from the peanut boys,
Loud in the lull, as the teams are changing sides) . . .   10
Hubbell takes the sign, nods, pumps, delivers—
A foul into the stands. Dunn takes a new ball out,
Hands it to Danning, who throws it down to Werber;
Werber takes off his glove, rubs the ball briefly,
Tosses it over to Hub, who goes to the rosin bag,   15
Takes the sign from Danning, pumps, delivers—
Low, outside, ball three. Danning goes to the mound,
Says something to Hub, Dunn brushes off the plate,
Adams starts throwing in the Giant bullpen,
Hub takes the sign from Danning, pumps, delivers,   20
Camilli gets hold of it, a *long* fly to the outfield,
Ott goes back, back, back, against the wall, gets under it,
Pounds his glove, and takes it for the out.
That's all for the Dodgers. . . .

Time is of the essence. The rhythms break,   25
More varied and subtle than any kind of dance;
Movement speeds up or lags. The ball goes out

In sharp and angular drives, or long, slow arcs,
Comes in again controlled and under aim;
The players wheel or spurt, race, stoop, slide, halt,   30
Shift imperceptibly to new positions,
Watching the signs, according to the batter,
The score, the inning. Time is of the essence.

Time is of the essence. Remember Terry?
Remember Stonewall Jackson, Lindstrom, Frisch,   35
When they were good? Remember Long George Kelly?
Remember John McGraw and Benny Kauff?
Remember Bridwell, Tenney, Merkel, Youngs,
Chief Meyers, Big Jeff Tesreau, Shufflin' Phil?
Remember Matthewson, and Ames, and Donlin,   40
Buck Ewing, Rusie, Smiling Mickey Welch?
Remember a left-handed catcher named Jack Humphries,
Who sometimes played the outfield, in '83?

Time is of the essence. The shadow moves
From the plate to the box, from the box to second base,   45
From second to the outfield, to the bleachers.

Time is of the essence. The crowd and players
Are the same age always, but the man in the crowd
Is older every season. Come on, play ball!

                                                            1942
                    Rolfe Humphries (1894–1969)

1. How does Humphries take a time-bound event like a baseball game and
   prove that "time is of the essence"?
2. How does Humphries make the historical past personal?

D.   **EASTER 1916**

I have met them at close of day
Coming with vivid faces
From counter or desk among grey
Eighteenth-century houses.
I have passed with a nod of the head   5
Or polite meaningless words,

What Happened?

Or have lingered awhile and said
Polite meaningless words,
And thought before I had done
Of a mocking tale or a gibe   10
To please a companion
Around the fire at the club,
Being certain that they and I
But lived where motley is worn:
All changed, changed utterly: 15
A terrible beauty is born.

That woman's days were spent
In ignorant good-will,
Her nights in argument
Until her voice grew shrill.   20
What voice more sweet than hers
When, young and beautiful,
She rode to harriers?
This man had kept a school
And rode our winged horse;   25
This other his helper and friend
Was coming into his force;
He might have won fame in the end,
So sensitive his nature seemed,
So daring and sweet his thought.   30
This other man I had dreamed
A drunken, vainglorious lout.
He had done most bitter wrong
To some who are near my heart,
Yet I number him in the song;   35
He, too, has resigned his part
In the casual comedy;
He, too, has been changed in his turn,
Transformed utterly:
A terrible beauty is born.   40

Hearts with one purpose alone
Through summer and winter seem
Enchanted to a stone
To trouble the living stream.
The horse that comes from the road,   45

Easter, 1968

The rider, the birds that range
From cloud to tumbling cloud,
Minute by minute they change;
A shadow of cloud on the stream
Changes minute by minute;   50
A horse-hoof slides on the brim,
And a horse plashes within it;
The long-legged moor-hens dive,
And hens to moor-cocks call;
Minute by minute they live: 55
The stone's in the midst of all.

Too long a sacrifice
Can make a stone of the heart.
O when may it suffice?
That is Heaven's part, our part   60
To murmur name upon name,
As a mother names her child
When sleep at last has come
On limbs that had run wild.
What is it but nightfall?   65
No, no, not night but death;
Was it needless death after all?
For England may keep faith
For all that is done and said.
We know their dream; enough   70
To know they dreamed and are dead;
And what if excess of love
Bewildered them till they died?
I write it out in a verse—
MacDonagh and MacBride   75
And Connolly and Pearse
Now and in time to be,
Wherever green is worn,
Are changed, changed utterly:
A terrible beauty is born.   80

1916
William Butler Yeats (1865–1939)

Like May Sarton's "Easter, 1968," Yeats's "Easter 1916" reflects a
specific incident and a specific point of view about that incident. On April

24, 1916 (Easter Monday), Irish republicans who sought to end British rule in Ireland seized buildings and a park in the center of Dublin. Within a week the rising was put down by superior British firepower, and the leaders of the rebellion were tried and executed.

1. What names and references require further research?*
2. How does Yeats link the Easter (resurrection) theme with the specific incidents of the rising?
3. How does Yeats himself indicate a changed attitude toward the people referred to in the poem?
4. To what extent, in reading the poem, do you feel the need for further information? What events of recent years give further resonances to Yeats's poem?

E.   **[COUPLET ON ISAAC NEWTON]**

Nature and Nature's Laws lay hid in Night:
God said, Let Newton be: And all was Light.

1730
Alexander Pope (1688–1744)

Pope's couplet refers to the discoveries about light and color made by Sir Isaac Newton (1642–1727), especially those reported in his *Opticks* (1704), which first described how light could be broken into its component colors. Other authors also reacted to these discoveries, and an account of them may be found in Marjorie Hope Nicolson's *Newton Demands the Muse* (Princeton University Press, 1946).

1. What allusion is contained in Pope's second line?
2. What does this allusion suggest about the impact of Newton's discoveries on his contemporaries and their thinking?

WRITING SUGGESTIONS⎯⎯⎯⎯⎯⎯⎯⎯⎯⎯⎯⎯⎯⎯⎯⎯⎯⎯⎯

1. Research the historical background of either "Woodstock" or "Kent State, May 4, 1970." Go to newspapers, magazines, or books on the period for

---

* The events of the Easter rising described in Yeats's poem are discussed in a contemporary account, James Stephens' *The Insurrection in Dublin* (London, 1916) and in a documentary collection, *1916: The Easter Rising*, ed. O. Dudley Edwards and Fergus Pyle (Dublin, 1968). Ruth Dudley Edwards is the author of a biography of Pearse (see lines 24–25): *Patrick Pearse: The Triumph of Failure* (London, 1977). A very useful study of the Easter rising is William I. Thompson's *The Imagination of an Insurrection* (Oxford, 1967). Kenneth Neill's *An Illustrated History of the Irish People* (New York, 1979) has some excellent photographs of the rising.

such background. In an essay explain how and why the poet has utilized the historical evidence. Consider the point of view that the poet takes on the historical events.

2. In 1816, the British government obtained a set of marble statues and friezes that had originally been on the Parthenon in Athens and that were brought to England by Lord Elgin. The following poem tells of John Keats's reaction to seeing these examples of Greek antiquity:

ON SEEING THE ELGIN MARBLES FOR THE FIRST TIME

My spirit is too weak; mortality
   Weighs heavily on me like unwilling sleep,
   And each imagined pinnacle and steep
Of godlike hardship tells me I must die
Like a sick eagle looking at the sky.   5
   Yet 'tis a gentle luxury to weep,
   That I have not the cloudy winds to keep
Fresh for the opening of the morning's eye.
Such dim-conceivéd glories of the brain
   Bring round the heart an indescribable feud;   10
So do these wonders a most dizzy pain,
   That mingles Grecian grandeur with the rude
Wasting of old Time—with a billowy main,
   A sun, a shadow of a magnitude.

1817
John Keats (1795–1821)

Investigate the circumstances of the bringing of the Elgin marbles to England and find a source that illustrates what they look like. Then write an essay discussing Keats's reaction to the marbles. Alternatively, you may wish to expand your research and write on the effect the Elgin marbles had on various poets and artists—for example, Benjamin Robert Haydon (to whom this poem and an accompanying one by Keats were addressed) and Lord Byron, whose poem on the marbles is called "The Curse of Minerva." Places to start your research: *Victorian Olympus*, by William Gaunt (Prologue); *Lord Elgin and his Collection*, by A. H. Smith; *Autobiography and Journals*, by Benjamin Robert Haydon; *Byron's Letters and Journals* (ed. Leslie A. Marchand), vol. 2. The Elgin marbles are still a subject of lively debate and controversy. See, for example, "Greece Wants Britain to Return Elgin Marbles," *The New York Times*, April 18, 1982, sec. 1, p. 10.

CHAPTER SEVEN

WHAT DID THEY MEAN?— THE WORLD OUTSIDE THE POEM

Poems depend on the time in which they were written even when they do not refer directly to historical events. Their words and their cultural assumptions necessarily reflect the time from which they come.

CHANGES IN LANGUAGE

Language is not static. From year to year, century to century, language changes. Old words go out of use, new words are created, some words become more specialized or more general in their usage, and others take on connotations not fully explained by dictionary definitions.

David Wagoner describes some of these transitions in the following poem:

AN ELEGY FOR YARDS, POUNDS, AND GALLONS

An unduly elected body of our elders
Is turning you out of office and schoolroom
through ten long years, is phasing you
Out of our mouths and lives forever.

An Elegy for Yards, Pounds, and Gallons

Words have been lost before: some hounded   5
Nearly to death, and some transplanted
With roots dead set against stone,
And some let slide into obscure senescence.

Some even murdered beyond recall like extinct animals—
(It would be cruel to rehearse their names: 10
They might stir from sleep on the dusty shelves
In pain for a moment).

Yet you, old emblems of distance and heaviness,
Solid and liquid companions, our good measures,
When have so many been forced to languish   15
For years through a deliberate deathwatch?

How can we name your colorless replacements
Or let them tell us for our time being
How much we weigh, how short we are,
Or how little we have left to drink?   20

Goodbye to Pounds by the Ton and all their Ounces,
To Gallons, Quarts, and Pints,
To Yards whose Feet are inching their last Mile,
Weighed down, poured out, written off,

And drifting slowly away from us   25
Like drams, like chains and gills,
To become as quaint as leagues and palms
In an old poem.

1973
David Wagoner (b. 1926)

Notice Wagoner's reference to "league," a word Tennyson used as a matter of course in "The Charge of the Light Brigade," and to other terms of measurement ("drams," "palms") that are now rarely used. If the word is obviously an "extinct animal," it will stand out because it is so unusual. But some words that *seem* familiar may have undergone shifts in meaning or implication. A passage from Geoffrey Chaucer's *The Canterbury Tales* (composed about 1387–1400) shows us words that have been lost to us and words whose meanings or spellings have changed:

from THE NUN'S PRIEST'S TALE

A poor *widwe somdeel stape* in age	widow somewhat advanced
Was *whilom* dwelling in a *narwe* cotage,	formerly narrow (that is, small)
Biside a grove, stonding in a dale:	
This widwe of which I telle you my tale,	
Sin thilke day that she was last a *wif,*	since that day wife 5
In pacience *ladde* a ful simple lif.	led
For litel was hir *catel* and hir *rente,*	property income
By *housbondrye* of *swich* as God hire sente	economy (that is, thrifty housekeeping) such
She *foond* hirself and *eek* hir doughtren two.	provided for also
Three large sowes hadde she and *namo,*	no more 10
Three *kin,* and eek a sheep that *highte Malle.*	cows was named Malle
Ful sooty was hir *bowr* and eek hir *halle.*	bedroom main room
In which she *eet* ful many a *sclendre meel;*	ate slender (that is, scanty) meal

Geoffrey Chaucer (1343–1400)

Even in this passage, filled as it is with unfamiliar terms, there are words that look familiar enough for us to think that we know exactly what they mean. "Catel" looks near enough to our "cattle," "rente" looks like "rent," "kin" looks the same as our word for relatives. In Chaucer's time, however, "catel" meant property—our word "chattel,"—"rente" meant income, and "kin" (=kine) meant cows.

Such words that look familiar but that have quite changed their meaning or implications pose a problem exactly because we may confuse them with our modern meaning. The poems below contain words whose most familiar meanings are not the ones the poets intend. Note, for example, Herrick's use of *lawn* and Shakespeare's use of *reeks* and *barks.*

DELIGHT IN DISORDER

A sweet disorder in the dress
Kindles in clothes a wantonness.
A lawn about the shoulders thrown
Into a fine distraction;
An erring lace, which here and there   5
Enthralls the crimson stomacher;
A cuff neglectful, and thereby
Ribbands to flow confusedly;

A winning wave, deserving note,
In the tempestuous petticoat;   10
A careless shoestring, in whose tie
I see a wild civility;
Do more bewitch me than when art
Is too precise in every part.

1648

Robert Herrick (1591–1674)

MY MISTRESS' EYES ARE NOTHING LIKE THE SUN

My mistress' eyes are nothing like the sun;
Coral is far more red than her lips' red;
If snow be white, why then her breasts are dun;
If hairs be wires, black wires grow on her head;
I have seen roses damask'd red and white,   5
But no such roses see I in her cheeks;
And in some perfumes is there more delight
Than in the breath that from my mistress reeks:
I love to hear her speak, yet well I know
That music hath a far more pleasing sound: 10
I grant I never saw a goddess go;
My mistress, when she walks, treads on the ground.
And yet, by heaven, I think my love as rare
As any she belied by false compare.

1609

William Shakespeare (1564–1616)

LET ME NOT TO THE MARRIAGE OF TRUE MINDS

Let me not to the marriage of true minds
Admit impediment. Love is not love
Which alters when it alteration finds,
Or bends with the remover to remove:
O, no, it is an ever-fixéd mark,   5
That looks on tempests and is never shaken;
It is the star to every wandering bark,

Whose worth's unknown, although his height be taken.
Love's not Time's fool, though rosy lips and cheeks
Within his bending sickle's compass come;   10
Love alters not with his brief hours and weeks,
But bears it out even to the edge of doom.
If this be error and upon me proved,
I never writ, nor no man ever loved.

1609
William Shakespeare (1564–1616)

Another example of a familiar word with another, less familiar, meaning is Matthew Arnold's use of *shingles* in his 1867 poem, "Dover Beach": "down the vast edges drear / And naked shingles of the world (lines 27–28). The familiar American definition—a piece of wood or other material used to cover the roof or sides of a house—does not seem to make much sense in Arnold's context: that context, as well as the date and the English setting, all suggest a different meaning of shingle is intended—a gravel-covered area of shore or beach.

A reader also needs to be ready for words that have taken on implications encompassed by no simple dictionary definition. In the 1970s, for example, *Watergate* was such a charged word. Its use came about as the result of a break-in at the Democratic Party's headquarters in an office-apartment complex named Watergate. Because the break-in implicated Richard Nixon's presidency, the use of the word came to be a kind of shorthand for a host of interrelated political scandals during Nixon's second term of office, 1972–1974. Writers could speak of a "Watergate mentality" or "the Watergate years" and could adapt the word for other scandals such as "Koreagate" with the knowledge that their readers needed no further explanation.

Since every poem is necessarily part of the time in which it was written, it is not at all surprising to find such shorthand words occurring in poems. Sometimes what the word signifies is so much a part of the world that the poet assumes a shared knowledge with the audience; sometimes, the poet educates the reader to the use of the shorthand word through associated images or ideas. When Thomas Wyatt uses the word *Fortune* in "They Flee from Me" (see Chapter Three), he assumes a knowledge of the implications of the word, and he also educates us to its meaning:

> Thankéd be Fortune, it hath been otherwise
> Twenty times better, but once in special.

Because the word *Fortune* is familiar, it is easy to pass over it without too much attention, particularly as the word still carries some of the same associations it did for Wyatt nearly four hundred years ago. Wyatt's phrase, "Thankéd be Fortune, it hath been otherwise," *might* be paraphrased as "Thank goodness," or "Thank God, it's been different in the past." Such a paraphrase, however, would lose some of the implications the word had outside the poem for Wyatt and his contemporaries. For them, the word was associated not just with good or bad luck but with a very specific image—the Wheel of Fortune—which the art and literature of the time used repeatedly.

In the *Mirror for Magistrates* (1563), written some forty years after Wyatt's poem, Thomas Sackville (1536–1608) describes this Wheel of Fortune:

> "Lo here," quoth Sorrow, "Princes of renown,
> That whilom sat on top of Fortune's wheel,
> Now laid full low, like wretches whirled down."

Examined with this image in mind, Wyatt's poem reveals that it is structured around this concept of fortune. The turn of fortune's wheel is suggested in the very first line of the poem: "They flee from me that sometime did me seek." The first stanza is developed by the opposition of *then*, when the speaker was at the top of the wheel and *now*, when the wheel of fortune has turned for him. Wyatt emphasizes this image in the third stanza with the phrase "But all is turnéd," and it becomes clear that Wyatt's speaker feels that the situation is not his fault, but that he is a victim of fortune's wheel.

CULTURAL ASSUMPTIONS

As Wyatt's poem illustrates, words reflect some of the cultural assumptions of the poet's time. These assumptions include a society's beliefs, its religious, political, and social values, and its ways of thinking about experience, which are shared—more or less—by the immediate audience of the poem.

This presents a challenge. Getting at the cultural assumptions of any age, even our own, is difficult, and recognizing these assumptions in a poem requires alertness. However talented the poet, he or she is writing for that age, not for a hundred or five hundred years in the future. The reader who lives in a different time and place may easily slip over places where shared values are assumed in a poem without recognizing their significance. With other poems, readers may experience a kind of culture shock because they *do* recognize the underlying assumptions, but find such values radically different from their own.

In addition to these problems, the reader also needs to be aware that poets do not always share the assumptions of their time or place. Sometimes they attack or question the assumptions of their society, putting one set of values or assumptions in contrast with another. In "The Convergence of the Twain," for example, Hardy does not believe that human progress is invincible, and in stanza 7 he opposes a fateful, inevitable force—the iceberg—to the overweening confidence represented by the "unsinkable" *Titanic:*

> And as the smart ship grew
> In stature, grace, and hue,
> In shadowy silent distance grew the Iceberg too.

The following two poems also present contrasts of one set of values with another:

BALLAD OF FAITH

> No dignity without chromium
> No truth but a glossy finish
> If she purrs she's virtuous
> If she hits ninety she's pure
> ZZZZZZZZZZ!   5
> Step on the gas, brother
> (The horn sounds hoarsely)

> 1950
> *William Carlos Williams*
> *(1883–1963)*

Like Hardy, Williams is able to count on his audience recognizing, if not necessarily sharing, certain assumptions—here, the value of the automobile in American society. Some Americans, Williams can assume, *have* believed in the value of fancy chrome and a glossy finish, in the importance of power and speed in the automobile. Williams humorously attacks these values by contrasting them to ideals of dignity, truth, virtue, and purity. Other cultural assumptions about automobiles are indicated by the pronoun "she" and the pun on "hoarsely."

The next poem shows the significance of the same kinds of cultural assumptions and, in addition, demonstrates the importance of place as it affects language. A. D. Hope is an Australian, and some of the words in the poem come from Australian English—"spanner," "bowser-boy," "poppet." At the same time, Hope reveals certain broader cultural assumptions with a clever comparison:

THE BRIDES

Down the assembly line they roll and pass
Complete at last, a miracle of design;
Their chromium fenders, the unbreakable glass,
The fashionable curve, the air-flow line.

Grease to the elbows Mum and Dad enthuse,   5
Pocket their spanners and survey the bride;
Murmur: 'A sweet job! All she needs is juice!
Built for a life-time—sleek as a fish. Inside

'He will find every comfort: the full set
Of gadgets; knobs that answer to the touch   10
For light or music; a place for his cigarette;
Room for his knees; a honey of a clutch.'

Now slowly through the show-room's flattering glare
See her wheeled in to love, console, obey,
Shining and silent! Parson with a prayer   15
Blesses the number-plate, she rolls away

To write her numerals in his book of life;
And now, at last, stands on the open road,
Triumphant, perfect, every inch a wife,
While the corks pop, the flash-light bulbs explode.   20

Her heavenly bowser-boy assumes his seat;
She prints the soft dust with her brand-new treads,
Swings towards the future, purring with a sweet
Concatenation of the poppet heads.

1951
A. D. Hope (b. 1907)

Another way in which we can perceive the significance of cultural assumptions is by contrasting poems on the same subject written at different times. Imagine, for instance, a poem about automobiles written in the 1980s.

---

spanners: wrenches. **bowser-boy:** British and Australian slang for a gasoline-pump attendant. **poppet heads:** valve heads; *poppet* is also slang for a young girl.

What assumptions in Williams' poem might be affected by inflation, higher gas prices, and the demand for more economical cars?

Different cultural assumptions are at work in the following two poems, both of which involve the relationship between men and women. In the passage from *Paradise Lost*, published in 1667, John Milton describes Adam and Eve before the Fall, in Eden:

from PARADISE LOST

Two of far nobler shape erect and tall,
God-like erect, with native Honor clad
In naked Majesty seemed Lords of all,
And worthy seemed, for in their looks Divine
The image of their glorious Maker shone,   5
Truth, Wisdom, Sanctitude severe and pure,
Severe, but in true filial freedom placed;
Whence true authority in men; *though both*
Not equal, as their sex not equal seemed;
For contemplation he and valor formed,   10
For softness she and sweet attractive Grace,
He for God only, she for God in him.

—Book IV, 288–99 (italics added)
John Milton (1608–1674)

The second poem was published in 1972:

FROM A SURVIVOR

The pact that we made was the ordinary pact
of men & women in those days

I don't know who we thought we were
that our personalities
could resist the failures of the race   5

Lucky or unlucky, we didn't know
the race had failures of that order
and that we were going to share them

From a Survivor

Like everybody else, we thought of ourselves as special

Your body is as vivid to me   10
as it ever was: even more

since my feeling for it is clearer:
I know what it could do and could not do

⸌it is no longer
the body of a god   15
or anything with power over my life

Next year it would have been 20 years
and you are wastefully dead
who might have made the leap
we talked, too late, of making   20

which I live now
not as a leap
but a succession of brief, amazing movements

each one making possible the next.

                                                        1972
                                    Adrienne Rich (b. 1929)

   Both poems talk about the relationship between man and woman (certainly a universal concern), and both poems are based on certain assumptions about that relationship. What assumptions does each passage contain, and how do these assumptions differ? Compare, for instance, Milton's line, "He for God only, she for God in him" and Rich's lines, "It is no longer / the body of a god / or anything with power over my life." What different values are being asserted, and how does the comparison of the two passages help clarify the values in each?

   Milton's description implies a God-centered universe in which every creature has an ordained and natural place; Rich's lines suggest, by contrast, a breakdown of that order or, to put it more positively, the development of a world in which these older (perhaps now stereotyped) values are replaced. Rich's descriptions are rooted, not only in her private experience, but in the broader social movement of the 1960s and 1970s that included a radical rethinking of a woman's role in society.

   But there is a potential trap for the reader here. It would be a misleading generalization to say that *everyone* in a particular time shares identical values and assumptions. Certainly, not every single person in 1667 agreed with Milton's views, nor did, in the 1970s, everyone agree with Adrienne Rich's. The variety of cultural assumptions and values possible within a given age can be more clearly appreciated by comparing two poets living at the same time reacting to the same event.

On July 20, 1969, Neil Armstrong, Buzz Aldrin, and Michael Collins—American astronauts—circled the moon in preparation for landing. In the early morning hours of July 21, Neil Armstrong became the first man to step onto the surface of the moon. Here is one poem written about that remarkable moment in human history:

VOYAGE TO THE MOON

Wanderer in our skies,
dazzle of silver in our leaves and on our
waters silver, O
silver evasion in our farthest thought—
"the visiting moon," "the glimpses of the moon,"   5

and we have found her.

               From the first of time
before the first of time, before the
first men tasted time we sought for her.
She was a wonder to us, unattainable,   10
a longing past the reach of longing,
a light beyond our lights, our lives—perhaps
a meaning to us—O, a meaning!

Now we have found her in her nest of night.

Three days and three nights we journeyed,   15
steered by farthest stars, climbed outward,
crossed the invisible tide rip where the floating dust
falls one way or the other in the void between,
followed that other down, encountered
cold, faced death, unfathomable emptiness.   20

---

the visiting moon: a phrase from Shakespeare's *Antony and Cleopatra*, IV, xv, 68. **glimpses of the moon:** from *Hamlet* I, iv, 51.

Now, the fourth day evening, we descend,
make fast, set foot at last upon her beaches,
   stand in her silence, lift our heads and see
above her, wanderer in her sky,
a wonder to us past the reach of wonder,   27
a light beyond our lights, our lives, the rising
earth,
         a meaning to us,
                  O, a meaning!

                                             1969
                  Archibald MacLeish (1892–1982)

But did everyone in 1969 agree with MacLeish on the meaning of the voyage
to the moon? Here is another poem:

MOON LANDING

It's natural the Boys should whoop it up for
So huge a phallic triumph, an adventure
   it would not have occurred to women
   to think worth while, made possible only

because we like huddling in gangs and knowing   5
the exact time: yes, our sex may in fairness
   hurrah the deed, although the motives
   that primed it were somewhat less than *menschlich*.

A grand gesture. But what does it period?
What does it osse? We were always adroiter   10
   with objects than lives, and more facile
   at courage than kindness: for the moment

the first flint was flaked, this landing was merely
a matter of time. But our selves, like Adam's,
   still don't fit us exactly, modern   15
   only in this—our lack of decorum.

---

menschlich: a Jewish expression describing a person or value strong enough to survive in the world
and good enough to deserve to exist in it. **period:** mark, as in a marking of chronological time.
osse: signify.

Homer's heroes were certainly no braver
Than our Trio, but more fortunate: Hector
    was excused the insult of having
    his valor covered by television.   20

Worth *going* to see? I can well believe it.
Worth *seeing?* Mneh! I once rode through a desert
    and was not charmed: give me a watered
    lively garden, remote from blatherers

about the New, the von Brauns, and their ilk, where   25
on August mornings I can count the morning
    glories, where to die has a meaning
    and no engine can shift my perspective.

Unsmudged, thank God, my Moon still queens the Heavens
as She ebbs and fulls, a Presence to glop at,   30
    Her Old Man, made of grit not protein,
    still visits my Austrian several

with His old detachment, and the old warnings
still have power to scare me: Hybris comes to
    an ugly finish. Irreverence   35
    is a greater oaf than Superstition.

Our apparatniks will continue making
the usual squalid mess called History:
    all we can pray for is that artists,
    chefs and saints may still appear to blithe it.   40

                        1969
               W. H. Auden (1907–1973)

    Auden uses the occasion of the moon landing to attack certain assumptions of his culture. He contrasts these assumptions with his own views on such broader issues as the difference between the sexes, the modern lack of manners

---

Hector: one of the Trojan heroes in the *Iliad*. **von Brauns:** refers to scientist-engineers such as Wernher von Braun (1912–1977), a German-born scientist who helped perfect rocketry. **glop:** stare. **several:** land that is privately owned or controlled or an enclosed plot of such property. **Hybris:** Greek term meaning excessive pride. **apparatniks:** operators of the technology. **blithe:** to make something happy, lighthearted.

and decorum, the contrast between art and science, the difference between ancient and modern heroes, and the ever-present eye of television.

Current readers may be startled by Auden's attitude toward the moon landing, particularly if they believe that everyone in 1969 saw it as a spectacular demonstration of mankind's ingenuity. But readers in the 1980s may, in fact, be more in tune with Auden's viewpoint than many of the first readers of the poem. If this is so, it is partly due to some changing assumptions. In the 1950s and 1960s, there was a certain amount of confidence that science could achieve great things and solve many, if not all, our problems. This particular assumption seems to wax and wane through history.

What we see in the words of a poem is just the tip of a world of ideas, assumptions, and values that give rise to the poem. We need to be aware that language undergoes changes—even radical changes—from century to century, year to year. We also need to be sensitive to the fact that our own assumptions about the world and our place in it are not necessarily the only assumptions that people have held. A poem is not about the world, it is part of the world. Wallace Stevens says it better: "The poem is the cry of its occasion."

EXERCISES

A.   SHALL I COMPARE THEE TO A SUMMER'S DAY?

Shall I compare thee to a summer's day?
Thou art more lovely and more temperate:
Rough winds do shake the darling buds of May,
And summer's lease hath all too short a date:
Sometimes too hot the eye of heaven shines,   5
And often is his gold complexion dimmed;
And every fair from fair sometimes declines,
By chance or nature's changing course untrimmed;
But thy eternal summer shall not fade,
Nor lose possession of that fair thou ow'st;   10
Nor shall death brag thou wander'st in his shade,
When in eternal lines to time thou grow'st:
So long as men can breathe, or eyes can see,
So long lives this, and this gives life to thee.

1609
William Shakespeare (1564–1616)

In the following poem, a modern poet has "translated" Shakespeare's poem into contemporary English:

SHALL I COMPARE THEE TO A SUMMER'S DAY?

Who says you're like one of the dog days?
You're nicer. And better.
Even in May, the weather can be gray,
And a summer sub-let doesn't last forever.
Sometimes the sun's too hot;   5
Sometimes it is not.
Who can stay young forever?
People break their necks or just drop dead!
But you? Never!
If there's just one condensed reader left   10
Who can figure out the abridged alphabet
    After you're dead and gone,
    In this poem you'll live on!

1957
Howard Moss (b. 1922)

1. What is the meaning of "dog days"? To what extent does this alter Shakespeare's original phrase, "summer's day"?
2. Compare Shakespeare's phrase "And summer's lease hath all too short a date" to Moss's version of the line, "And a summer sub-let doesn't last forever." What does Shakespeare's original line mean? What meaning of "lease" does Shakespeare have in mind? What kind of change has Moss made and what is the effect of the change?
3. Moss has replaced Shakespeare's more general phrase "By chance, or Nature's changing course untrimmed" with a more specific phrase, "People break their necks or just drop dead." What might be the rationale for this change?
4. What details of Shakespeare's poem does Moss leave out of his version?
5. What does Moss mean by "*condensed* reader"? What modern idea is Moss referring to by that expression?
6. How do the two poems, written in different times, also differ in tone?

B. The following six poems concern women and involve significant cultural assumptions. They are not in chronological or any other order. Determine what cultural assumptions are at work and how these assumptions are thought about by the poet/speaker of each poem. Authors and dates are given at the end of the exercise.

1. TO MY DEAR AND LOVING HUSBAND

If ever two were one, then surely we.
If ever man were lov'd by wife, then thee;
If ever wife was happy in a man,
Compare with me ye women if you can.

I prize thy love more than whole Mines of gold,   5
Or all the riches that the East doth hold.
My love is such that Rivers cannot quench,
Nor ought but love from thee, give recompence.
Thy love is such I can no way repay,
The heavens reward thee manifold I pray.   10

Then while we live, in love let's so persever,
That when we live no more, we may live ever.

2. LIVING IN SIN

She had thought the studio would keep itself;
no dust upon the furniture of love.
Half heresy, to wish the taps less vocal,
the panes relieved of grime. A plate of pears,
a piano with a Persian shawl, a cat   5
stalking the picturesque amusing mouse
had risen at his urging.
Not that at five each separate stair would writhe
under the milkman's tramp; that morning light
so coldly would delineate the scraps   10
of last night's cheese and three sepulchral bottles;
that on the kitchen shelf among the saucers
a pair of beetle-eyes would fix her own—
Envoy from some village in the moldings . . .
Meanwhile, he, with a yawn,   15
sounded a dozen notes upon the keyboard,
declared it out of tune, shrugged at the mirror,
rubbed at his beard, went out for cigarettes;
while she, jeered by the minor demons,

pulled back the sheets and made the bed and found   20
a towel to dust the table-top,
and let the coffee-pot boil over on the stove.
By evening she was back in love again,
though not so wholly but throughout the night
she woke sometimes to feel the daylight coming   25
like a relentless milkman up the stairs.

3. OH, OH, YOU WILL BE SORRY FOR THAT WORD

Oh, oh, you will be sorry for that word!
Give back my book and take my kiss instead.
Was it my enemy or my friend I heard,
"What a big book for such a little head!"
Come, I will show you now my newest hat,   5
And you may watch me purse my mouth and prink!
Oh, I shall love you still, and all of that.
I never again shall tell you what I think.
I shall be sweet and crafty, soft and sly;
You will not catch me reading any more: 10
I shall be called a wife to pattern by;
And some day when you knock and push the door,
Some sane day, not too bright and not too stormy,
I shall be gone, and you may whistle for me.

4. AN ANSWER TO ANOTHER PERSUADING A LADY TO MARRIAGE

Forbear, bold youth; all's heaven here,
    And what you do aver
To others courtship may appear,
    'Tis sacrilege to her.

She is a public deity;   5
    And were't not very odd
She should depose herself to be
    A petty household god?

First make the sun in private shine
   And bid the world adieu,   10
That so he may his beams confine
   In compliment to you:

But if of that you do despair,
   Think how you did amiss
To strive to fix her beams which are   15
   More bright and large than this.

5. THE EMERALD TREE BOA

It was Eve it chose at last,
having studied them
until it knew surely
which was first made
unresisting and would hear.   5

It watched the lord of Eden
lord it with lions and speak
with the head-high horses ringing.
It watched her walk away
the nights beside the great   10
reticulated python, lean all afternoon
against the trees through which it lay,
touch, touch, touch, the patterns
of its skin, or watching it moving
in its ways rapt   15
with her chin in her hands.

Long after, old men
writing it down could only say,
explaining how that conversation moved her
to lay their sacred history in ruins,   20
she was weak, and the serpent
of all things most subtle.

She who knew the truth was dead.
They could not write for her:

it had the perfection of color   25
leaves of the grass and first trees
foreshadowed. When it closed its eyes
against the irritants of paradise,
it hid them in membranes
of luminous gold.   30

She heard nothing spoken:
only that and the delicate
silence of its tongue
told her of wisdom
more and other than her own.   35

For that only her daughters
bear the names of death,
and all women who weave
beauty into magic still
go to the snakes for their power,   40
or call them.

6. ON MYSELF

Good Heaven, I thank thee, since it was designed
I should be framed, but of the weaker kind,
That yet, my soul, is rescued from the love
Of all those trifles, which their passions move.
Pleasures, and praise, and plenty have with me   5
But their just value. If allowed they be,
Freely, and thankfully as much I taste,
As will not reason, or religion waste.
If they're denied, I on my self can live,
And slight those aids, unequal chance does give.   10
When in the sun, my wings can be displayed,
And in retirement, I can bless the shade.

1. "To My Dear and Loving Husband" (1678): Anne Bradstreet (1612–1672)
2. "Living in Sin" (1955): Adrienne Rich (b. 1929)

3. "Oh, Oh, You Will Be Sorry for That Word" (1923): Edna St. Vincent Millay (1892–1950)
4. "An Answer to Another Persuading a Lady to Marriage" (1667): Katherine Philips (1631–1664)
5. "The Emerald Tree Boa" (1979): Suzanne Gross (b. 1933)
6. "On Myself" (1713): Anne Finch, Countess of Winchelsea (1661–1720)

C. Here are two poems concerned with Sunday, one written in the seventeenth century and the other written in the twentieth century. Herbert's original spelling and punctuation in "Sunday" have been retained. What cultural values and religious beliefs are evident in each poem? What individual values are apparent?

SUNDAY

O Day most calm, most bright,
    The fruit of this, the next worlds bud,
Th' indorsement of supreme delight,
Writ by a friend, and with his bloud;
The couch of time; cares balm and bay: 5
The week were dark, but for thy light:
    Thy torch doth show the way.

        The other dayes and thou
Make up one man; whose face thou art,
Knocking at heaven with thy brow: 10
The worky-daies are the back-part;
The burden of the week lies there,
Making the whole to stoup and bow,
        Till thy release appeare.

        Man had straight forward gone   15
To endlesse death: but thou dost pull
And turn us round to look on one,
Whom, if we were not very dull,
We could not choose but look on still;
Since there is no place so alone,   20
        The which he doth not fill.

Sundaies the pillars are,
On which heav'ns palace arched lies:
The other dayes fill up the spare
And hollow room with vanities.   25
They are the fruitfull beds and borders
In gods rich garden: that is bare,
   Which parts their ranks and orders.

  The Sundaies of mans life,
Thredded together on times string,   30
Make bracelets to adorn the wife
Of the eternall glorious King.
On Sunday heavens gate stands ope;
Blessings are plentifull and rife,
   More plentifull than hope.   35

  This day my Saviour rose,
And did inclose this light for his:
That, as each beast his manger knows,
Man might not of his fodder misse.
Christ hath took in this piece of ground,   40
And made a garden there for those
   Who want herbs for their wound.

  The rest of our Creation
Our great Redeemer did remove
With the same shake, which at his passion   45
Did th' earth and all things with it move.
As Sampson bore the doores away,
Christs hands, though nail'd, wrought our salvation,
   And did unhinge that day.

  The brightnesse of that day   50
We sullied by our foul offence:
Wherefore that robe we cast away,
Having a new at his expence,
Whose drops of bloud paid the full price,
That was requir'd to make us gay,   55
   And fit for Paradise.

Thou art a day of mirth:
And where the week-dayes trail on ground,
Thy flight is higher, as thy birth.
O let me take thee at the bound.   60
Leaping with thee from sev'n to sev'n,
Till that we both, being toss'd from earth,
            Flie hand in hand to heav'n!

                                        1633
                    George Herbert (1593–1633)

SUNDAY MORNING

1

Complacencies of the peignoir, and late
Coffee and oranges in a sunny chair,
And the green freedom of a cockatoo
Upon a rug mingle to dissipate
The holy hush of ancient sacrifice.   5
She dreams a little, and she feels the dark
Encroachment of that old catastrophe,
As a calm darkens among water-lights.
The pungent oranges and bright, green wings
Seem things in some procession of the dead,   10
Winding across wide water, without sound.
The day is like wide water, without sound,
Stilled for the passing of her dreaming feet
Over the seas, to silent Palestine,
Dominion of the blood and sepulchre.   15

2

Why should she give her bounty to the dead?
What is divinity if it can come
Only in silent shadows and in dreams?
Shall she not find in comforts of the sun,
In pungent fruit and bright, green wings, or else   20
In any balm or beauty of the earth,
Things to be cherished like the thought of heaven?
Divinity must live within herself:

Passions of rain, or moods in falling snow;
Grievings in loneliness, or unsubdued   25
Elations when the forest blooms; gusty
Emotions on wet roads on autumn nights;
All pleasures and all pains, remembering
The bough of summer and the winter branch.
These are the measures destined for her soul.   30

3

Jove in the clouds had his inhuman birth.
No mother suckled him, no sweet land gave
Large-mannered motions to his mythy mind
He moved among us, as a muttering king,
Magnificent, would move among his hinds,   35
Until our blood, commingling, virginal,
With heaven, brought such requital to desire
The very hinds discerned it, in a star.
Shall our blood fail? Or shall it come to be
The blood of paradise? And shall the earth   40
Seem all of paradise that we shall know?
The sky will be much friendlier then than now,
A part of labor and a part of pain,
And next in glory to enduring love,
Not this dividing and indifferent blue.   45

4

She says, "I am content when wakened birds,
Before they fly, test the reality
Of misty fields, by their sweet questionings;
But when the birds are gone, and their warm fields
Return no more, where, then, is paradise?"   50
There is not any haunt of prophecy,
Nor any old chimera of the grave,
Neither the golden underground, nor isle
Melodious, where spirits gat them home,
Nor visionary south, nor cloudy palm   55
Remote on heaven's hill, that has endured
As April's green endures; or will endure
Like her remembrance of awakened birds,
Or her desire for June and evening, tipped
By the consummation of the swallow's wings.   60

5

She says, "But in contentment I still feel
The need of some imperishable bliss."
Death is the mother of beauty; hence from her,
Alone, shall come fulfilment to our dreams
And our desires. Although she strews the leaves   65
Of sure obliteration on our paths,
The path sick sorrow took, the many paths
Where triumph rang its brassy phrase, or love
Whispered a little out of tenderness,
She makes the willow shiver in the sun   70
For maidens who were wont to sit and gaze
Upon the grass, relinquished to their feet.
She causes boys to pile new plums and pears
On disregarded plate. The maidens taste
And stray impassioned in the littering leaves.   75

6

Is there no change of death in paradise?
Does ripe fruit never fall? Or do the boughs
Hang always heavy in that perfect sky,
Unchanging, yet so like our perishing earth,
With rivers like our own that seek for seas   80
They never find, the same receding shores
That never touch with inarticulate pang?
Why set the pear upon those river-banks
Or spice the shores with odors of the plum?
Alas, that they should wear our colors there,   85
The silken weavings of our afternoons,
And pick the strings of our insipid lutes!
Death is the mother of beauty, mystical,
Within whose burning bosom we devise
Our earthly mothers waiting, sleeplessly.   90

7

Supple and turbulent, a ring of men
Shall chant in orgy on a summer morn
Their boisterous devotion to the sun,
Not as a god, but as a god might be,
Naked among them, like a savage source.   95

Their chant shall be a chant of paradise,
Out of their blood, returning to the sky;
And in their chant shall enter, voice by voice,
The windy lake wherein their lord delights,
The trees, like serafin, and echoing hills,   100
That choir among themselves long afterward.
They shall know well the heavenly fellowship
Of men that perish and of summer morn.
And whence they came and whither they shall go
The dew upon their feet shall manifest.   105

8

She hears, upon that water without sound,
A voice that cries, "The tomb in Palestine
Is not the porch of spirits lingering.
It is the grave of Jesus, where he lay."
We live in an old chaos of the sun,   110
Or old dependency of day and night,
Or island solitude, unsponsored, free,
Of that wide water, inescapable.
Deer walk upon our mountains, and the quail
Whistle about us their spontaneous cries;   115
Sweet berries ripen in the wilderness;
And, in the isolation of the sky,
At evening, casual flocks of pigeons make
Ambiguous undulations as they sink,
Downward to darkness, on extended wings.   120

1923
Wallace Stevens (1879–1955)

D. We saw how Archibald MacLeish in "Voyage to the Moon," and W. H.
Auden in "Moon Landing" expressed assumptions about the use of technology. Here are three additional poems that concern, in one way or another, the interrelationships among nature, humans, and technology. What
assumptions are at issue in each poem? What is being praised or criticized
or considered? What historical events or attitudes prompt each poem?

THE GOLF LINKS

The golf links lie so near the mill
That almost every day

The laboring children can look out
And see the men at play.

1917
Sarah N. Cleghorn (1876–1959)

THE MOUTH OF THE HUDSON

(For Esther Brooks)

A single man stands like a bird-watcher,
and scuffles the pepper and salt snow
from a discarded, gray
Westinghouse Electric cable drum.
He cannot discover America by counting   5
the chains of condemned freight-trains
from thirty states. They jolt and jar
and junk in the siding below him.
He has trouble with his balance.
His eyes drop,   10
and he drifts with the wild ice
ticking seaward down the Hudson,
like the blank sides of a jig-saw puzzle.

The ice ticks seaward like a clock.
A Negro toasts   15
wheat-seeds over the coke-fumes
of a punctured barrel.
Chemical air
sweeps in from New Jersey,
and smells of coffee.   20

Across the river,
ledges of suburban factories tan
in the sulphur-yellow sun
of the unforgivable landscape.

1964
Robert Lowell (1917–1978)

ALL WATCHED OVER BY MACHINES OF LOVING GRACE

I like to think (and
the sooner the better!)
of a cybernetic meadow
where mammals and computers
live together in mutually   5
programming harmony
like pure water
touching clear sky.

I like to think
  (right now, please!)   10
of a cybernetic forest
filled with pines and electronics
where deer stroll peacefully
past computers
as if they were flowers   15
with spinning blossoms.

I like to think
  (it has to be!)
of a cybernetic ecology
where we are free of our labors   20
and joined back to nature,
returned to our mammal
brothers and sisters,
and all watched over
by machines of loving grace.   25

1968

Richard Brautigan (b. 1935)

E. In any age, there are ideas simmering in the culture that surface in its
poetry. In 1850, Tennyson published a long poem, *In Memoriam A. H.
H.* In that elegy, Tennyson links questions raised by the untimely death of
his friend, Arthur Henry Hallam, with some broader questions:

from IN MEMORIAM A.H.H.

Are God and Nature then at strife
  That Nature lends such evil dreams?

In Memoriam A.H.H.

So careful of the type she seems,
So careless of the single life.

(from stanza 55)

56

'So careful of the type?' but no.
    From scarped cliff and quarried stone
    She cries, 'A thousand types are gone:
I care for nothing, all shall go.

'Thou makest thine appeal to me: 5
    I bring to life, I bring to death:
    The spirit does but mean the breath:
I know no more.' And he, shall he,

Man, her last work, who seemed so fair,
    Such splendid purpose in his eyes,   10
    Who rolled the psalm to wintry skies,
Who built him fanes of fruitless prayer,

Who trusted God was love indeed
    And love Creation's final law—
    Though Nature, red in tooth and claw   15
With ravine, shrieked against his creed—

Who loved, who suffered countless ills,
    Who battled for the True, the Just,
    Be blown about the desert dust,
Or sealed within the iron hills?   20

No more? A monster then, a dream,
    A discord. Dragons of the prime,
    That tear each other in their slime,
Were mellow music matched with him.

O life as futile, then, as frail!   25
    O for thy voice to soothe and bless!
    What hope of answer, or redress?
Behind the veil, behind the veil.

1850

Alfred, Lord Tennyson (1809–1892)

Tennyson asks the question, "Are God and Nature then at strife / That Nature lends such evil dreams?" This question takes on added significance because of a specific idea—speculation on evolution and natural selection—that intrigued and perplexed many individuals in the nineteenth century.

Charles Darwin's *Origin of Species* (1859) was the most detailed and scientific statement about evolution up to that time, but some of the ideas that Darwin expressed in his book were being discussed long before he finally published his theory. They were being expressed and debated, in fact, before Darwin took his epoch-making voyage (1831–1835) on the ship *Beagle*, a journey that provided him with the evidence for his theory of natural selection.

Charles Lyell's *Principles of Geology*, published in 1834, contained this thought-provoking passage on its title page:

> The inhabitants of the globe, like all the other parts of it, are subject to change. It is not only the individual that perishes, but the whole species.

And, in 1844, Robert Chambers in *Vestiges of Creation* had written:

> It is clear, moreover, from the whole scope of natural laws, that the individual, as far as the present sphere of being is concerned, is to the author of Nature a consideration of inferior moment. Everywhere we see the arrangements of the species perfect: the individual is left, as it were, to take his chance amidst the melee of the various laws affecting him. If he be found inferiorly endowed, or ill befalls him, there was at least not partiality against him. The system has the fairness of a lottery, in which every one has the like chance of drawing the prize.

At the end of *Origin of Species*, Darwin put the case somewhat more optimistically:

> It is interesting to contemplate a tangled bank, clothed with many plants of many kinds, with birds singing on the bushes, with various insects flitting about, and with worms crawling through the damp earth, and to reflect that these elaborately constructed forms, so different from each other, and dependent upon each other in so complex a manner, have all been produced by laws acting around us. These laws, taken in the largest sense, being growth with reproduction; inheritance which is almost implied by reproduction; variability from the indirect and direct action of the conditions of life, and from use and disuse: a ratio of increase so high as to lead to a struggle for life, and as a consequence to natural selection, entailing divergence

of character and the extinction of less-improved forms. Thus, from the war of nature, from famine and death, the most exalted object which we are capable of conceiving, namely, the production of the higher animals, directly follows. There is grandeur in this view of life, with its several powers, having been originally breathed by the Creator into a few forms or into one; and that, whilst this planet has gone cycling on according to the fixed law of gravity, from so simple a beginning endless forms most beautiful and most wonderful have been, and are being evolved.

The following poems are just a sampling of the effects that speculation on evolution and natural selection had on poets and poetry:

WITH WHOM IS NO VARIABLENESS, NEITHER SHADOW OF TURNING

It fortifies my soul to know
That, though I perish, Truth is so:
That, howso'er I stray and range,
Whate'er I do, Thou dost not change.
I steadier step when I recall   5
That, if I slip, Thou dost not fall.

1869
Arthur Hugh Clough (1819–1861)

from THROUGH A GLASS DARKLY

Ah yet, when all is thought and said,
The heart still overrules the head;
Still what we hope we must believe,
And what is given us receive;—

Must still believe, for still we hope   5
That, in a world of larger scope,

---

through a glass darkly: Clough's title is taken from I Corinthians 13: 11–12: "When I was a child, I spake as a child, I understood as a child: but when I became a man, I put away childish things. For now we see through a glass darkly; but then face to face: now I know in part; but then shall I know even as I am known."

What here is faithfully begun
Will be completed, not undone.

1869
Arthur Hugh Clough (1819–1861)

James Thomson's "The City of Dreadful Night" (at 1122 lines, much too long to be cited in full) contains these stanzas:

from THE CITY OF DREADFUL NIGHT

We bow down to the universal laws,
Which never had for man a special clause
  Of cruelty or kindness, love or hate;
If toads and vultures are obscene to sight,
If tigers burn with beauty and with might   5
  Is it by favor or by wrath of fate?
All substance lives and struggles evermore
Through countless shapes continually at war,
  By countless interactions interknit;
If one is born a certain day on earth,   10
All times and forces tended to that birth,
  Not all the world could change or hinder it.
I find no hint throughout the Universe
Of good or ill, of blessing or of curse:
  I find alone Necessity Supreme. . . .   15

(Canto 14, lines 746–760)
1874
James Thomson (1834–1882)

The impact of these ideas on evolution and natural selection is not limited to English poetry alone:

from SONG OF MYSELF

Before I was born out of my mother generations guided me,
My embryo has never been torpid, nothing could overlay it.

---

if tigers . . . with might: see William Blake's "The Tyger."

For it the nebula cohered to an orb,
The long slow strata piled to rest it on,
Vast vegetables gave it sustenance,
Monstrous sauroids transported it in their mouths and deposited
   it with care.

All forces have been steadily employ'd to complete and delight
   me,
Now on this spot I stand with my robust soul.

(Section 44, lines 1163–68)

1855

Walt Whitman (1819–1892)

    Poems in the twentieth century also reflect something of this idea, as in Philip Appleman's "October Spring":

This new year lights
no dogwood, no magnolia to find us
limping through our shrunken moments or
calling courage from our stubborn past,
the long pilgrimage of algae
sponges, reptiles, flowers,
men. . . .

(lines 8–14; italics added)

    Appleman also wrote a poem on the journey that led Darwin to his *Origin of Species:*

ON THE *BEAGLE*

There are men who hold the world
in their fingertips and
are part of what they hold.

The *Beagle* set sail
to easy summer—five years on sea   5
and land the watchful man
from Cambridge put
his fingers on a universe
of cuttlefish, sea-slugs, condors,

the ancient monsters' bones,   10
megatherium, mastodon: all
fixed forever in immutable forms, creatures
of a benign
Intelligence.
It was written.   15

And yet . . .

The young man put his fingers on
the pulse of rivers, coral reefs,
pampas and mountains,
the flotsam of earthquakes—and   20
on futures of learning, from
pigeons' plumage, the beaks of finches, bones
of rabbits and ducks—decades
of learning,
dissecting ten thousand   25
barnacles—pondering:
"If
we choose to let
conjecture run wild, then animals—
our fellow brethren in pain,   30
disease, death, suffering, and famine—
they may partake from our origin
in one common ancestor:
we may be all
netted together."   35

The *Beagle* labored on: in the winter
of Cape Horn,
twenty-three days of beating
against the icy bluster
came to broken boats   40
and spoiled collections.
The good ship rode to shelter—
and there on a rocky point
of Tierra del Fuego, naked

"**if we choose** . . .": This quotation and those later in the poem are from Darwin's *Journal of Researches into the Geology & Natural History of the Various Countries Visited during the Voyage of H.M.S. Beagle Round the World* (1839).

in snow, a mother   45
suckled her child
("whilst the sleet fell and thawed
on her naked bosom, and on the skin
of her naked baby")—there, in a little band,
stood   50
"man in his primitive wildness,"
ringed by the dark beech forest:
"As they threw their arms wildly
around their heads,
their long hair streaming,   55
they seemed the troubled spirits
of another world."
There
in the Bay of Good Success,
Charles Darwin, on the foredeck of the *Beagle*,   60
our future in his freezing fingertips,
stared into the faces
of our past.

1976
Philip Appleman (b. 1926)

1. Most of these passages are extracts from larger works, so any absolute generalization about them would need to be made in that context; however,
   what ideas as expressed by Lyell, Chambers, and Darwin find expression
   in Tennyson's poem? in Clough's? in Whitman's? in Appleman's?
2. How does Tennyson's passage in *In Memoriam* differ in attitude and tone
   from Whitman's? What information about the cultural background and
   autobiographical experiences of each author needs to be considered in
   comparing and contrasting their attitudes?
3. What does Appleman do in "October Spring" with the speculation on
   evolution and natural selection that is different from the other examples?
   What would account for this change?
4. What viewpoint does he bring to "On the *Beagle*"? How do Darwin's comments, incorporated in the poem, provide a perspective?

WRITING SUGGESTIONS————————————————————

1. Choose one of the poems in Exercise B and, in an essay, explain what
   cultural assumptions are at work and how these assumptions are handled

---

"whilst the sleet fell . . ."; "man in his primitive wildness . . ."; "as they threw . . .": These
quotations are from Darwin's *Journal*.

by the poet. You may, for this essay, wish to compare or contrast two of the poems, emphasizing a single comparison or contrast that links the two poems.

2. In stanza 4 of "Sunday Morning" (Exercise C) the speaker asks, "Where, then, is paradise?" In an essay explain the poem's answer to that question and discuss how this answer is a "modern" one, reflecting certain cultural assumptions.

PART

IV

HOW?

CHAPTER EIGHT

RHYME, OTHER REPEATING SOUNDS, AND METER

Poems are words that reflect the human beings who write them, the place and time in which they were written, and the cultural assumptions their writers accept or reject. But the first thing that may be apparent about a poem is that it is an *arrangement* of words that has a visible pattern or shape. Rhyme makes these patterns, rhythm makes them, the lines on the page make them, and more subtly, the ordering of argument and associations within poems makes these patterns. How do these patterns create enjoyment and meaning?

SOUND LIKENESSES

Sounds affect us: The ring of an alarm clock jars sleepers into action; the steady hum of an air-conditioner lulls insomniacs to sleep. The screech of chalk on blackboard sends shivers up some people's backs. The sound of an automobile engine tells the mechanic what's wrong with it. The explosive rhythms of a rock song and the harmonies of a Mozart symphony have real, but quite different effects on their audiences. Exactly why such sound repetitions are effective and some are enjoyable is a mystery. It may be a physical cause connected with the rhythms of heartbeat, breathing, and other bodily processes. It may be a psychological pleasure that has to do with the way the brain works. It could be a cultural cause connected with our distant tribal past. Whatever the causes, we are attuned to sound and find it meaningful as well as affecting:

SOME GOOD THINGS TO BE SAID FOR THE IRON AGE

A ringing tire iron
  dropped on the pavement

Whang of a saw
brusht on limbs
   the taste   5
  of rust

      1970
   Gary Snyder (b. 1930)

Even before they learn to talk, children love to hear the sounds of words, and they repeat nonsense syllables and meaningless rhymes. They continue to enjoy repeating sound patterns after they have learned the language. Consider the tongue-twister that begins:

Peter Piper picked a peck of pickled peppers.

This line has a sound pattern called ALLITERATION—the repetition of the beginning sounds of words and syllables—in this case *p*. Alliteration is more than a child's pleasure and goes back in English poetry to its beginnings. The following poem gives an example of the oldest kind of English poetry as well as a modern version of alliterative verse:

JUNK

Huru Welandes
   worc ne geswiceð
monna ænigum
   ðara ðe Mimming can
heardne gehealdan.

      —"Waldere" (c. 1000 A.D.)

An axe angles
   from my neighbor's ashcan;

Huru . . . gehealdan: The epigraph, from the Old English poem "Waldere," translates, "Truly Weland's work—the sword Mimming—will not fail any man who knows how to hardily wield it."

Junk

It is hell's handiwork,
        the wood not hickory,
The flow of the grain
        not faithfully followed.
The shivered shaft
        rises from a shellheap
Of plastic playthings,
        paper plates,   5
And the sheer shards
        of shattered tumblers
That were not annealed
        for the time needful.
At the same curbside,
        a cast-off cabinet
Of wavily-warped
        unseasoned wood
Waits to be trundled
        in the trash-man's truck.   10
Haul them off! Hide them!
        The heart winces
For junk and gimcrack,
        for jerrybuilt things
And the men who make them
        for a little money,
Bartering pride
        like the bought boxer
Who pulls his punches,
        or the paid-off jockey   15
Who in the home stretch
        holds in his horse.
Yet the things themselves
        in thoughtless honor
Have kept composure,
        like captives who would not
Talk under torture.
        Tossed from a tailgate
Where the dump displays
        its random dolmens,   20
Its black barrows
        and blazing valleys,

---

dolmens: prehistoric stone structures.

They shall waste in the weather
                                  toward what they were.
The sun shall glory
                    in the glitter of glass-chips,
Foreseeing the salvage
                      of the prisoned sand,
And the blistering paint
                        peel off in patches,   25
That the good grain
                  be discovered again.
Then burnt, bulldozed,
                      they shall all be buried
To the depth of diamonds,
                      in the making dark
Where halt Hephaestus
                    keeps his hammer
And Wayland's work
                is worn away.   30

1961
Richard Wilbur (b. 1921)

Wilbur imitates the old English alliteration of three or four words in each line and the strong break between halves of a line. Such a break or pause within a line is called CAESURA.

Other pleasing devices of sound, in addition to alliteration, are illustrated by the following poem:

HISTORY OF EDUCATION

The decent docent doesn't doze:
He teaches standing on his toes.
His student dassn't doze—and does,
And that's what teaching is and was.

1945
David McCord (b. 1897)

How do the repeating sound patterns in the three poems by Snyder, Wilbur, and McCord create not only pleasure but meaning? It is always dangerous to

---

halt Hephaestus: Greek god of metal-working, who was lame.

generalize about what creates pleasure, but in Snyder's poem the repeated *i* and *r* sounds in "ringing tire iron" sound like what's being described. In Wilbur's poem, the alliteration falls on important words and emphasizes them:

> a cast-off cabinet
> Of wavily-warped
> unseasoned wood.

In McCord's poem the humor is reinforced by many devices of repeating sounds: the tongue-twisting difficulties of the first line and the very heavy alliteration are only two of them. In addition, the poem has RHYME—words or syllables that sound alike except for their beginning sounds: *doze/toes, does/was*. When the vowel sounds of successive words or syllables are the same, the device is called ASSONANCE: dEcEnt / tEAchEs. When everything *but* the vowel sound is the same, the device is called CONSONANCE: pick/peck, doze/does.

Sound Likenesses and Their Names		
beginnings alike	decent docent doesn't doze	ALLITERATION
endings alike	goes/doze/froze/toes	RHYME
vowels alike	go load a slow boat	ASSONANCE
consonants alike	dirt/dart tick/tock	CONSONANCE

METER

McCord's poem also has a repeating pattern of STRESSES—syllables that get more time and breath force spent on them by the speaking voice:

> The DEcent DOcent DOESn't DOZE.

If the stressed syllables are marked / and the unstressed syllables are marked ⌣, the following repeating pattern of stresses becomes apparent:

> ⌣ / ⌣ / ⌣ / ⌣ /
> The decent docent doesn't doze.

Such a regularly occurring pattern of stressed and unstressed syllables is called METER. Each pattern has a name based on the unit of stressed and unstressed syllables which recurs most often in the line. These patterns are the raw materials out of which poets create—as this chapter will illustrate—the meaning and pleasure inherent in sound. But first, some names for these patterns and some examples.

In "History of Education" the repeating unit or FOOT is ⌣ /, a two-syllable pattern with the unstressed syllable coming first. This particular pattern is one of IAMBIC feet or IAMBS, the most common pattern in English poetry. The Peter Piper tongue-twister has another pattern:

Péter Píper pícked a péck of píckled péppers.

Here the repeating unit, / ⌣, has the stressed syllable first; this pattern is called a TROCHAIC foot or TROCHEE.

Two kinds of poetic feet can be mixed in a line, but one will predominate, as in this line from Keats's "To Autumn":

Séason | of místs | and mél|low frúit|fulnéss.

The vertical markings divide the line into feet. Although the line starts with a trochee in the word *season*, the most common unit here (and in the rest of Keats's poem), is the iamb.

A poetic foot must have at least two syllables, since it is the regular *alternation* of stressed and unstressed syllables that makes up meter.

ON THE ANTIQUITY OF MICROBES

Adam
Had 'em.
Anonymous

Occasionally within a poetic line, a two-syllable foot may have no stresses (⌣ ⌣) or it may have two stresses(//), as in the second line of Keats's "To Autumn":

Close bós|om-friénd | of the | matúr|ing sún.

The first foot, //, is a SPONDAIC foot or SPONDEE, and the third one, ⌣⌣, is a PYRRHIC foot or PYRRHIC. A line may not have a number of pyrrhics or spondees in succession, because *some* syllables, but not all, must be stressed.

Two-Syllable Feet		
stress pattern	*example*	*name*
⌣ /	submít, awáit	IAMB or IAMBIC FOOT
/ ⌣	hélpful, fórward	TROCHEE or TROCHAIC FOOT
⌣⌣ (occurs only in combination with other feet)	salt of the earth	PYRRHIC or PYRRHIC FOOT
//	Lóok óut!	SPONDEE or SPONDAIC FOOT

Some very well-known poems are written in *three-syllable* feet. Here is the beginning of one:

from A VISIT FROM ST. NICHOLAS

⏑ ⏑ ´ | ⏑ ⏑ ´ | ⏑ ⏑ ´ | ⏑ ⏑ ´
'Twas the night | before Christ|mas, and all | through the house,

⏑ ⏑ ´ ⏑ ⏑ ´ ⏑ ⏑ ´ ⏑ ⏑ ´
Not a crea|ture was stir|ring, not e|ven a mouse.

1823
Clement Moore (1779–1863)

This is ANAPESTIC rhythm; an ANAPEST, ⏑ ⏑ ´, is a three-syllable foot with the stress coming on the last syllable. Its reverse, with the stress coming on the first syllable, ´ ⏑ ⏑, is called a DACTYLIC foot or DACTYL. Tennyson's "Charge of the Light Brigade" (p. 156) is mostly in DACTYLIC rhythm, which imitates the thundering cavalry charge its lines describe. Here is the first stanza:

from THE CHARGE OF THE LIGHT BRIGADE

´ ⏑ ⏑ ´ ⏑ ⏑
Half a league, half a league,

´ ⏑ ⏑ ´ ⏑
Half a league onward,

´ ⏑ ⏑ ´ ⏑ ⏑ ´
All in the valley of Death

´ ⏑ ⏑ ´ ⏑
Rode the six hundred.

´ ⏑ ⏑ ´ ⏑ ⏑
"Forward the Light Brigade!   5

´ ⏑ ⏑ ´ ⏑ ⏑
Charge for the guns!" he said.

´⏑ ⏑ ´ ⏑ ⏑ ´
Into the valley of Death

´ ⏑ ⏑ ´ ⏑
Rode the six hundred.

1854
Alfred, Lord Tennyson (1809–1892)

Two other three-syllable feet occasionally occur, the AMPHIBRACH, ⏑ ´ ⏑ , and the AMPHIMACER, ´ ⏑ ´, but neither is ever the most common rhythm of a whole poem.

Three-Syllable Feet

stress pattern	example	name
⌣ ⌣ /	cavalier	ANAPEST or ANAPESTIC FOOT
/ ⌣ ⌣	agency, aggravate	DACTYL or DACTYLIC FOOT
⌣ / ⌣	ballooning, museum	AMPHIBRACH or AMPHIBRACHIC FOOT
/ ⌣ /	Hurry home! difficult	AMPHIMACER or AMPHIMACRIC FOOT

Meter refers not only to the kind of rhythm or poetic foot in a line, but also to the number of such feet per line. The Greek prefixes mono- (1), di- (2), tri- (3), tetra- (4), penta- (5), hexa- (6), hepta- (7), and octa- (8) indicate the number of feet, although few English poems have anything other than three-, four-, or five-foot lines. For example, to identify the meter of Shakespeare's "That Time of Year Thou Mayst in Me Behold," we need to say not only that it is iambic, but IAMBIC PENTAMETER, since there are five iambic feet in each line:

That time | of year | thou mayst | in me | behold

When yel|low leaves, | or none, | or few, | do hang

Upon | those boughs | which shake | against | the cold.

Just as iambic rhythm is the most common in English poetry, so iambic pentameter is the most common combination of rhythm and line length. But there are many poems in TETRAMETER, or four-foot lines, such as "History of Education":

The de|cent do|cent does|n't doze:

He teach|es stan|ding on | his toes.

His stu|dent dass|n't doze|—and does,

And that's | what tea|ching is | and was.

These lines are in regular IAMBIC TETRAMETER.

All the meters discussed so far are ACCENTUAL—that is, recurring accents or stresses determine the pattern of each line. The meter of some poems does not depend on the number of accents, but merely on the number of syllables;

this kind of meter is called SYLLABIC. The following poem is in syllabic meter; the pattern of each stanza is 5-8-8-4 syllables:

ROSE-CHEEKED LAURA

Rose-cheeked Laura, come,
Sing thou smoothly with thy beauty's
Silent music, either other
    Sweetly gracing.

Lovely forms do flow   5
From concent divinely framed;
Heav'n is music, and thy beauty's
    Birth is heav'nly.

These dull notes we sing
Discords need for helps to grace them;   10
Only beauty purely loving
    Knows no discord,

But still moves delight,
Like clear springs renewed by flowing,
Ever perfect, ever in them-   15
    Selves eternal.

                1602
    Thomas Campion (1567–1620)

Dylan Thomas's "Fern Hill" (p. 67) has a rigid syllabic pattern in each of its stanzas of 14-14-9-6-9-14-14-6 (or 7)-9. Syllabic meter is perhaps best known in the HAIKU, which comes into English from Japanese. What, from the following examples, do you find to be the syllabic pattern of haiku?

TWO HAIKU

My two plum trees are
So gracious . . . See, they flower
One now, one later.
            Buson (1716–1783)

---

concent: harmony.

Under cherry-trees
Soup, the salad, fish and all . . .
Seasoned with petals.
                Basho (1644–1694)

both translated by Peter Beilenson

What other generalizations about the form can be made from these examples?
Here is a modern example which conveys a very different world:

HAIKU

1

Eastern guard tower
glints in sunset; convicts rest
like lizards on rocks.

2

The piano man
is sting at 3 am
his songs drop like plum.

3

Morning sun slants cell.
Drunks stagger like cripple flies
On Jailhouse floor.

4

To write a blues song
is to regiment riots
and pluck gems from graves.

5

A bare pecan tree
slips a pencil shadow down
a moonlit snow slope.

6

The falling snow flakes
Can not blunt the hard aches nor
Match the steel stillness.

7

Under moon shadows
A tall boy flashes knife and
Slices star bright ice.

8

In the August grass
Struck by the last rays of sun
The cracked teacup screams.

9

Making jazz swing in
Seventeen syllables AIN'T
No square poet's job.

1968
Etheridge Knight (b. 1933)

Some poems are written in FREE VERSE, which does not use regular stress alternations or a recurring number of syllables per line but substitutes other kinds of rhythms, usually those of repeated word, phrase, or sentence patterns, or some other auditory or visual cadences. In some poets' practice, this can mean writing long lines arranged somewhat like the verses of the King James Version of the Old Testament. That translation is an example of verse that occasionally falls into almost regular metrical patterns, especially in the Psalms— for example, the anapests of the beginning of Psalm 19:

The heav|ens declare | the glo|ry of God;

And the fir|mament show|eth his han|diwork.

But much more frequently the strong rhythms and cadences of Old Testament verse do not use regular metrical patterns, but rely on other kinds of repetition, such as repetition of parallel phrases (phrases in succession that have the same grammatical pattern, such as *in the house, on the road, by a stream*) or repetition of first words of phrases. Job's lament for his misfortunes will illustrate:

Let the day perish wherein I was born,
And the night in which it was said,
There is a man child conceived.
Let that day be darkness;
Let not God regard it from above,
Neither let the light shine upon it.

—Job 3: 3–4

One of the best-known poets to write in lines resembling the verses of the English version of the Old Testament was Walt Whitman:

from SONG OF MYSELF

We sail the arctic sea. . . .
Through the clear atmosphere I stretch around on the wonderful beauty,
The enormous masses of ice pass me and I pass them, the scenery is plain in
all directions,
The white-topt mountains show in the distance, I fling out my fancies toward
them,
We are approaching some great battle-field in which we are soon to be
engaged.

> (Section 33, lines 806–810)
> 1855/1891–92
> *Walt Whitman (1819–1892)*

Compare also these lines by an eighteenth-century poet, Christopher Smart, in the poem "Jubilate Agno" ("Rejoice in the Lamb"). Smart (who was going mad) included many personal and topical references, some of which may seem comic now:

from JUBILATE AGNO

For the word of God is a sword on my side—no matter what other
weapon a stick or a straw.
For I have adventured myself in the name of the Lord, and he hath
mark'd me for his own.
For I bless God for the Postmaster general & all conveyancers of letters
under his care especially Allen & Shelvock.
For my grounds in New Canaan shall infinitely compensate for the flats
& mains of Staindrop Moor.
For the praise of God can give to a mute fish the notes of a nightingale.   5
For I have seen the White Raven & Thomas Hall of Willingham & am
myself a greater curiosity than both.

composed 1759–1763   1939
> *Christopher Smart (1722–1771)*

Although Robert Frost once suggested that free verse was rather like play-ing tennis with the net down, its use does convey a sense of the mind or speaking voice discovering ideas as it proceeds. Arranged on the page, free verse often takes the form of very irregular line lengths such as we have seen in Ammons' "Corsons Inlet" and Levertov's "Merritt Parkway." But irregular lines are not always an indication of free verse. Earle Birney's "Irapuato" will be seen to scan quite regularly if the lines are considered continuous:

$$\smile \quad / \quad \smile \quad / \smile$$
For rea|sons a|ny--

$$--/ \quad \smile \quad /$$
--brig|adier|--

$$--\quad \smile \quad /$$
- could tell

$$/ \quad \smile \quad \smile \quad / \quad \smile \quad /$$
this is | a fav|orite nook | for--

$$--/ \quad \smile /$$
- mass|acre.

Many modern poems will not be found so regular, however. Here are the first lines of Robert Bly's "Waking from Sleep":

$$\smile \smile \smile \quad / \quad \smile \quad \smile \quad / \quad \smile \smile \quad / \quad \smile \quad / \quad /\smile$$
It is the morning. The country has slept the whole winter.

$$/ \quad \smile \quad / \quad \smile \quad / \quad \smile \smile \quad / \quad / \quad \smile \quad / \quad \smile \quad /$$
Window seats were covered with fur skins, the yard was full

$$\smile \quad / \quad / \quad \smile \quad / \quad \smile \quad / \smile\smile / \quad / \smile \quad /$$
Of stiff dogs, and hands that clumsily held heavy books.

Robert Frost has also said that a modern poet has only two choices for his line rhythms: loose iambic and strict iambic. Frost exaggerated, as the variety of metrics in this chapter should show, but the examples from Whitman and Bly may demonstrate the substantial truth of his statement.

METER AT WORK

It takes no complicated metrical analysis to get pleasure out of the rhythm of a poem like the following; children especially, as Longfellow anticipated, like its rolling gait:

from PAUL REVERE'S RIDE

Listen, my children, and you shall hear
Of the midnight ride of Paul Revere,

On the eighteenth of April, in Seventy-five;
Hardly a man is now alive
Who remembers that famous day and year.   5

1863
Henry Wadsworth Longfellow (1807–1882)

In poems like this one and Tennyson's "Charge of the Light Brigade," the triple rhythms do more than please; they actually serve the poem's meaning because they imitate the canter or gallop of horses.

But horses' hooves are not the only sounds that triple rhythm can imitate. Since poetry and music have common origins, it is not surprising to see the metrics of poems imitate the effects of music and dancing, as in the following poem:

THE DANCE

In Breughel's great picture, The Kermess,
the dancers go round, they go round and
around, the squeal and the blare and the
tweedle of bagpipes, a bugle and fiddles
tipping their bellies (round as the thick-   5
sided glasses whose wash they impound)
their hips and their bellies off balance
to turn them. Kicking and rolling about
the Fair Grounds, swinging their butts, those
shanks must be sound to bear up under such   10
rollicking measures, prance as they dance
in Breughel's great picture, The Kermess.

1944
William Carlos Williams (1883–1963)

How does the rhythm of this poem reproduce the sound and the movement of the group dancing? Aside from Williams' very accurate descriptions and comparisons—of the dancers' bellies and their beer glasses, for example—the rhythm is the *oom-pa-pa* of the dance itself:

Kermess: a feast and dance celebrating a yearly outdoor fair in Holland and Belgium. **Breughel:** Pieter Breughel (c. 1525–1569), Flemish painter, who also painted the picture referred to in Auden's "Musée des Beaux Arts" (Chapter 4).

The Dance

⏑ / ⏑ ⏑ / ⏑ ⏑ ⏑ / ⏑
the dancers go round, they go round and

⏑ / ⏑ / ⏑ ⏑ / ⏑ ⏑
around, the squeal and the blare and the

/ ⏑ ⏑ / ⏑ ⏑ / ⏑ ⏑ / ⏑
tweedle of bagpipes, a bugle and fiddles

The stresses seem obvious enough, but trying to divide this line by line into feet creates problems; just as the sense of the passage is ENJAMBED, or RUN-ON—having grammatical units that do not stop at the end of the line—so also are the metrics:

⏑ / ⏑ ⏑ / ⏑ ⏑ / ⏑
the dan|cers go round, | they go round | and

⏑ / ⏑ / ⏑ ⏑ / ⏑ ⏑
around,| the squeal | and the blare | and the

/ ⏑ ⏑ / ⏑ ⏑ / ⏑ ⏑ / ⏑
twee|dle of bag|pipes, a bug|le and fid|dles

To evoke more of the sound of the dance music, Williams uses the device of ONOMATOPOEIA—the use of words whose sound imitates what they describe, such as *Bang!* and *Pop!* Here three onomatopoeic words describe the sound of the bagpipes:

the *squeal* and the *blare* and the
tweedle of bagpipes.

A subtler metrical music can be heard in Roethke's "My Papa's Waltz." Roethke also uses triple meter, but not purely anapestic:

⏑ / ⏑ ⏑ ⏑ /
The whiskey | on your breath

⏑ / ⏑ ⏑ ⏑ / ⏑
Could make a | small boy diz|zy;

⏑ / ⏑ ⏑ ⏑ /
But I hung | on like death:

⏑ / ⏑ ⏑ ⏑ / ⏑
Such waltzing | was not ea|sy.

The basic pattern is two triple feet per line, but Roethke combines anapests with amphibrachs to make his waltz rhythm. It is not a regular waltz rhythm—that would go *dum*-da-da *dum*-da-da—but an irregular one with a kind of bump to it at the end of some lines: "your *breath* . . . like *death*." The dance is awkward and irregular, appropriate to the poem's portrayal of the father as a slightly drunk, clumsy, yet gentle man. All such metrics that imitate other sounds merely help to work on the suggestion the lines themselves make.

Using the basic meter of a poem to imitate another sound commits the poet to one metric pattern. This can become monotonous, especially in a long poem. A much more subtle technique, capable of many different effects, is to establish a basic pattern of iambic rhythm and then make exceptions to it where a special sound effect is desired. Iambic rhythm, being the rhythm of common speech, will not strike the ear with any special effect; it will not recall the sound of horses' hooves or the sounds of music, for example. It is the ordinary rhythm we hear in conversation every day:

> ˘ / ˘ / ˘ / ˘ / ˘ /
> "I didn't call the Smiths today; did you?"

If iambics are made *very* regular they may indeed catch our notice as too sing-song. The effect is used by Shakespeare, stressing the clock's tick-tock regularity:

> ˘ / ˘ / ˘ / ˘ / ˘ /
> When I do count the clock that tells the time

Poets vary the metrics of their lines unless they are trying to achieve an effect such as Shakespeare's here. Usually a trochee or a spondee is substituted for an iambic foot. Keats uses a trochee for the first foot in "To Autumn":

> / ˘ | ˘ / | ˘ / | ˘ / | ˘ /
> Season | of mists | and mel|low fruit|fulness

The effect is to *emphasize* the word or words where the substitution occurs. The emphasis with a spondee substitution is greater, since two strong stresses come together. Consider the second line of Milton's sonnet on his blindness (p. 39):

> When I consider how my light is spent

> ˘ / | ˘ / | ˘ / | / / | ˘ /
> Ere half | my days, | in this | dark world | and wide

/ / /
This dark world is a poignant underlining of the poet's blindness; for him the whole world has changed. A spondee has the effect of slowing down a line of verse, a pyrrhic of speeding it up. With substitutions, the poet is able to imitate the sound of what is being described, to control the speed of his verse, and to emphasize important words.

Alexander Pope demonstrates metric substitutions and other devices the poet has at his disposal in this passage:

from AN ESSAY ON CRITICISM

> True ease in writing comes from art, not chance,
> As those move easiest who have learned to dance.

'Tis not enough no harshness gives offence;
The sound must seem an Echo to the sense:
Soft is the strain when Zephyr gently blows,   5
And the smooth stream in smoother numbers flows;
But when loud surges lash the sounding shore,
The hoarse, rough verse should like the torrent roar:
When Ajax strives some rock's vast weight to throw,
The line too labors, and the words move slow;   10
Not so, when swift Camilla scours the plain,
Flies o'er th' unbending corn, and skims along the main.

1711

Alexander Pope (1688–1744)

Pope triumphantly reaches his goal of suiting sound to sense by carefully choosing vowel and consonant combinations and tuning his metrical groupings as if the poem were a musical instrument. An initial trochee emphasizes *soft* in

$$\text{/ } \smile \quad \smile \text{ / } \mid \smile \text{ / } \smile \text{ / } \smile \text{ /}$$

Soft is | the strain | when Zeph|yr gent|ly blows,

The next line's metrics illustrate what it says; from an initial pyrrhic and spondee the rest of the line turns into "smoother numbers"—that is, more regular metrics:

And the | smooth stream | in smooth|er num|bers flows:

In the following lines there is a dramatic change:

But when loud surges lash the sounding shore,
The hoarse, rough verse should like the torrent roar:
When Ajax strives some rock's vast weight to throw,
The line too labors, and the words move slow;

Here the effects are only partly metrical. The *vast weight* is emphasized by a spondee, which also slows down the line, as do the spondaic substitutions in the next line:

When A|jax strives | some rock's | vast weight | to throw,

The line | too la|bors, and | the words | move slow;

Zephyr: wind god. **numbers:** meter. **Ajax:** a Greek warrior in Homer's *Iliad,* famous for his strength. **Camilla:** an Amazon queen in Virgil's *Aeneid,* supposedly so fast a runner she could go over a field of wheat (the English call it *corn*) without bending the blades.

Moreover Pope clusters consonants together:

> When Ajax strives some rock's vast weight to throw
> ksstr   zs   mr   ksv   stw

Such consonant groups cannot be pronounced rapidly; they too slow down the line and increase its difficulty of pronunciation, so that "The line too labours, and the words move slow." On the other hand, speed is the effect of the metrics in the next passage:

> Not so, when swift Camilla scours the plain,
> Flies o'er th' unbending corn, and skims along the main.

The speed comes not only from avoiding consonant clusters, but also from the use of metrical combinations that allow unstressed syllables to come together:

> Flies o'er | th' unben|ding corn, | and skims | along | the main.

Notice that Pope gains this appearance of speed even though the line is one foot longer than the others. It is what is technically called an ALEXANDRINE, that is, a six-foot iambic line, or an iambic hexameter.

To summarize, meter can help suit the sound to the sense in a number of ways:

(1) Basic meter imitates the action described:

> *Boldly* they *rode* and *well*
> the *dan*cers go *round*, they go *round* and a*round*
> When *I* do *count* the *clock* that *tells* the *time*

(2) Metric substitutions emphasize key words:

> *Soft* is the strain when Zephyr gently blows

(3) Metric substitutions speed up or slow down the verse to fit the sense:

> When Ajax *strives* some *rock's vast weight* to *throw*
>
> *Flies* o'er th' un*ben*ding *corn*, and *skims* along the *main*.

RHYME AT WORK

The simplest and most fundamental job of rhyme is to give pleasure. We have already spoken of the delight children take in rhyming, even if the rhymed sounds are nonsense words. But adults have always enjoyed rhymes, too, and J. R. R. Tolkien may have had both in mind when he wrote the following poem:

CAT

The fat cat on the mat
   may seem to dream
of nice mice that suffice
   for him, or cream;
but he free, maybe,   5
   walks in thought
unbowed, proud, where loud
   roared and fought
his kin, lean and slim,
   or deep in den   10
in the East feasted on beasts
   and tender men.
The giant lion with iron
   claw in paw,
and huge ruthless tooth   15
   in gory jaw;
the pard dark-starred,
   fleet upon feet,
that oft soft from aloft
   leaps on his meat   20
where woods loom in gloom—
   far now they be,
   fierce and free,
   and tamed is he;
but fat cat on the mat   25
   kept as a pet,
   he does not forget.

1962
J. R. R. Tolkien (1892–1973)

"Cat" is a poem that uses INTERNAL RHYME—where the rhyme words occur within each line ("claw in paw," "fleet upon feet")—as well as the more common END RHYME, where the rhymes come at the ends of lines.

Rhyme has useful functions besides the pleasure it gives. It is, for example, a MNEMONIC DEVICE—rhyme makes it easier to remember a saying or a rule such as the "Thirty Days Hath September" verse, which helps many people recall the number of days in each month.

Rhyme also functions to signal the ends of lines, or to put it another way, to signal when a metrical unit or a whole poem is at an end. Here is a verse that Alexander Pope had engraved on the collar of a dog he gave Prince Frederick:

ENGRAVED ON THE COLLAR OF A DOG WHICH I GAVE TO HIS ROYAL HIGHNESS

I am his Highness' Dog at Kew;
Pray tell me sir, whose dog are you?

1736
Alexander Pope (1688–1744)

At the end of the couplet the last stress and the rhyme occur together, closing the sense and the recurring sound patterns (rhyme and meter) at once:

Pray tell me sir, whose dog are *you?*

Like the last beat of the meter (with which it coincides), the rhyme closes things and makes them seem final:

THE SPAN OF LIFE

The old dog barks backward without getting up.
I can remember when he was a pup.

1936
Robert Frost (1874–1963)

The poem need not be ending for a rhyme to occur, of course. In longer poems the rhyme helps group together lines that are related to each other by their sense—rhyme has a *structural* function, in other words. A poem from the seventeenth century will illustrate:

TO LUCASTA, ON GOING TO THE WARS

Tell me not, Sweet, I am unkind	*a*
That from the nunnery	*b*
Of thy chaste breast and quiet mind,	*a*
To war and arms I fly.	*b*

True, a new mistress now I chase,	*c*	5
The first foe in the field;	*d*	
And with a stronger faith embrace	*c*	
A sword, a horse, a shield.	*d*	

Yet this inconstancy is such	*e*	
As you too shall adore;	*f*	10
I could not love thee, dear, so much,	*e*	
Loved I not honor more.	*f*	

1649

Richard Lovelace (1618–1658)

The short stanzas divide the sense of the poem neatly, and the new rhymes in each stanza indicate new matter in the structure of the poem. The italic letters indicate when a new rhyme is introduced; thus the *unkind/mind* rhyme is *a*, the *nunnery/fly* rhyme (really a *near* rhyme—see page 238) is *b*, the *chase/ embrace* rhyme is *c*, and so on. The RHYME SCHEME of the poem—the pattern of its rhymes indicated by these letters—is *abab cdcd efef*.

		rhymes
Stanza 1	The speaker asks	*a*
	his beloved not to	*b*
	blame him for going	*a*
	to war.	*b*
Stanza 2	The speaker introduces the	*c*
	metaphor of the "new mistress"	*d*
	and talks of "embracing" the accouter-	*c*
	ments of war.	*d*
Stanza 3	The speaker resolves this new	*e*
	love / old love conflict by saying he	*f*
	could not love his beloved so much	*e*
	if he did not love honor (and there-	*f*
	fore the necessity of embracing his	
	"new mistress") more.	

This clumsy paraphrase of an elegant and deservedly famous love lyric may at least show how the new rhymes correspond with different parts of the poem's structure. Much more will be said about this structural function of rhyme in the next chapter, where different poetic forms will be discussed.

The most important function of rhyme is *emphasis*. Words that rhyme force us to pay attention to them and to compare them. Good poets use these emphatic and comparative qualities of rhyme. Turn back to Wordsworth's poem on Westminster Bridge in Chapter Four, this time paying special attention to the rhymes. The poem has the carefully interwoven rhymes of an Italian sonnet, a form that will be more fully described in Chapter Nine. (Briefly, a *sonnet* is a fourteen-line poem in iambic pentameter.) The first line of Wordsworth's poem ends in *fair*, and rhymes for this word occur in lines 4, 5, and 8: *wear, bare*, and *air*. You will recall that Wordsworth has chosen for the special emphasis of rhyme the key words in his celebration of the city's beauty: his attention was first caught because the scene was so beautiful or *fair*; because the smokeless *air* of the city is *bare* of its usual smoke, it can *wear* the beauty of the morning like a garment. Wordsworth juxtaposes rhymes such as *wear* and *bare* to highlight the city's paradoxes. Because the words sound *alike*, we are more struck by the fact that in meaning they are close to *opposites*. But reconciling opposites is what Wordsworth is doing—the usually radically different city and country are at this moment almost indistinguishable; by being more *still* than usual the city seems more *alive*; being *bare* of smoke enables the city to be *clothed* with beauty.

The last rhymes exemplify the emphatic and comparative functions of rhyme:

steep
hill
deep
will
asleep
still

It is the stillness and deep calm that enable the city to look as if it were alive and part of nature like the hills and valleys around. It can seem to have a will and to be asleep because of this stillness from its usual smoky and mechanical activity.

Another function of rhyme is humor, which often results when the rhyme words have more than one syllable. Ogden Nash was a master of such rhymes:

THE TURTLE

The turtle lives 'twixt plated decks
Which practically conceal its sex.
I think it clever of the turtle
In such a fix to be so fertile.

1929

Ogden Nash (1902–1971)

When two syllables of a word rhyme, the result is called DOUBLE RHYME: *turtle/fertile*.

from DON JUAN

'Tis pity learned virgins ever wed
With persons of no sort of education
Or gentlemen, who, though well born and bred,
Grow tired of scientific conversation:
I don't choose to say much upon this head,   5
I'm a plain man, and in a single station,
But—Oh! ye lords of ladies intellectual,
Inform us truly, have they not henpecked you all?

1819

George Gordon, Lord Byron (1788–1824)

The last rhymes—inte*llectual*/hen*pecked you all*—involve three syllables and are called TRIPLE RHYMES. Both double and triple rhymes are known as FEMININE RHYMES—multisyllabic rhymes in which the first syllable is stressed. They contrast with the ordinary single-syllable MASCULINE RHYMES, which always occur on a stressed syllable: *ate/straight/debate*. Multisyllabic rhyme is most frequently used for comic verse, but there are notable exceptions. Wilfred Owen uses feminine rhyme in serious poems such as "Dulce et Decorum Est," p. 168, and even triple rhyme has been used for a serious purpose:

from BRIDGE OF SIGHS

One more Unfortunate,
Weary of breath,

Rashly importunate,
Gone to her death!

Take her up tenderly,   5
Lift her with care;
Fashion'd so slenderly,
Young, and so fair!

1846
Thomas Hood (1799–1846)

Another kind of rhyme needs to be mentioned. In many poems we have looked at, you may have noticed line endings that are similar but not quite rhymes—for example, in "My Papa's Waltz":

The whiskey on your breath
Could make a small boy dizzy;
But I hung on like death:
Such waltzing was not easy.

We romped until the pans
Slid from the kitchen shelf;
My mother's countenance
Could not unfrown itself.

The pairs *dizzy/easy* and *pans/countenance* are NEAR RHYMES or SLANT RHYMES. Other examples may be found in "Bells for John Whiteside's Daughter" (*body/study, window/shadow, little/scuttle, ready/study*) and in Wyatt's "They Flee from Me" (*chamber/remember, special/fall*), both in Chapter Three. A special case of near rhyme is the EYE RHYME, where pairs of words look as if they ought to rhyme but do not: *laughter/daughter, care/are*.

To summarize, the poetic uses of rhyme include giving pleasure, signaling the ends of lines and grouping structural units of lines together, emphasizing key words, getting us to compare the sense of words that sound alike, and sometimes contributing to a comic tone.

EXERCISES_____

It may seem that meter and rhyme are things that critics and English teachers worry about more than poets, but here is what two poets have to say about them:

Words in themselves do not convey meaning. . . . let us take the example of two people who are talking on the other side of a closed door, whose voices can be heard but whose words cannot be distinguished. Even though the words do not carry, the sound of them does, and the listener can catch the meaning of the conversation. This is because every meaning has a sound posture.

—Robert Frost, "Getting the Sound of Sense": An Interview

Poetry has both meaning and meter, and in a good poem they are so closely related that they seem one thing.

—Louis Simpson, *An Introduction to Poetry*, 2nd ed.

A. Meter, as we have seen, not only contributes to pleasure but also conveys meaning. In order to analyze this function it is useful to be able to describe the meter of a poem—that is, to determine its SCANSION. To scan a poem, read it aloud or listen to someone else read it. Then proceed with the following steps. Don't let these technical steps obscure the point of the procedure—casting light on the meaning of a poem.

1. Read through the poem and mark the syllables you stress with the symbol ⁄ . Don't look for a pattern at this point or mark a stress just because you think one belongs there; just try to faithfully reflect the way you are reading the poem.

2. Go through and mark the rest of the syllables with the symbol ‿ .

3. Find the most common recurring unit and make divisions between units with a vertical line, |. This is the most difficult part because, as you will have noticed, the *middle* of an iambic line looks just like a trochaic one, with alternate stressed and unstressed syllables, while the middle of an anapestic line looks just like a dactylic one, with two unstressed syllables between each stress. You need to listen carefully to your own voice. Does it seem to be going da-da-*dum*, da-da-*dum*, or does it sound more like *dum*-da-da, *dum*-da-da? Look also at the *ends* of phrases and sentences; if they consistently end da-da-*dum*, then anapests, not dactyls, are the basic metrical feet.

4. Finally, to determine the whole metrical description of a poem, you need to count the number of feet in each line. Many poems will have the same count and the same metrical foot for each line; the sonnets we have read, for instance, have fourteen lines, all of which are iambic pentameter. But some poems alternate longer and shorter lines, for example tetrameters and trimeters, as in "Western Wind":

‿ ⁄ ‿ ⁄ ‿ ⁄ ‿ ⁄ [O] Wes|tern Wind, | when wilt | thou blow,	tetrameter
‿ ⁄ ‿ ⁄ ‿ ⁄ The small | rain down | can rain.	trimeter
⁄ ‿ ‿ ⁄ ‿ ⁄ ‿ ⁄ Christ! that | my love | were in | my arms,	tetrameter
‿ ⁄ ‿ ⁄ ‿ ⁄ And I | in my bed | again.	trimeter

Rhyme and Meter

Matthew Arnold's "Dover Beach" uses dimeters, trimeters, tetrameters, and pentameters:

The sea | is calm | tonight.   trimeter

The tide | is full, | the moon | lies fair   tetrameter

Upon | the straits; | on the | French coast | the light   pentameter

Gleams . . .

The Sea | of Faith   dimeter

Was once, too, at the full.

Scan the first five lines of the following poem:

BUICK

As a sloop with a sweep of immaculate wing on her
    delicate spine
And a keel as steel as a root that holds in the sea as she leans,
Leaning and laughing, my warm-hearted beauty, you ride,
    you ride,
You tack on the curves with parabola speed and a kiss
    of goodbye,
Like a thoroughbred sloop, my new high-spirited spirit, my kiss.   5

As my foot suggests that you leap in the air with your hips of
    a girl,
My finger that praises your wheel and announces your voices
    of song,
Flouncing your skirts, you blueness of joy, you flirt of politeness,
You leap, you intelligence, essence of wheelness with
    silvery nose,
And your platinum clocks of excitement stir like the hairs of
    a fern.   10

But how alien you are from the booming belts of your birth and
    the smoke

The Death of a Toad

Where you turned on the stinging lathes of Detroit and Lansing
    at night
And shrieked at the torch in your secret parts and the
    amorous tests,
But now with your eyes that enter the future of roads you forget;
You are all instinct with your phosphorous glow and your
    streaking hair.   15

And now when we stop it is not as the bird from the shell that
    I leave
Or the leathery pilot who steps from his bird with a sneer
    of delight,
And not as the ignorant beast do you squat and watch
    me depart,
But with exquisite breathing you smile, with satisfaction of love,
And I touch you again as you tick in the silence and settle
    in sleep.   20

1942
Karl Shapiro (b. 1913)

1. What is the meter of the poem?
2. What is the simile Shapiro uses in the first five lines? How does the meter help this simile?
3. What other devices of sound repetition (such as alliteration, consonance, and rhyme) does Shapiro use? Which ones seem to help reinforce the poem's lines? How do they do this?

B. Scan the first two lines of the following poem. Can you find reasons for the rhythm of line 2 in the content of the line?

THE DEATH OF A TOAD

A toad the power mower caught,
Chewed and clipped of a leg, with a hobbling hop has got
    To the garden verge, and sanctuaried him
    Under the cineraria leaves, in the shade
      Of the ashen heartshaped leaves, in a dim,   5
      Low, and final glade.

The rare original heartsblood goes,
Spends on the earthen hide, in the folds and wizening, flows
In the gutters of the banked and staring eyes. He lies
As still as if he would return to stone,   10
And soundlessly attending, dies
Toward some deep monotone.

Toward misted and ebullient seas
And cooling shores, towards lost Amphibia's emperies.
Day dwindles, drowning, and at length is gone   15
In the wide and antique eyes, which still appear
To watch, across the castrate lawn,
The haggard daylight steer.

1950
Richard Wilbur (b. 1921)

1. Why does Wilbur use alliteration in such phrases as "hobbling hop" and
   "Day dwindles, drowning"? How does the meter help the sense of line 15?
2. Look at the rhyme pairs in this poem. How do the pairs in 4–6, 7–8, and
   10–12 emphasize and contrast meanings?

C. Scan Henry Reed's "Naming of Parts" in Chapter Two. What metrical
differences can be found in the poem? Why does Reed make this metrical
distinction?

D.   *from* **THE CLOUD**

I bring fresh showers for the thirsting flowers,
     From the seas and the streams;
I bear light shade for the leaves when laid
     In their noonday dreams.
From my wings are shaken the dews that waken   5
     The sweet buds every one,
When rocked to rest on their mother's breast,
     As she dances about the sun.
I wield the flail of the lashing hail,
     And whiten the green plains under,   10
And then again I dissolve it in rain,
     And laugh as I pass in thunder.

1820
Percy Bysshe Shelley (1792–1822)

1. What is the meter of "The Cloud"? Why does Shelley use this meter?
2. How many of the sound repetition devices mentioned in this chapter can be found in "The Cloud"? In what ways do they reinforce meaning?

E.
I LIKE TO SEE IT LAP THE MILES

I like to see it lap the Miles—
And lick the Valleys up—
And stop to feed itself at Tanks—
And then—prodigious step

Around a Pile of Mountains—   5
And supercilious peer
In Shanties—by the sides of Roads
And then a Quarry pare

To fit its sides
And crawl between   10
Complaining all the while
In horrid—hooting stanza—
Then chase itself down Hill—

And neigh like Boanerges—
Then—prompter than a Star   15
Stop—docile and omnipotent
At its own stable door—

                                        1891
                        Emily Dickinson (1830–1886)

LIMITED

I am riding on a limited express, one of the crack trains of
    the nation.
Hurtling across the prairie into blue haze and dark air go
    fifteen all-steel coaches holding a thousand people.
(All the coaches shall be scrap and rust and all the men and
    women laughing in the diners and sleepers shall pass to
    ashes.)

I ask a man in the smoker where he is going and he answers:
"Omaha."

1916

Carl Sandburg (1878–1967)

1. Identify the meter of Dickinson's poem. What is the predominant meter of Sandburg's first line? Is the rest of the Sandburg poem metrically regular? Which of the two poets is more concerned with the train's movement? How does this help explain metrical differences?
2. What kind of rhyme is used in Dickinson's poem? What sound device is exemplified in the pairs *like/lick, stop/step*? Why does she use this device?
3. Count the feet in each of Dickinson's lines. Which lines have the fewest feet? How is the meaning of these lines related to their length?

F.   **SIR BEELZEBUB**

When
Sir
Beelzebub called for his syllabub in the hotel in Hell
        Where Proserpine first fell,
Blue as the gendarmerie were the waves of the sea   5

      (Rocking and shocking the bar-maid).

Nobody comes to give him his rum but the
Rim of the sky hippopotamus-glum
Enhances the chances to bless with a benison
Alfred Lord Tennyson crossing the bar laid   10
With cold vegetation from pale deputations
Of temperance workers (all signed in Memoriam)
Hoping with glory to trip up the Laureate's feet

      (Moving in classical metres) . . .

Like Balaclava, the lava came down from the   15

Proserpine: the queen of the underworld in Roman mythology. **Alfred, Lord Tennyson:** a great experimenter with metrics, which may help explain the references to him; **"Crossing the Bar"** and **"In Memoriam"** are titles of his poems. **Balaclava:** an allusion to Tennyson's "The Charge of the Light Brigade."

Roof, and the sea's blue wooden gendarmerie
Took them in charge while Beelzebub roared for his rum.

    . . . None of them come!

1922

Edith Sitwell (1887–1964)

1. Review the functions of rhyme summarized on page 238. Which of them does rhyme perform here?
2. Consider how the poem's effect would be different if rhyme ended the lines, as follows:

> Nobody comes
> to give him his rum
> but the rim of the sky hippopotamus-glum
> Enhances
> the chances
> to bless with a benison
> Alfred Lord Tennyson.

3. Does Sitwell seem to you more concerned with the sound of these words, more concerned with their meaning, or equally concerned with the two? What is the tone of the poem?
4. How does the rhyme (often multisyllabic) contribute to its tone?

G.   **A BLESSING**

> From what, sometimes, seems an arbitrary
> form or discipline often come two words
> that rhyme and, in the rhyming, fully marry
> the world of spoons and sheets and common birds
> to another world that we have always known,   5
> where the waterfall of dawn does not drown
> even the haloed gnat, where we are shown
> how to find and hold the pale day moon, round
> and blessed in the silver lake of a coffee spoon.

1981

Mekeel McBride (b. 1950)

1. What different kinds of rhyme does the poem contain?
2. What function of rhyme does McBride discuss in the first four lines? How

do the lines' rhymes underscore this point? What illustrations of this point can be found in the poems in this chapter?

3. How do the internal rhymes of the last two lines reinforce the visual image?

WRITING SUGGESTIONS

1. Examine the rhyme words in Gerard Manley Hopkins' "Spring and Fall" on page 50. In an essay, discuss the ways in which these rhymes underscore the THEME of Hopkins' poem—that is, the thesis, major idea, or central point.

2. Reread Richard Lovelace's "To Althea, From Prison." Scan the poem and identify metric substitutions. Examine the rhyme words. Look for other devices such as assonance and onomatopoeia. Then write an essay discussing Lovelace's use of sound in this poem.

CHAPTER NINE

SHAPES AND FORMS

A poem is, among other things, an arrangement of lines on the page and of words within lines. It has a shape, a pattern, or a design, created by the order of words and lines, the length of lines, the meter, the placement of rhymes, the repetition of words or phrases or ideas, spacing, capitalization, even the typeface. These groupings of a poem's lines constitute its FORM. It may be a form established by tradition for a kind of subject (the limerick, for example), or it may be a unique form, created by the poet for a single poem.

Asking questions about the form of a poem can help make clear its relation to meaning. How does form itself convey meaning or help to underline and reinforce meaning?

SHAPED POEMS AND CONCRETE POEMS

In some poems, the reinforcing role of form is immediately obvious because the poet has chosen a design that is the pictorial equivalent of what the words say. In George Herbert's "Easter Wings" the lines begin long, reflecting the content: "man in wealth and store." Then they shorten, again reflecting the content: "he became / Most poor." The lines expand again after the envisioned union with Christ as the speaker imagines sharing Christ's Easter victory:

EASTER WINGS

Lord, who createdst man in wealth and store,
    Though foolishly he lost the same,
        Decaying more and more,
            Till he became
                Most poor:
                With thee
            O let me rise
        As larks, harmoniously,
    And sing this day thy victories:
Then shall the fall further the flight in me.

My tender age in sorrow did begin;
    And still with sicknesses and shame
        Thou didst so punish sin,
            That I became
                Most thin.
                With thee
            Let me combine,
        And feel this day thy victory;
    For, if I imp my wing on thine,
Affliction shall advance the flight in me.

1633
George Herbert (1593–1633)

Poems like "Easter Wings," whose pattern of lines pictures what their lines describe, are called SHAPED POEMS. Here is a recent example:

---

store: abundance. **imp:** in falconry, to graft new feathers on a wing.

WINTER WAS A WHITE PAGE

Winter was a white page
    soon to be ripped
        from the calendar
            says the rippling script
                of Canada geese
                    in a language
                      their quills
                          bring creaking
                              from valleys
                                  and bristling hills
                                      where it entered
                                          the redman's deep
                                            ancestral sleep
                                      a message
                                  that stirred
                        the bear in its bed
                    the grasses
                under snow
            a message heard
        and read
      at an open
     window
    by one
   whose
  pen
 passes
the
word

                                          1979
Jon Stallworthy (b. 1935)

A. R. Ammons' "Corsons Inlet" and Denise Levertov's "Merritt Parkway," both in Chapter Four, may also be considered shaped poems.

A modern variation of shaped verse is CONCRETE POETRY, which approaches graphic art in its pictorial representation of meaning and is more likely to consist of single words than statements—that is, concrete poetry tends to rely more on the visual component and less on words to convey its meaning. E. E. Cummings' "1(a" (p. 15) is an early example of concrete poetry; another example is Mary Ellen Solt's "Forsythia."

FORSYTHIA

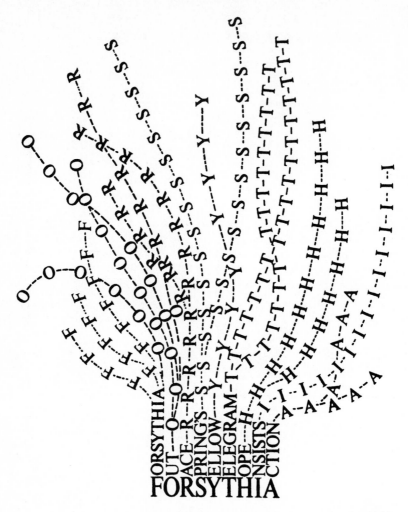

1966
Mary Ellen Solt (b. 1920)

FIXED OR TRADITIONAL FORMS

Common Stanza Forms

Form is usually less bold in calling attention to itself than in the preceding examples of pictorial or concrete poetry. In English poetry until the last half century, the most common method of creating pattern or design within a poem has been grouping lines by rhyming their end words. The result has been a series of stanza forms with simple or complex rhyme schemes, sometimes called FIXED FORMS because their arrangement is fixed by tradition.

The COUPLET—a pair of lines that rhyme—is the simplest of these forms:

LITTLE LYRIC (OF GREAT IMPORTANCE)

I wish the rent
Was heaven sent.

1942
Langston Hughes (1902–1967)

Various meters within couplets are possible: Langston Hughes' couplet is in *dimeters*; the third section of Auden's "In Memory of W. B. Yeats" is in *tetrameter* couplets. Elizabeth Barrett Browning's "Lord Walter's Wife" is in *octameter* couplets. Most couplets, however, are in *pentameters*, and examples in this book include Browning's "My Last Duchess" (Chapter Five) and the excerpt from Chaucer's "Nun's Priest's Tale" in Chapter Seven. Pentameter couplets such as Pope's are sometimes called HEROIC COUPLETS because of their use for heroic or epic subjects during the seventeenth and eighteenth centuries. But whatever their length or meter, couplets emphasize *twos*: the two rhyming lines are set off against each other, and the two halves of each line are also often balanced or opposed. Thus when we ask what form has to do with meaning in couplets, the answer is likely to be that the poet is comparing or contrasting two things, as in the following lines:

from AN ESSAY ON CRITICISM

'Tis hard to say, if greater want of skill
Appear in writing or in judging ill;
But of the two less dangerous is th' offense
To tire our patience, than mislead our sense:
Some few in that, but numbers err in this,   5
Ten censure wrong for one who writes amiss;
A fool might once himself alone expose,
Now one in verse makes many more in prose.

1711
Alexander Pope (1688–1744)

Here the major comparison in the passage is between the errors of critics and those of poets, but further comparisons and contrasts go on *between* and *within* couplets. Want of skill in writing and criticizing is compared with harm done by each (lines 3–4). The errors of one fool (7) are compared with the errors of many (8). And within single lines, writing badly is contrasted with criticizing badly (2), tiring our patience with misleading us (4), and the few or one with the many (5, 6, 7, 8).

Couplet Contrasts

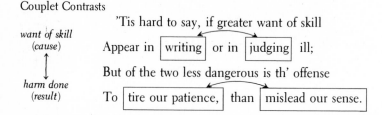

These couplets of Pope's are END-STOPPED—that is, the rhyme word closes (completes) both the grammatical unit and the sense of a statement at the end of the couplet. If line endings are made less obvious by being ENJAMBED or RUN ON—that is, allowing the sense of a sentence to continue past the rhyme word at the end of the line—they lose this comparative emphasis. Such enjambed lines are often found in narrative or dramatic poems. Robert Browning's "My Last Duchess" begins:

> That's my last Duchess painted on the wall,
> Looking as if she were alive. I call
> That piece a wonder, now: Fra Pandolf's hands
> Worked busily a day, and there she stands.

We scarcely notice the rhymes when the lines are enjambed or run on in this way.

The TRIPLET or TERCET is a three-line stanza. Thomas Hardy's "The Convergence of the Twain" is in tercets, and Robert Herrick used them in the following poem:

UPON JULIA'S CLOTHES

> Whenas in silks my Julia goes,
> Then, then, methinks, how sweetly flows
> That liquefaction of her clothes.

Next, when I cast mine eyes and see
That brave vibration, each way free,   5
O, how that glittering taketh me!

1648
Robert Herrick (1591–1674)

The term TRIPLET usually refers to a group in which the same rhyme is used for all three lines (*aaa, bbb, ccc*, and so on), while the term TERCET is generally reserved for other rhyme combinations within three-line groups. An example is TERZA RIMA, in which rhymed lines enclose a middle line that furnishes the outer rhyme for the next group of three lines (*aba bcb cdc*, and so on). This verse form was invented by Dante Alighieri (1265–1321) for his long, three-part poem *The Divine Comedy*. Shelley altered the form slightly when he wrote the following poem. Instead of letting the triplets continue, he cut them off after each group of four with a couplet:

ODE TO THE WEST WIND

1

O wild West Wind, thou breath of Autumn's being,
Thou, from whose unseen presence the leaves dead
Are driven, like ghosts from an enchanter fleeing,

Yellow, and black, and pale, and hectic red,
Pestilence-stricken multitudes: O Thou,   5
Who chariotest to their dark wintry bed

The wingéd seeds, where they lie cold and low,
Each like a corpse within its grave, until
Thine azure sister of the Spring shall blow

Her clarion o'er the dreaming earth, and fill   10
(Driving sweet buds like flocks to feed in air)
With living hues and odours plain and hill:

Wild Spirit, which art moving everywhere;
Destroyer and Preserver, hear, O hear!

2

Thou on whose stream, 'mid the steep sky's commotion,   15
Loose clouds like Earth's decaying leaves are shed,
Shook from the tangled boughs of Heaven and Ocean,

Angels of rain and lightning: there are spread
On the blue surface of thine aery surge,
Like the bright hair uplifted from the head   20

Of some fierce Mænad, even from the dim verge
Of the horizon to the zenith's height,
The locks of the approaching storm. Thou Dirge

Of the dying year, to which this closing night
Will be the dome of a vast sepulchre,   25
Vaulted with all thy congregated might

Of vapours, from whose solid atmosphere
Black rain and fire and hail will burst: O hear!

3

Thou who didst waken from his summer dreams
The blue Mediterranean, where he lay,   30
Lulled by the coil of his chrystálline streams,

Beside a pumice isle in Baiæ's bay,
And saw in sleep old palaces and towers
Quivering within the wave's intenser day,

All overgrown with azure moss and flowers   35
So sweet, the sense faints picturing them! Thou
For whose path the Atlantic's level powers

Cleave themselves into chasms, while far below
The sea blooms and the oozy woods which wear
The sapless foliage of the ocean, know   40

Thy voice, and suddenly grow grey with fear,
And tremble and despoil themselves; O hear!

4

If I were a dead leaf thou mightest bear;
If I were a swift cloud to fly with thee;
A wave to pant beneath thy power, and share   45

Ode to the West Wind

The impulse of thy strength, only less free
Than thou, O Uncontrollable! If even
I were as in my boyhood, and could be

The comrade of thy wanderings over Heaven,
As then, when to outstrip thy skiey speed   50
Scarce seemed a vision; I would n'er have striven

As thus with thee in prayer in my sore need,
Oh! lift me as a wave; a leaf, a cloud!
I fall upon the thorns of life! I bleed!

A heavy weight of hours has chained and bowed   55
One too like thee: tameless, and swift, and proud.

                    5

Make me thy lyre, even as the forest is:
What if my leaves are falling like its own!
The tumult of thy mighty harmonies

Will take from both a deep, autumnal tone,   60
Sweet though in sadness. Be thou, Spirit fierce,
My spirit! Be thou me, impetuous one!

Drive my dead thoughts over the universe
Like withered leaves to quicken a new birth;
And, by the incantation of this verse,   65

Scatter, as from an unextinguished hearth
Ashes and sparks, my words among mankind!
Be through my lips to unawakened Earth

The trumpet of a prophecy! O Wind,
If Winter comes, can Spring be far behind?   70

                                        1820
Percy Bysshe Shelley (1792–1822)

How does terza rima work in this instance? The linking rhyme connects individual tercets since there is an echo from the last in each succeeding three-line group. At the same time, the links work to tie together a longer grammatical or descriptive passage.

The QUATRAIN is a group of four lines, with or without rhyme, but most frequently rhymed. One possibility alternates rhymes *abab*:

DIRCE

Stand close around, ye Stygian set,
With Dirce in one boat conveyed!
Or Charon, seeing, may forget
That he is old and she a shade.

1831
Walter Savage Landor (1775–1864)

This rhyme scheme ties the lines together in a close-knit unit of sense.

Another rhyming stanza form is what is usually called the IN MEMORIAM STANZA, after Tennyson's use of it in his long poem *In Memoriam A. H. H.* (1850), commemorating the death of his friend Arthur Hallam. The rhyme scheme here is *abba*. Although Tennyson believed he had invented this stanza scheme, it had been used by some earlier poets, including Ben Jonson:

AN ELEGY

Though beauty be the mark of praise,
  And yours of whom I sing be such
  As not the world can praise too much,
Yet is 't your virtue now I raise.

A virtue, like allay, so gone   5
  Throughout your form as, though that move
  And draw and conquer all men's love,
This subjects you to love of one.

Wherein you triumph yet; because
  'Tis of yourself, and that you use   10

Stygian: having to do with the river Styx, which separates the land of the living from the land of the dead (Hades) in Greek mythology. The dead are called **shades**, and are ferried across the Styx by the ancient boatman **Charon.**

allay: alloy, a union of component parts.

An Elegy

The noblest freedom, not to choose
Against or faith or honor's laws.

But who should less expect from you,
 In whom alone Love lives again?
 By whom he is restored to men,   15
And kept, and bred, and brought up true.

His falling temples you have reared,
 The withered garlands ta'en away;
 His altars kept from the decay
That envy wished, and nature feared;   20

And on them burn so chaste a flame,
 With so much loyalties' expense,
 As Love, t' acquit such excellence,
Is gone himself into your name.

And you are he; the deity   25
 To whom all lovers are designed
 That would their better objects find;
Among which faithful troop am I.

Who, as an offspring at your shrine,
 Have sung this hymn, and here entreat 30
 One spark of your diviner heat
To light upon a love of mine.

Which, if it kindle not, but scant
 Appear, and that to shortest view,
 Yet give me leave t' adore in you   35
What I in her am grieved to want.

        1640
    Ben Jonson (1573–1637)

Another poem using this rhyme scheme is the "accidental" poem of William Whewell's in Chapter One, Exercise E.

A more frequent form is the BALLAD STANZA, *abcb*. Since English is a rhyme-poor language, the ballad stanza is a much easier stanza to write, so it is frequently encountered not only in poems composed five hundred years ago, but in songs that are popular now. The ballad stanza gets its name from its use in FOLK BALLADS, anonymous songs passed on by word of mouth until they were collected in the eighteenth and nineteenth centuries. Some of these may date back as far as the thirteenth century. Here is one of the best-known examples of folk or popular ballads:

BARBARA ALLAN

It was in and about the Martinmas time,
    When the green leaves were a-fallin',
That Sir John Graeme in the West Country
    Fell in love with Barbara Allan.

He sent his man down through the town   5
    To the place where she was dwellin':
"O haste and come to my master dear,
    Gin ye be Barbara Allan."

O slowly, slowly rase she up,
    To the place where he was lyin',   10
And when she drew the curtain by:
    "Young man, I think you're dyin'."

"O it's I'm sick, and very, very sick,
    And 'tis a' for Barbara Allan."
"O the better for me ye sal never be,   15
    Though your heart's blood were a-spillin'.

"O dinna ye mind, young man," said she,
    "When ye the cups were fillin',
That ye made the healths gae round and round,
    And slighted Barbara Allan?"   20

He turned his face unto the wall,
    And death with him was dealin':
"Adieu, adieu, my dear friends all,
    And be kind to Barbara Allan."

---

gin: if. **mind:** remember.

And slowly, slowly, rase she up,   25
    And slowly, slowly left him;
And sighing said she could not stay,
    Since death of life had reft him.

She had not gane a mile but twa,
    When she heard the dead-bell knellin',   30
And every jow that the dead-bell ga'ed
    It cried, "Woe to Barbara Allan!"

"O mother, mother, make my bed,
    O make it soft and narrow:
Since my love died for me today,   35
    I'll die for him tomorrow."

   c. 15th century

                                     Anonymous

Some Other Rhymed Forms

The VILLANELLE is a French verse form which uses a recurring rhyme scheme in tercets and repetition of whole lines to achieve its effect. It has not been a popular form in English but there are a few memorable examples, of which this poem by Dylan Thomas may be the best:

DO NOT GO GENTLE INTO THAT GOOD NIGHT

Do not go gentle into that good night,	*a*
Old age should burn and rave at close of day;	*b*
Rage, rage against the dying of the light.	*a*

Though wise men at their end know dark is right,	*a*	
Because their words had forked no lightning they	*b*	5
Do not go gentle into that good night.	*a—line 1*	
	repeated	

Good men, the last wave by, crying how bright	*a*
Their frail deeds might have danced in a green bay,	*b*
Rage, rage against the dying of the light.	*a—line 3*
	repeated

---

jow: stroke. **ga'ed:** struck.

Wild men who caught and sang the sun in flight,	*a*	*10*
And learn, too late, they grieved it on its way,	*b*	
Do not go gentle into that good night.	*a—line 1*	

Grave men, near death, who see with blinding sight	*a*	
Blind eyes could blaze like meteors and be gay,	*b*	
Rage, rage against the dying of the light.	*a—line 3*	*15*

And you, my father, there on the sad height,	*a*
Curse, bless me now with your fierce tears, I pray.	*b*
Do not go gentle into that good night.	*a—line 1*
Rage, rage against the dying of the light.	*a—line 3*

1952
Dylan Thomas (1914–1953)

RHYME ROYAL, a seven-line stanza rhyming *ababbcc*, is also called the Chaucerian stanza because it was sometimes used by Geoffrey Chaucer (1343?–1400). Edmund Spenser also used it, as did Shakespeare in a narrative poem, *The Rape of Lucrece:*

from THE RAPE OF LUCRECE

"Lucrece," quoth he, "this night I must enjoy thee.	*a*	
If thou deny, then force must work my way;	*b*	
For in thy bed I purpose to destroy thee.	*a*	
That done, some worthless slave of thine I'll slay,	*b*	
To kill thine honor with thy live's decay;	*b*	*5*
And in thy dead arms do I mean to place him,	*c*	
Swearing I slew him, seeing thee embrace him."	*c*	

1594
William Shakespeare (1564–1616)

The SPENSERIAN STANZA is a nine-line stanza rhyming *ababbcbcc* and ending in an ALEXANDRINE or twelve-syllable, six-foot line. Invented by Edmund Spenser for his epic poem *The Faerie Queene*, it was used by later poets such as Wordsworth, Keats, and Shelley.

from THE FAERIE QUEENE

A little lowly Hermitage it was	*a*
Downe in a dale, hard by a forest's side,	*b*
Far from resort of people, that did pas	*a*
In travell to and froe: a little wyde	*b*
There was an holy Chappell edifyde,	*b* 5
Wherein the Hermite dewly went to say	*c*
His holy things each morne and eventyde:	*b*
Thereby a Christall streame did gently play,	*c*
Which from a sacred fountaine welled forth alway.	*c*

(I, 1, 34)

1590

Edmund Spenser (c. 1552–1599)

OTTAVA RIMA, an eight-line stanza rhyming *ababab cc*, was first used in English by Sir Thomas Wyatt (1503–1542). Its most successful use is in *Don Juan*, a long narrative poem by Lord Byron, who saw the comic potential of the stanza and exploited it by using frequent feminine rhymes (see Chapter 8 for another excerpt):

from DON JUAN

'Tis a sad thing, I cannot choose but say,	*a*
And all the fault of that indecent sun,	*b*
Who cannot leave alone our helpless clay,	*a*
But will keep baking, broiling, burning on,	*b*
That howsoever people fast and pray,	*a* 5
The flesh is frail, and so the soul undone:	*b*
What men call gallantry, and gods adultery,	*c*
Is much more common where the climate's sultry.	*c*

1819

George Gordon, Lord Byron (1788–1824)

Some Comic Forms

The LIMERICK is always comic and usually obscene. The form is probably familiar to you, but you may not have heard it described as a five-line poem in anapestic trimeter and dimeter, rhyming *aabba*. Here are two examples. The first plays with the tradition of *pastoral poetry*, where the young man is often named Daphnis and his sweetheart, Chloe; the second plays with the limerick's metrical regularity:

TWO LIMERICKS

"For the tenth time, dull Daphnis," said Chloe,
"You have told me my bosom is snowy;
You have made much fine verse on
Each part of my person,
Now *do* something—there's a good boy!"

A decrepit old gas man named Peter
While hunting around for the meter,
Touched a leak with his light;
He rose out of sight—
And, as everyone who knows anything about poetry
    can tell you, he also ruined the meter.

Though the form of limericks makes them memorable, their authors are often forgotten; most examples are anonymous, and their dates of composition unknown.

The CLERIHEW at least has the advantages of being slightly more intellectually clever than the limerick and more certain of authorship. Named after its inventor, Edmund Clerihew Bentley (1875–1956)—author of the famous detective novel *Trent's Last Case*—the clerihew consists of two irregular couplets, sometimes with even more irregular rhymes, making some comment about the biography of a famous person. One of Bentley's own will serve as an example:

CLERIHEW

Sir Christopher Wren
Said, "I am going to dine with some men.
If anybody calls
Say I am designing St. Paul's."

1951

The DOUBLE DACTYL also uses people's names, but only people who are fortunate (or unfortunate) enough to have double-dactyl names:

Ralph Waldo Emerson   Henry S. Kissinger

HISTORICAL REFLECTIONS

Higgledy-piggledy,
Benjamin Harrison,
Twenty-third President,
Was, and, as such,

Served between Clevelands, and
Save for this trivial
Idiosyncrasy,
Didn't do much.

1966
John Hollander (b. 1929)

The double dactyl's form is a little stricter than the clerihew's: All lines except the last in each stanza are composed of two dactyls. The first is a nonsense line, the second a double dactyl name. Only the fourth and last shorter lines need rhyme, and there must also be a single word double dactyl—like *idiosyncrasy*—somewhere.

The Sonnet

Of all the fixed forms in English, the sonnet has been the most consistently popular. Since the Renaissance, when the sonnet form was introduced into English from Italian, almost every major English and American poet has attempted the form.

A SONNET is a fourteen-line poem in iambic pentameter. There are several varieties, each with a distinctive rhyme scheme. When the sonnet was introduced into English in the first half of the sixteenth century, it was modeled on poems by Petrarch—Francesco Petrarca (1304–1374)—and other Italian poets, so this early sonnet form is called the ITALIAN or PETRARCHAN SONNET. The first eight lines of the Italian sonnet rhyme *abbaabba*. The last six lines introduce new rhymes, but they may be arranged in any way the poet pleases. Here is an example:

ON THE GRASSHOPPER AND THE CRICKET

The poetry of earth is never dead:
When all the birds are faint with the hot sun,
And hide in cooling trees, a voice will run
From hedge to hedge about the new-mown mead;
That is the grasshopper's—he takes the lead   5
In summer luxury—he has never done
With his delights; for when tired out with fun
He rests at ease beneath some pleasant weed.
The poetry of earth is ceasing never:
On a lone winter evening, when the frost   10
Has wrought a silence, from the stove there shrills
The cricket's song, in warmth increasing ever,
And seems to one in drowsiness half lost,
The grasshopper's among some grassy hills.

1817

John Keats (1795–1821)

How does the sonnet form organize the content in this poem? The title suggests the subjects—the grasshopper and the cricket. The first eight lines talk about the grasshopper, while the last six talk about the cricket. In the last line the two subjects are brought together: the cricket's song seems to the drowsy listener to be the grasshopper's. The division between parts is marked by the repetition of a phrase: both the first eight and the last six lines begin, "The poetry of earth. . . ." The two parts also contrast seasons: the first eight lines are talking about summer; the last six, winter. At least one other contrast is implied: the outdoor world of birds, trees, hedges, and weeds opposed to the indoor world of the warming stove.

How does the sonnet's form underline or reinforce these contrasts? The rhyme scheme of the Italian sonnet knits the first eight lines together with only two rhymes: *abbaabba*. The last six lines have new rhymes. Therefore, when you see an Italian sonnet form you can look for some kind of difference in matter or tone between these two groups of lines.

The first eight lines of a sonnet are called the OCTAVE; the last six lines are called the SESTET. The relationship of these two parts defines the structure, or principle of organization, of an Italian sonnet. The poet may go from one part of the subject to another between octave and sestet, as Keats does in "On the Grasshopper and the Cricket." Or the poet may use the octave to present a problem and the sestet to resolve it, as Milton does in the sonnet "When I Consider How My Light Is Spent" (p. 39). Another way poets use the Italian sonnet is to describe a scene in the octave and then use the sestet to comment on what the scene means to them. Wordsworth's sonnet on Westminster Bridge (p. 99) develops in that way, and so does this poem:

DESIGN

I found a dimpled spider, fat and white	*a*
On a white heal-all, holding up a moth	*b*
Like a white piece of rigid satin cloth—	*b*
Assorted characters of death and blight	*a*
Mixed ready to begin the morning right,	*a* 5
Like the ingredients of a witches' broth—	*b*
A snow-drop spider, a flower like a froth,	*b*
And dead wings carried like a paper kite.	*a*
What had that flower to do with being white,	*a*
The wayside blue and innocent heal-all?	*c* 10
What brought the kindred spider to that height,	*a*
Then steered the white moth thither in the night?	*a*
What but design of darkness to appall?	*c*
If design govern in a thing so small.	*c*

1936
Robert Frost (1874–1963)

Frost takes the unusual step of repeating the *a* rhyme of the octave, using it with only one new rhyme (*c*) in the sestet. This is an extraordinary feat because it is already difficult enough to find four *a* rhymes, let alone seven. Why does Frost do it? The metric substitution in line 2 emphasizes *white*—the word so essential to the poem's theme; notice that this word is not only the first *a* rhyme, but also the first repetition of the *a* rhyme in the sestet.

As you read through the following poem, notice how Hopkins' divisions of the lines into groups reflect the movement of the poem:

THE LANTERN OUT OF DOORS

Sometimes a lantern moves along the night,
That interests our eyes. And who goes there?
I think; where from and bound, I wonder, where,
With, all down darkness wide, his wading light?

Men go by me whom either beauty bright   5
In mould or mind or what not else makes rare:
They rain against our much-thick and marsh air
Rich beams, till death or distance buys them quite.

Death or distance soon consumes them: wind
What most I may eye after, be in at the end   10
I cannot, and out of sight is out of mind.

Christ minds; Christ's interest, what to avow or amend
There, eyes them, heart wants, care haunts, foot follows kind,
Their ransom, their rescue, and first, fast, last friend.

composed 1877   1918
Gerard Manley Hopkins (1844–1889)

In the octave the speaker describes his fellow human beings, moving
through the world, going by him with real lanterns or with figurative ones—
"beauty bright," either of body or mind, until they are lost from sight through
"death or distance." The sestet then comments on this passing of fellow creatures. The poet cannot attend to them once death or distance has swallowed
them, but Christ can, and he sees them, "minds" them always.

Smaller divisions within the sonnet help accomplish Hopkins' purpose.
The octave breaks into two quatrains, and they have separate but closely related
subjects: the first quatrain treats the actual sight of lanterns going by and the
poet's curiosity about who is carrying them, while the second is less literal and
more metaphorical, about people who "go by" throughout his life whose "light"
is beauty of spirit or body. The sestet also breaks into divisions. The rhymes
are *cdc dcd*, and each tercet, or group of three lines, has a separate subject: the
first about the poet's inability to follow these lanterns as they are consumed by
death or distance; the second about Christ's ability to do so and his interest.
But the tercets are linked logically (both are about "minding" or paying attention to other people) and linked by rhyme, since they are joined as in *terza
rima*.

The ENGLISH or SHAKESPEAREAN SONNET is an easier form to write in English since it requires no more than two rhyme words for any single rhyme. It
rhymes *abab cdcd efef gg*. Shakespeare did not introduce this form; it is named
for him because he is its most famous practitioner, having used it for more
than 150 poems in his SONNET SEQUENCE—a series of sonnets on similar themes
and sometimes addressed to the same person.

Here is an example of a Shakespearean sonnet. The rhymes give some
indication of the way such a sonnet is structured:

---

mould: body. **wind . . . after:** no matter how much I try to look for them.

THAT TIME OF YEAR THOU MAYST IN ME BEHOLD

That time of year thou mayst in me behold
When yellow leaves, or none, or few, do hang
Upon those boughs which shake against the cold,
Bare ruined choirs, where late the sweet birds sang.
In me thou see'st the twilight of such day   5
As after sunset fadeth in the west;
Which by and by black night doth take away,
Death's second self, that seals up all in rest.
In me thou see'st the glowing of such fire,
That on the ashes of his youth doth lie,   10
As the deathbed whereon it must expire,
Consumed with that which it was nourished by.
This thou perceiv'st, which makes thy love more strong,
To love that well which thou must leave ere long.

1609
William Shakespeare (1564–1616)

One way of seeing the structure of this poem more clearly, aside from looking
at the rhymes, is to look at those points in the poem when the speaker addresses
his hearer/reader directly: those lines in which "thou" is used. At every four
lines there is a similar line: "That time of year thou may'st in me behold," "In
me thou see'st," "In me thou see'st," "This thou perceiv'st." Each four-line
group begins with the speaker saying, "You can see this in me," and the *this*
in each case is a comparison for a time of life: winter, twilight, a dying fire.
The last two lines differ. In them the speaker gives a kind of "moral" of the
story: since I am getting older and will not be around much longer, that makes
your love stronger. As the following diagram shows, the thought-structure of
the poem follows the same groupings as the rhyme, organizing itself into three
quatrains and a concluding couplet that sums up and comments on the previous twelve lines.

first quatrain *compares writ-* *er's time of life* *to winter*	That time of year thou mayst in me behold	*a*	1
	When yellow leaves, or none, or few, do hang	*b*	2
	Upon those boughs which shake against the cold,	*a*	3
	Bare ruined choirs, where late the sweet birds sang.	*b*	4
second quatrain *compares writ-* *er's time of life* *to evening*	In me thou see'st the twilight of such day	*c*	5
	As after sunset fadeth in the west;	*d*	6
	Which by and by black night doth take away,	*c*	7
	Death's second self, that seals up all in rest.	*d*	8

third quatrain compares writer's time of life to dying fire	In me thou see'st the glowing of such fire,	*e* 9
	That on the ashes of his youth doth lie,	*f* 10
	As the deathbed whereon it must expire,	*e* 11
	Consumed with that which it was nourished by.	*f** 12

* Note the separate rhymes in each quatrain, but all twelve lines have same subject: writer's time of life.

major break between first twelve and last two lines

The couplet comments on or draws a moral from the subject of the first twelve lines.	This thou perceiv'st, which makes thy love more strong,	*g* 13
	To love that well which thou must leave ere long.	*g* 14

Edmund Spenser introduced another variation of the sonnet in his sonnet sequence *Amoretti*. The SPENSERIAN SONNET is more like the Shakespearean than the Italian in structure, but as difficult as the Italian, since there are four *b* and *c* rhymes: *abab bcbc cdcd ee*. In Spenser's version the three quatrains are more closely tied together:

ONE DAY I WROTE HER NAME UPON THE STRAND

One day I wrote her name upon the strand,
But came the waves and washed it away:
Again I wrote it with a second hand,
But came the tide, and made my pains his prey.
"Vain man," said she, "that dost in vain essay,   5
A mortal thing so to immortalize,
For I my self shall like to this decay,
And eek my name be wiped out likewise."
"Not so," quod I, "let baser things devise
To die in dust, but you shall live by fame: 10
My verse your virtues rare shall eternize,
And in the heavens write your glorious name.
Where whenas death shall all the world subdue,
Our love shall live, and later life renew."

1595
Edmund Spenser (c.1552–1599)

The three quatrains are unified by rhyme and subject: they narrate a conversation between the two lovers. But as the following diagram shows, they are

**One Day I Wrote Her Name
upon the Strand**

separate in that the first quatrain relates his action, the second her comment, and the third his reply. The sonnet concludes with a summarizing and generalizing couplet, as does the Shakespearean sonnet.

first quatrain describes his attempt and its failure	One day I wrote her name upon the strand,	a	1
	But came the waves and washéd it away:	b	2
	Again I wrote it with a second hand,	a	3
	But came the tide, and made my pains his prey.	b	4
second quatrain contains her response to the vanity of the attempt	"Vain man," said she, "that dost in vain essay,	b	5
	A mortal thing so to immortalize,	c	6
	For I my self shall like to this decay,	b	7
	And eek my name be wipéd out likewise."	c	8
third quatrain: his denial of the vanity of the attempt	"Not so," quod I, "let baser things devise	c	9
	To die in dust, but you shall live by fame:	d	10
	My verse your virtues rare shall eternize,	c	11
	And in the heavens write your glorious name.	d*	12

* Note the twelve lines have close connection and the
quatrains are linked by continuous rhymes.

break as in Shakespearean sonnet

The couplet works as in Shakespearean sonnet.	Where whenas death shall all the world subdue,	e	13
	Our love shall live, and later life renew."	e	14

Blank Verse

Besides the sonnet, one other fixed form deserves its own section—BLANK VERSE, which is unrhymed iambic pentameter. Although not so colloquial as free verse, it is the fixed form that best approximates ordinary speech in its rhythms and length of utterances. Like rhymed verse, blank verse can be either end-stopped or enjambed. Because of its closeness to speech patterns, blank verse is a common medium for dramatic poetry, and the serious plays of Shakespeare are mostly in this form. Blank verse, as an influential form in English poetry, was introduced by Henry Howard, Earl of Surrey (1517–1547) in his translation of Virgil's Latin epic poem *The Aeneid*. The appropriateness of blank verse to the serious purpose of epic poetry was most successfully proven by John Milton's *Paradise Lost* (1667) and William Wordsworth's *The Prelude* (1850).

But blank verse is very adaptable to the individual voice of the poet and to many different moods and tones. It can handle the fervor of young romance and the melancholy of mature reflection:

Shapes and Forms

from ROMEO AND JULIET

It is my lady; O it is my love!
O that she knew she were!
She speaks, yet she says nothing. What of that?
Her eye discourses; I will answer it.
I am too bold; 'tis not to me she speaks.   5
Two of the fairest stars in all the heaven,
Having some business, do entreat her eyes
To twinkle in their spheres till they return.
What if her eyes were there, they in her head?
The brightness of her cheek would shame those stars   10
As daylight doth a lamp; her eyes in heaven
Would through the airy region stream so bright
That birds would sing and think it were not night.

(II, i, 10–22)

1599

William Shakespeare (1564–1616)

TEARS, IDLE TEARS

Tears, idle tears, I know not what they mean,
Tears from the depth of some divine despair
Rise in the heart, and gather to the eyes,
In looking on the happy autumn-fields,
And thinking of the days that are no more.   5

Fresh as the first beam glittering on a sail,
That brings our friends up from the underworld,
Sad as the last which reddens over one
That sinks with all we love below the verge;
So sad, so fresh, the days that are no more.   10

Ah, sad and strange as in dark summer dawns
The earliest pipe of half-awakened birds
To dying ears, when unto dying eyes
The casement slowly grows a glimmering square;
So sad, so strange, the days that are no more.   15

Dear as remembered kisses after death,
And sweet as those by hopeless fancy feigned

On lips that are for others; deep as love,
Deep as first love, and wild with all regret;
O Death in Life, the days that are no more!   20

1847

Alfred, Lord Tennyson (1809–1892)

Blank verse's ability to accommodate the rhythms of colloquial speech is illustrated by Frost's use of it in the following poem:

MENDING WALL

Something there is that doesn't love a wall,
That sends the frozen-ground-swell under it
And spills the upper boulders in the sun,
And makes gaps even two can pass abreast.
The work of hunters is another thing: 5
I have come after them and made repair
Where they have left not one stone on a stone,
But they would have the rabbit out of hiding,
To please the yelping dogs. The gaps I mean,
No one has seen them made or heard them made,   10
But at spring mending-time we find them there.
I let my neighbor know beyond the hill;
And on a day we meet to walk the line
And set the wall between us once again.
We keep the wall between us as we go.   15
To each the boulders that have fallen to each.
And some are loaves and some so nearly balls
We have to use a spell to make them balance:
"Stay where you are until our backs are turned!"
We wear our fingers rough with handling them.   20
Oh, just another kind of outdoor game,
One on a side. It comes to little more:
There where it is we do not need the wall:
He is all pine and I am apple orchard.
My apple trees will never get across   25
And eat the cones under his pines, I tell him.
He only says, "Good fences make good neighbors."
Spring is the mischief in me, and I wonder

If I could put a notion in his head:
"*Why* do they make good neighbors? Isn't it   30
Where there are cows? But here there are no cows.
Before I built a wall I'd ask to know
What I was walling in or walling out,
And to whom I was like to give offense.
Something there is that doesn't love a wall,   35
That wants it down." I could say, "Elves" to him,
But it's not elves exactly, and I'd rather
He said it for himself. I see him there,
Bringing a stone grasped firmly by the top
In each hand, like an old-stone savage armed.   40
He moves in darkness as it seems to me,
Not of woods only and the shade of trees.
He will not go behind his father's saying,
And he likes having thought of it so well
He says again, "Good fences make good neighbors."   45

1914
Robert Frost (1874–1963)

    To sum up, asking questions about the external shapes and the line group-
ings of a poem can lead us directly to its internal structure and to its meaning.
The shape and its relation to meaning may be obvious, but when it is not, we
need to look more closely at how rhyme links and separates parts of a poem,
how fixed forms are appropriate for particular kinds of themes and develop-
ments of thought, and how blank verse can be adapted to suit different poetic
purposes.

EXERCISES_____

A.   **HOW EVERYTHING HAPPENS**
            (Based on a Study of the Wave)

```
                                              happen.
                                          to
                                        up
                                  stacking
                               is
                        something
       When nothing is happening

       When it happens
                     something
                           pulls
                                back
                                 not
                                  to
                                     happen.

       When                          has happened.
           pulling back      stacking up
                      happens

                has happened                        stacks up.
       When it              something           nothing
                              pulls back while


       Then nothing is happening.


                                     happens.
                                  and
                             forward
                          pushes
                        up
                     stacks
             something
       Then
```

                                    1970
                        May Swenson (b. 1919)

1. How does Swenson translate the wave's three dimensions into two dimensions on the page?
2. How does the phrase "stacking up" connect the wave's motion with what Swenson is doing in the poem?
3. What line marks the point where the wave is at its quietest point? How does the appearance of the line indicate this?
4. If you were asked to number the lines of this poem, how would you do so? Give a reason for your answer.

B. Reread Blake's "The Tyger" (Chapter 1) and answer the following questions:

1. The poem has a form that seems simple—it is in couplets. Why are the pairs of couplets grouped into quatrains?
2. What is the effect of the broken sentences in the two middle stanzas, surrounded by two stanzas of complete questions?
3. Notice the beginning and ending stanzas are nearly, but not exactly, the same. What is the effect of the REFRAIN (a repeated line or group of lines; in songs, the refrain is called a CHORUS) of the repeated stanzas? What is changed by the difference between "Could" and "Dare"?
4. Notice this poem is entirely composed of questions. What is the effect of these questions? How do they imply or assert some answers?

C.   **PARADISE**

I bless thee, Lord, because I GROW
Among thy trees, which in a ROW
To thee both fruit and order OW.

What open force, or hidden CHARM
Can blast my fruit, or bring me HARM   5
While the inclosure is thine ARM?

Inclose me still for fear I START.
Be to me rather sharp and TART,
Then let me want thy hand and ART.

When thou dost greater judgments SPARE,   10
And with thy knife but prune and PARE,
Ev'n fruitful trees more fruitful ARE.

Such sharpness shows the sweetest FRIEND:
Such cuttings rather heal than REND:
And such beginnings touch their END.   15

1633
George Herbert (1593–1633)

1. Do Herbert's comments about *order* and *a row* apply only to trees in the first triplet? To what else might they apply?
2. How do the rhyme words in each triplet apply to what the lines are saying?

D. Petrarch's construction of the sonnet and his subject matter—idealized love—were influential on English poetry. Here is a sonnet from Petrarch's sequence of love-lyrics (number 190 from the *Rime Sparse*) addressed to Laura, followed first by a prose translation by Robert M. Durling, then by Thomas Wyatt's English version of the same poem, and finally by Edmund Spenser's version from his sonnet sequence *Amoretti:*

UNA CANDIDA CERVA SOPRA L'ERBA

Una candida cerva sopra l'erba
verde m'apparve con duo corna d'oro,
fra due riviere all'ombra d'un alloro,
levando 'l sole a la stagione acerba.

Era sua vista sì dolce superba   5
ch' i'lasciai per seguirla ogni lavoro,
come l'avaro che 'n cercar tesoro
con diletto l'affanno disacerba.

"Nessun mi tocchi," al bel collo d'intorno
scritto avea di diamanti et di topazi.   10
"Libera farmi al mio Cesare parve."

Et era 'l sol già vòlto al mezzo giorno,
gli occhi miei stanchi di mirar, non sazi,
quand' io caddi ne l'acqua et ella sparve.

composed about 1327
Francesco Petrarca (1304–1374)

A white doe on the green grass appeared to me, with two golden horns, between two rivers, in the shade of a laurel, when the sun was rising in the unripe season.

Her look was so sweet and proud that to follow her I left every task, like the miser who as he seeks treasure sweetens his trouble with delight.

"Let no one touch me," she bore written with diamonds and topazes around her lovely neck. "It has pleased my Caesar to make me free."

And the sun had already turned at midday; my eyes were tired by looking but not sated, when I fell into the water, and she disappeared.

WHOSO LIST TO HUNT

Whoso list to hunt, I know where is an hind,
   But as for me, alas, I may no more,
   The vain travail hath wearied me so sore,
  I am of them that furthest come behind.
Yet may I by no means my wearied mind   5
   Draw from the deer, but as she fleeth afore
   Fainting I follow; I leave off therefore,
  Since in a net I seek to hold the wind.
Who list her hunt, I put him out of doubt,
   As well as I, may spend his time in vain.   10
   And graven with diamonds in letters plain,
There is written her fair neck round about,
   "*Noli me tangere*, for Caesar's I am,
   And wild for to hold, though I seem tame."

composed about 1534

        Sir Thomas Wyatt (1503–1542)

LYKE AS A HUNTSMAN AFTER WEARY CHACE

Lyke as a huntsman after weary chace,
   Seeing the game from him escapt away,

"Let no one touch me": Caesar freed stags and put collars on them inscribed "*Noli me tangere. Caesaris sum*" ("Do not touch me, I am Caesar's").

•

Sits downe to rest him in some shady place,
  With panting hounds beguiléd of their pray:
So after long pursuit and vaine assay,   5
When I all weary had the chace forsooke,
The gentle deare returnd the selfe-same way,
Thinking to quench her thirst at the next brooke.
There she beholding me with mylder looke,
Sought not to fly, but fearelesse still did bide: 10
Till I in hand her yet halfe trembling tooke,
And with her owne goodwill hir fyrmely tyde.
Strange thing me seemed to see a beast so wyld,
So goodly wonne with her owne will beguyld.

                                              1595
                   Edmund Spenser (c.1552–1599)

1. What is the rhyme scheme of Petrarch's Italian sonnet? How strict is Wyatt in following it?
2. What is the subject in each quatrain of Wyatt's poem? How are these subjects linked from stanza to stanza, and how are they unified in the concluding couplet?
3. What problem is posed in the octave? How is it resolved in the sestet?
4. What contrasts of attitude and tone can be found between Petrarch's version and Wyatt's?
5. What is the sonnet form of Spenser's poem?
6. Compare Spenser's treatment of the problem in the octave and the resolution in the sestet with Wyatt's poem. How do they differ?
7. What is the subject of each of Spenser's quatrains, and how does the concluding couplet unify these subjects?
8. What is the tone of Spenser's poem, and how does it differ from Petrarch's? From Wyatt's?

E.   **GOD'S GRANDEUR**

The world is charged with the grandeur of God.
  It will flame out, like shining from shook foil;
  It gathers to a greatness, like the ooze of oil
Crushed. Why do men then now not reck his rod?
Generations have trod, have trod, have trod;   5
  And all is seared with trade; bleared, smeared with toil;
  And wears man's smudge and shares man's smell: the soil
Is bare now, nor can foot feel, being shod.
And for all this, nature is never spent;
  There lives the dearest freshness deep down things;   10

And though the last lights off the black West went
  Oh, morning, at the brown brink eastward, springs—
Because the Holy Ghost over the bent
  World broods with warm breast and with ah! bright wings.

composed 1877   1918
                              Gerard Manley Hopkins (1844–1889)

1. What is the form of "God's Grandeur"?
2. What is stated in the first quatrain? How does the second quatrain compli-
   cate or develop these first lines?
3. What problem does Hopkins pose in the octave? Is this problem resolved
   in the sestet?

F.   **THE SILKEN TENT**

          She is as in a field a silken tent
          At midday when a sunny summer breeze
          Has dried the dew and all its ropes relent,
          So that in guys it gently sways at ease,
          And its supporting central cedar pole,   5
          That is its pinnacle to heavenward
          And signifies the sureness of the soul,
          Seems to owe naught to any single cord,
          But strictly held by none, is loosely bound
          By countless silken ties of love and thought   10
          To everything on earth the compass round,
          And only by one's going slightly taut
          In the capriciousness of summer air
          Is of the slightest bondage made aware.

                                           1942
                              Robert Frost (1874–1963)

1. Which of the traditional sonnet forms is Frost working with in "The Silken
   Tent"?
2. What does the pattern of alliteration in this poem, especially that on the *s*
   sound, do to reinforce the poem's meaning? Look at the following phrases,
   for instance: "sunny summer," "sways at ease," "supporting central cedar,"
   "signifies the sureness of the soul," "countless silken ties," "capriciousness
   of summer."
3. Notice that the poem has several *internal* rhymes: *naught/taut*,
   guys/signifies/ties. How do these rhymes reinforce meaning (that is, do they
   support the poem in any way)?

G.   *from* **THE PRELUDE**

One summer evening (led by her) I found
A little boat tied to a willow tree
Within a rocky cave, its usual home.
Straight I unloosed her chain, and stepping in
Pushed from the shore. It was an act of stealth   5
And troubled pleasure, nor without the voice
Of mountain-echoes did my boat move on;
Leaving behind her still, on either side,
Small circles glittering idly in the moon,
Until they melted all into one track   10
Of sparkling light. But now, like one who rows,
Proud of his skill, to reach a chosen point
With an unswerving line, I fixed my view
Upon the summit of a craggy ridge,
The horizon's utmost boundary; for above   15
Was nothing but the stars and the grey sky.
She was an elfin pinnace; lustily
I dipped my oars into the silent lake,
And, as I rose upon the stroke, my boat
Went heaving through the water like a swan;   20
When, from behind that craggy steep till then
The horizon's bound, a huge peak, black and huge,
As if with voluntary power instinct
Upreared its head. I struck and struck again,
And growing still in stature the grim shape   25
Towered up between me and the stars, and still,
For so it seemed, with purpose of its own
And measured motion like a living thing,
Strode after me. With trembling oars I turned,
And through the silent water stole my way   30
Back to the covert of the willow tree;
There in her mooring-place I left my bark,—
And through the meadows homeward went, in grave
And serious mood; but after I had seen
That spectacle, for many days, my brain   35
Worked with a dim and undetermined sense
Of unknown modes of being; o'er my thoughts

---

led by her: led by Nature.

There hung a darkness, call it solitude
Or blank desertion. No familiar shapes
Remained, no pleasant images of trees,   40
Of sea or sky, no colours of green fields;
But huge and mighty forms, that do not live
Like living men, moved slowly through the mind
By day, and were a trouble to my dreams.

(I, 357–400)

composed 1799–1805   1850

William Wordsworth (1770–1850)

1. What is the form of this passage?
2. Wordsworth said in his Preface to the *Lyrical Ballads* (1798), which he wrote together with Coleridge, that the language in a good poem was the same as in prose:

> And it would be a most easy task to prove . . . that not only the language of a large portion of every good poem, even of the most elevated character, must necessarily, except with reference to the metre, in no respect differ from that of good prose, but likewise that some of the most interesting parts of the best poems will be found to be strictly the language of prose when prose is well written.

To what extent does this passage from *The Prelude* follow Wordsworth's comments about the language of a good poem? How closely does this passage approximate prose, or seem to? Keep in mind the effects of enjambment in creating this effect. Look at the syntax of sentences to see when Wordsworth uses inversions of normal word order—how often does this occur? How often does Wordsworth use periphrasis or "poetic" language?

WRITING SUGGESTIONS

1. Choose either Cummings' "next to of course god america i" (Exercise N in Chapter 1) or George Barker's "To My Mother" in Poems for Further Reading. Write an essay that identifies the form of the poem, points out any variations or departures from this form, and gives the author's possible reasons for these changes.
2. In the manuscript, the original title of Frost's "The Silken Tent" (Exercise F) was "In Praise of Her Poise." In an essay, explain how the idea of *poise* is expressed through the form of the poem—its organization, imagery, rhyme scheme, and sentence structure.

CHAPTER TEN

ARGUMENT AND ASSOCIATION

Poems are not organized only by line lengths, rhymes, and groupings of sound. If a poem were nothing but formally arranged sound, it would be music. If it were only formally arranged figures of black and white, it would be graphic art. But a poem is a pattern of *meaning* as well as one of sound and appearance on the page. Its sequence of thought can give it structure. Sometimes the sequence is purely that of events in time: first A happened; then B happened. Sometimes cause is added: B happened *because* A happened. Events might be simultaneous but *described* in sequence: A happened while B was going on:

A PRIMER OF THE DAILY ROUND

A peels an apple, while B kneels to God,
C telephones to D, who has a hand
On E's knee, F coughs, G turns up the sod
For H's grave, I do not understand
But J is bringing one clay pigeon down   5
While K brings down a nightstick on L's head,
And M takes mustard, N drives into town,
O goes to bed with P, and Q drops dead,
R lies to S, but happens to be heard
By T, who tells U not to fire V   10
For having to give W the word
That X is now deceiving Y with Z,

Who happens just now to remember A
Peeling an apple somewhere far away.

1958
Howard Nemerov (b. 1920)

Nemerov's sonnet illustrates other logical sequences: since H has died, H must be buried, and therefore G turns up the sod for the grave. Often a poem proceeds by association, and Nemerov illustrates this as well:

But J is bringing one clay pigeon down
While K brings down a nightstick on L's head.

J and K are acting simultaneously, but often such a description of two things or events occurs in a poem not because of any simultaneity or sequence or logical connection, but simply because the poet's mind perceives a resemblance and thus associates the two.

Such thought patterns in poems may be supported and reinforced by the fixed forms discussed in the last chapter, and Nemerov's poem is an excellent example. But the developing order of thoughts may give its own form—often called OPEN FORM—to the poem. In either case the reader needs to grasp the movement of thought in the poem. How do we do this? How do we figure out the thought sequence and find the key to structure?

ARGUMENT AND FORM

If the poem is in a fixed form, that form can provide our starting clues:

WHEN I HAVE FEARS

When I have fears that I may cease to be
   Before my pen has gleaned my teeming brain,
Before high-piled books, in charact'ry,
   Hold like rich garners the full-ripened grain;
When I behold, upon the night's starred face,   5
   Huge cloudy symbols of a high romance,
And think that I may never live to trace
   Their shadows, with the magic hand of chance;

---

charact'ry: characters, that is, letters of the alphabet. **unreflecting:** untroubled by either introspection or self-consciousness.

And when I feel, fair creature of an hour,
   That I shall never look upon thee more,   10
Never have relish in the faery power
   Of unreflecting love!—then on the shore
Of the wide world I stand alone, and think
   Till Love and Fame to nothingness do sink.

composed 1818   1848

John Keats (1795–1821)

The structure of this Shakespearean sonnet provides clues to its sequence of thought. Each of the three quatrains deals with a different fear. Each describes something the poet is afraid he will fail to do before he dies—"cease to be": getting his brain's contents into books, experiencing enough of chance and high romance, spending enough time with fleeting, "unreflecting" love. And when he has such fears, then he "stands alone" and thinks until "Love and Fame" no longer matter—this last thought is in the concluding two-and-one-half lines of the poem. The three quatrains express the fears, and the couplet explains what happens when he has them:

> *When* I have fears . . .
> *Then* on the shore . . . I stand
> Till Love and Fame to nothingness do sink.

The sequence of thought, which matches the formal parts of the sonnet, is this development of a fear and its consequences: *When* I think about dying, *then* love and fame become much less important.

    The thought sequence *When/Then*, which we have just seen used in a Shakespearean sonnet, also fits the two-part structure of the Italian sonnet—perhaps even better. Milton uses it in "When I Consider How My Light Is Spent," for example. But the same logical structure will be found in poems that are not sonnets or any other fixed form. The beginning of Philip Appleman's "October Spring" is an example:

> When crisp catalpa leaves
> come tumbling down the frosty morning air
> like tarpaulins for tulips.
> [then] it's spring again in little college towns.

Here, the time cue "when" is our first clue to the sequence of thought, and we can supply the "then."

    The *When/Then* sequence gives structure to both the following poems, but as in Appleman's poem above, the *Then* is understood rather than written:

Argument and Association

O MOON

O Moon, when I gaze on thy beautiful face,
Careering along through the boundaries of space,
The thought has often come into my mind
If I ever shall see thy glorious behind.

1911
Sir Edmund Gosse (1849–1928)

WHEN I HEARD THE LEARN'D ASTRONOMER

When I heard the learn'd astronomer,
When the proofs, the figures, were ranged in columns before me,
When I was shown the charts and diagrams, to add, divide, and
    measure them,
When I sitting heard the astronomer where he lectured with much
    applause in the lecture-room,
How soon unaccountable I became tired and sick,   5
Till rising and gliding out I wander'd off by myself,
In the mystical moist night air, and from time to time,
Look'd up in perfect silence at the stars.

1865
Walt Whitman (1819–1892)

Whitman makes the structure slightly more complex in this poem (italics added):

WHEN I PERUSE THE CONQUER'D FAME

When I peruse the conquer'd fame of heroes and the victories of
    mighty generals, I do not envy the generals,
Nor the President in his Presidency, nor the rich in his great house,
But when I hear of the brotherhood of lovers, how it was with them,
How together through life, through dangers, odium, unchanging,
    long and long,
Through youth and through middle and old age, how unfaltering,   5
    how affectionate and faithful they were,
Then I am pensive—I hastily walk away fill'd with the bitterest envy.

1860
Walt Whitman (1819–1892)

Looking for key words such as "when" and "then" can be very helpful in following the poem's sequence of thoughts, and therefore in seeing its structure.

Another important clue to structure can be paragraph division:

TO HIS COY MISTRESS

Had we but world enough, and time,
This coyness, lady, were no crime.
We would sit down, and think which way
To walk and pass our long love's day.
Thou by the Indian Ganges' side   5
Shouldst rubies find; I by the tide
Of Humber would complain. I would
Love you ten years before the Flood,
And you should, if you please, refuse
Till the conversion of the Jews.   10
My vegetable love should grow
Vaster than empires, and more slow;
An hundred years should go to praise
Thine eyes, and on thy forehead gaze;
Two hundred to adore each breast,   15
But thirty thousand to the rest;
An age at least to every part,
And the last age should show your heart.
For, lady, you deserve this state,
Nor would I love at lower rate.   20
   But at my back I always hear
Time's wingéd chariot hurrying near;
And yonder all before us lie
Deserts of vast eternity.
Thy beauty shall no more be found,   25
Nor, in thy marble vault, shall sound
My echoing song; then worms shall try
That long-preserved virginity,
And your quaint honor turn to dust,
And into ashes all my lust: 30

---

coy: hesitant; reluctant. **Humber:** a river in Northern England. **conversion of the Jews:** an event that in Christian tradition will not take place until the end of the world. **vegetable:** slow-growing. **state:** treatment.

The grave's a fine and private place,
But none, I think, do there embrace.
    Now therefore, while the youthful hue
Sits on thy skin like morning dew,
And while thy willing soul transpires   35
At every pore with instant fires,
Now let us sport us while we may;
And now, like amorous birds of prey,
Rather at once our time devour
Than languish in his slow-chapped power.   40
Let us roll all our strength and all
Our sweetness up into one ball,
And tear our pleasures with rough strife
Through the iron gates of life.
Thus, though we cannot make our sun   45
Stand still, yet we will make him run.

1681
Andrew Marvell (1621–1678)

The three paragraphs of the poem reveal themselves to be three parts of an argument:

line 1   *Had we but time* [that is, if we only had enough time]

line 3   *We would* [love slowly]

line 21   *But* [we don't have time]

line 33   *Now therefore* [let us love now, quickly]

PATTERNS OF ASSOCIATION

But structure is not always marked by time cues and paragraph divisions. We saw when discussing James Dickey's "The Lifeguard" (Chapter 5) how a state of mind—the lifeguard's chagrin at failing to save the drowning child—could generate a whole train of imagined or hallucinated images. Many poems work on a similar basis of *association:* in the following examples, the speaker begins with one thought—what would happen if he married—and what follows is a number of scenes or images, all of which are associated in his head with the idea of marriage:

---

slow-chapped: slow-jawed.

MARRIAGE

Should I get married? Should I be good?
Astound the girl next door with my velvet suit and faustus hood?
Don't take her to movies but to cemeteries
tell all about werewolf bathtubs and forked clarinets
then desire her and kiss her and all the preliminaries   5
and she going just so far and I understanding why
not getting angry saying You must feel! It's beautiful to feel!
Instead take her in my arms lean against an old crooked tombstone
and woo her the entire night the constellations in the sky—

When she introduces me to her parents   10
back straightened, hair finally combed, strangled by a tie,
should I sit knees together on their 3rd degree sofa
and not ask Where's the bathroom?
How else to feel other than I am,
often thinking Flash Gordon soap—   15
O how terrible it must be for a young man
seated before a family and the family thinking
We never saw him before! He wants our Mary Lou!
After tea and homemade cookies they ask What do you do for
   a living?
Should I tell them? Would they like me then?   20
Say All right get married, we're losing a daughter
but we're gaining a son—
And should I then ask Where's the bathroom?

O God, and the wedding! All her family and her friends
and only a handful of mine all scroungy and bearded   25
just wait to get at the drinks and food—
And the priest! he looking at me as if I masturbated
asking me Do you take this woman for your lawful wedded wife?
And I trembling what to say say Pie Glue!
I kiss the bride all those corny men slapping me on the back   30
She's all yours, boy! Ha-ha-ha!
And in their eyes you could see some obscene honeymoon
   going on—

---

faustus hood: such as that worn by the title character, a scholar, in Christopher Marlowe's play
Doctor Faustus (1604).

Then all that absurd rice and clanky cans and shoes
Niagara Falls! Hordes of us! Husbands! Wives! Flowers! Chocolates!
All streaming into cozy hotels   35
All going to do the same thing tonight
The indifferent clerk he knowing what was going to happen
The lobby zombies they knowing what
The whistling elevator man he knowing
The winking bellboy knowing   40
Everybody knowing! I'd be almost inclined not to do anything!
Stay up all night! Stare that hotel clerk in the eye!
Screaming: I deny honeymoon! I deny honeymoon!
running rampant into those almost climactic suites
yelling Radio belly! Cat shovel!   45
O I'd live in Niagara forever! in a dark cave beneath the Falls
I'd sit there the Mad Honeymooner
devising ways to break marriages, a scourge of bigamy
a saint of divorce—

But I should get married I should be good   50
How nice it'd be to come home to her
and sit by the fireplace and she in the kitchen
aproned young and lovely wanting my baby
and so happy about me she burns the roast beef
and comes crying to me and I get up from my big papa chair   55
saying Christmas teeth! Radiant brains! Apple deaf!
God what a husband I'd make! Yes, I should get married!
So much to do! like sneaking into Mr. Jones' house late at night
and cover his golf clubs with 1920 Norwegian books
Like hanging a picture of Rimbaud on the lawnmower   60
like pasting Tannu Tuva postage stamps all over the picket fence
like when Mrs. Kindhead comes to collect for the Community Chest
grab her and tell her There are unfavorable omens in the sky!
And when the mayor comes to get my vote tell him
When are you going to stop people killing whales!   65
And when the milkman comes leave him a note in the bottle
Penguin dust, bring me penguin dust, I want penguin dust—

Yet if I should get married and it's Connecticut and snow
and she gives birth to a child and I am sleepless, worn,

Rimbaud: Arthur Rimbaud (1854–1891), a French poet.

Marriage

up for nights, head bowed against a quiet window, the past   70
   behind me
finding myself in the most common of situations a trembling man
knowledged with responsibility not twig-smear nor Roman
   coin soup—
O what would that be like!
Surely I'd give it for a nipple a rubber Tacitus
For a rattle a bag of broken Bach records   75
Tack Della Francesca all over its crib
Sew the Greek alphabet on its bib
And build for its playpen a roofless Parthenon

No, I doubt I'd be that kind of father
not rural not snow no quiet window   80
but hot smelly tight New York City
seven flights up roaches and rats in the walls
a fat Reichian wife screeching over potatoes Get a job!
And five nose running brats in love with Batman
And the neighbors all toothless and dry haired   85
like those hag masses of the 18th century
all wanting to come in and watch TV
The landlord wants his rent
Grocery store Blue Cross Gas & Electric Knights of Columbus
Impossible to lie back and dream Telephone snow, ghost parking—   90
No! I should not get married I should never get married!
But—imagine if I were married to a beautiful sophisticated woman
tall and pale wearing an elegant black dress and long black gloves
holding a cigarette holder in one hand and a highball in the other
and we lived high up in a penthouse with a huge window   95
from which we could see all of New York and ever farther on clearer
   days
No, can't imagine myself married to that pleasant prison dream—

O but what about love? I forget love
not that I am incapable of love
it's just that I see love as odd as wearing shoes—   100
I never wanted to marry a girl who was like my mother
And Ingrid Bergman was always impossible

Tacitus: Cornelius Tacitus (57?–117), a Roman historian. **Della Francesca:** Piero della Francesca (1420?–1492), an Italian Renaissance painter.

And there's maybe a girl now but she's already married
And I don't like men and—
but there's got to be somebody!   105
Because what if I'm 60 years old and not married,
all alone in a furnished room with pee stains on my underwear
and everybody else is married! All the universe married but me!

Ah, yet well I know that were a woman possible as I am possible
then marriage would be possible—   110
Like SHE in her lonely alien gaud waiting her Egyptian lover
so I wait—bereft of 2,000 years and the bath of life.

1960
Gregory Corso (b. 1930)

Corso works with two sets of associated thoughts in the poem. One set is composed mostly of comically stereotypical views of marriage derived from various sources, some of them popular and others more limited, such as Wilheim Reich (1897–1957), a psychiatrist who wrote on personal relationships and who is obliquely referred to in line 83. The other set of thoughts pictures the speaker doing, saying, and thinking various outrageous things such as replying "Pie Glue!" instead of "I do" to the priest's question at the wedding. These humorous idiosyncrasies make a contrast to the marriage scenes; they are at once more real—because they express something about the speaker's own unique personality—and symbolic of his wish for freedom, for avoiding the constricting scenarios he imagines marriage to be.

Sometimes the process of thought is governed by a single controlling image—often expressed in a metaphor or simile—that generates all the other associated images in the poem:

A VALEDICTION: FORBIDDING MOURNING

As virtuous men pass mildly away,
    And whisper to their souls to go,
While some of their sad friends do say,
    The breath goes now, and some say, no:

So let us melt, and make no noise,   5
    No tear-floods, nor sigh-tempests move,

Marriage   She: the name of a novel (1887) by H. Rider Haggard; its heroine becomes ageless by bathing in flame, then waits thousands of years for her Egyptian lover to return.

A Valediction: saying farewell.

A Valediction: Forbidding Mourning

'Twere profanation of our joys
   To tell the laity our love.

Moving of th' earth brings harms and fears,
   Men reckon what it did and meant,   10
But trepidation of the spheres,
   Though greater far, is innocent.

Dull sublunary lovers' love
   (Whose soul is sense) cannot admit
Absence, because it doth remove   15
   Those things which elemented it.

But we by a love so much refined,
   That ourselves know not what it is,
Inter-assuréd of the mind,
   Care less, eyes, lips, and hands to miss.   20

Our two souls therefore, which are one,
   Though I must go, endure not yet
A breach, but an expansion,
   Like gold to airy thinness beat.

If they be two, they are two so   25
   As stiff twin compasses are two;
Thy soul, the fixed foot, makes no show
   To move, but doth, if th' other do.

And though it in the center sit,
   Yet when the other far doth roam,   30
It leans, and hearkens after it,
   And grows erect, as that comes home.

Such wilt thou be to me, who must
   Like th' other foot, obliquely run;
Thy firmness makes my circle just,   35
   And makes me end, where I begun.

1633
John Donne (1572–1631)

---

laity: those who are not clergy; Donne is making the love of the two people in the poem a kind of religious order. **trepidation of the spheres:** movement of the spheres thought to contain the planets and stars. **sublunary:** earthly, underneath the moon. **elemented:** composed.

Argument and Association

The speaker urges his beloved not to mourn their temporary leavetaking, and he uses an argument rooted in a controlling simile:

> As virtuous men pass mildly away,
>   And whisper to their souls to go,
> While some of their sad friends do say,
>   The breath goes now, and some say, no:
>
> So let us melt. . . .

Here is an argument based on a series of associations which emerge out of a single comparison. The speaker, in the first comparison, argues that the two lovers should take their leave of each other without making a fuss, just as "virtuous men" take leave of their souls—mildly, with no fear or hesitation—while friends ignorant of this inner calm foolishly debate whether the dying still breathe, an issue of no real importance to truly virtuous souls.

This comparison of the parting of the two lovers to the parting of the body and the virtuous soul (in contrast to the fuss made by the ignorant observers) is continued by an association in the next stanza:

> So let us melt, and make no noise,
>   No tear-floods, nor sigh-tempests move
> 'Twere profanation of our joys
>   To tell the laity our love.

Donne suggests that their love is like a religious order, an idea associated with the virtuous men in the first stanza. It would be profane to tell the laity of their love. The reference to laity also connects to the ignorant observers in stanza 1. This contrast of the religious and the laity is continued in stanza 3 where the heavenly spheres and the earthly sphere are contrasted. Then, developing this point in stanza 4, Donne suggests that their love is more refined than that of mere earthly lovers. Their love does not depend on material things and therefore can survive the absence of the other lover's body, as virtuous men can take untroubled leave of their souls. The unity of the lovers' souls is developed in that section of the poem comparing their souls first to beaten gold and then to drafting compasses. These images, too, emerge out of the initial simile: the lovers' parting from each other, like the virtuous parting with their souls, is no real separation.

The following poem is a more modern example of the subtle use of argument and association we saw in Donne:

PETER QUINCE AT THE CLAVIER

1

Just as my fingers on these keys
Make music, so the selfsame sounds
On my spirit make a music, too.

Music is feeling, then, not sound;
And thus it is that what I feel,   5
Here in this room, desiring you,

Thinking of your blue-shadowed silk,
Is music. It is like the strain
Waked in the elders by Susanna.

Of a green evening, clear and warm,   10
She bathed in her still garden, while
The red-eyed elders watching, felt

The basses of their beings throb
In witching chords, and their thin blood
Pulse pizzicati of Hosanna.   15

2

In the green water, clear and warm,
Susanna lay.
She searched
The touch of springs,
And found   20
Concealed imaginings.
She sighed,
For so much melody.

Peter Quince: a comic character in Shakespeare's A *Midsummer Night's Dream*. **clavier:** any keyboard instrument. **the elders, Susanna:** In one of the books of Daniel not usually included in the Old Testament, Susanna, the beautiful wife of a rich Babylonian, bathes every day in her locked garden. Two elders—older men of influence in the city—hide themselves in the garden, see her bathing, and demand that she either yield to them or be accused of adultery with a young man. She refuses them, but is saved from condemnation when Daniel interrogates the elders separately and catches them in conflicting stories. **pizzicati:** sounds made by plucking rather than bowing the strings of a musical instrument.

Upon the bank, she stood
In the cool   25
Of spent emotions.
She felt, among the leaves,
The dew
Of old devotions.

She walked upon the grass,   30
Still quavering.
The winds were like her maids,
On timid feet,
Fetching her woven scarves,
Yet wavering.   35

A breath upon her hand
Muted the night.
She turned—
A cymbal crashed,
And roaring horns.   40

3

Soon, with a noise like tambourines,
Came her attendant Byzantines.

They wondered why Susanna cried
Against the elders by her side;

And as they whispered, the refrain   45
Was like a willow swept by rain.

Anon, their lamps' uplifted flame
Revealed Susanna and her shame.

And then, the simpering Byzantines
Fled, with a noise like tambourines.   50

4

Beauty is momentary in the mind—
The fitful tracing of a portal;
But in the flesh it is immortal.

Peter Quince at the Clavier

The body dies; the body's beauty lives.
So evenings die, in their green going,   55
A wave, interminably flowing.
So gardens die, their meek breath scenting
The cowl of winter, done repenting.
So maidens die, to the auroral
Celebration of a maiden's choral.   60
Susanna's music touched the bawdy strings
Of those white elders; but, escaping,
Left only Death's ironic scraping.
Now, in its immortality, it plays
On the clear viol of her memory,   65
And makes a constant sacrament of praise.

                                          1923
                   Wallace Stevens (1879–1955)

Asking the usual battery of questions yields no answers about time or place at the beginning of this poem, but there is a speaker, who is playing a keyboard instrument of some sort and either talking to or thinking about another person to whom he is attracted ("desiring you. / Thinking of your blue-shadowed silk"). And then the speaker begins to tell the story of Susanna. Why Susanna?

He gets there by association. He starts by saying that just as his fingers on the keys make music, the sound acting on his soul makes music too. This leads to a metaphoric equation of music with feeling: "Music is feeling then, not sound" (line 4). But the speaker then turns his statement around, arguing not that music is feeling, but that feeling is music: "And thus it is that what I feel / . . . is Music" (5, 8). And it is *this* metaphor that he illustrates with the particular example of Susanna and the elders. The poem is working as a kind of argument, in other words, with an example in support of a metaphoric generalization.

But why Susanna and the elders instead of Antony and Cleopatra, Romeo and Juliet, Dido and Aeneas, or Pocahontas and John Smith? What in the speaker's desires resembles that of the elders? When we read through the poem we never get back to the initial situation of the speaker and the woman he desires. Perhaps he never spoke to her about it, never brought it to the question of her agreement or refusal. This might be a sense in which his desire resembles that of the elders: it is unsatisfied. Perhaps it is illicit, as theirs was.

In any case it is the story of Susanna and the elders which the speaker associates with his desire. The desire aroused in the elders by Susanna is a "strain"—a tune, although Stevens is not ignoring the more frequent sense of the word. She makes the "basses" (or *bases*, again a word with other meanings) of their beings play chords, and their very heartbeat a song of praise. Susanna's sense of well-being is "melody." The rest of the poem has many more of these metaphoric equations of feeling with song or sounds of particular musical instruments.

The greatest difficulties come in the last stanza. For one thing, Stevens makes a paradoxical statement about beauty and time:

> Beauty is momentary in the mind . . .
> But in the flesh it is immortal.
> The body dies; the body's beauty lives.

For another, Stevens never seems to return to the original situation in the first eight lines of the poem. Susanna's story is concluded, extending the metaphor which has been the poem's main theme: Susanna's beauty is seen as music which could not be played on the "bawdy strings" of the elders, who are seen as instruments. Her music escapes them. The sound they make is only that of their own mortality: "death's ironic scraping." Susanna's music—her beauty—is played on a different instrument—"the clear viol of her memory"—that is, all our memories of her and her story. What does this have to do with beauty's transitoriness in the mind and permanence in flesh? And what does it have to do with the speaker's desire for the woman in blue-shadowed silk?

Stevens (or his speaker) seems to be condemning a certain kind of fruitless thinking about beauty. Instead, he argues, beauty only exists finally and permanently in its objects. The objects themselves—maidens, gardens, and so on, die, but their beauty lives in other maidens and gardens—just as Susanna's desirable beauty seems to live in the woman in blue-shadowed silk, who, after all, started the association with Susanna's story.

At each point in the poem the verse fits what is going on. It slows down at Susanna's bath:

> In the green water, clear and warm,
> Susanna lay.
> She searched
> The touch of springs,
> And found
> Concealed imaginings.
> She sighed,
> For so much melody.

It is loud and strident at the moment of suspense and drama:

> A breath upon her hand
> Muted the night.
> She turned—
> A cymbal crashed,
> And roaring horns.

It has silly feminine rhymes to fit Susanna's silly maids: "And then, the simpering Byzantines / Fled, with a noise like tambourines." It seeks out rhymes that parallel and reinforce each other: *plays/praise, Susanna/Hosanna*.

The sequence of Stevens' poem is controlled by the movement of his speaker's mind, whether he is associating one desire with another and one woman with another, illustrating a generalization about feeling and music, or arriving at conclusions about all of these things.

We need to be alert for cues to the thought sequences presented in a poem, whether it is in a fixed form or not. Time indications (*when/then*, for instance), stanza divisions, governing metaphors or similes, and sequences of connected images all give us cues to the structure of argument and association.

EXERCISES

A.   **STILL TO BE NEAT**

> Still to be neat, still to be dressed,
> As you were going to a feast;
> Still to be powdered, still perfumed;
> Lady, it is to be presumed,
> Though art's hid causes are not found,   5
> All is not sweet, all is not sound.
>
> Give me a look, give me a face
> That makes simplicity a grace;
> Robes loosely flowing, hair as free;
> Such sweet neglect more taketh me   10
> Than all th' adulteries of art.
> They strike mine eyes, but not my heart.

> 1609
> *Ben Jonson (1573–1637)*

1. What is contrasted in the two stanzas of Jonson's poem?
2. According to the poem, what "is to be presumed" about the person who is always neatly dressed, powdered, and perfumed?
3. What does Jonson mean by "th' adulteries of art" in line 11?
4. What does the word "sound" mean (line 6)? In what way might this woman he speaks of not be *sound*, and what might be the cause?
5. What is the poem's fixed form? How does the thought sequence work within this form?

---

still: always. **as you were going**: as if you were going.

B.   **BEWARE   :   DO NOT READ THIS POEM**

tonite   ,   thriller was
abt an ol woman   , so vain she
surrounded herself w/
        many mirrors

it got so bad that finally she   5
locked herself indoors & her
whole life became the
        mirrors

one day the villagers broke
into her house   ,   but she was too   10
swift for them   .   she disappeared
        into a mirror

each tenant who bought the house
after that   ,   lost a loved one to
        the ol woman in the mirror   :   15
        first a little girl
        then a young woman
        then the young woman/s husband

the hunger of this poem is legendary
it has taken in many victims   20
back off from this poem
it has drawn in yr feet
back off from this poem
it has drawn in yr legs

back off from this poem   25
it is a greedy mirror
you are into this poem   from
        the waist down
nobody can hear you can they   ?
this poem has had you up to here   30
        belch
this poem aint got no manners
you cant call out frm this poem
relax now & go w/ this poem   35

move & roll on to this poem
do not resist this poem
this poem has yr eyes
this poem has his head
this poem has his arms
this poem has his fingers   40
this poem has his fingertips
this poem is the reader & the
reader this poem

statistic :   the us bureau of missing persons reports
                 that in 1968 over 100,000 people disappeared
                 leaving no solid clues
                       nor trace   only
         a space   in the lives of their friends

                                                1970
                            Ishmael Reed (b. 1938)

1. Why does Reed begin with the movie about mirrors? What associations does Reed develop from this first image? In what way is this or any other poem like a mirror?
2. How have we been prepared for Reed's next to last stanza? How does the comparison to the movie thriller help prepare for this stanza? Is this a statement we could have accepted without his comparison with the movie thriller? Is the statement true of other poems?
3. Explain the significance of the spaces in the last two lines of the poem.

C.   **THE GREEDY THE PEOPLE**

            the greedy the people
            (as if as can yes)
            they sell and they buy
            and they die for because
            though the bell in the steeple   5
            says Why

            the chary the wary
            (as all as can each)
            they don't and they do
            and they turn to a which   10
            though the moon in her glory
            says Who

the busy the millions
(as you're as can i'm)
they flock and they flee   15
through a thunder of seem
though the stars in their silence
say Be

the cunning the craven
(as think as can feel)   20
they when and they how
and they live for until
though the sun in his heaven
says Now

the timid the tender   25
(as doubt as can trust)
they work and they pray
and they bow to a must
though the earth in her splendor
says May   30

1960

E. E. Cummings (1894–1963)

1. What sorts of people are described in the first lines of each stanza? What kinds of words are associated with these people in the third and fourth lines of each stanza?
2. What does Cummings contrast with the people and attitudes described at the beginning of each stanza?
3. Each stanza ends "says ———". To what other word in the stanza is the concluding word explicitly contrasted?
4. What likenesses and associations organize this poem?

D.   **THE VICTOR DOG**

For Elizabeth Bishop

Bix to Buxtehude to Boulez,
The little white dog on the Victor label
Listens long and hard as he is able.
It's all in a day's work, whatever plays.

The Victor Dog

From judgment, it would seem, he has refrained.   5
He even listens earnestly to Bloch,
Then builds a church upon our acid rock.
He's man's—no—he's the Leiermann's best friend,

Or would be if hearing and listening were the same.
Does he hear? I fancy he rather smells   10
Those lemon-gold arpeggios in Ravel's
"Les jets d'eau du palais de ceux qui s'aiment."

He ponders the Schumann Concerto's tall willow hit
By lightning and stays put. When he surmises
Through one of Bach's eternal boxwood mazes   15
The oboe pungent as a bitch in heat,

Or when the calypso decants its raw bay rum
Or the moon in *Wozzeck* reddens ripe for murder,
He doesn't sneeze or howl; just listens harder.
Adamant needles bear down on him from   20

Whirling of outer space, too black, too near—
But he was taught as a puppy not to flinch,
Much less to imitate his bête noire Blanche
Who barked, fat foolish creature, at King Lear.

Still others fought in the road's filth over Jezebel,   25
Slavered on hearths of horned and pelted barons.
His forebears lacked, to say the least, forbearance.
Can nature change in him? Nothing's impossible.

Musicians and composers mentioned or alluded to, in order, are Bix Beiderbecke (1903–1931), a popular jazz trumpet-player; Dietrich Buxtehude (1637–1707); Pierre Boulez (b. 1925); Ernest Bloch (1880–1959); Franz Schubert (1797–1828), whose "Der Leiermann" ("The Organ Grinder") has dogs for his audience; Maurice Ravel (1875–1937); Robert Schumann (1810–1856); Johann Sebastian Bach (1685–1750); Alban Berg (1885–1935), who wrote the opera *Wozzeck*, in which the main character kills his mistress as the moon rises; and George Frideric Handel (1685–1759). **the Victor label:** the labels on RCA Victor records had for many years a white dog listening to an old gramophone. **arpeggios:** the notes of a chord played quickly one after another rather than all at once. **"Les jets . . . s'aiment":** "The palace fountains of those who love each other." **boxwood mazes:** boxwood hedges were sometimes planted and pruned into mazes on large estates; Merrill compares Bach's complex fugal music to these mazes. **bête noire:** literally, "black beast"—used of someone or something regarded as obnoxious. **Blanche:** in Shakespeare's *King Lear* (III, vi, 61). **Jezebel:** Ahab's wife, who was thrown from a window and whose body was eaten by dogs (2 Kings 9:33–36).

The last chord fades. The night is cold and fine.
His master's voice rasps through the grooves' bare groves.   30
Obediently, in silence like the grave's
He sleeps there on the still-warm gramophone

Only to dream he is at the premiere of a Handel
Opera long thought lost—*Il Cane Minore.*
Its allegorical subject is his story!   35
A little dog revolving round a spindle

Gives rise to harmonies beyond belief,
A cast of stars. . . . Is there in Victor's heart
No honey for the vanquished? Art is art.
The life it asks of us is a dog's life.   40

1972
James Merrill (b. 1926)

1. What is this rhyme scheme called? How strictly does Merrill rhyme?
2. What point of view and associations hold together all the musical references and stanzas of this poem?
3. Look at Merrill's plays on words such as *forebears/forbearance, grooves/groves/graves, Victor/vanquished*—how do these affect the poem's tone?
4. How frequently does Merrill alliterate in this poem? Why?

E. The following poem is a kind of argument. Trace the main points in its train of thought.

TERENCE, THIS IS STUPID STUFF

"Terence, this is stupid stuff:
You eat your victuals fast enough;
There can't be much amiss, 'tis clear,
To see the rate you drink your beer.
But oh, good Lord, the verse you make,   5

The Victor Dog   Il Cane Minore: the constellation Canis Minor (Little Dog).

Terence: Housman originally planned to call the collection in which this poem appeared *The Poems of Terence Hearsay*. Although he changed his mind and titled the book A *Shropshire Lad,* the fictional poet-persona still remains, and this is the Terence being addressed.

It gives a chap the belly-ache.
The cow, the old cow, she is dead;
It sleeps well, the horned head:
We poor lads, 'tis our turn now
To hear such tunes as killed the cow.   10
Pretty friendship 'tis to rhyme
Your friends to death before their time
Moping melancholy mad:
Come, pipe a tune to dance to, lad."

    Why, if 'tis dancing you would be,   15
There's brisker pipes than poetry.
Say, for what were hop-yards meant,
Or why was Burton built on Trent?
Oh many a peer of England brews
Livelier liquor than the Muse,   20
And malt does more than Milton can
To justify God's ways to man.
Ale, man, ale's the stuff to drink
For fellows whom it hurts to think:
Look into the pewter pot   25
To see the world as the world's not.
And faith, 'tis pleasant till 'tis past.
The mischief is that 'twill not last.
Oh I have been to Ludlow fair
And left my necktie God knows where,   30
And carried half-way home, or near,
Pints and quarts of Ludlow beer:
Then the world seemed none so bad,
And I myself a sterling lad;
And down in lovely muck I've lain,   35
Happy till I woke again.
Then I saw the morning sky:
Heigho, the tale was all a lie;
The world, it was the old world yet,
I was I, my things were wet,   40
And nothing now remained to do
But begin the game anew.

Burton: Burton-on-Trent was renowned for its ale. **to justify God's ways to man:** Housman slightly changes John Milton's words describing his purpose in writing the epic poem *Paradise Lost* (1667), Book I, 25–26.

Therefore, since the world has still
Much good, but much less good than ill,
And while the sun and moon endure   45
Luck's a chance, but trouble's sure,
I'd face it as a wise man would,
And train for ill and not for good.
'Tis true, the stuff I bring for sale
Is not so brisk a brew as ale: 50
Out of a stem that scored the hand
I wrung it in a weary land.
But take it: if the smack is sour,
The better for the embittered hour;
It should do good to heart and head   55
When your soul is in my soul's stead;
And I will friend you, if I may,
In the dark and cloudy day.

There was a king reigned in the East:
There, when kings will sit to feast,   60
They get their fill before they think
With poisoned meat and poisoned drink.
He gathered all that springs to birth
From the many-venomed earth;
First a little, thence to more,   65
He sampled all her killing store;
And easy, smiling, seasoned sound,
Sate the king when healths went round.
They put arsenic in his meat
And stared aghast to watch him eat;   70
They poured strychnine in his cup
And shook to see him drink it up:
They shook, they stared as white's their shirt:
Them it was their poison hurt.
—I tell the tale that I heard told.   75
Mithridates, he died old.

1896
A. E. Housman (1859–1936)

1. Why is the first verse paragraph in quotation marks? How many speakers
   are there in this poem?

Mithridates: a first-century ruler in Asia Minor who ruled for over fifty years.

2. Remember the verse paragraph division of Marvell's argument in "To His Coy Mistress." The next to last verse paragraph in Housman's poem begins "Therefore." If it is the conclusion, why is there yet another verse paragraph?
3. What is the argument *answering* (first verse paragraph)?

F.   **PHILLIS, BE GENTLER I ADVISE**

> Phillis, be gentler I advise,
> Make up for time misspent,
> When beauty on its death-bed lies,
> 'Tis high time to repent.
>
> Such is the malice of your fate,   5
> That makes you old so soon,
> Your pleasure ever comes too late,
> How early e'er begun.
>
> Think what a wretched thing is she,
> Whose stars contrive in spite,   10
> The morning of her love should be,
> Her fading beauty's night.
>
> Then if to make your ruin more,
> You'll peevishly be coy,
> Die with the scandal of a whore,   15
> And never know the joy.

                        1680

          John Wilmot, 2nd Earl of Rochester
                  (1647–1680)

1. Compare this poem with Marvell's "To His Coy Mistress." How are the two poems similar? How different?
2. What other argument besides that of time does Rochester's speaker use? What is the tone of the poem? In what ways does it differ from that of Marvell's poem?

G.   **THE INSTRUCTION MANUAL**

> As I sit looking out of a window of the building
> I wish I did not have to write the instruction manual on the uses
>   of a new metal.

I look down into the street and see people, each walking with an
    inner peace,
And envy them—they are so far away from me!
Not one of them has to worry about getting out this manual   5
    on schedule.
And, as my way is, I begin to dream, resting my elbows on the
    desk and leaning out of the window a little,
Of dim Guadalajara! City of rose-colored flowers!
City I wanted most to see, and most did not see, in Mexico!
But I fancy I see, under the press of having to write the
    instruction manual,
Your public square, city, with its elaborate little bandstand!   10
The band is playing *Scheherazade* by Rimsky-Korsakov.
Around stand the flower girls, handing out rose- and lemon-
    colored flowers,
Each attractive in her rose-and-blue striped dress (Oh! such
    shades of rose and blue),
And nearby is the little white booth where women in green serve
    you green and yellow fruit.
The couples are parading; everyone is in a holiday mood.   15
First, leading the parade, is a dapper fellow
Clothed in deep blue. On his head sits a white hat
And he wears a mustache, which has been trimmed for
    the occasion.
His dear one, his wife, is young and pretty; her shawl is rose,
    pink and white.
Her slippers are patent leather, in the American fashion,   20
And she carries a fan, for she is modest, and does not want the
    crowd to see her face too often.
But everybody is so busy with his wife or loved one
I doubt they would notice the mustachioed man's wife.
Here come the boys! They are skipping and throwing little things
    on the sidewalk
Which is made of gray tile. One of them, a little older, has a   25
    toothpick in his teeth.
He is silenter than the rest, and affects not to notice the pretty
    young girls in white.
But his friends notice them, and shout their jeers at the
    laughing girls.
Yet soon all this will cease, with the deepening of their years,
And love bring each to the parade grounds for another reason.

But I have lost sight of the young fellow with the toothpick.   30
Wait—there he is—on the other side of the bandstand,
Secluded from his friends, in earnest talk with a young girl
Of fourteen or fifteen. I try to hear what they are saying
But it seems they are just mumbling something—shy words of
    love, probably.
She is slightly taller than he, and looks quietly down into his   35
    sincere eyes.
She is wearing white. The breeze ruffles her long fine black hair
    against her olive cheek.
Obviously she is in love. The boy, the young boy with the
    toothpick, he is in love too;
His eyes show it. Turning from this couple,
I see there is an intermission in the concert.
The paraders are resting and sipping drinks through straws   40
(The drinks are dispensed from a large crock by a lady in
    dark blue),
And the musicians mingle among them, in their creamy white
    uniforms, and talk
About the weather, perhaps, or how their kids are doing
    at school.
Let us take this opportunity to tiptoe into one of the side streets.
Here you may see one of those white houses with green trim   45
That are so popular here. Look—I told you!
It is cool and dim inside, but the patio is sunny.
An old woman in gray sits there, fanning herself with a palm
    leaf fan.
She welcomes us to her patio, and offers us a cooling drink.
"My son is in Mexico City," she says. "He would welcome   50
    you too
If he were here. But his job is with a bank there.
Look, here is a photograph of him."
And a dark-skinned lad with pearly teeth grins out at us from the
    worn leather frame.
We thank her for her hospitality, for it is getting late
And we must catch a view of the city, before we leave, from a   55
    good high place.
That church tower will do—the faded pink one, there against the
    fierce blue of the sky. Slowly we enter.
The caretaker, an old man dressed in brown and gray, asks us
    how long we have been in the city, and how we like it here.

His daughter is scrubbing the steps—she nods to us as we pass
    into the tower.
Soon we have reached the top, and the whole network of the
    city extends before us.
There is the rich quarter, with its houses of pink and white, and   60
    its crumbling, leafy terraces.
There is the poorer quarter, its homes a deep blue.
There is the market, where men are selling hats and
    swatting flies
And there is the public library, painted several shades of pale
    green and beige.
Look! There is the square we just came from, with
    the promenaders.
There are fewer of them, now that the heat of the day   65
    has increased,
But the young boy and girl still lurk in the shadows of
    the bandstand.
And there is the home of the little old lady—
She is still sitting in the patio, fanning herself.
How limited, but how complete withal, has been our experience
    of Guadalajara!
We have seen young love, married love, and the love of an aged   70
    mother for her son.
We have heard the music, tasted the drinks, and looked at
    colored houses.
What more is there to do, except stay? And that we cannot do.
And as a last breeze freshens the top of the weathered old tower,
    I turn my gaze
Back to the instruction manual which has made me dream
    of Guadalajara.

                                     1956
                          John Ashbery (b. 1927)

1. The poet W. S. Merwin says that "open forms are in some concerns the strictest. Here only the poem itself can be seen as its form. In a peculiar sense if you criticize how it happens you criticize what it is." The open form of Ashbery's poem might suggest that it could go on for many more than its 74 lines or end at any point earlier. What associations made at the beginning of the poem act to organize the poem and prepare for the appropriateness of its ending when it comes?
2. What tensions in the poem—stresses between one wish and another, contrasts of images, contrasts of setting and incidents—serve to unify the poem?

3. What associations develop from line to line, sentence to sentence?
4. In a note on this poem, John Frederick Nims says that "solemn readers, not content with enjoying an exercise in fantasy, might say that this is a poem about levels of reality and the power of the imagination." Comment on Nims' remark.

WRITING SUGGESTIONS_____

1. List in order the things which the speaker encounters or describes in the following poem. Write an essay discussing how these various images are associated in the poem, and what reasons there might be for their order in the poem:

LONDON

I wander through each chartered street,
Near where the chartered Thames does flow,
And mark in every face I meet
Marks of weakness, marks of woe.

In every cry of every man,   5
In every Infant's cry of fear,
In every voice, in every ban,
The mind-forged manacles I hear.

How the Chimney-sweeper's cry
Every black'ning Church appalls;   10
And the hapless Soldier's sigh
Runs in blood down Palace walls.

But most through midnight streets I hear
How the youthful Harlot's curse
Blasts the new-born Infant's tear,   15
And blights with plagues the Marriage hearse.

1794
William Blake (1757–1827)

2. In an essay, state the argument of the following poem and discuss the ways in which contrasts of images, structural units, and word choice combine to support that argument.

THE NAKED AND THE NUDE

For me, the naked and the nude
(By lexicographers construed
As synonyms that should express
The same deficiency of dress
Or shelter) stand as wide apart   5
As love from lies, or truth from art.

Lovers without reproach will gaze
On bodies naked and ablaze;
The hippocratic eye will see
In nakedness, anatomy;   10
And naked shines the Goddess when
She mounts her lion among men.

The nude are bold, the nude are sly
To hold each treasonable eye.
While draping by a showman's trick   15
Their dishabille in rhetoric,
They grin a mock-religious grin
Of scorn at those of naked skin.

The naked, therefore, who compete
Against the nude may know defeat;   20
Yet when they both together tread
The briary pastures of the dead,
By Gorgons with long whips pursued,
How naked go the sometime nude!

1958
Robert Graves (b. 1895)

PART
V

WHY?

CHAPTER ELEVEN

THE POET IN QUESTION

We suggested in Chapter One that the poetry reader's question "What does it all mean?" is too broad to answer and that the reader must ask more specific questions. These specific line-by-line inquiries can then be organized into questions that derive from the human origin of the poem. Who is speaking? What is the time and setting? What events does the poem describe and what cultural assumptions does it reflect? How does its structure and form reinforce its meaning? In the preceding ten chapters, we have explored how all these questions can be answered. But yet one overarching question remains: *Why* do all these elements come together in a single poem—often in such a curious way? The simple answer is that they come together in the poem because they are yoked together by one human being. This human act links us to the poem. The most convincing proof of the meaningfulness of a poem—its delight and wisdom—comes from our certain knowledge that poems are written by people.

PUBLIC AND PRIVATE ORDERS

To be human is to be unique. The poet Adrienne Rich remarked that she likes to have a reader say, "But I always thought a poem was something written on a piece of paper," so that she could ask the important question, "But look, how did those words get on that piece of paper?" This allows her, she says, to make the point that behind a poem there must be a mind.

It is this individual mind at work in the poem that introduces the complexity. This mind has a unique way of looking at experience, of trying to order it, and of expressing that ordering attempt in language and form that will lead the poet's audience toward shared discovery and delight.

A poem is the intersection of these shared and private aspects of being human. A writer uses the public language, but with individual phrasing, choice of words, and perspective. When the poet writes about love and sports and work and play and good and evil and birth and death, we can understand because these are the experiences of our lives as well; at the same time the sequence and combination of experiences is singular. The poet may utilize the publicly held beliefs of the culture and refer to familiar myths and allusions; however, when these beliefs find their way into a poem they are expressed in a highly individualized way.

When John Donne in "A Valediction: Forbidding Mourning" wrote about the private experience of two lovers parting, he used details and images that were public property—references to religious ideas, to Ptolemaic astronomy, to drafting, to goldsmithing; however, the way all these details were put into a single poem was uniquely Donne's. In such ways, a private experience—real or imagined—is shared with the poem's audience. And, similarly, Donne described the private experience of waking up in the morning with a lover at one's side with images and details that were also public property:

THE GOOD MORROW

I wonder, by my troth, what thou and I
Did till we loved? were we not weaned till
   then,
But sucked on country pleasures childishly?
Or snorted we in the seven sleepers' den?
'Twas so; but this, all pleasures fancies be.   5
If ever any beauty I did see,
Which I desired, and got, 'twas but a dream of
   thee.

And now good-morrow to our waking souls,
Which watch not one another out of fear;
For love all love of other sights controls,
And makes one little room an everywhere.   10
Let sea-discoverers to new worlds have gone;
Let maps to other, worlds on worlds have
   shown;
Let us possess one world; each hath one, and is
   one.

My face in thine eye, thine in mine appears,   15
And true plain hearts do in the faces rest;
Where can we find two better hemispheres

seven sleepers' den: A reference to the Christian legend in which seven youths of Ephesus were imprisoned in a cave by their pagan persecutors. They slept miraculously for 200 years and woke to find that Christianity had triumphed.

If ever beauty . . . 'twas but a dream: A reference to Plato's idea that reality is only the shadow of the Ideal. Here, the lady is the ideal; all those other women were just shadows.

And makes one little room an everywhere: A reference to the notion that man/the earth, etc. (the microcosm) is a mirror of the universe (the macrocosm)

Let sea-discoverers . . . Let maps . . . : References to contemporary history—recent explorations to the New World and the making of new astronomical maps.

My face . . . faces rest: A reference to the belief that a person's true self is reflected in the face, particularly the eyes.

Without sharp north, without declining west?
Whatever dies was not mixed equally;
If our two loves be one, or thou and I   20
Love so alike that none can slacken, none can
    die.

dies . . . mixed equally: A reference to theories of medicine which said the body must be composed of elements equally mixed or it will sicken and die; *die* is also a Renaissance pun equating sexual climax with death.

                                        1633
                John Donne (1572–1631)

In writing this poem, Donne was drawing on a rich store of natural lore, philosophic systems, and traditional mythologies, which his audience would recognize as a matter of course. Yet, Donne's combination of these gives us insight into his particular way of seeing things.

Since many of Donne's once-current public systems and mythologies are no longer current, in order to fully understand the poem we must inquire into these past cultural assumptions. It is also useful to read a number of Donne's poems, such as "A Valediction: Forbidding Mourning" and "The Sun Rising," to see his view of these systems in "The Good Morrow." The special way in which a poet looks at the world may be only partially revealed by a single poem, but if we look at several, we can get a clearer idea of what concepts, words, and perceptions are important to that poet's attempt to order experience within poems. In Chapter Six, we looked at Thomas Hardy's "The Convergence of the Twain" and discussed its connections with some of the assumptions of the time about progress. In that poem, Hardy used such phrases as "The Immanent Will that stirs and urges everything" (line 18) and "The Spinner of the Years" (31) to describe the force that brought the *Titanic* and the iceberg together. In the context of the poem, we can easily understand the general meaning of these phrases; however, reading more of Hardy's poetry and fiction aids us in comprehending more precisely why he emphasizes and personifies this force at work on human destiny. In such poems as "Hap" and "Channel Firing" and in his novels such as *The Return of the Native* and *Tess of the D'Urbervilles*, we discover further evidence that in Hardy's view, humans are subject to forces over which they have no real control; whatever control they think they have is merely illusory. Thus, "The Convergence of the Twain" is not just a single poem on the page but one that is part of a mind behind the poem, meditating on the meaning of existence. Reading more than one work by a poet can be even more useful when he or she is not using public systems and mythologies, but imposing a personal order on experience.

"PUTTING THINGS WHERE THEY DON'T HAVE TO GO"

In responding to this natural urge to order experience, many poets, especially many contemporary poets, find the traditional poetic strategies for such ordering inadequate. Why? Or to turn around the question posed at the beginning of this chapter, "Why *don't* so many of the expected, traditional elements of poetry now come together in poems?" Why do so many contemporary poems seem to ignore those familiar orderings of fixed form, of meaningful locality and time setting, and of a recognizable universality in the actions or feelings described?

These questions have both a simple and a more complex answer. The simple answer is that many contemporary poets experiment with content and form in order to mirror the confusing variety of human experience, rather than impose what they see as an artificial order upon it. In one of his poems, Ted Berrigan wrote:

> I make up each
> poem (i.e. "verse form") as
> it arrives by putting
> things where they have to go
> tho I sometimes vary this by putting
> things where they don't have to go.
>
> —from *Sonnet LXXV*

The following poem by Michael McClure expands on Berrigan's comment:

from HYMN TO ST. GERYON

THE GESTURE THE GESTURE THE GESTURE THE GESTURE THE GES-
TURE THE GESTURE THE GESTURE THE GESTURE   to make fists of it.

> Clyfford Still: "We are committed to an unqualified act,
> not illustrating outworn myths or contemporary alibis. One must
>   accept total responsibility for what he executes.
> And the measure of his greatness will be the depths of his
>   insight and courage in realizing   5
> his own vision. Demands for communication are pre-
>   sumptuous and irrelevant."

St. Geryon: In Greek mythology, Geryon was reputedly the strongest man alive, born as he was with three heads, six hands, and three bodies joined at the waist. According to Robert Graves, Geryon = geranon = crane. In both Greek and Irish legend, cranes were associated with alphabetical secrets and with poets (*The Greek Myths*, II, p. 143). **Clyfford Still:** American artist (b. 1904) usually described as part of the Abstract Expressionist school of painting.

Hymn to St. Geryon

To hit with the thing. To make a robe of it
    TO WEAR.
    To fill out the thing as we see it!   10
    To clothe ourselves in the action,
to remove from the precious to the full swing.
    To hit the object over the head. To step
        into what we conjecture.
    Name it the *stance*. Not politics   15

    but ourselves—is the question.

HERE I SEE IT WITH FLOWERS ENTERING INTO IT
    that way.
    Not caring except for my greatness, caring
    only for my size I would enter it.   20

    THE SELFS FREE HERO
THOREAU is there, LAWRENCE, BLAKE, GOYA
ST. POLLOCK is there and KLINE whom I imagine
    in a world of nerves and nightsweats. . . .

                          1959
              Michael McClure (b. 1932)

As such passages by Berrigan and McClure suggest, some artists have turned from seeing their actions and creations as part of a larger, ordering system to portraying in all its complexities the randomness of experience and the essential idiosyncrasies of the self. The movement away from ordering systems is not confined to poets and artists, but is a cultural phenomenon of our time. As Louis Auchincloss writes in his recent novel *The House of the Prophet*:

    Until the Industrial Revolution our European forebears had lived in a society where the universe was deemed to have a purpose and where a deity judged men, rewarding them or condemning them according to an absolute standard of right and wrong. And the dethronement of the deity

---

Thoreau . . . Kline: a selection of writers and painters who in one way or another rebelled against conventional life styles and methods of artistic expression. Henry David Thoreau (1817–1862), American author of *Walden* and "Of Civil Disobedience"; D. H. Lawrence (1885–1930), English author; William Blake (1757–1827), English artist and poet; Francisco Goya (1746–1828), Spanish painter renowned for his freedom of interpretation, violent technique, and use of distortion. **St. Pollock:** Jackson Pollock (1912–1962), American abstract painter; Franz Kline (1910–1962), abstract expressionist who in his later paintings experimented with forms in which accident and chance were guiding principles.

was followed by a long succession of political theories as to who was to judge men and by what standards: a king, a parliament, a congress, the people. But now we exist in a cold, mechanical universe where we are obliged to accept the lonely responsibility of each man for his own soul.

How does this loss of historical purpose and sense, with its accompanying emphasis on the self, affect poetry? Not all poetry *is* affected. Poems continue to be written within traditional philosophic systems, in traditional forms, and with traditional subjects. But in much contemporary poetry, with the loss of historical continuity goes the possibility of neat philosophical systems and explanations. With the loss of systems goes the idea that fixed forms in poetry can mirror philosophical order. So one consequence is a *formal* one: poets are free to use traditional forms if they wish, but most of them cannot any longer do so with a conviction that the forms reflect something fixed and sure in the human psyche or the world. The contemporary poet William Matthews has said that "one of the functions of art should be to disarrange patterns of certainty in the psyche," and he relates this idea to the notion of form. It never occurred to him to write in traditional forms, he says, because "I'm so much a believer in the notion of surprising yourself, and taking risks and preferring disorder to order, that it would be almost temperamentally impossible for me to do it."

FOUL SHOTS: A CLINIC

for Paul Levitt

Be perpendicular to the basket,
toes avid for the line.

Already this description
is perilously abstract: the ball
and basket are round, the nailhead   5
centered in the centerplank
of the foul-circle is round,
and though the rumpled body
isn't round, it isn't
perpendicular. You have to draw   10
"an imaginary line," as the breezy

coaches say, "through your shoulders."
Here's how to cheat: remember

your collarbone. Now the instructions
grow spiritual—deep breathing,   15
relax and concentrate both; aim
for the front of the rim but miss it
deliberately so the ball goes in.
Ignore this part of the clinic

and shoot 200 foul shots   20
every day. Teach yourself not to be
bored by any boring one of them.

You have to do this, and chances
are you don't; you'd love to be good
at it but not by a love that drives   25
you to shoot 200 foul shots
every day, and the lovingly unlaunched
foul shots we're talking about now—
the clinic having served to bring us
together—circle eccentrically   30
in a sky of stolid orbits
as unlike as you and I are
from the arcs those foul shots
leave behind when they go in.

                              1979
           William Matthews (b. 1942)

Matthews is saying that both discipline and form are important: one must practice two hundred shots a day; how one stands and where is very important. But
at the same time he says this discipline and form is very hard to achieve and
certainly not as easy as the coaches make out: "be perpendicular to the basket"
is a description which is already "perilously abstract." It is possible to see the
whole discussion of form in basketball here as a metaphor for all activities in
which form is important—and poetry is one of these activities. Matthews suggests metaphorically that form is important—even essential—but not describ-
able in traditional terms or reducible to easy, set prescriptions.

Matthews is just one of many writers dealing with the problems of tradition
and poetic conventions. Another contemporary poet, Mark Strand, talks about
rhyme and poetry in an interview in *The Ohio Review* (Spring, 1972):

INTERVIEWER: . . . to what extent [do] you think there is very
firmly embedded in contemporary poetry now, the poetry of today, a dis-

trust of what once on a time would have been called "poetic conventions," and now which we would probably put in quotation marks? . . .

STRAND: Well, I don't know. I can say that we distrust rhyme because it sounds a little tinny, a little false, a little decorative, and a little unnatural. The point of writing a version of plain-style verse, it seems, is to affect as much as possible the naturalness of conversation, or plain discourse, not overly-excited discourse. Rhymes would get in the way . . . I'm not talking about my own poetry when I say this. . . . I still rhyme. I mean, I've rhymed fairly recently, and I find it useful. I don't mind that, and I don't mind meters either. It sometimes seems quite natural to me.

INTERVIEWER: But your work still has this sense of great—great control, great form, as if you were containing it. You're still very much in control, and yet your poems are just as mad, it seems to me, in their own way.

STRAND: Well I am really aware, too, that when I am writing a poem, I am writing a poem. I think that that makes certain demands. There are certain concessions made to that inner debate, artistic concessions, and they're important. You know, one of the horrifying things about many poets is that they lost, somewhere along the line, in the fervor of this inner debate, the idea of poetry. . . . They become, in fact, "chroniclers" or "notators." They write notebooks or leaflets or what have you. As if to say, "I am connected to my times in this way, and I am connected to this debate in this way." But there's no sense of getting absorbed in the idea of the poem. . . .

Poetry has always seemed to me the most truthful medium of all. To say that the poem gets in the way is to say that you don't trust what the poem can do. I mean I've always believed poems. Sir Thomas Wyatt's "They Flee From Me, That Sometime Did Me Seek" strikes me as terribly honest, yet it's a poem and a very formal one, and I certainly don't say, "Gee, I wish he'd written that as a confession and not as a poem, because as a poem it lacks reality," or "I don't believe it because it rhymes." And the same goes for Shakespeare's sonnets—they're very sad, and some of them are heartbreaking, and just because they're sonnets, that doesn't mean you don't believe them. And so on and so forth, right up to the present.

KEEPING THINGS WHOLE

In a field
I am the absence
of field.
This is
always the case.

5

Milk

Wherever I am
I am what is missing.

When I walk
I part the air
and always   10
the air moves in
to fill the spaces
where my body's been.

We all have reasons
for moving.   15
I move
to keep things whole.

1968
Mark Strand (b. 1934)

Poets have a variety of ways of attempting what Strand calls "the natural-ness of conversation, of plain discourse," in order to achieve a poetry that is "the most truthful medium of all." Sometimes the result looks like prose:

MILK

Milk used to come in tall glass, heavy and uncrystalline as frozen melted snow. It rose direct and thick as horse-chestnut tree trunks that do not spread out upon the ground even a little; a shaft of white drink narrowing at the cream and rounded off in a thick-lipped grin. Empty and unrinsed, a diluted milk ghost entrapped and dulled light and vision.

Then things got a little worse: squared, high-shouldered and rounded off in the wrong places, a milk replica of a hand made Danish wooden milk bat. But that was only the beginning. Things got worse than that.

Milk came in waxed paper that swelled and spilled and oozed flat pieces of milk. It had a little lid that didn't close properly or resisted when pulled so that when it did give way milk jumped out.

Things are getting better now. Milk is bigger—half a gallon, at least—in thin milky plastic with a handle, a jug founded on an oblong. Pick it up and the milk moves, rising enthusiastically in the neck as it shifts its center of weight. Heavy as a breast, but lighter, shaping itself without much changing shape: like bringing home the milk in a bandana, a neckerchief or a scarf, strong as canvas waterwings whose strength was only felt dragged under water.

On the highway this morning at the go-round about where you leave New Hampshire, there had been an accident. Milk was sloshed on the gray-blue-black so much like a sheet of early winter ice you drove over it slowly, no matter what the temperature of the weather that eddied in through the shatterproof glass gills. There were milk-skins all around, the way dessert plates look after everyone has left the table in the Concord grape season. Only bigger, unpigmented though pretty opaque, not squashed but no less empty.

Trembling, milk is coming into its own.

1969
James Schuyler (b. 1923)

Poets usually have a clear sense of what they are *not* doing when writing—a sense that is illustrated by the following poem:

WHY I AM NOT A PAINTER

I am not a painter, I am a poet.
Why? I think I would rather be
a painter, but I am not. Well,

For instance, Mike Goldberg
is starting a painting. I drop in.   5
"Sit down and have a drink" he
says. I drink; we drink. I look
up. "You have SARDINES in it."
"Yes, it needed something there."
"Oh." I go and the days go by   10
and I drop in again. The painting

is going on, and I go, and the days
go by. I drop in. The painting is
finished. "Where's SARDINES?"
All that's left is just   15
letters, "It was too much," Mike says.

But me? One day I am thinking of
a color: orange. I write a line

about orange. Pretty soon it is a
whole page of words, not lines.   20
Then another page. There should be
so much more, not of orange, of
words, of how terrible orange is
and life. Days go by. It is even in
prose, I am a real poet. My poem   25
is finished and I haven't mentioned
orange yet. It's twelve poems, I call
it ORANGES. And one day in a gallery
I see Mike's painting, called SARDINES.

1956
Frank O'Hara (b. 1926)

"THE SELF'S FREE HERO"

When poets make decisions about form—what to leave out, where to place
things, what to put in—they cannot any longer do so because a tradition fixes
the choices. Formal decisions finally come back to the individual poet, as John
Ashbery points out in the following selection:

from THREE POEMS

I thought that if I could put it all down, that would be
one way. And next the thought came to me that to leave
all out would be another, and truer, way.

clean-washed sea

The flowers were.

These are examples of leaving out. But, forget as we will,
something soon comes to stand in their place. Not the
truth, perhaps, but—yourself. It is you who made this,
therefore you are true. But the truth has passed on

to divide all.

1972
John Ashbery (b. 1927)

"Not the truth, perhaps, but—yourself." What does Ashbery's phrase mean? For many poets, the truth embodied in philosophic systems or in the fixed forms of poetry no longer serves or is no longer attainable. The self, then, becomes the only reliable "I" or eye through which to explain the world and the individual's place in it. Often, now as in the past, the experience related by the poet may be intensely private, but we are given enough of that experience to be able to recognize that it reflects or extends our own:

AFTER DRINKING ALL NIGHT WITH A FRIEND, WE GO OUT IN A BOAT AT DAWN TO SEE WHO CAN WRITE THE BEST POEM

These pines, these fall oaks, these rocks,
This water dark and touched by wind—
I am like you, you dark boat,
Drifting over water fed by cool springs.

Beneath the waters, since I was a boy,   5
I have dreamt of strange and dark treasures,
Not of gold, or strange stones, but the true
Gift, beneath the pale lakes of Minnesota.

This morning also, drifting in the dawn wind,
I sense my hands, and my shoes, and this ink—   10
Drifting, as all of this body drifts,
Above the clouds of the flesh and the stone.

A few friendships, a few dawns, a few glimpses of grass,
A few oars weathered by the snow and the heat,
So we drift toward shore, over cold waters,   15
No longer caring if we drift or go straight.

1962
Robert Bly (b. 1926)

The experience related by the self of the poem, however, can occasionally be obscure, almost deliberately secret, and hidden in private language and autobiographical experiences:

A VALEDICTION FORBIDDING MOURNING

My swirling wants. Your frozen lips.
The grammar turned and attacked me.

A Valediction Forbidding Mourning

Themes, written under duress.
Emptiness of the notations.

They gave me a drug that slowed the healing of wounds.   5

I want you to see this before I leave:
the experience of repetition as death
the failure of criticism to locate the pain
the poster in the bus that said:
my bleeding is under control.   10

A red plant in a cemetery of plastic wreaths.

A last attempt: the language is a dialect called metaphor.
These images go unglossed: hair, glacier, flashlight.
When I think of a landscape I am thinking of a time.   15
When I talk of taking a trip I mean forever.
I could say: those mountains have a meaning
but further than that I could not say.

To do something very common, in my own way.

1971
Adrienne Rich (b. 1929)

The title's allusion to Donne's "A Valediction: Forbidding Mourning" is likely to give the impression that the poem concerns a similar leavetaking, but the "red plant in a cemetery of wreaths" indicates something more. Checking up on Rich's biography will tell us that her husband died in 1970, the year before the poem's publication. (Compare Rich's lines about her husband's being "wastefully dead" in "From a Survivor.") This information makes some lines of the poem clearer, but the speaker states flatly that some of it is not going to be made clear, perhaps even to herself:

> These images go unglossed: hair, glacier, flashlight.
>   . . .
> I could say: those mountains have a meaning
> but further than that I could not say.

If intense autobiographical images remain too unglossed, a poem turns in on itself, and readers are prevented from sharing the experience. One way out of this predicament is for the poet to gloss the images of private experience:

PERSONAL HELICON

For Michael Longley

As a child, they could not keep me from wells
And old pumps with buckets and windlasses.
I loved the dark drop, the trapped sky, the smells
Of waterweed, fungus and dank moss.

One, in a brickyard, with a rotted board top.   5
I savoured the rich crash when a bucket
Plummeted down at the end of a rope.
So deep you saw no reflection in it.

A shallow one under a dry stone ditch
Fructified like any aquarium.   10
When you dragged out long roots from the soft mulch
A white face hovered over the bottom.

Others had echoes, gave back your own call
With a clean new music in it. And one
Was scaresome for there, out of ferns and tall   15
Foxgloves, a rat slapped across my reflection.

Now, to pry into roots, to finger slime,
To stare big-eyed Narcissus, into some spring
Is beneath all adult dignity. I rhyme
To see myself, to set the darkness echoing.   20

1966
Seamus Heaney (b. 1939)

Heaney uses here an apparently private childhood experience, but he glosses
its meaning for us. The childhood experience of looking into wells becomes a
parallel for looking into the self to make poems.

Another way out of the private and enclosed self is through breaking it into

Helicon: a mountain in Greece sacred to the Muses and Apollo, god of poetry. A well or spring is
there, also associated with the Muses. **big-eyed Narcissus:** in Greek mythology, Narcissus chanced
on a glassy pool and fell hopelessly in love with his own reflection.

separate, often contradictory, characters so that the audience participates in the drama of the self. John Berryman's "Henry" is such a character:

from THE DREAM SONGS
14

> Life, friends, is boring. We must not say so.
> After all, the sky flashes, the great sea yearns,
> we ourselves flash and yearn,
> and moreover my mother told me as a boy
> (repeatingly) 'Ever to confess you're bored   5
> means you have no
>
> Inner Resources.' I conclude now I have no
> inner resources, because I am heavy bored.
> Peoples bore me,
> literature bores me, especially great literature,   10
> Henry bores me, with his plights & gripes
> as bad as achilles,
>
> who loves people and valiant art, which bores me.
> And the tranquil hills, & gin, look like a drag
> and somehow a dog   15
> has taken itself & its tail considerably away
> into mountains or sea or sky, leaving
> behind: me, wag.

1964

John Berryman (1914–1972)

Troubled by people who took the "Henry" of his poems to be too autobiographical, Berryman, perhaps somewhat disingenuously, cautioned:

> The poem, then, whatever its wide cast of characters, is essentially about an imaginary character (not the poet, not me) named Henry, a white American in early middle age sometimes in blackface, who has suffered an irreversible loss and talks about himself sometimes in the first person, sometimes in the third, sometimes even in the second; he has a friend, never named, who addresses him as Mr Bones and variants thereof.

Achilles: The Greek warrior who withdrew from the fighting at Troy because he felt that he had been dishonored by Agamemnon, the Greek general.

from THE DREAM SONGS
76
Henry's Confession

Nothin very bad happen to me lately.
How you explain that?—I explain that, Mr Bones.
terms o' your bafflin odd sobriety.
Sober as man can get, no girls, no telephones,
what could happen bad to Mr Bones?   5
—If life is a handkerchief sandwich,

in a modesty of death I join my father
who dared so long agone leave me.
A bullet on a concrete stoop
close by a smothering southern sea   10
spreadeagled on an island, by my knee.
—You is from hunger, Mr Bones,

I offers you this handkerchief, now set
your left foot by my right foot,
shoulder to shoulder, all that jazz,   15
arm in arm, by the beautiful sea,
hum a little, Mr Bones.
—I saw nobody coming, so I went instead.

1964

John Berryman (1914–1972)

Still another way out of exclusive concentration on the self is through
reference to poetic tradition, as in Adrienne Rich's "Valediction Forbidding
Mourning," with its allusion to Donne's poem. This is scarcely a modern phenomenon, of course. Ralegh played his "The Nymph's Reply to the Shepherd"
against Marlowe's "The Passionate Shepherd to His Love"; Spenser played with
the influence of Petrarch and Wyatt in writing his sonnet "Lyke as a Huntsman
after Weary Chace."

Denise Levertov uses and transforms poetic tradition in the following poem:

---

my father . . . : When Berryman was eleven years old and his family was living in Tampa,
Florida, his father shot himself on a porch outside the boy's bedroom window.

O TASTE AND SEE

The world is
not with us enough.
O taste and see

the subway Bible poster said,
meaning The Lord, meaning   5
if anything all that lives
in the imagination's tongue,

grief, mercy, language,
tangerine, weather, to
breathe them, bite,   10
savor, chew, swallow, transform

into our flesh our
deaths, crossing the street, plum, quince,
living in the orchard and being

hungry and plucking   15
the fruit.

1964
Denise Levertov (b. 1923)

Levertov's first lines are allusions to William Wordsworth's sonnet "The World
Is Too Much with Us" (in Poems for Further Reading). Levertov not only
revises and extends Wordsworth's observations into a modern setting, but she
transforms other pieces of the cultural past: the poster slogan seen in the subway comes from the Bible—"O taste and see that the Lord is good" (Psalms
xxiv: 8); the reference to "plum, quince," comes from lines in John Keats's
"Eve of St. Agnes" with perhaps an allusion to stanza 5 of Wallace Stevens'
"Sunday Morning." The last three lines of Levertov's poem refer to the temptation of Adam and Eve described in Genesis and in English poetry, most
notably in John Milton's epic, *Paradise Lost*. These allusions do not dominate
her poem; they serve rather to illustrate a new perception about the individual
in the modern world.

"THE EXACT FEEL AND SLANT OF A FIELD"

The loss of historical continuity described earlier in this chapter often turns
writers to the self for the only reliable "given" in experience. All that is certain

are memory and perceptions: what is remembered and what is seen, heard, smelt, touched, or tasted. The world of the senses has always been important in poetry, but in contemporary poetry it can become the sole reason for a poem's being. John Ashbery says that the best poets

> describe the exact feel
> and slant of a field in such a way as
> to
> Make you wish you were in it, or
> better yet
> To make you realize that you ac-
> tually are in it
> For better or for worse, with no
> Conceivable way of getting out.
>
> —from "Litany," 1979

We can see this technique—what might be called "verbal photography"—in the work of several poets:

THE RED WHEELBARROW

> so much depends
> upon
>
> a red wheel
> barrow
>
> glazed with rain   5
> water
>
> beside the white
> chickens.
>
> 1923
> *William Carlos Williams*
> *(1883–1963)*

Williams explained the significance of this focus upon the particularity of the objective world:

> To make a start
> out of particulars

and make them general, rolling
up the sum. . . .
                rolling up out of chaos   5
a nine months' wonder, the city
the man, an identity.

—from *Paterson*, Preface

The poet may find it enough "to make a start out of particulars" or to try to fix a passing impression. Ezra Pound described the challenge of finding apt words for such a transitory experience:

Three years ago [1913] in Paris I got out of a "metro" [subway] train at La Concorde, and saw suddenly a beautiful face, and then another and another, and then a beautiful child's face, and then another beautiful woman, and I tried all that day to find words for what this had meant to me, and I could not find any words that seemed to me worthy, or as lovely as that sudden emotion. And that evening . . . I was still trying and found, suddenly, the expression. I do not mean that I found words, but there came an equation . . . not in speech, but in little splotches of colour. . . . I wrote a thirty-line poem, and destroyed it. . . . Six months later I made a poem half that length; a year later I made [this] hokku-like [haiku-like] sentence":

IN A STATION OF THE METRO

The apparition of these faces in the crowd;
Petals on a wet, black bough.

1916
Ezra Pound (1885–1972)

The challenges and rewards of this attempt to "fix the transitory spectacle" are still evident in the most recent contemporary poetry. Here are two examples:

from LITANY

I photographed all things,
All things as happening
As prelude, as prelude to the impatience
Of enormous summer nights opening

Out farther and farther, like the billowing   5
Of a parachute, with only that slit
Of starlight. The old, old
Wonderful story, and it's all right
As far as it goes, but impatience
Is the true ether that surrounds us.   10
Without it everything would be asphalt.

Now that the things of autumn
Have been sequestered too in their chain
The other parts of the year become
Visible   15
And the summer night is like a goldfish bowl
With everything in full view, yet only parts
Are what is actually seen, and these supply
The rest. It's not like cheating
Since it *is* all there, but more like   20
Helping the truth along a little:
The artifice lets it become itself,
Nestling in truth. These are long days
And we need all the help we can get.

We are to become ashamed only much later,   25
Much later on, under the old bench.
And it is not like the old days
When we used to sing off-key
For hours in the rain-drenched schoolroom
On purpose. Here, whatever is forgotten   30
Or stored away is imbued with vitality.
Whatever is to come is too.

                                                              1979
                                               John Ashbery (b. 1927)

THE EEL GROUNDS

On warm nights, the tide out,
my father, uncle, and I
wade the flats above the nun buoy
to raid the eel grounds.

**Not Ideas about the Thing
but the Thing Itself**

My uncle touches a match   5
to the windproof lantern
and our shadows flare
halfway across the bay.

The eels boil up toward the light,
knotted thick as mooring cable,   10
almost knocking us off our feet.

We drag the wire trap
until it can't be lifted,
and lug it ashore.

Secret as bootleggers, we pack   15
bushels brimmed with ice,
and gun the ancient flatbed
through the saw grass.

                        1979
              Aaron Fischer (b. 1952)

Whether they are working within fixed forms or experimental ones, whether their poems have as focus the self or the closely observed detail, poets still do what they have always done—provide us with language that allows us to see both them as private and unique human beings, and ourselves and our experiences in new and remarkable ways:

NOT IDEAS ABOUT THE THING BUT THE THING ITSELF

At the earliest ending of winter,
In March, a scrawny cry from outside
Seemed like a sound in his mind.

He knew that he heard it,
A bird's cry, at daylight or before,   5
In the early March wind.

The sun was rising at six,
No longer a battered panache above snow . . .
It would have been outside.

---

panache: a plume, as on a helmet.

It was not from the vast ventriloquism   10
Of sleep's faded papier-mâché . . .
The sun was coming from outside.

That scrawny cry—it was
A chorister whose c preceded the choir.
It was part of the colossal sun,   15

Surrounded by its choral rings,
Still far away. It was like
A new knowledge of reality.

1954
Wallace Stevens (1879–1955)

Poetry is part of that "thing itself" which gives us a new knowledge of reality.

EXERCISES————————————————————————————

A. Greek and Roman mythology has provided poets with a storehouse of material from which they can draw for personal reinterpretations of those myths (see, for example, Tennyson's "Ulysses" in Poems for Further Reading).

MYTH

Long afterward, Oedipus, old and blinded, walked the
roads.   He smelled a familiar smell.   It was
the Sphinx.   Oedipus said, "I want to ask one question.
Why didn't I recognize my mother?"   "You gave the
wrong answer," said the Sphinx.   "But that was what
made everything possible," said Oedipus.   "No," she said.
"When I asked, What walks on four legs in the morning,
two at noon, and three in the evening, you answered,
Man.   You didn't say anything about woman."
"When you say Man," said Oedipus, "you include women
too. Everyone knows that."   She said, "That's what
you think."

1973
Muriel Rukeyser (1913–1980)

1. What details of the Oedipus myth does Rukeyser use in this poem?
2. What changes or inventions does she use?
3. What suggests that this is very much a contemporary poem (compare, for example, the poems in Chapter Seven, Exercise B)?

B. Using details of biblical sources and/or classical mythology, poets can still construct their own mythologies:

LEDA AND THE SWAN

A sudden blow: the great wings beating still
Above the staggering girl, her thighs caressed
By the dark webs, her nape caught in his bill,
He holds her helpless breast upon his breast.

How can those terrified vague fingers push   5
The feathered glory from her loosening thighs?
And how can body, laid in that white rush,
But feel the strange heart beating where it lies?

A shudder in the loins engenders there
The broken wall, the burning roof and tower
And Agamemnon dead.   10
                    Being so caught up,
So mastered by the brute blood of the air,
Did she put on his knowledge with his power
Before the indifferent beak could let her drop?

1924
William Butler Yeats (1865–1939)

1. In "Leda and the Swan," Yeats uses the Greek myths that tell about Leda, the mother of Helen of Troy. In one, Leda was assaulted by Zeus in the form of a swan and bore a daughter Helen, who was at least one cause of the Trojan Wars. For accounts of that myth, consult a handbook of mythology such as Edith Hamilton, *Mythology*; H. J. Rose, A *Handbook of Greek Mythology*; Robert Graves, *The Greek Myths*; or *The New Century Classical Handbook*, ed. Catherine Avery. What details of the myth does Yeats interpret or reinterpret?
2. According to the poem, what are the violent consequences of the rape? What historical era does the rape initiate?

3. You may wish to research Yeats's personal view of history as background to "Leda and the Swan." In addition to many poems that express this view, Yeats's *Michael Robartes and the Dancer* (1921) and *A Vision* (1938) set out his detailed system.

C. Samuel Johnson (1709–1894)—critic, novelist, and poet—has a character in his novel *Rasselas* (1759) describe the task of the poet:

> The business of a poet, said Imlac, is to examine, not the individual, but the species; to remark general properties and large appearances; he does not number the streaks of the tulip, or describe the different shades of the verdure of the forest. He is to exhibit in his portraits of nature such prominent and striking features, as recall the original in every mind; and neglect the minuter discriminations, which one may have remarked and another neglected, for those characteristics which are alike obvious to vigilance and carelessness.
>
> But the knowledge of nature is only half of the task of a poet.

Imlac goes on to tell his pupil, Rasselas, that a poet must be acquainted with all experiences of life; be able to evaluate the happiness or misery in every situation; be skillful enough to trace the changes in the human mind as it is affected by institutions, climate, and social custom; and rise above the prejudices of his own time and country in order to perceive enduring and universal truths. The poet, according to Imlac, writes as "legislator of mankind," presiding, through his character and his poems, over the thoughts and manners of the human race.

Even then, Imlac is not finished describing the comprehensive tasks of the poet, but Rasselas cries out, "Enough! Thou has convinced me that no human being can ever be a poet."

Two hundred years later the American poet Frank O'Hara describes the work of the poet much differently:

> I am mainly preoccupied with the world as I experience it. . . . I don't think of fame or posterity (as Keats so grandly and genuinely did), nor do I care about clarifying experiences for anyone or bettering (other than accidentally) anyone's state or social relation. . . . What is happening to me, allowing for lies and exaggerations which I try to avoid, goes into my poems. I don't think my experiences are clarified or made beautiful for myself or anyone else, they are just there in whatever form I can find them.
>
> —quoted in Donald M. Allen, ed., *The New American Poetry*

Here are two poems, one by Johnson and one by O'Hara:

ON THE DEATH OF DR. ROBERT LEVET

Condemn'd to hope's delusive mine,
  As on we toil from day to day,
By sudden blasts, or slow decline,
  Our social comforts drop away.

Well tried through many a varying year,   5
  See LEVET to the grave descend;
Officious, innocent, sincere,
  Of ev'ry friendless name the friend.

Yet still he fills affection's eye,
  Obscurely wise, and coarsely kind;   10
Nor, letter'd arrogance, deny
  Thy praise to merit unrefin'd.

When fainting nature call'd for aid,
  And hov'ring death prepar'd the blow,
His vig'rous remedy display'd   15
  The power of art without the show.

In misery's darkest caverns known,
  His useful care was ever nigh,
Where hopeless anguish pour'd his groan,
  And lonely want retir'd to die.   20

No summons mock'd by chill delay,
  No petty gain disdain'd by pride,
The modest wants of ev'ry day
  The toil of ev'ry day supplied.

His virtues walk'd their narrow round,   25
  Nor made a pause, nor left a void;
And sure th' Eternal Master found
  The single talent well employ'd.

Robert Levet (1705–1782) was a self-trained physician who lived in Johnson's house and treated the poor of the neighborhood. **officious:** eager to help.

The busy day, the peaceful night,
    Unfelt, uncounted, glided by;   30
His frame was firm, his powers were bright,
    Tho' now his eightieth year was nigh.

Then with no throbbing fiery pain,
    No cold gradations of decay,
Death broke at once the vital chain,   35
    And free'd his soul the nearest way.

1783
Samuel Johnson (1709–1784)

THE DAY LADY DIED

It is 12:20 in New York a Friday
three days after Bastille day, yes
it is 1959 and I go get a shoeshine
because I will get off the 4:19 in Easthampton
at 7:15 and then go straight to dinner   5
and I don't know the people who will feed me

I walk up the muggy street beginning to sun
and have a hamburger and a malted and buy
an ugly NEW WORLD WRITING to see what the poets
in Ghana are doing these days   10
          I go on to the bank
and Miss Stillwagon (first name Linda I once heard)
doesn't even look up my balance for once in her life
and in the GOLDEN GRIFFIN I get a little Verlaine
for Patsy with drawings by Bonnard although I do   15
think of Hesiod, trans. Richmond Lattimore or
Brendan Behan's new play or *Le Balcon* or *Les Nègres*
of Genet, but I don't, I stick with Verlaine
after practically going to sleep with quandariness

and for Mike I just stroll into the PARK LANE   20
Liquor Store and ask for a bottle of Strega and
then I go back where I came from to 6th Avenue

Lady: Billie Holiday (1915–1959), the great American blues singer, whose nickname was "Lady Day."

and the tobacconist in the Ziegfeld Theatre and
casually ask for a carton of Gauloises and a carton
of Picayunes, and a NEW YORK POST with her face on it   25

and I am sweating a lot by now and thinking of
leaning on the john door in the 5 SPOT
while she whispered a song along the keyboard
to Mal Waldron and everyone and I stopped breathing

1964

Frank O'Hara (1926–1966)

Both Johnson, through his character Imlac, and O'Hara have given a description of the poetic task. To what extent do their poems exemplify their statements? Consider, for example, the following more specific questions:

1. How does Johnson place Levet's death in relation to all his readers? in relation to philosophic systems? in relation to himself?
2. How does O'Hara place Holiday's death in relation to all the above categories?
3. How does O'Hara's poem illustrate his statement: "What is happening to me . . . goes into my poem?" What of Johnson gets into his poem?
4. Why is O'Hara concerned with location in such detail, and why does Johnson not seem to have this concern?

D.   LOVE CALLS US TO THE THINGS OF THIS WORLD

The eyes open to a cry of pulleys,
And spirited from sleep, the astounded soul
Hangs for a moment bodiless and simple
As false dawn.
                    Outside the open window
The morning air is all awash with angels.   5

Some are in bed-sheets, some are in blouses,
Some are in smocks: but truly there they are.
Now they are rising together in calm swells
Of halcyon feeling, filling whatever they wear
With the deep joy of their impersonal breathing;   10

Now they are flying in place, conveying
The terrible speed of their omnipresence, moving

Mal Waldron: the pianist who was Billie Holiday's last accompanist.

And staying like white water; and now of a sudden
They swoon down into so rapt a quiet
That nobody seems to be there.
The soul shrinks   15

From all that it is about to remember,
From the punctual rape of every blessèd day,
And cries,
      "Oh, let there be nothing on earth but laundry,
Nothing but rosy hands in the rising steam
And clear dances done in the sight of heaven."   20

Yet, as the sun acknowledges
With a warm look the world's hunks and colors,
The soul descends once more in bitter love
To accept the waking body, saying now
In a changed voice as the man yawns and rises,   25

"Bring them down from their ruddy gallows;
Let there be clean linen for the backs of thieves;
Let lovers go fresh and sweet to be undone,
And the heaviest nuns walk in a pure floating
Of dark habits,
      keeping their difficult balance."   30

1956
Richard Wilbur (b. 1921)

A critic, John J. Keenan, has raised some "heretical questions," as he calls them, in response to Wilbur's poem:

> Listening to Richard Wilbur introduce his poem, "Love Calls Us to the Things of This World," at a poetry reading, I suddenly had a startling, heretical thought pop into my head.
> Mr. Wilbur was merely explaining that the poem had its beginning when he was awakened one morning by the sound of squeaky clotheslines outside his apartment window. I had always liked the poem, but never felt that I understood all of the allusions and images until that moment. The poet's comment had given me the context I needed, and the poem became clearer in tone, imagery, and allusions because of something I had learned that was not actually stated in the poem itself.

Examine the first few lines of the poem with the above information in mind and you can see for yourself how it helps open up the poem to the reader:

> The eyes open to a cry of pulleys,
> And spirited from sleep, the astounded soul
> Hangs for a moment bodiless and simple
> As false dawn.
> Outside the open window
> The morning air is all awash with angels.

How long would it have taken you to appreciate the pun on "awash" or the metaphor of "angels" if you didn't associate "the cry of pulleys" with clotheslines?

The heretical questions I found myself entertaining were simply this: "Why don't more contemporary poets furnish us with the context we need in order to read the poem intelligently? Why can't they tell the reader in print what they would normally tell an audience in a reading?" . . . From the large number of readers who comfortably ignore contemporary poetry, it is apparent that many have withdrawn their agreement to accept poetry on conventional terms. If poets are not to find themselves playing private word games as personal therapy, they may rediscover the communicative pleasures of poetry, which may lead them to see that there is nothing subversive or patronizing about sharing more of the poetic process with the reader.

—from "Why Can't Our Poets Play Fair?"

1. Keenan argues that Wilbur's opening image—"the cry of pulleys"—is so unglossed within the context of the poem as to make the other allusions and images of the poem unclear. What evidence does he give to support this claim? Do you agree or disagree?
2. What in the poems in this or the other chapters of this book supports Keenan's argument? What evidence from these poems might be used to counter his argument?

E.   **A PACT**

> I make a pact with you, Walt Whitman—
> I have detested you long enough.
> I come to you as a grown child
> Who has had a pig-headed father;
> I am old enough now to make friends.   5
> It was you that broke the new wood,

Now it is time for carving.
We have one sap and one root—
Let there be commerce between us.

1916

Ezra Pound (1885–1972)

WALT WHITMAN AT BEAR MOUNTAIN

. . . life which does not give the preference to any other life,
of any previous period, which therefore prefers its own existence . . .

—Ortega y Gasset

Neither on horseback nor seated,
But like himself, squarely on two feet,
The poet of death and lilacs
Loafs by the footpath. Even the bronze looks alive
Where it is folded like cloth. And he seems friendly.   5

"Where is the Mississippi panorama
And the girl who played the piano?
What are you, Walt?
The Open Road goes to the used-car lot.

"Where is the nation you promised?   10
These houses built of wood sustain
Colossal snows,
And the light above the street is sick to death.

"As for the people—see how they neglect you!
Only a poet pauses to read the inscription."   15

"I am here," he answered.
"It seems you have found me out.
Yet, did I not warn you that it was Myself
I advertised? Were my words not sufficiently plain?

"I gave no prescriptions,   20
And those who have taken my moods for prophecies
Mistake the matter."

Then, vastly amused—"Why do you reproach me?
I freely confess I am wholly disreputable.
Yet I am happy, because you have found me out."   25

A crocodile in wrinkled metal loafing . . .

Then all the realtors,
Pickpockets, salesmen, and the actors performing
Official scenarios,
Turned a deaf ear, for they had contracted   30
American dreams.

But the man who keeps a store on a lonely road,
And the housewife who knows she's dumb,
And the earth, are relieved.

All that grave weight of America   35
Cancelled! Like Greece and Rome.
The future in ruins!
The castles, the prisons, the cathedrals
Unbuilding, and roses
Blossoming from the stones that are not there . . .   40

The clouds are lifting from the high Sierras.
The Bay mists clearing;
And the angel in the gate, the flowering plum,
Dances like Italy, imagining red.

                              1960
                    Louis Simpson (b. 1923)

As these poems may suggest, the poetry of Walt Whitman (1819–1872) has been tremendously influential not only on American poetry but on modern poetry in general. Of the preceding poem, Louis Simpson says:

> "Walt Whitman at Bear Mountain" springs from an actual experience, as do most of my poems. About three years ago I traveled up the Hudson River to Bear Mountain with my wife and the poet Robert Bly and his wife. We came upon the Jo Davidson (I believe that's the right spelling) statue of Walt Whitman. The statue was very impressive under the leaves. A few days later I started this poem. I didn't finish it for months, not until I had moved to California. The

fragments of what I had attempted then cohered all at once—this is the way it happens with me, if I'm lucky.

Whitman means a great deal to me. When I came to America, at the age of seventeen, an intelligent cousin gave me a copy of *Leaves of Grass*. I recognized immediately that Whitman was a great, original poet. I now think that he is the greatest poet we have had in America. But I think that most of his prophecies have been proved wrong. It is a strange fact, when you think about it—that a poet can be great and yet be mistaken in his ideas. The Whitman who heralds an inevitable march of Democracy, who praises the intelligence of the masses, is nearly always mistaken. At least, if there ever was an America like that, it no longer exists. But the Whitman who uses his own eyes and ears, who describes things, who expresses his own sly humor or pathos, is unbeatable. I tried to show the two Whitmans in my poem. I used my ideas about Whitman as a way of getting at my own ideas about America. And I think a great deal about the country I live in; indeed, it seems an inexhaustible subject, one that has hardly been tapped. By America, I mean the infinitely complex life we have. Sometimes when I look at Main Street, I feel like a stranger looking at the Via Aurelia, or the Pyramids. But our monuments are ephemeral. Poetry is the art of the ephemeral.

It is hard to talk about a poem, for talking about poetry leads you out in every direction. I do not see the art of poetry as separated from life.

—from *Poet's Choice*, ed. Paul Engle and Joseph Langland

1. Why would a poet "detest" another poet? Why does Pound "detest" Whitman?
2. What does Pound say about Whitman's importance as a poet? What is it that Pound both admires and needs to break with in Whitman?
3. Which of Whitman's prophecies about America does Simpson suggest have been proved wrong? How does Simpson's view affect his poem about Whitman?

F. LYING IN A HAMMOCK AT WILLIAM DUFFY'S FARM IN PINE ISLAND, MINNESOTA

Over my head, I see the bronze butterfly,
Asleep on the black trunk,
Blowing like a leaf in green shadow.
Down the ravine behind the empty house,
The cowbells follow one another   5

Into the distances of the afternoon.
To my right,
In a field of sunlight between two pines,
The droppings of last year's horses
Blaze up into golden stones.
I lean back, as the evening darkens and comes on.   10
A chicken hawk floats over, looking for home.
I have wasted my life.

1963
James Wright (1927–1980)

1. How specific is place in this poem? How important is it?
2. Look at the natural details in the poem. Is there an arrangement of any sort? In earlier chapters we have seen examples of natural details reflecting the speaker's mood, changing that mood, and influencing the organization of the poem. Are any of these things going on here? If so, which one(s), and if not, how do the details work?
3. Do the observed details prepare in any way—temporally, symbolically, or some other way—for the poem's last line?

WRITING SUGGESTIONS_____

1. In a recent book, *The Culture of Narcissism: American Life in an Age of Diminishing Expectations* (1978), Christopher Lasch wrote:

   > To live for the moment is the prevailing passion—to live for yourself, not for your predecessors or posterity. We are fast losing the sense of historical continuity, the sense of belonging to a succession of generations originating in the past and stretching into the future.

   In an essay, discuss the validity of this statement as a description of the contemporary poems discussed in this chapter. You may wish to focus on two or three poems only, such as Michael McClure's "Hymn to St. Geryon," James Schuyler's "Milk," and Robert Bly's "After Drinking All Night with a Friend. . . ."

2. Write an essay comparing and contrasting the following two poems:

THE PICTURE OF LITTLE T. C. IN A PROSPECT OF FLOWERS

See with what simplicity
This nymph begins her golden days!
In the green grass she loves to lie,
And there with her fair aspect tames
The wilder flowers, and gives them names;   5
But only with the roses plays,
    And them does tell
What color best becomes them, and what smell.

Who can foretell for what high cause
This darling of the gods was born?   10
Yet this is she whose chaster laws
The wanton Love shall one day fear,
And, under her command severe,
See his bow broke and ensigns torn.
    Happy who can   15
Appease this virtuous enemy of man!

O then let me in time compound
And parley with those conquering eyes,
Ere they have tried their force to wound;
Ere with their glancing wheels they drive   20
In triumph over hearts that strive,
And them that yield but more despise:
    Let me be laid
Where I may see thy glories from some shade.

Meantime, whilst every verdant thing   25
Itself does at thy beauty charm,
Reform the errors of the spring;
Make that the tulips may have share
Of sweetness, seeing they are fair;
And roses of their thorns disarm;   30
    But most procure
That violets may a longer age endure.

T.C.: probably Theophila Cornewall, a child of a family known to Marvell. The family had lost
several children as a result of the plague and infant mortality.

But, O young beauty of the woods
Whom nature courts with fruits and flowers,
Gather the flowers, but spare the buds,   35
Lest Flora, angry at thy crime
To kill her infants in their prime,
Do quickly make the example yours;
    And ere we see,
Nip in the blossom all our hopes and thee.

1681

Andrew Marvell (1621–1678)

THE PICTURE OF J. T. IN A PROSPECT OF STONE

What should one
  wish a child
    and that, one's own
      emerging
from between   5
  the stone lips   .
of a sheep-stile
  that divides
    village graves
and village green?   10
  —Wish her
    the constancy of stone.
—But stone
  is hard.
    —Say, rather   15
it resists
  the slow corrosives
    and the flight
of time
  and yet it takes   20

The Picture of Little T. C.   **Flora:** goddess of flowers.

The Picture of J. T.   **sheep stile:** a step or gate in a wall that allows a person to pass through but that prevents the passage of sheep or cattle.

```
        the play, the fluency
    from light.
        —How would you know
        the gift you'd give
    was the gift                                    25
        she'd wish to have?
        —Gift is giving,
    gift is meaning:
        first
            I'd give                                30
    then let her
        live with it
            to prove
    its quality the better and
        thus learn                                  35
            to love
    what (to begin with)
        she might spurn.
            —You'd
    moralize a gift?                                40
        —I'd have her
        understand
    the gift I gave her.
        —And so she shall
            but let her play                        45
    her innocence away
        emerging
            as she does
    between
        her doom (unknown),                         50
            her unmown green.
```

1963

Charles Tomlinson (b. 1927)

The following questions may be useful in preparing your essay:

1. What in Marvell's poem—in addition to the title—influences Tomlinson's poem?
2. What changes in speaker, attitude, setting, and situation does Tomlinson make in reference to Marvell's poem?
3. In both poems, the situation seems to be a response to a literal experi-

ence—seeing a child in a garden, seeing a child crossing through a stile set in a stone wall. How are the details of the observed scene treated in each poem?

4. How are those details of the scene connected to the wishes each speaker has for the child?

5. What ordering systems are at work in Marvell's poem that are absent in Tomlinson's poem? What takes the place of these ordering systems?

6. To what extent does Tomlinson's poem require that the reader know Marvell's poem? What is gained by comparing the two?

POEMS FOR FURTHER READING

LORD RANDALL

"Oh where ha'e ye been, Lord Randall my son?
O where ha'e ye been, my handsome young man?"
  "I ha'e been to the wild wood: mother, make my bed soon,
  For I'm weary wi' hunting, and fain wald lie down."

"Where gat ye your dinner, Lord Randall my son?   5
Where gat ye your dinner, my handsome young man?"
  "I dined wi' my true love; mother, make my bed soon,
  For I'm weary wi' hunting, and fain wald lie down."

"What gat ye to your dinner, Lord Randall my son?
What gat ye to your dinner, my handsome young man?"   10
  "I gat eels boiled in broo: mother, make my bed
        soon,
For I'm weary wi' hunting and fain wald lie down."

"What became of your bloodhounds, Lord Randall my son?
What became of your bloodhounds, my handsome young man?"
  "O they swelled and they died: mother, make my bed soon,   15
  For I'm weary wi' hunting and fain wald lie down."

"O I fear ye are poisoned, Lord Randall my son!
O I fear ye are poisoned, my handsome young man!"
  "O yes, I am poisoned: mother, make my bed soon,
  For I'm sick at the heart, and I fain wald lie down."   20

composed about 1500

                                        Anonymous

---

fain: gladly. **wald:** would. **broo:** broth.

WITH HOW SAD STEPS, O MOON, THOU CLIMB'ST THE SKIES!

With how sad steps, O Moon, thou climb'st the skies!
How silently, and with how wan a face!
What, may it be that even in heavenly place
That busy archer his sharp arrows tries?
Sure, if that long-with-love-acquainted eyes   5
Can judge of love, thou feel'st a lover's case,
I read it in thy looks; thy languished grace,
To me, that feel the like, thy state descries.
Then, even of fellowship, Oh Moon, tell me,
Is constant love deemed there but want of wit?   10
Are beauties there as proud as here they be?
Do they above love to be loved, and yet
Those lovers scorn whom that love doth possess?
Do they call virtue there ungratefulness?

1591/1598
Sir Philip Sidney (1554–1586)

WHEN I DO COUNT THE CLOCK THAT TELLS THE TIME

When I do count the clock that tells the time,
And see the brave day sunk in hideous night;
When I behold the violet past prime,
And sable curls, all silvered o'er with white;
When lofty trees I see barren of leaves,   5
Which erst from heat did canopy the herd,
And summer's green all girded up in sheaves,
Borne on the bier with white and bristly beard,
Then of thy beauty do I question make,
That thou among the wastes of time must go,   10
Since sweets and beauties do themselves forsake
And die as fast as they see others grow;
And nothing 'gainst time's scythe can make defense
Save breed, to brave him when he takes thee hence.

1609
William Shakespeare (1564–1616)

ON MY FIRST SON

Farewell, thou child of my right hand, and joy;
My sin was too much hope of thee, loved boy:
Seven years thou wert lent to me, and I thee pay,
Exacted by thy fate, on the just day.
O could I lose all father now! for why   5
Will man lament the state he should envy,
To have so soon 'scaped world's and flesh's rage,
And, if no other misery, yet age?
Rest in soft peace, and asked, say, "Here doth lie
Ben Jonson his best piece of poetry."   10
For whose sake henceforth all his vows be such
As what he loves may never like too much.

1616

Ben Jonson (1572–1637)

CORINNA'S GOING A-MAYING

Get up! get up for shame! the blooming morn
Upon her wings presents the god unshorn.
  See how Aurora throws her fair
  Fresh-quilted colors through the air:
  Get up, sweet slug-a-bed, and see   5
  The dew bespangling herb and tree.
Each flower has wept and bowed toward the east
Above an hour since, yet you not dressed;
  Nay, not so much as out of bed?
  When all the birds have matins said,   10
  And sung their thankful hymns, 'tis sin,
  Nay, profanation to keep in,
Whenas a thousand virgins on this day
Spring, sooner than the lark, to fetch in May.   15

On My First Son   child of my right hand: Jonson's son was named Benjamin, which means "child of the right hand." **the just day:** Benjamin died on his seventh birthday in 1603.

Corinna's Going A-Maying   The god unshorn: Apollo, the sun god. **to fetch in May:** to bring in May flowers to decorate the house.

Rise, and put on your foliage, and be seen
To come forth, like the springtime, fresh and green,
    And sweet as Flora. Take no care
    For jewels for your gown or hair;
    Fear not; the leaves will strew
    Gems in abundance upon you;   20
Besides, the childhood of the day has kept,
Against you come, some orient pearls unwept;
    Come and receive them while the light
    Hangs on the dew-locks of the night,
    And Titan on the eastern hill   25
    Retires himself, or else stands still
Till you come forth. Wash, dress, be brief in praying:
Few beads are best when once we go a-Maying.

Come, my Corinna, come; and, coming, mark
How each field turns a street, each street a park   30
    Made green and trimmed with trees; see how
    Devotion gives each house a bough
    Or branch: each porch, each door ere this,
    An ark, a tabernacle is,
Made up of whitethorn neatly interwove,   35
As if here were those cooler shades of love.
    Can such delights be in the street
    And open fields, and we not see 't?
    Come, we'll abroad; and let's obey
    The proclamation made for May,   40
And sin no more, as we have done, by staying;
But, my Corinna, come, let's go a-Maying.

There's not a budding boy or girl this day
But is got up and gone to bring in May;
    A deal of youth, ere this, is come   45
    Back, and with whitethorn laden home.
    Some have dispatched their cakes and cream
    Before that we have left to dream;
And some have wept, and wooed, and plighted troth,
And chose their priest, ere we can cast off sloth.   50
    Many a green-gown has been given,

Titan: also a sun god.

Many a kiss, both odd and even;
Many a glance, too, has been sent
From out the eye, love's firmament;
Many a jest told of the keys betraying   55
This night, and locks picked; yet we're not a-Maying.

Come, let us go while we are in our prime,
And take the harmless folly of the time.
  We shall grow old apace, and die
  Before we know our liberty.   60
  Our life is short, and our days run
  As fast away as does the sun;
And, as a vapor or a drop of rain
Once lost, can ne'er be found again;
  So when or you or I are made   65
  A fable, song, or fleeting shade,
  All love, all liking, all delight
  Lies drowned with us in endless night.
Then while time serves, and we are but decaying,
Come, my Corinna, come, let's go a-Maying.   70

> 1648
> *Robert Herrick (1591–1674)*

THE GARDEN

  How vainly men themselves amaze
To win the palm, the oak, or bays,
And their incessant labors see
Crowned from some single herb, or tree,
Whose short and narrow-vergéd shade   5
Does prudently their toils upbraid;
While all flowers and all trees do close
To weave the garlands of repose!

  Fair Quiet, have I found thee here,
And Innocence, thy sister dear?
Mistaken long, I sought you then   10
In busy companies of men.
Your sacred plants, if here below,

Only among the plants will grow;
Society is all but rude   15
To this delicious solitude.

No white nor red was ever seen
So amorous as this lovely green.
Fond lovers, cruel as their flame,
Cut in these trees their mistress' name: 20
Little, alas, they know or heed
How far these beauties hers exceed!
Fair trees, wheresoe'er your barks I wound,
No name shall but your own be found.

When we have run our passion's heat,   25
Love hither makes his best retreat.
The gods, that mortal beauty chase,
Still in a tree did end their race:
Apollo hunted Daphne so,
Only that she might laurel grow;   30
And Pan did after Syrinx speed,
Not as a nymph, but for a reed.

What wondrous life is this I lead!
Ripe apples drop about my head;
The luscious clusters of the vine   35
Upon my mouth do crush their wine;
The nectarine and curious peach
Into my hands themselves do reach;
Stumbling on melons, as I pass,
Insnared with flowers, I fall on grass.   40

Meanwhile the mind, from pleasure less,
Withdraws into its happiness;
The mind, that ocean where each kind
Does straight its own resemblance find;
Yet it creates, transcending these,   45
Far other worlds and other seas,

The gods, that mortal beauty chase: In myths, nymphs pursued by gods—such as Daphne by Apollo, Syrinx by Pan—turn into plants or trees to escape. **resemblance:** each land creature was thought to have a counterpart in the sea.

The Garden

Annihilating all that's made
To a green thought in a green shade.

   Here at the fountain's sliding foot,
Or at some fruit tree's mossy root,   50
Casting the body's vest aside,
My soul into the boughs does glide:
There, like a bird, it sits and sings,
Then whets and combs its silver wings,
And, till prepared for longer flight,   55
Waves in its plumes the various light.

   Such was that happy garden-state,
While man there walked without a mate:
After a place so pure and sweet,
What other help could yet be meet!   60
But 'twas beyond a mortal's share
To wander solitary there:
Two paradises 'twere in one
To live in paradise alone.

   How well the skillful gardener drew   65
Of flowers and herbs this dial new,
Where, from above, the milder sun
Does through a fragrant zodiac run;
And as it works, th' industrious bee
Computes its time as well as we!   70
How could such sweet and wholesome hours
Be reckoned but with herbs and flowers?

                     1681
Andrew Marvell (1621–1678)

My soul: compare Yeats's "Sailing to Byzantium," stanza 4. **What other help could yet be meet!:** God created Eve because, before her existence, "for Adam there was not found an help meet for him" (Genesis: 2:20).

A SONG FOR ST. CECILIA'S DAY

1

From harmony, from heavenly harmony
    This universal frame began:
    When Nature underneath a heap
      Of jarring atoms lay,
      And could not heave her head,   5
The tuneful voice was heard from high:
    "Arise, ye more than dead."
Then cold, and hot, and moist, and dry,
In order to their stations leap,
      And Music's power obey.   10
From harmony, from heavenly harmony
    This universal frame began:
    From harmony to harmony
Through all the compass of the notes it ran,
The diapason closing full in man.   15

2

What passion cannot Music raise and quell!
    When Jubal struck the corded shell,
    His listening brethren stood around,
    And, wondering, on their faces fell
    To worship that celestial sound.   20
Less than a god they thought there could not dwell
    Within the hollow of that shell
    That spoke so sweetly and so well.
What passion cannot Music raise and quell!

3

The trumpet's loud clangor   25
    Excites us to arms,
With shrill notes of anger,
    And mortal alarms.

St. Cecilia's Day: November 22. Cecilia is the patron saint of music. In England, from about 1683 to 1703, the day was celebrated with religious services and concerts. Dryden's ode was set to music first by G. B. Draghi in 1687 and then, in a more famous setting, by George Frideric Handel (1685–1759) in 1739. **Jubal:** the inventor of the harp and organ (Genesis 4: 21).

The double double double beat
　　Of the thundering drum　　　　　　　　　　30
Cries: "Hark! the foes come;
Charge, charge, 'tis too late to retreat."

4

The soft complaining flute
In dying notes discovers
The woes of hopeless lovers,　　　　　　　　　35
Whose dirge is whispered by the warbling lute.

5

　　Sharp violins proclaim
Their jealous pangs, and desperation,
Fury, frantic indignation,
Depth of pains, and height of passion,　　　　40
　　For the fair, disdainful dame.

6

　　But O! what art can teach,
　　What human voice can reach,
The sacred organ's praise?
　　Notes inspiring holy love,　　　　　　　　45
Notes that wing their heavenly ways
　　To mend the choirs above.

7

Orpheus could lead the savage race;
And trees unrooted left their place,
　　Sequacious of the lyre;　　　　　　　　　50
But bright Cecilia raised the wonder higher:
When to her organ vocal breath was given,
An angel heard, and straight appeared,
　　Mistaking earth for heaven.

GRAND CHORUS

As from the power of sacred lays　　　　　　55
　　The spheres began to move,

Orpheus: the legendary poet and musician whose music was able to tame wild beasts.

And sung the great Creator's praise
  To all the blest above;
So, when the last and dreadful hour
This crumbling pageant shall devour,   60
The trumpet shall be heard on high,
The dead shall live, the living die,
And Music shall untune the sky.

1687
John Dryden (1631–1700)

ELEGY WRITTEN IN A COUNTRY CHURCHYARD

The curfew tolls the knell of parting day,
  The lowing herd wind slowly o'er the lea,
The plowman homeward plods his weary way,
  And leaves the world to darkness and to me.

Now fades the glimmering landscape on the sight,   5
  And all the air a solemn stillness holds,
Save where the beetle wheels his droning flight,
  And drowsy tinklings lull the distant folds;

Save that from yonder ivy-mantled tower
  The moping owl does to the moon complain   10
Of such, as wandering near her secret bower,
  Molest her ancient solitary reign.

Beneath those rugged elms, that yew tree's shade,
  Where heaves the turf in many a moldering heap,
Each in his narrow cell forever laid,   15
  The rude forefathers of the hamlet sleep.

The breezy call of incense-breathing morn,
  The swallow twittering from the straw-built shed,
The cock's shrill clarion, or the echoing horn,
  No more shall rouse them from their lowly bed.   20

This crumbling pageant: the universe. **The trumpet**: "for the trumpet shall sound, and the dead shall be raised incorruptible, and we shall be changed" (I Corinthians 15: 52).

Elegy Written in a Country Churchyard

For them no more the blazing hearth shall burn,
    Or busy housewife ply her evening care;
No children run to lisp their sire's return,
    Or climb his knees the envied kiss to share.

Oft did the harvest to their sickle yield,   25
    Their furrow oft the stubborn glebe has broke;
How jocund did they drive their team afield!
    How bowed the woods beneath their sturdy stroke!

Let not Ambition mock their useful toil,
    Their homely joys, and destiny obscure;   30
Nor Grandeur hear with a disdainful smile
    The short and simple annals of the poor.

The boast of heraldry, the pomp of power,
    And all that beauty, all that wealth e'er gave,
Awaits alike the inevitable hour.   35
    The paths of glory lead but to the grave.

Nor you, ye proud, impute to these the fault,
    If Memory o'er their tomb no trophies raise,
Where through the long-drawn aisle and fretted vault
    The pealing anthem swells the note of praise.   40

Can storied urn or animated bust
    Back to its mansion call the fleeting breath?
Can Honor's voice provoke the silent dust,
    Or Flattery soothe the dull cold ear of Death?

Perhaps in this neglected spot is laid   45
    Some heart once pregnant with celestial fire;
Hands that the rod of empire might have swayed,
    Or waked to ecstasy the living lyre.

But Knowledge to their eyes her ample page
    Rich with the spoils of time did ne'er unroll;   50
Chill Penury repressed their noble rage,
    And froze the genial current of the soul.

---

storied urn: funeral urn with inscription or design.

Poems for Further Reading

Full many a gem of purest ray serene,
    The dark unfathomed caves of ocean bear:
Full many a flower is born to blush unseen,   55
    And waste its sweetness on the desert air.

Some village Hampden, that with dauntless breast
    The little tyrant of his fields withstood;
Some mute inglorious Milton here may rest,
    Some Cromwell guiltless of his country's blood.   60

The applause of listening senates to command,
    The threats of pain and ruin to despise,
To scatter plenty o'er a smiling land,
    And read their history in a nation's eyes,

Their lot forbade: nor circumscribed alone   65
    Their growing virtues, but their crimes confined;
Forbade to wade through slaughter to a throne,
    And shut the gates of mercy on mankind,

The struggling pangs of conscious truth to hide,
    To quench the blushes of ingenuous shame,   70
Or heap the shrine of Luxury and Pride
    With incense kindled at the Muse's flame.

Far from the madding crowd's ignoble strife,
    Their sober wishes never learned to stray;
Along the cool sequestered vale of life   75
    They kept the noiseless tenor of their way.

Yet even these bones from insult to protect
    Some frail memorial still erected nigh,
With uncouth rhymes and shapeless sculpture decked,
    Implores the passing tribute of a sigh.   80

Their name, their years, spelt by the unlettered Muse,
    The place of fame and elegy supply:

Hampden . . . Milton . . . Cromwell: John Hampden was a member of Parliament who, in 1637, refused to pay a tax levied by Charles I. John Milton (1608–1674); Oliver Cromwell (1599–1658) was Lord Protector of England (1653–1658). All three figures were involved in the English Civil War.

Elegy Written in a Country Churchyard

And many a holy text around she strews,
    That teach the rustic moralist to die.

For who to dumb Forgetfulness a prey,   85
    This pleasing anxious being e'er resigned,
Left the warm precincts of the cheerful day,
    Nor cast one longing lingering look behind?

On some fond breast the parting soul relies,
    Some pious drops the closing eye requires;   90
Even from the tomb the voice of Nature cries,
    Even in our ashes live their wonted fires.

For thee, who mindful of the unhonored dead
    Dost in these lines their artless tale relate;
If chance, by lonely contemplation led,   95
    Some kindred spirit shall inquire thy fate,

Haply some hoary-headed swain may say,
    "Oft have we seen him at the peep of dawn
Brushing with hasty steps the dews away
    To meet the sun upon the upland lawn.   100

"There at the foot of yonder nodding beech
    That wreathes its old fantastic roots so high,
His listless length at noontide would he stretch,
    And pore upon the brook that babbles by.

"Hard by yon wood, now smiling as in scorn,   105
    Muttering his wayward fancies he would rove,
Now drooping, woeful wan, like one forlorn,
    Or crazed with care, or crossed in hopeless love.

"One morn I missed him on the customed hill,
    Along the heath and near his favorite tree;   110
Another came; nor yet beside the rill,
    Nor up the lawn, nor at the wood was he;

"The next with dirges due in sad array
    Slow through the churchway path we saw him borne.
Approach and read (for thou canst read) the lay,   115
    Graved on the stone beneath yon aged thorn."

The Epitaph

Here rests his head upon the lap of Earth
  A youth to Fortune and to Fame unknown.
Fair Science frowned not on his humble birth,
  And Melancholy marked him for her own.   120

Large was his bounty, and his soul sincere,
  Heaven did a recompense as largely send:
He gave to Misery all he had, a tear,
  He gained from Heaven ('twas all he wished) a friend.

No farther seek his merits to disclose,   125
  Or draw his frailties from their dread abode
(There they alike in trembling hope repose),
  The bosom of his Father and his God.

                                            1751
                        Thomas Gray (1716–1771)

A RED, RED ROSE

O my luve's like a red, red rose,
  That's newly sprung in June;
O my luve's like the melodie
  That's sweetly played in tune.

As fair art thou, my bonnie lass,   5
  So deep in luve am I:
And I will luve thee still, my dear,
  Till a' the seas gang dry.

Till a' the seas gang dry, my dear,
  And the rocks melt wi' the sun: 10
O I will love thee still, my dear,
  While the sands o' life shall run.

And fare thee weel, my only luve,
  And fare thee weel awhile!
And I will come again, my luve,   15
  Though it were ten thousand mile.

                                            1796
                        Robert Burns (1759–1796)

THE WORLD IS TOO MUCH WITH US

The world is too much with us; late and soon,
Getting and spending, we lay waste our powers,
Little we see in Nature that is ours;
We have given our hearts away, a sordid boon!
This Sea that bares her bosom to the moon,   5
The winds that will be howling at all hours,
And are up-gathered now like sleeping flowers,
For this, for everything, we are out of tune;
It moves us not.—Great God! I'd rather be
A Pagan suckled in a creed outworn;   10
So might I, standing on this pleasant lea,
Have glimpses that would make me less forlorn;
Have sight of Proteus rising from the sea;
Or hear old Triton blow his wreathéd horn.

1807

William Wordsworth (1770–1850)

ODE
Intimations of Immortality from Recollections of Early Childhood

The Child is father of the Man;
And I could wish my days to be
Bound each to each by natural piety.

1

There was a time when meadow, grove, and stream,
The earth, and every common sight,
　　To me did seem
　　Appareled in celestial light,
The glory and the freshness of a dream.   5
It is not now as it hath been of yore—
　　Turn whereso'er I may,
　　By night or day,
The things which I have seen I now can see no more.

Proteus: a sea-god capable of changing his shape. **Triton:** son of the sea-god Neptune.

The Child is father of the Man: from Wordsworth's "My Heart Leaps Up."

2

The Rainbow comes and goes,   10
And lovely is the Rose,
The Moon doth with delight
Look round her when the heavens are bare,
Waters on a starry night
Are beautiful and fair;   15
The sunshine is a glorious birth;
But yet I know, where'er I go,
That there hath passed away a glory from the earth.

3

Now, while the birds thus sing a joyous song,
And while the young lambs bound   20
As to the tabor's sound,
To me alone there came a thought of grief:
A timely utterance gave that thought relief,
And I again am strong:
The cataracts blow their trumpets from the steep,   25
No more shall grief of mine the season wrong;
I hear the Echoes through the mountains throng,
The Winds come to me from the fields of sleep,
And all the earth is gay;
Land and sea   30
Give themselves up to jollity,
And with the heart of May
Doth every Beast keep holiday—
Thou Child of Joy,
Shout round me, let me hear thy shouts, thou happy Shepherd-boy!   35

4

Ye blessed Creatures, I have heard the call
Ye to each other make; I see
The heavens laugh with you in your jubilee;
My heart is at your festival,   40
My head hath its coronal,
The fullness of your bliss, I feel—I feel it all.
Oh, evil day! if I were sullen
While Earth herself is adorning,
This sweet May morning,   45

And the Children are culling
    On every side,
In a thousand valleys far and wide,
Fresh flowers; while the sun shines warm,
And the Babe leaps up on his Mother's arm—   50
    I hear, I hear, with joy I hear!
    —But there's a Tree, of many, one,
A single Field which I have looked upon,
Both of them speak of something that is gone:
    The Pansy at my feet   55
    Doth the same tale repeat:
Whither is fled the visionary gleam?
Where is it now, the glory and the dream?

5

Our birth is but a sleep and a forgetting:
The Soul that rises with us, our life's Star,   60
    Hath had elsewhere its setting,
    And cometh from afar:
    Not in entire forgetfulness,
    And not in utter nakedness,
But trailing clouds of glory do we come   65
    From God, who is our home:
Heaven lies about us in our infancy!
Shades of the prison-house begin to close
    Upon the growing Boy
    But he   70
Beholds the light, and whence it flows,
    He sees it in his joy;
The Youth, who daily farther from the east
    Must travel, still is Nature's Priest,
    And by the vision splendid   75
    Is on his way attended;
At length the Man perceives it die away,
And fade into the light of common day.

6

Earth fills her lap with pleasures of her own;
Yearnings she hath in her own natural kind,   80
And, even with something of a Mother's mind,
    And no unworthy aim,
    The homely Nurse doth all she can

To make her foster child, her Inmate Man,
    Forget the glories he hath known,   85
And that imperial palace whence he came.

        7

Behold the Child among his newborn blisses,
A six-years' Darling of a pygmy size!
See, where 'mid work of his own hand he lies,
Fretted by sallies of his mother's kisses,   90
With light upon him from his father's eyes!
See, at his feet, some little plan or chart,
Some fragment from his dream of human life,
Shaped by himself with newly-learnéd art;
    A wedding or a festival,   95
    A mourning or a funeral;
      And this hath now his heart,
    And unto this he frames his song;
      Then will he fit his tongue
To dialogues of business, love, or strife;   100
    But it will not be long
    Ere this be thrown aside,
    And with new joy and pride
The little Actor cons another part;
Filling from time to time his "humorous stage"   105
With all the Persons, down to palsied Age,
That Life brings with her in her equipage;
    As if his whole vocation
    Were endless imitation.

        8

Thou, whose exterior semblance doth belie   110
    Thy Soul's immensity;
Thou best Philosopher, who yet dost keep
Thy heritage, thou Eye among the blind,
That, deaf and silent, read'st the eternal deep,
Haunted forever by the eternal mind—   115
    Mighty Prophet! Seer blest!
    On whom those truths do rest,

The little Actor . . . "humorous stage": It is a commonplace in Shakespeare, for example, that
people of various "humours," or temperaments, and people of various ages are actors on life's stage.

Which we are toiling all our lives to find,
In darkness lost, the darkness of the grave;
Thou, over whom thy Immortality   120
Broods like the Day, a Master o'er a Slave,
A Presence which is not to be put by;
Thou little Child, yet glorious in the might
Of heaven-born freedom on thy being's height,
Why with such earnest pains dost thou provoke   125
The years to bring the inevitable yoke,
Thus blindly with thy blessedness at strife?
Full soon thy Soul shall have her earthly freight,
And custom lie upon thee with a weight,
Heavy as frost, and deep almost as life!   130

                              9

          O joy! that in our embers
          Is something that doth live,
          That nature yet remembers
          What was so fugitive!
The thought of our past years in me doth breed   135
Perpetual benediction: not indeed
For that which is most worthy to be blest;
Delight and liberty, the simple creed
Of Childhood, whether busy or at rest,
With new-fledged hope still fluttering in his breast—   140
          Not for these I raise
          The song of thanks and praise;
        But for those obstinate questionings
          Of sense and outward things,
          Fallings from us, vanishings;   145
        Blank misgivings of a Creature
Moving about in worlds not realized,
High instincts before which our mortal Nature
Did tremble like a guilty Thing surprised;
        But for those first affections,   150
        Those shadowy recollections,
      Which, be they what they may,
Are yet the fountain light of all our day,
Are yet a master light of all our seeing;
        Uphold us, cherish, and have power to make   155
Our noisy years seem moments in the being

Of the eternal Silence: truths that wake,
     To perish never;
Which neither listlessness, nor mad endeavor,
     Nor Man nor Boy,   160
Nor all that is at enmity with joy,
Can utterly abolish or destroy!
     Hence in a season of calm weather
     Though inland far we be,
Our Souls have sight of that immortal sea   165
     Which brought us hither,
     Can in a moment travel thither,
And see the Children sport upon the shore,
And hear the mighty waters rolling evermore.

10

Then sing, ye Birds, sing, sing a joyous song!   170
     And let the young Lambs bound
     As to the tabor's sound!
We in thought will join your throng,
     Ye that pipe and ye that play,
     Ye that through your hearts today   175
     Feel the gladness of the May!
What though the radiance which was once so bright
Be now forever taken from my sight,
     Though nothing can bring back the hour
Of splendor in the grass, of glory in the flower;   180
     We will grieve not, rather find
     Strength in what remains behind;
     In the primal sympathy
     Which having been must ever be;
     In the soothing thoughts that spring   185
     Out of human suffering;
     In the faith that looks through death,
In years that bring the philosophic mind.

11

And O, ye Fountains, Meadows, Hills, and Groves,
Forebode not any severing of our loves!   190
Yet in my heart of hearts I feel your might;
I only have relinquished one delight

To live beneath your more habitual sway.
I love the Brooks which down their channels fret,
Even more than when I tripped lightly as they;   195
The innocent brightness of a newborn Day
      Is lovely yet;
The clouds that gather round the setting sun
Do take a sober coloring from an eye
That hath kept watch o'er man's mortality;   200
Another race hath been, and other palms are won.
Thanks to the human heart by which we live,
Thanks to its tenderness, its joys, and fears,
To me the meanest flower that blows can give
Thoughts that do often lie too deep for tears.   205

1807

William Wordsworth (1770–1850)

KUBLA KHAN

[Coleridge's note]:

    The following fragment is here published at the request of a poet of great and deserved celebrity, and, as far as the author's own opinions are concerned, rather as a psychological curiosity, than on the ground of any supposed *poetic* merits.

    In the summer of the year 1797, the author, then in ill health, had retired to a lonely farmhouse between Porlock and Linton, on the Exmoor confines of Somerset and Devonshire. In consequence of a slight indisposition, an anodyne had been prescribed, from the effects of which he fell asleep in his chair at the moment that he was reading the following sentence, or words of the same substance, in *Purchas's Pilgrimage*: "Here the Khan Kubla commanded a palace to be built, and a stately garden thereunto. And thus ten miles of fertile ground were inclosed with a wall." The author continued for about three hours in a profound sleep, at least of the external senses, during which time he has the most vivid confidence that he could not have composed less than from two to three hundred lines; if that indeed can be called composition in which all the images rose up before him as *things*, with a parallel production of the correspondent expressions, without any sensation or consciousness of effort. On awaking he appeared to himself to have a distinct recollection of the whole,

---

a poet of great and deserved celebrity: Lord Byron.

and taking his pen, ink, and paper, instantly and eagerly wrote down the lines that are here preserved. At this moment he was unfortunately called out by a person on business from Porlock, and detained by him above an hour, and on his return to his room, found, to his no small surprise and mortification, that though he still retained some vague and dim recollection of the general purport of the vision, yet, with the exception of some eight or ten scattered lines and images, all the rest had passed away like the images on the surface of a stream into which a stone has been cast, but, alas! without the after restoration of the latter!

>   Then all the charm
> Is broken—all that phantom world so fair
> Vanishes, and a thousand circlets spread,
> And each misshape[s] the other. Stay awhile,
> Poor youth! who scarcely dar'st lift up thine eyes—
> The stream will soon renew its smoothness, soon
> The visions will return! And lo, he stays,
> And soon the fragments dim of lovely forms
> Come trembling back, unite, and now once more
> The pool becomes a mirror.

> > [from Coleridge's *The Picture; or,*
> > *the Lover's Resolution,* lines 91–100]

    Yet from the still surviving recollections in his mind, the author has frequently purposed to finish for himself what had been originally, as it were, given to him. Σαμερον αδιον ασω: but the tomorrow is yet to come.

> In Xanadu did Kubla Khan
> A stately pleasure dome decree:
> Where Alph, the sacred river, ran
> Through caverns measureless to man
>   Down to a sunless sea.   5
> So twice five miles of fertile ground
> With walls and towers were girdled round:
> And there were gardens bright with sinuous rills,
> Where blossomed many an incense-bearing tree;
> And here were forests ancient as the hills,   10
> Enfolding sunny spots of greenery.

Σαμερον αδιον ασω: "I shall sing a sweeter song today." In later editions Σαμερον, "today," was changed to αὔριον, "tomorrow."

Kubla Khan

But oh! that deep romantic chasm which slanted
Down the green hill athwart a cedarn cover!
A savage place! as holy and enchanted
As e'er beneath a waning moon was haunted   15
By woman wailing for her demon lover!
And from this chasm, with ceaseless turmoil seething,
As if this earth in fast thick pants were breathing,
A mighty fountain momently was forced:
Amid whose swift half-intermitted burst   20
Huge fragments vaulted like rebounding hail,
Or chaffy grain beneath the thresher's flail:
And 'mid these dancing rocks at once and ever
It flung up momently the sacred river.
Five miles meandering with a mazy motion   25
Through wood and dale the sacred river ran,
Then reached the caverns measureless to man,
And sank in tumult to a lifeless ocean:
And 'mid this tumult Kubla heard from far
Ancestral voices prophesying war!   30
   The shadow of the dome of pleasure
   Floated midway on the waves;
   Where was heard the mingled measure
   From the fountain and the caves.
It was a miracle of rare device,   35
A sunny pleasure dome with caves of ice!

   A damsel with a dulcimer
   In a vision once I saw:
   It was an Abyssinian maid,
   And on her dulcimer she played,   40
   Singing of Mount Abora.
Could I revive within me
Her symphony and song,
To such a deep delight 'twould win me,
That with music loud and long,   45
I would build that dome in air,
That sunny dome! those caves of ice!
And all who heard should see them there,
And all should cry, Beware! Beware!
His flashing eyes, his floating hair!   50
Weave a circle round him thrice,

And close your eyes with holy dread,
For he on honeydew hath fed,
And drunk the milk of Paradise.

1816
Samuel Taylor Coleridge (1772–1834)

ON A STUPENDOUS LEG OF GRANITE

Discovered Standing by Itself in the Deserts of Egypt,
With the Inscription Inserted Below:

In Egypt's sandy silence, all alone,
Stands a gigantic Leg, which far off throws
The only shadow that the desert knows.
"I am great Ozymandias," saith the stone,
"The King of kings; this mighty city shows   5
The wonders of my hand." The city's gone!
Naught but the leg remaining to disclose
The sight of that forgotten Babylon.
We wonder, and some hunter may express
Wonder like ours, when through the wilderness   10
Where London stood, holding the wolf in chase,
He meets some fragment huge, and stops to guess
What wonderful, but unrecorded, race
Once dwelt in that annihilated place.

1818
Horace Smith (1779–1849)

OZYMANDIAS

I met a traveler from an antique land
Who said: Two vast and trunkless legs of stone
Stand in the desert . . . Near them, on the sand,
Half sunk, a shattered visage lies, whose frown,
And wrinkled lip, and sneer of cold command,   5

Ozymandias: Ramses II (1292–1225 B.C.).

Tell that its sculptor well those passions read
Which yet survive, stamped on these lifeless things,
The hand that mocked them, and the heart that fed:
And on the pedestal these words appear:
"My name is Ozymandias, king of kings: 10
Look on my works, ye Mighty, and despair!"
Nothing beside remains. Round the decay
Of that colossal wreck, boundless and bare
The lone and level sands stretch far away.

1818

Percy Bysshe Shelley (1792–1822)

See the Appendix: Writing about Poems for a sample essay on these two poems.

ODE ON A GRECIAN URN

1

Thou still unravished bride of quietness,
    Thou foster child of silence and slow time,
Sylvan historian, who canst thus express
    A flowery tale more sweetly than our rhyme:
What leaf-fringed legend haunts about thy shape   5
    Of deities or mortals, or of both,
        In Tempe or the dales of Arcady?
    What men or gods are these? What maidens loath?
What mad pursuit? What struggle to escape?
        What pipes and timbrels? What wild ecstasy?   10

2

Heard melodies are sweet, but those unheard
    Are sweeter; therefore, ye soft pipes, play on;
Not to the sensual ear, but, more endeared,
    Pipe to the spirit ditties of no tone:
Fair youth, beneath the trees, thou canst not leave   15
    Thy song, nor ever can those trees be bare;
        Bold Lover, never, never canst thou kiss,
Though winning near the goal—yet, do not grieve;
        She cannot fade, though thou hast not thy bliss,
    Forever wilt thou love, and she be fair!   20

Tempe . . . Arcady: locations in Greece symbolic of ideal beauty. **timbrels:** tambourines.

3

Ah, happy, happy boughs! that cannot shed
    Your leaves, nor ever bid the Spring adieu;
And, happy melodist, unweariéd,
    Forever piping songs forever new;
More happy love! more happy, happy love!   25
    Forever warm and still to be enjoyed,
        Forever panting, and forever young;
All breathing human passion far above,
    That leaves a heart high-sorrowful and cloyed,
        A burning forehead, and a parching tongue.   30

4

Who are these coming to the sacrifice?
    To what green altar, O mysterious priest,
Lead'st thou that heifer lowing at the skies,
    And all her silken flanks with garlands dressed?
What little town by river or sea shore,   35
    Or mountain-built with peaceful citadel,
        Is emptied of this folk, this pious morn?
And, little town, thy streets forevermore
    Will silent be; and not a soul to tell
        Why thou art desolate, can e'er return.   40

5

O Attic shape! Fair attitude! with brede
    Of marble men and maidens overwrought,
With forest branches and the trodden weed;
    Thou, silent form, dost tease us out of thought
As doth eternity: Cold Pastoral!   45
    When old age shall this generation waste,
        Thou shalt remain, in midst of other woe
Than ours, a friend to man, to whom thou say'st,
"Beauty is truth, truth beauty,"—that is all
    Ye know on earth, and all ye need to know.   50

1820
John Keats (1795–1821)

Attic: pertaining to Athens, in Greece. **brede:** an ornamental band.

LORD WALTER'S WIFE

"But why do you go?" said the lady, while both sate under the yew,
And her eyes were alive in their depth, as the kraken beneath the sea-
    blue.

"Because I fear you," he answered;—"because you are far too fair,
And able to strangle my soul in a mesh of your gold-coloured hair."

"Oh, that," she said, "is no reason! Such knots are quickly undone,   5
And too much beauty, I reckon, is nothing but too much sun."

"Yet farewell so," he answered;—"the sunstroke's fatal at times.
I value your husband, Lord Walter, whose gallop rings still from the
    limes."

"Oh, that," she said, "is no reason. You smell a rose through a fence;
If two should smell it, what matter? who grumbles, and where's the
    pretence?"   10

"But I," he replied, "have promised another, when love was free,
To love her alone, alone, who alone and afar loves me."

"Why, that," she said, "is no reason. Love's always free, I am told.
Will you vow to be safe from the headache on Tuesday, and think it
    will hold?"

"But you," he replied, "have a daughter, a young little child, who was
    laid   15
In your lap to be pure; so I leave you; the angels would make me
    afraid."

"Oh, that," she said, "is no reason. The angels keep out of the way;
And Dora, the child, observes nothing, although you should please
    me and stay."

At which he rose up in his anger,—"Why, now, you no longer are
    fair!
Why, now, you no longer are fatal, but ugly and hateful, I swear."   20

Kraken: a mythical sea-monster.

At which she laughed out in her scorn,—"These men! Oh, these men over-nice,
Who are shocked if a colour not virtuous, is frankly put on by a vice."

Her eyes blazed upon him—"And *you!* You bring us your vices so near,
That we smell them! You think in our presence a thought 'twould defame us to hear!

"What reason had you, and what right,—I appeal to your soul from my life,—   25
To find me too fair as a woman? Why, sir, I am pure, and a wife.

"Is the day-star too fair up above you? It burns you not. Dare you imply
I brushed you more close than the star does, when Walter had set me as high?

"If a man finds a woman too fair, he means simply adapted too much,
To uses unlawful and fatal. The praise!—shall I thank you for such?   30

"Too fair?—not unless you misuse us! and surely if, once in a while,
You attain to it, straightway you call us no longer too fair, but too vile.

"A moment,—I pray your attention!—I have a poor word in my head,
I must utter, though womanly custom would set it down better unsaid.

"You grew, sir, pale to impertinence, once when I showed you a ring,   35
You kissed my fan when I dropped it. No matter!—I've broken the thing.

"You did me the honour, perhaps, to be moved at my side now and then,
In the senses—a vice, I have heard, which is common to beasts and some men.

"Love's a virtue for heroes!—as white as the snow on high hills,
And immortal as every great soul is that struggles, endures, and fulfils.   40

Lord Walter's Wife

"I love my Walter profoundly,—you, Maude, though you faltered a
    week,
For the sake of . . . what was it? an eyebrow? or, less still, a mole on
    a cheek?

"And since, when all's said, you're too noble to stoop to the frivolous
    cant,
About crimes irresistible, virtues that swindle, betray, and supplant,

"I determined to prove to yourself that, whate'er you might dream or
    avow,   45
By illusion, you wanted precisely no more of me than you have now.

"There! Look me full in the face!—in the face. Understand, if you
    can,
That the eyes of such women as I am, are clean as the palm of a
    man.

"Drop his hand, you insult him. Avoid us for fear we should cost you
    a scar—
You take us for harlots, I tell you, and not for the women we are.   50

"You wronged me; but then I considered . . . there's Walter! And so
    at the end,
I vowed that he should not be mulcted, by me, in the hand of a
    friend.

"Have I hurt you indeed? We are quits then. Nay, friend of my Wal-
    ter, be mine!
Come Dora, my darling, my angel, and help me to ask him to dine."

1862
Elizabeth Barrett Browning (1806–1861)

Maude: the wife of the man being addressed. **mulcted:** defrauded, swindled.

ULYSSES

It little profits that an idle king,
By this still hearth, among these barren crags,
Matched with an aged wife, I mete and dole
Unequal laws unto a savage race,
That hoard, and sleep, and feed, and know not me.   5

I cannot rest from travel; I will drink
Life to the lees. All times I have enjoyed
Greatly, have suffered greatly, both with those
That loved me, and alone; on shore, and when
Through scudding drifts the rainy Hyades   10
Vexed the dim sea. I am become a name;
For always roaming with a hungry heart
Much have I seen and known—cities of men
And manners, climates, councils, governments,
Myself not least, but honored of them all—   15
And drunk delight of battle with my peers,
Far on the ringing plains of windy Troy.
I am a part of all that I have met;
Yet all experience is an arch wherethrough
Gleams that untraveled world whose margin fades   20
Forever and forever when I move.
How dull it is to pause, to make an end,
To rust unburnished, not to shine in use!
As though to breathe were life! Life piled on life
Were all too little, and of one to me   25
Little remains; but every hour is saved
From that eternal silence, something more,
A bringer of new things; and vile it were
For some three suns to store and hoard myself,
And this gray spirit yearning in desire   30
To follow knowledge like a sinking star,
Beyond the utmost bound of human thought.
   This is my son, mine own Telemachus,
To whom I leave the scepter and the isle—

Ulysses: the Greek Odysseus. Tennyson derives his monologue from the prediction in Homer's *Odyssey* that after Odysseus' homecoming, he will wander once again (*Odyssey* 23) and from a scene in Dante's *Inferno* in which Ulysses in old age urges his followers to leave Ithaca and follow virtue and knowledge (*Inferno* 26). **lees:** sediment at the bottom of a wine jug or bottle. **Hyades:** a group of stars in the constellation Taurus, thought to indicate rain.

Well-loved of me, discerning to fulfill   35
This labor, by slow prudence to make mild
A rugged people, and through soft degrees
Subdue them to the useful and the good.
Most blameless is he, centered in the sphere
Of common duties, decent not to fail   40
In offices of tenderness, and pay
Meet adoration to my household gods,
When I am gone. He works his work, I mine.
    There lies the port; the vessel puffs her sail;
There gloom the dark, broad seas. My mariners,   45
Souls that have toiled, and wrought, and thought with me—
That ever with a frolic welcome took
The thunder and the sunshine, and opposed
Free hearts, free foreheads—you and I are old;
Old age hath yet his honor and his toil.   50
Death closes all; but something ere the end,
Some work of noble note, may yet be done,
Not unbecoming men that strove with Gods.
The lights begin to twinkle from the rocks;
The long day wanes; the slow moon climbs; the deep   55
Moans round with many voices. Come, my friends,
'Tis not too late to seek a newer world.
Push off, and sitting well in order smite
The sounding furrows; for my purpose holds
To sail beyond the sunset, and the baths   60
Of all the western stars, until I die.
It may be that the gulfs will wash us down;
It may be we shall touch the Happy Isles,
And see the great Achilles, whom we knew.
Though much is taken, much abides; and though   65
We are not now that strength which in old days
Moved earth and heaven, that which we are, we are—
One equal temper of heroic hearts,
Made weak by time and fate, but strong in will
To strive, to seek, to find, and not to yield.   70

1842
Alfred, Lord Tennyson (1809–1892)

---

opposed: countered with. **Happy Isles:** in mythology, the place where virtuous souls were thought
to live.

PORPHYRIA'S LOVER

The rain set early in tonight,
    The sullen wind was soon awake,
It tore the elm-tops down for spite,
    And did its worst to vex the lake:
    I listened with heart fit to break.   5
When glided in Porphyria; straight
    She shut the cold out and the storm,
And kneeled and made the cheerless grate
    Blaze up, and all the cottage warm;
    Which done, she rose, and from her form   10
Withdrew the dripping cloak and shawl,
    And laid her soiled gloves by, untied
Her hat and let the damp hair fall,
    And, last, she sat down by my side
    And called me. When no voice replied,   15
She put my arm about her waist,
    And made her smooth white shoulder bare,
And all her yellow hair displaced,
    And, stooping, made my cheek lie there,
    And spread, o'er all, her yellow hair,   20
Murmuring how she loved me—she
    Too weak, for all her heart's endeavor,
To set its struggling passion free
    From pride, and vainer ties dissever,
    And give herself to me forever.   25
But passion sometimes would prevail,
    Nor could tonight's gay feast restrain
A sudden thought of one so pale
    For love of her, and all in vain:
    So, she was come through wind and rain.   30
Be sure I looked up at her eyes
    Happy and proud; at last I knew
Porphyria worshiped me: surprise
    Made my heart swell, and still it grew
    While I debated what to do.   35
That moment she was mine, mine, fair,
    Perfectly pure and good: I found
A thing to do, and all her hair
    In one long yellow string I wound
    Three times her little throat around,   40

And strangled her. No pain felt she;
    I am quite sure she felt no pain.
As a shut bud that holds a bee,
    I warily oped her lids: again
    Laughed the blue eyes without a stain.   45
And I untightened next the tress
    About her neck; her cheek once more
Blushed bright beneath my burning kiss:
    I propped her head up as before.
    Only, this time my shoulder bore   50
Her head, which droops upon it still:
    The smiling rosy little head,
So glad it has its utmost will,
    That all it scorned at once is fled,
    And I, its love, am gained instead!   55
Porphyria's love: she guessed not how
    Her darling one wish would be heard.
And thus we sit together now,
    And all night long we have not stirred,
    And yet God has not said a word!   60

1842
Robert Browning (1812–1889)

THE BERG
A Dream

I saw a ship of martial build
(Her standards set, her brave apparel on)
Directed as by madness mere
Against a stolid iceberg steer,
Nor budge it, though the infatuate ship went down.   5
The impact made huge ice-cubes fall
Sullen, in tons that crashed the deck;
But that one avalanche was all—
No other movement save the foundering wreck.

The Berg: Compare Melville's poem with Thomas Hardy's description of the sinking of the *Titanic* (1912) in "The Convergence of the Twain."

Along the spurs of ridges pale,   10
Not any slenderest shaft and frail,
A prism over glass-green gorges lone,
Toppled; nor lace of traceries fine,
Nor pendent drops in grot or mine
Were jarred, when the stunned ship went down.   15

Nor sole the gulls in cloud that wheeled
Circling one snow-flanked peak afar,
But nearer fowl the floes that skimmed
And crystal beaches, felt no jar.
No thrill transmitted stirred the lock   20
Of jack-straw needle-ice at base;
Towers undermined by waves—the block
Atilt impending—kept their place.
Seals, dozing sleek on sliddery ledges
Slipt never, when by loftier edges   25
Through very inertia overthrown,
The impetuous ship in bafflement went down.

Hard Berg (methought), so cold, so vast,
With mortal damps self-overcast;
Exhaling still thy dankish breath—   30
Adrift dissolving, bound for death;
Though lumpish thou, a lumbering one—
A lumbering lubbard loitering slow,
Impingers rue thee and go down,
Sounding thy precipice below,   35
Nor stir the slimy slug that sprawls
Along thy dead indifference of walls.

                                                     1888
                          Herman Melville (1819–1891)

I HEAR AMERICA SINGING

I hear America singing, the varied carols I hear,
Those of mechanics, each one singing his as it should be blithe and
    strong,
The carpenter singing his as he measures his plank or beam,

The mason singing his as he makes ready for work, or leaves off work,
The boatman singing what belongs to him in his boat, the deck-hand
    singing on the steamboat deck,   5
The shoemaker singing as he sits on his bench, the hatter singing as
    he stands,
The wood-cutter's song, the ploughboy's on his way in the morning,
    or at noon intermission or at sundown,
The delicious singing of the mother, or of the young wife at work, or
    of the girl sewing or washing,
Each singing what belongs to him or her and to none else,
The day what belongs to the day—at night the party of young fellows,
    robust, friendly,   10
Singing with open mouths their strong melodious songs.

1860
Walt Whitman (1819–1892)

RICHARD CORY

Whenever Richard Cory went down town,
We people on the pavement looked at him:
He was a gentleman from sole to crown,
Clean favored, and imperially slim.

And he was always quietly arrayed,   5
And he was always human when he talked;
But still he fluttered pulses when he said,
"Good-morning," and he glittered when he walked.

And he was rich—yes, richer than a king—
And admirably schooled in every grace: 10
In fine, we thought that he was everything
To make us wish that we were in his place.

So on we worked, and waited for the light,
And went without the meat, and cursed the bread;
And Richard Cory, one calm summer night,   15
Went home and put a bullet through his head.

1897
Edwin Arlington Robinson (1869–1935)

THE AIM WAS SONG

Before man came to blow it right
   The wind once blew itself untaught,
And did its loudest day and night
   In any rough place where it caught.

Man came to tell it what was wrong: 5
   It hadn't found the place to blow;
It blew too hard—the aim was song.
   And listen—how it ought to go!

He took a little in his mouth,
   And held it long enough for north   10
To be converted into south,
   And then by measure blew it forth.

By measure. It was word and note,
   The wind the wind had meant to be—
A little through the lips and throat.   15
   The aim was song—the wind could see.

1923
Robert Frost (1874–1963)

THE RIVER-MERCHANT'S WIFE: A LETTER

While my hair was still cut straight across my forehead
I played about the front gate, pulling flowers.
You came by on bamboo stilts, playing horse,
You walked about my seat, playing with blue plums.
And we went on living in the village of Chokan: 5
Two small people, without dislike or suspicion.

At fourteen I married My Lord you.
I never laughed, being bashful.
Lowering my head, I looked at the wall.
Called to, a thousand times, I never looked back.   0

Chokan: a suburb of Nanking, China.

At fifteen I stopped scowling,
I desired my dust to be mingled with yours
Forever and forever and forever.
Why should I climb the look out?

At sixteen you departed,   15
You went into far Ku-to-yen, by the river of swirling eddies,
And you have been gone five months.
The monkeys make sorrowful noise overhead.

You dragged your feet when you went out.
By the gate now, the moss is grown, the different mosses,   20
Too deep to clear them away!
The leaves fall early this autumn, in wind.
The paired butterflies are already yellow with August
Over the grass in the West garden;
They hurt me. I grow older.   25
If you are coming down through the narrows of the river Kiang,
Please let me know beforehand,
And I will come out to meet you
                    As far as Cho-fu-Sa.

By Rihaku
1915
Ezra Pound (1885–1972)

POETRY

I too, dislike it: there are things that are important beyond all this fiddle.
   Reading it, however, with a perfect contempt for it, one discovers
        that there is in
it after all, a place for the genuine.
    Hands that can grasp, eyes
  that can dilate, hair that can rise   5
      if it must, these things are important not because a

high sounding interpretation can be put upon them but because they are
   useful; when they become so derivative as to become unintelligible,

---

By Rihaku: Pound's poem is a version of a Japanese translation into English of a poem by the Chinese poet Li Po (701–762), whose name in Japanese is Rihaku.

the same thing may be said for all of us—that we
  do not admire what   10
  we cannot understand. The bat,
    holding on upside down or in quest of something to

eat elephants pushing, a wild horse taking a roll, a tireless wolf under
  a tree, the immovable critic twinkling his skin like a horse that feels
    a flea, the base-
ball fan, the statistician—case after case   15
  could be cited did
  one wish it; nor is it valid
    to discriminate against "business documents and

school-books"; all these phenomena are important. One must make a
    distinction
however: when dragged into prominence by half poets, the result is
    not poetry,   20
  nor till the autocrats among us can be
  "literalists of
  the imagination"—above
    insolence and triviality and can present

for inspection, imaginary gardens with real toads in them, shall we have   25
  it. In the meantime, if you demand on one hand, in defiance of their
    opinion—
the raw material of poetry in
  all its rawness and
  that which is, on the other hand,
    genuine then you are interested in poetry.   30

1921
Marianne Moore (1887–1972)

Moore annotates two of her quotations in the poem: " **'Business documents and school-books'** is from the *Diary of Tolstoy*: 'Where the boundary between prose and poetry lies, I shall never be able to understand. The question is raised in manuals of style, yet the answer to it lies beyond me. Poetry is verse: prose is not verse. Or else poetry is everything with the exception of business documents and school books' (p. 84). **'Literalist of the imagination'** is a phrase Yeats uses to describe William Blake in *Ideas of Good and Evil* (1903)."

THE LOVE SONG OF J. ALFRED PRUFROCK

S'io credessi che mia risposta fosse
a persona che mai tornasse al mondo,
questa fiamma staria senza più scosse.
Ma per ciò che giammai di questo fondo
non tornò vivo alcun, si'i'odo il vero,
senza tema d'infamia ti rispondo.

Let us go then, you and I,
When the evening is spread out against the sky
Like a patient etherised upon a table;
Let us go, through certain half-deserted streets,
The muttering retreats   5
Of restless nights in one-night cheap hotels
And sawdust restaurants with oyster-shells:
Streets that follow like a tedious argument
Of insidious intent
To lead you to an overwhelming question . . .   10
Oh, do not ask, 'What is it?'
Let us go and make our visit.

In the room the women come and go
Talking of Michelangelo.

The yellow fog that rubs its back upon the window-panes,   15
The yellow smoke that rubs its muzzle on the window-panes,
Licked its tongue into the corners of the evening,
Lingered upon the pools that stand in drains,
Let fall upon its back the soot that falls from chimneys,
Slipped by the terrace, made a sudden leap,   20
And seeing that it was a soft October night,
Curled once about the house, and fell asleep.

And indeed there will be time
For the yellow smoke that slides along the street

S'io credessi . . . : In Dante's *Inferno* (about 1320), one of the damned is asked by the poet to tell his story. He replies "If I believed that my answer could get back to the world, this flame [he speaks through a tongue of flame] would stop moving. But because no one has ever returned from this place alive, if I hear the truth, I will answer you without fear of disgrace" (27).

Rubbing its back upon the window-panes;   25
There will be time, there will be time
To prepare a face to meet the faces that you meet;
There will be time to murder and create,
And time for all the works and days of hands
That lift and drop a question on your plate;   30
Time for you and time for me,
And time yet for a hundred indecisions,
And for a hundred visions and revisions,
Before the taking of a toast and tea.

In the room the women come and go   35
Talking of Michelangelo.

And indeed there will be time
To wonder, 'Do I dare?' and, 'Do I dare?'
Time to turn back and descend the stair,
With a bald spot in the middle of my hair—   40
(They will say: 'How his hair is growing thin!')
My morning coat, my collar mounting firmly to the chin,
My necktie rich and modest, but asserted by a simple pin—
(They will say: "But how his arms and legs are thin!')
Do I dare   45
Disturb the universe?
In a minute there is time
For decisions and revisions which a minute will reverse.

For I have known them all already, known them all—
Have known the evenings, mornings, afternoons,   50
I have measured out my life with coffee spoons;
I know the voices dying with a dying fall
Beneath the music from a farther room.
   So how should I presume?

And I have known the eyes already, known them all—   55
The eyes that fix you in a formulated phrase,
And when I am formulated, sprawling on a pin,
When I am pinned and wriggling on the wall,
Then how should I begin
To spit out all the butt-ends of my days and ways?   60
   And how should I presume?

The Love Song of J. Alfred Prufrock

And I have known the arms already, known them all—
Arms that are braceleted and white and bare
(But in the lamplight, downed with light brown hair!)
Is it perfume from a dress   65
That makes me so digress?
Arms that lie along a table, or wrap about a shawl.
    And should I then presume?
    And how should I begin?

    . . . . .

Shall I say, I have gone at dusk through narrow streets   70
And watched the smoke that rises from the pipes
Of lonely men in shirt-sleeves, leaning out of windows? . . .

I should have been a pair of ragged claws
Scuttling across the floors of silent seas.

    . . . . .

And the afternoon, the evening, sleeps so peacefully!   75
Smoothed by long fingers,
Asleep . . . tired . . . or it malingers,
Stretched on the floor, here beside you and me.
Should I, after tea and cakes and ices,
Have the strength to force the moment to its crisis?   80
But though I have wept and fasted, wept and prayed,
Though I have seen my head (grown slightly bald)
    brought in upon a platter,
I am no prophet—and here's no great matter;
I have seen the moment of my greatness flicker,
And I have seen the eternal Footman hold my coat,
    and snicker,   85
And in short, I was afraid.

And would it have been worth it, after all,
After the cups, the marmalade, the tea,
Among the porcelain, among some talk of you and me,
Would it have been worth while,   90
To have bitten off the matter with a smile,
To have squeezed the universe into a ball
To roll it towards some overwhelming question,
To say: 'I am Lazarus, come from the dead,
Come back to tell you all, I shall tell you all'—   95

If one, settling a pillow by her head,
   Should say: 'That is not what I meant at all.
   That is not it, at all.'
And would it have been worth it, after all,
Would it have been worth while,   100
After the sunsets and the dooryards and the sprinkled streets,

After the novels, after the teacups, after the skirts that trail
   along the floor—
And this, and so much more?—
It is impossible to say just what I mean!
But as if a magic lantern threw the nerves in patterns
   on a screen: 105
Would it have been worth while
If one, settling a pillow or throwing off a shawl,
And turning toward the window, should say:
   'That is not it at all,
   That is not what I meant, at all.'   110

      . . . . .

No! I am not Prince Hamlet, nor was meant to be;
Am an attendant lord, one that will do
To swell a progress, start a scene or two,
Advise the prince; no doubt, an easy tool,
Deferential, glad to be of use,   115
Politic, cautious, and meticulous;
Full of high sentence, but a bit obtuse;
At times, indeed, almost ridiculous—
Almost, at times, the Fool.

I grow old . . . I grow old . . .   120
I shall wear the bottoms of my trousers rolled.

Shall I part my hair behind? Do I dare to eat a peach?
I shall wear white flannel trousers, and walk upon the beach.
I have heard the mermaids singing, each to each.

I do not think that they will sing to me.   125

I have seen them riding seaward on the waves
Combing the white hair of the waves blown back
When the wind blows the water white and black.

We have lingered in the chambers of the sea
By sea-girls wreathed with seaweed red and brown   130
Till human voices wake us, and we drown.

1917
T. S. Eliot (1888–1965)

THEME FOR ENGLISH B

The instructor said,

> *Go home and write*
> *a page tonight.*
> *And let that page come out of you—*
> *Then, it will be true.*   5

I wonder if it's that simple?
I am twenty-two, colored, born in Winston-Salem.
I went to school there, then Durham, then here
to this college on the hill above Harlem.
I am the only colored student in my class.   10
The steps from the hill lead down into Harlem,
through a park, then I cross St. Nicholas,
Eighth Avenue, Seventh, and I come to the Y,
the Harlem Branch Y, where I take the elevator
up to my room, sit down, and write this page: 15

It's not easy to know what is true for you or me
at twenty-two, my age. But I guess I'm what
I feel and see and hear, Harlem, I hear you:
hear you, hear me—we two—you, me, talk on this page.
(I hear New York, too.) Me—who?   20

Well, I like to eat, sleep, drink, and be in love.
I like to work, read, learn, and understand life.
I like a pipe for a Christmas present,
or records—Bessie, bop, or Bach.
I guess being colored doesn't make me *not* like   25

Bessie: Bessie Smith (1898?–1937), a blues singer.

the same things other folks like who are other races.
So will my page be colored that I write?

Being me, it will not be white.
But it will be
a part of you, instructor.   30
You are white—
yet a part of me, as I am a part of you.
That's American.
Sometimes perhaps you don't want to be a part of me.
Nor do I often want to be a part of you.   35
But we are, that's true!
As I learn from you,
I guess you learn from me—
although you're older—and white—
and somewhat more free.   40

This is my page for English B.

> 1951
> *Langston Hughes (1902–1967)*

INCIDENT

Once, riding in old Baltimore,
    Heart-filled, head-filled with glee,
I saw a Baltimorean
    Keep looking straight at me.

Now I was eight and very small,   5
    And he was no whit bigger;
And so I smiled, but he poked out
    His tongue, and called me "Nigger."

I saw the whole of Baltimore
    From May until December;   10
Of all the things that happened there
    That's all that I remember.

> 1925
> *Countee Cullen (1903–1946)*

IN MEMORY OF W. B. YEATS

(d. January, 1939)

1

He disappeared in the dead of winter:
The brooks were frozen, the airports almost deserted,
And snow disfigured the public statues;
The mercury sank in the mouth of the dying day.
What instruments we have agree   5
The day of his death was a dark cold day.

Far from his illness
The wolves ran on through the evergreen forests,
The peasant river was untempted by the fashionable quays;
By mourning tongues   10
The death of the poet was kept from his poems.

But for him it was his last afternoon as himself,
An afternoon of nurses and rumors;
The provinces of his body revolted,
The squares of his mind were empty,   15
Silence invaded the suburbs,
The current of his feeling failed; he became his admirers.

Now he is scattered among a hundred cities
And wholly given over to unfamiliar affections,
To find his happiness in another kind of wood   20
And be punished under a foreign code of conscience.
The words of a dead man
Are modified in the guts of the living.

But in the importance and noise of tomorrow
When the brokers are roaring like beasts on the floor of the Bourse,   25
And the poor have the sufferings to which they are fairly accustomed,
And each in the cell of himself is almost convinced of his freedom,
A few thousand will think of this day
As one thinks of a day when one did something slightly unusual.
What instruments we have agree   30
The day of his death was a dark cold day.

Bourse: the Paris stock exchange.

2

You were silly like us; your gift survived it all:
The parish of rich women, physical decay,
Yourself. Mad Ireland hurt you into poetry.
Now Ireland has her madness and her weather still,   35
For poetry makes nothing happen: it survives
In the valley of its making where executives
Would never want to tamper, flows on south
From ranches of isolation and the busy griefs,
Raw towns that we believe and die in; it survives,   40
A way of happening, a mouth.

3

Earth, receive an honored guest:
William Yeats is laid to rest.
Let the Irish vessel lie
Emptied of its poetry.   45

Time that is intolerant
Of the brave and innocent,
And indifferent in a week
To a beautiful physique,

Worships language and forgives   50
Everyone by whom it lives;
Pardons cowardice, conceit,
Lays its honours at their feet.

Time that with this strange excuse
Pardoned Kipling and his views,   55
And will pardon Paul Claudel,
Pardons him for writing well.

In the nightmare of the dark
All the dogs of Europe bark,
And the living nations wait,   60
Each sequestered in its hate;

Kipling: Rudyard Kipling (1865–1936), whose poetry celebrated English nationalism and the British Empire. **Claudel:** Paul Claudel (1868–1955), a conservative French poet and dramatist. **Pardons him:** pardons Yeats, that is; Auden objected to the political views of Kipling, Claudel, and Yeats.

Intellectual disgrace
Stares from every human face,
And the seas of pity lie
Locked and frozen in each eye.   65

Follow, poet, follow right
To the bottom of the night,
With your unconstraining voice
Still persuade us to rejoice;

With the farming of a verse   70
Make a vineyard of the curse,
Sing of human unsuccess
In a rapture of distress;

In the deserts of the heart
Let the healing fountain start,   75
In the prison of his days
Teach the free man how to praise.

1940
W. H. Auden (1907–1973)

ELEGY FOR JANE

My Student, Thrown by a Horse

I remember the neckcurls, limp and damp as tendrils;
And her quick look, a sidelong pickerel smile;
And how, once startled into talk, the light syllables leaped for her,
And she balanced in the delight of her thought,
A wren, happy, tail into the wind,   5
Her song trembling the twigs and small branches.
The shade sang with her;
The leaves, their whispers turned to kissing;
And the mold sang in the bleached valleys under the rose.

Oh, when she was sad, she cast herself down into such a pure depth,   10
Even a father could not find her:
Scraping her cheek against straw;
Stirring the clearest water.

My sparrow, you are not here,
Waiting like a fern, making a spiny shadow.   15
The sides of wet stones cannot console me,
Nor the moss, wound with the last light.

If only I could nudge you from this sleep,
My maimed darling, my skittery pigeon.
Over this damp grave I speak the words of my love: 20
I, with no rights in this matter,
Neither father nor lover.

1953

Theodore Roethke (1908–1963)

THE MAN-MOTH

        Here, above,
cracks in the buildings are filled with battered moonlight.
The whole shadow of Man is only as big as his hat.
It lies at his feet like a circle for a doll to stand on,
and he makes an inverted pin, the point magnetized to the moon.   5
He does not see the moon; he observes only her vast properties,
feeling the queer light on his hands, neither warm nor cold,
of a temperature impossible to record in thermometers.

        But when the Man-Moth
pays his rare, although occasional, visits to the surface,   10
the moon looks rather different to him. He emerges
from an opening under the edge of one of the sidewalks
and nervously begins to scale the faces of the buildings.
He thinks the moon is a small hole at the top of the sky,
proving the sky quite useless for protection.   15
He trembles, but must investigate as high as he can climb.

        Up the façades,
his shadow dragging like a photographer's cloth behind him,
he climbs fearfully, thinking that this time he will manage

Man-Moth: According to Bishop's own note to the poem, the title is from a newspaper misprint for *mammoth.*

to push his small head through that round clean opening   20
and be forced through, as from a tube, in black scrolls on the light.
(Man, standing below him, has no such illusions.)
But what the Man-Moth fears most he must do, although
he fails, of course, and falls back scared but quite unhurt.

        Then he returns   25
to the pale subways of cement he calls his home. He flits,
he flutters, and cannot get aboard the silent trains
fast enough to suit him. The doors close swiftly.
The Man-Moth always seats himself facing the wrong way
and the train starts at once at its full, terrible speed,   30
without a shift in gears or a gradation of any sort.
He cannot tell the rate at which he travels backwards.

        Each night he must
be carried through artificial tunnels and dream recurrent dreams.
Just as the ties recur beneath his train, these underlie   35
his rushing brain. He does not dare look out the window,
for the third rail, the unbroken draught of poison,
runs there beside him. He regards it as a disease
he has inherited the susceptibility to. He has to keep
his hands in his pockets, as others must wear mufflers.   40

        If you catch him,
hold up a flashlight to his eye. It's all dark pupil,
an entire night itself, whose haired horizon tightens
as he stares back, and closes up the eye. Then from the lids
one tear, his only possession, like the bee's sting, slips.   45
Slyly he palms it, and if you're not paying attention
he'll swallow it. However, if you watch, he'll hand it over,
cool as from underground springs and pure enough to drink.

                                   1946
                  Elizabeth Bishop (1911–1979)

ISRAELIS

It is themselves they trust and no one else;
Their fighter planes that screech across the sky,

Real, visible as the glorious sun;
Riflesmoke, gunshine, and rumble of tanks.

Man is a fanged wolf, without compassion   5
Or ruth: Assyrians, Medes, Greeks, Romans,
And devout pagans in Spain and Russia
—Allah's children, most merciful of all.

Where is the Almighty if murder thrives?
He's dead as mutton and they buried him   10
Decades ago, covered him with their own
Limp bodies in Belsen and Babi Yar.

Let the strong compose hymns and canticles,
Live with the Lord's radiance in their hard skulls
Or make known his great benevolences;   15
Stare at the heavens and feel glorified

Or humbled and awestruck buckle their knees:
They are done with him now and forever.
Without a whimper from him they returned,
A sign like an open hand in the sky.   20

The pillar of fire: Their flesh made it;
It burned briefly and died—you all know where.
Now in their own blood they temper the steel,
God being dead and their enemies not.

1971
Irving Layton (b. 1912)

TO MY MOTHER

Most near, most dear, most loved and most far,
Under the window where I often found her
Sitting as huge as Asia, seismic with laughter,
Gin and chicken helpless in her Irish hand,
Irresistible as Rabelais, but most tender for   5

Rabelais: François Rabelais (1494?–1553), French humorist and satirist, known for his ribald stories.

The lame dogs and hurt birds that surround her,—
She is a procession no one can follow after
But be like a little dog following a brass band.

She will not glance up at the bomber, or condescend
To drop her gin and scuttle to a cellar,   10
But lean on the mahogany table like a mountain
Whom only faith can move, and so I send
O all my faith, and all my love to tell her
That she will move from mourning into morning.

1957

George Barker (b. 1913)

SESTINA: TRAVEL NOTES

Directed by the eyes of others,
Blind to the long, deceptive voyage,
We walked across the bridge in silence
And said "Goodnight," and paused, and walked away.
Ritual of apology and burden: 5
The evening ended; not a soul was harmed.

But then I thought: we all are harmed
By the indifference of others;
Being corrupt, corruptible, they burden
All who would vanish on some questioned voyage,   10
Tunneling through the longest way away
To maps of bitterness and silence.

We are concerned with that destructive silence
Impending in the dark, that never harms
Us till it strikes, washing the past away.   15
Remote from intrigues of the others,
We must chart routes that ease the voyage,
Clear passageways and lift the burden.

---

bomber . . . cellar: allusions to the bombing of England by the Germans during World War II.

Sestina: Travel Notes: see Donald Justice's "Sestina on Six Words by Weldon Kees."

But where are routes? Who names the burden?
The night is gifted with a devious silence   20
That names no promises of voyage
Without contagion and the syllables of harm.
—I see ahead the hands of others
In frantic motion, warning me away.

To pay no heed, and walk away   25
Is easy; but the familiar burden
Of a later time, when certainties of others
Assume the frigid shapes of silence
And build new winters, echoing harm,
May banish every passageway for voyage.   30

You knew before the fear of voyage,
You saw before the hands that warned away,
You heard before the voices trained to harm
Listeners grown weak through loss and burdens.
Even in city streets at noon that silence   35
Waited for you, but not, you thought, for others.

Storms will break silence. Seize on harm,
Play idiot or seer to others, make the burden
Theirs, though no voyage is, no tunnel, door, nor way.

1947
Weldon Kees (1914–1955)

LOVE POEM

My clumsiest dear, whose hands shipwreck vases,
At whose quick touch all glasses chip and ring,
Whose palms are bulls in china, burs in linen,
And have no cunning with any soft thing

Except all ill at ease fidgeting people: 5
The refugee uncertain at the door
You make at home; deftly you steady
The drunk clambering on his undulant floor.

Unpredictable dear, the taxi drivers' terror,
Shrinking from far headlights pale as a dime   10
Yet leaping before red apoplectic streetcars—
Misfit in any space. And never on time.

A wrench in clocks and solar system. Only
With words and people and love you move at ease.
In traffic of wit expertly manoeuvre   15
And keep us, all devotion, at your knees.

Forgetting your coffee spreading on our flannel,
Your lipstick grinning on our coat,
So gayly in love's unbreakable heaven
Our souls in glory of spilt bourbon float.   20

Be with me darling early and late. Smash glasses—
I will study wry music for your sake.
For should your hands drop white and empty
All the toys of the world would break.

1947
John Frederick Nims (b. 1914)

A REFUSAL TO MOURN THE DEATH, BY FIRE, OF A CHILD IN LONDON

Never until the mankind making
Bird beast and flower
Fathering and all humbling darkness
Tells with silence the last light breaking
And the still hour   5
Is come of the sea tumbling in harness

And I must enter again the round
Zion of the water bead
And the synagogue of the ear of corn
Shall I let pray the shadow of a sound   10
Or sow my salt seed
In the least valley of sackcloth to mourn

The majesty and burning of the child's death.
I shall not murder
The mankind of her going with a grave truth   15
Nor blaspheme down the stations of the breath
With any further
Elegy of innocence and youth.

Deep with the first dead lies London's daughter,
Robed in the long friends,   20
The grains beyond age, the dark veins of her mother,
Secret by the unmourning water
Of the riding Thames.
After the first death, there is no other.

1946
Dylan Thomas (1914–1953)

WE REAL COOL

The Pool Players.
Seven at the Golden Shovel.

We real cool. We
Left school. We

Lurk late. We
Strike straight. We

Sing sin. We
Thin gin. We

Jazz June. We
Die soon.

1959
Gwendolyn Brooks
(b. 1917)

AFTER THE SURPRISING CONVERSIONS

September twenty-second, Sir: today
I answer. In the latter part of May,
Hard on our Lord's Ascension, it began
To be more sensible. A gentleman
Of more than common understanding, strict   5
In morals, pious in behavior, kicked
Against our goad. A man of some renown,
An useful, honored person in the town,
He came of melancholy parents; prone
To secret spells, for years they kept alone—   10
His uncle, I believe, was killed of it:
Good people, but of too much or little wit.
I preached one Sabbath on a text from Kings;
He showed concernment for his soul. Some things
In his experience were hopeful. He   15
Would sit and watch the wind knocking a tree
And praise this countryside our Lord has made.
Once when a poor man's heifer died, he laid
A shilling on the doorsill; though a thirst
For loving shook him like a snake, he durst   20
Not entertain much hope of his estate

The Surprising Conversions: The title refers to conversions that took place in the religious community of Jonathan Edwards (1703–1758), in Massachusetts, during late 1734 and early 1735. Edwards described this period in a letter to a Boston clergyman. Lowell's poem concerns what happened following this period of religious activity. The relevant portion of Edwards' letter begins with events in May, 1735:

"In the latter part of May, it began to be very sensible that the Spirit of God was gradually withdrawing from us, and after this time Satan seemed to be more let loose, and raged in a dreadful manner. The first instance wherein it appeared, was a person's putting an end to his life by cutting his throat. He was a gentleman of more than common understanding, of strict morals, religious in his behavior, and a useful, honorable person in the town; but was of a family that are exceeding prone to melancholy, and his mother was killed with it. He had, from the beginning of this extraordinary time, been exceedingly concerned about the state of his soul, and there were some things in his experience, that appeared very hopefully, but he durst entertain no hope concerning his own good estate. Towards the latter end of his time, he grew much discouraged, and melancholy grew amain upon him, till he was wholly overpowered by it, and was, in great measure, past a capacity of receiving advice, or being reasoned with to any purpose: the devil took the advantage, and drove him into despairing thoughts. He was kept awake nights meditating upon terror, so that he had scarce any sleep at all, for a long time together. And it was observable at last, that he was scarcely well capable of managing his ordinary business, and was judged delirious by the coroner's inquest. The news of this extraordinarily affected the minds of people here, and struck them as it were with astonishment. After this, multitudes in this and other towns seemed to have it strongly suggested to them, and pressed upon them, to do as this person had done. And many that seemed to be under no melancholy, some pious persons, that had no special darkness or doubts about the goodness of their state, nor were under any special trouble or concern of mind about any thing spiritual or temporal, yet had it urged upon them, as if somebody had spoken to them, *Cut your own throat, now is a good opportunity.* Now! Now! So that they were obliged to fight with all their might to resist it, and yet no reason suggested to them why they should do it" (*The Works of President Edwards*, New York, 1851, III, 69–72).

In heaven. Once we saw him sitting late
Behind his attic window by a light
That guttered on his Bible; through that night
He meditated terror, and he seemed   25
Beyond advice or reason, for he dreamed
That he was called to trumpet Judgment Day
To Concord. In the latter part of May
He cut his throat. And though the coroner
Judged him delirious, soon a noisome stir   30
Palsied our village. At Jehovah's nod
Satan seemed more let loose amongst us: God
Abandoned us to Satan, and he pressed
Us hard, until we thought we could not rest
Till we had done with life. Content was gone.   35
All the good work was quashed. We were undone.
The breath of God had carried out a planned
And sensible withdrawal from this land;
The multitude, once unconcerned with doubt,
Once neither callous, curious nor devout,   40
Jumped at broad noon, as though some peddler groaned
At it in its familiar twang: "My friend,
Cut your own throat. Cut your own throat. Now! Now!"
September twenty-second, Sir, the bough
Cracks with the unpicked apples, and at dawn
The small-mouth bass breaks water, gorged with spawn.

1946
Robert Lowell (1917–1977)

THE WATCH

When I
took my
watch to the watchfixer I
felt privileged but also pained to watch the operation. He
had long fingernails and a voluntary squint. He   5
fixed a magnifying cup over his
squint eye. He
undressed my
watch. I
watched him   10

The Watch

split her
in three layers and lay her
middle—a quivering viscera—in a circle on a little plinth. He
shoved shirtsleeves up and leaned like an ogre over my
naked watch. With critical pincers he   15
poked and stirred. He
lifted out little private things with a magnet too tiny for me
to watch almost. "Watch out!" I
almost said. His
eye watched, enlarged, the secrets of my   20
watch, and I
watched anxiously. Because what if he
touched her
ticker too rough, and she
gave up the ghost out of pure fright? Or put her   25
things back backwards so she'd
run backwards after this? Or he
might lose a minuscule part, connected to her
exquisite heart, and mix her
up, instead of fix her.   30
And all the time,
all the time-
pieces on the walls, on the shelves, told the time,
told the time
in swishes and ticks,   35
swishes and ticks,
and seemed to be gloating, as they watched and told. I
felt faint, I
was about to lose my
breath—my   40
ticker going lickety-split—when watchfixer clipped her
three slices together with a gleam and two flicks of his
tools like chopsticks. He
spat out his
eye, lifted her   45
high, gave her
a twist, set her
hands right, and laid her
little face, quite as usual, in its place on my
wrist.   50

1967

May Swenson (b. 1919)

CHURCH GOING

Once I am sure there's nothing going on
I step inside, letting the door thud shut.
Another church: matting, seats, and stone,
And little books; sprawlings of flowers, cut
For Sunday, brownish now; some brass and stuff   5
Up at the holy end; the small neat organ;
And a tense, musty, unignorable silence,
Brewed God knows how long. Hatless, I take off
My cycle-clips in awkward reverence,

Move forward, run my hand around the font.   10
From where I stand, the roof looks almost new—
Cleaned, or restored? Someone would know: I don't.
Mounting the lectern, I peruse a few
Hectoring large-scale verses, and pronounce
"Here endeth" much more loudly than I'd meant.   15
The echoes snigger briefly. Back at the door
I sign the book, donate an Irish sixpence,
Reflect the place was not worth stopping for.

Yet stop I did: in fact I often do,
And always end much at a loss like this,   20
Wondering what to look for; wondering, too,
When churches fall completely out of use
What we shall turn them into, if we shall keep
A few cathedrals chronically on show,
Their parchment, plate and pyx in locked cases,   25
And let the rest rent-free to rain and sheep.
Shall we avoid them as unlucky places?

Or, after dark, will dubious women come
To make their children touch a particular stone;
Pick simples for a cancer; or on some   30
Advised night see walking a dead one?
Power of some sort or other will go on
In games, in riddles, seemingly at random;
But superstition, like belief, must die,
And what remains when disbelief has gone?   35
Grass, weedy pavement, brambles, buttress, sky,

A shape less recognizable each week,
A purpose more obscure. I wonder who
Will be the last, the very last, to seek
This place for what it was; one of the crew   40
That tap and jot and know what rood-lofts were?
Some ruin-bibber, randy for antique,
Or Christmas-addict, counting on a whiff
Of gown-and-bands and organ-pipes and myrrh?
Or will he be my representative,   45

Bored, uninformed, knowing the ghostly silt
Dispersed, yet tending to this cross of ground
Through suburb scrub because it held unspilt
So long and equably what since is found
Only in separation—marriage, and birth,   50
And death, and thoughts of these—for whom was built
This special shell? For, though I've no idea
What this accoutred frowsty barn is worth,
It pleases me to stand in silence here;

A serious house on serious earth it is,   55
In whose blent air all our compulsions meet,
Are recognized, and robed as destinies.
And that much never can be obsolete,
Since someone will forever be surprising
A hunger in himself to be more serious,   60
And gravitating with it to this ground,
Which, he once heard, was proper to grow wise in,
If only that so many dead lie round.

1955
Philip Larkin (b. 1922)

FUNERAL ORATION FOR A MOUSE

This, Lord, was an anxious brother and
a living diagram of fear: full of health himself,
he brought diseases like a gift
to give his hosts. Masked in a cat's moustache

but sounding like a bird, he was a ghost   5
   of lesser noises and a kitchen pest
for whom some ladies stand on chairs. So,
   Lord, accept our felt though minor guilt
     for an ignoble foe and ancient sin:
      the murder of a guest   10
   who shared our board: just once he ate
     too slowly, dying in our trap
from necessary hunger and a broken back.

Humors of love aside, the mousetrap was our own
   opinion of the mouse, but for the mouse   15
     it was the tree of knowledge with
     its consequential fruit, the true cross
     and the gate of hell. Even to approach
      it makes him like or better than
its maker: his courage as a spoiler never once   20
impressed us, but to go out cautiously at night,
   into the dining room;—what bravery, what
     hunger! Younger by far, in dying he
was older than us all: his mobile tail and nose
spasmed in the pinch of our annoyance. Why,   25
then, at that snapping sound, did we, victorious,
   begin to laugh without delight?

   Our stomachs, deep in an analysis
     of their own stolen baits
(and asking, "Lord, Host, to whom are we the pests?"),   30
   contracted and demanded a retreat
   from our machine and its effect of death,
     as if the mouse's fingers, skinnier
than hairpins and as breakable as cheese,
   could grasp our grasping lives, and in   35
   their drowning movement pull us under too,
into the common death beyond the mousetrap.

                        1961
                Alan Dugan (b. 1923)

SESTINA ON SIX WORDS BY WELDON KEES

I often wonder about the others
Where they are bound for on the voyage,
What is the reason for their silence,
Was there some reason to go away?
It may be they carry a dark burden,   5
Expect some harm, or have done harm.

How can we show we mean no harm?
Approach them? But they shy from others.
Offer, perhaps, to share the burden?
They change the subject to the voyage,   10
Or turn abruptly, walk away,
To brood against the rail in silence.

What is defeated by their silence
More than love, less than harm?
Many already are looking their way,   15
Pretending not to. Eyes of others
Will follow them now the whole voyage
And add a little to the burden.

Others touch hands to ease the burden,
Or stroll, companionable in silence,   20
Counting the stars which bless the voyage,
But let the foghorn speak of harm,
Their hearts will stammer like the others',
Their hands seem in each other's way.

It is so obvious, in a way.   25
Each is alone, each with his burden.
To others always they are others,
And they can never break the silence,
Say, lightly, *thou*, but to their harm
Although they make many a voyage.   30

What do they wish for from the voyage
But to awaken far away
By miracle free from every harm,

See Kees' "Sestina: Travel Notes."

Hearing at dawn that sweet burden
The birds cry after a long silence?   35
Where is that country not like others?

There is no way to ease the burden.
The voyage leads on from harm to harm,
A land of others and of silence.

1959
Donald Justice (b. 1925)

I KNOW A MAN

As I sd to my
friend, because I am
always talking,—John, I

sd, which was not his
name, the darkness sur-   5
rounds us, what

can we do against
it, or else, shall we &
why not, buy a goddamn big car,

drive, he sd, for   10
christ's sake, look
out where yr going.

1957
Robert Creeley (b. 1926)

APRIL INVENTORY

The green catalpa tree has turned
All white; the cherry blooms once more.
In one whole year I haven't learned
A blessed thing they pay you for.
The blossoms snow down in my hair;   5
The trees and I will soon be bare.

April Inventory

The trees have more than I to spare.
The sleek, expensive girls I teach,
Younger and pinker every year,
Bloom gradually out of reach.   10
The pear tree lets its petals drop
Like dandruff on a tabletop.

The girls have grown so young by now
I have to nudge myself to stare.
This year they smile and mind me how   15
My teeth are falling with my hair.
In thirty years I may not get
Younger, shrewder, or out of debt.

The tenth time, just a year ago,
I made myself a little list   20
Of all the things I'd ought to know,
Then told my parents, analyst,
And everyone who's trusted me
I'd be substantial, presently.

I haven't read one book about   25
A book or memorized one plot.
Or found a mind I did not doubt.
I learned one date. And then forgot.
And one by one the solid scholars
Get the degrees, the jobs, the dollars.   30

And smile above their starchy collars.
I taught my classes Whitehead's notions;
One lovely girl, a song of Mahler's.
Lacking a source-book or promotions,
I showed one child the colors of   35
A luna moth and how to love.

I taught myself to name my name,
To bark back, loosen love and crying;
To ease my woman so she came,

Whitehead: Alfred North Whitehead (1861–1947), English philosopher and mathematician.
Mahler: Gustav Mahler (1860–1911), Austrian composer and conductor.

To ease an old man who was dying.   40
I have not learned how often I
Can win, can love, but choose to die.

I have not learned there is a lie
Love shall be blonder, slimmer, younger;
That my equivocating eye   45
Loves only by my body's hunger;
That I have forces, true to feel,
Or that the lovely world is real.

While scholars speak authority
And wear their ulcers on their sleeves,   50
My eyes in spectacles shall see
These trees procure and spend their leaves.
There is a value underneath
The gold and silver in my teeth.

Though trees turn bare and girls turn wives,   55
We shall afford our costly seasons;
There is a gentleness survives
That will outspeak and has its reasons.
There is a gentleness survives
That will outspeak and has its reasons.
There is a loveliness exists,
Preserves us, not for specialists.   60

1959

W. D. Snodgrass (b. 1926)

FOR THE ANNIVERSARY OF MY DEATH

Every year without knowing it I have passed the day
When the last fires will wave to me
And the silence will set out
Tireless traveler
Like the beam of a lightless star   5

Then I will no longer
Find myself in life as in a strange garment
Surprised at the earth

And the love of one woman
And the shamelessness of men   10
As today writing after three days of rain
Hearing the wren sing and the falling cease
And bowing not knowing to what

                                          1967
                    W. S. Merwin (b. 1927)

MARVELL'S GARDEN

Marvell's garden, that place of solitude,
is not where I'd choose to live
yet is the fixed sundial
that turns me round
unwillingly   5
in a hot glade
as closer, closer I come to contradiction,
to the shade green within the green shade.

The garden where Marvell scorned love's solicitude—
that dream—and played instead an arcane solitaire,   10
shuffling his thoughts like shadowy chance
across the shrubs of ecstasy,
and cast the myths away to flowering hours
as yes, his mind, that sea, caught at green
thoughts shadowing a green infinity.   15

And yet Marvell's garden was not Plato's
garden—and yet—he *did* care more for the form
of things than for the thing itself—
ideas and visions,
resemblances and echoes,   20
things seeming and being
not quite what they were.

That was his garden, a kind of attitude
struck out of an earth too carefully attended,
wanting to be left alone.   25

Marvell's garden: See Andrew Marvell's "The Garden."

And I don't blame him for that.
God knows, too many fences fence us out
and his garden closed in on Paradise.

On Paradise! When I think of his hymning
Puritans in the Bermudas, the bright oranges   30
lighting up that night! When I recall
his rustling tinsel hopes
beneath the cold decree of steel,
Oh, I have wept for some new convulsion
to tear together this world and his.   35

But then I saw his luminous plumed Wings
prepared for flight,
and then I heard him singing glory
in a green tree,
and then I caught the vest he'd laid aside   40
all blest with fire.

And I have gone walking slowly in
his garden of necessity
leaving brothers, lovers, Christ
outside my walls   45
where they have wept without
and I within.

                                                          1971
                              Phyllis Webb (b. 1927)

THOSE WERE THE DAYS

The sun came up before breakfast,
perfectly round and yellow, and we
dressed in the soft light and shook out
our long blond curls and waited
for Maid to brush them flat and place   5
the part just where it belonged.
We came down the carpeted stairs

Puritans in the Bermudas: The allusion is to Marvell's poem "Bermudas."

Those Were the Days

one step at a time, in single file,
gleaming in our sailor suits, two
four-year-olds with unscratched knees   10
and scrubbed teeth. Breakfast came
on silver dishes with silver covers
and was set in table center, and Mother
handed out the portions of eggs
and bacon, toast, and juice. We could   15
hear the ocean not far off, and boats
firing up their engines, and the shouts
of couples in white on the tennis courts.
I thought, Yes, this is the beginning
of another summer, and it will go on   20
until the sun tires of us or the moon
rises in its place on a silvered dawn
and no one wakens. My brother flung
his fork on the polished wooden floor
and cried out, "My eggs are cold, cold!"   25
and turned his plate over. I laughed
out loud, and Mother slapped my face,
and when I cleared my eyes the table
was bare of even a simple white cloth
and the steaming plates had vanished.   30
My brother said, "It's time," and we
struggled into our galoshes and snapped
them up, slumped into our peacoats,
one year older now and on our way
to the top through the freezing rains   35
of the end of November, lunch boxes
under our arms, tight fists pocketed,
out the door and down the front stoop,
heads bent low, tacking into the wind.

1981
Philip Levine (b. 1928)

HOBBES, 1651

When I returned at last from Paris hoofbeats pounded
   Over the harsh and unrelenting road;
It was cold, the snow high; I was old, and the winter
   Sharp, and the dead mid-century sped by
In ominous, blurred streaks as, brutish, the wind moaned   5
   Among black branches. I rode through a kind
Of graceless winter nature, bled of what looked like life.
   My vexing horse threw me. If it was not safe
In England yet, or ever, that nowhere beneath the gray
   Sky would be much safer seemed very plain.   10

1962
John Hollander (b. 1929)

DEATH OF A SON

(who died in a mental hospital aged one)

Something has ceased to come along with me.
Something like a person: something very like one.
   And there was no nobility in it
   Or anything like that.

Something was there like a one year   5
Old house, dumb as stone. While the near buildings
   Sang like birds and laughed
   Understanding the pact

They were to have with silence. But he
Neither sang nor laughed. He did not bless silence   10
   Like bread, with words.
   He did not forsake silence.

Hobbes, 1651: Thomas Hobbes (1588–1679), English philosopher. Hobbes had been a tutor to Prince Charles (later Charles II), the son of Charles I (executed 1649). The publication of Hobbes' *Leviathan* in 1651 scandalized the exiled court of Charles II in Paris; Hobbes was banished and he returned to England. **brutish:** echoes Hobbes' phrase from *Leviathan:* "and the life of man, solitary, poor, nasty, brutish, and short" (I, xiii).

Death of a Son

But rather, like a house in mourning
Kept the eye turned in to watch the silence while
      The other houses like birds   15
          Sang around him.

And the breathing silence neither
Moved nor was still.

      I have seen stones: I have seen brick
But this house was made up of neither bricks nor stone   20
          But a house of flesh and blood
             With flesh of stone

      And bricks for blood. A house
Of stones and blood in breathing silence with the other
          Birds singing crazy on its chimneys.   25
          But this was silence,

      This was something else, this was
Hearing and speaking though he was a house drawn
          Into silence, this was
             Something religious in his silence,   30

      Something shining in his quiet,
This was different this was altogether something else:
          Though he never spoke, this
             Was something to do with death.

      And then slowly the eye stopped looking   35
Inward. The silence rose and became still.
The look turned to the outer place and stopped,
          With the birds still shrilling around him.
          And as if he could speak

He turned over on his side with his one year   40
Red as a wound
He turned over as if he could be sorry for this
And out of his eyes two great tears rolled, like stones,
      and he died.
                    1954

             Jon Silkin (b. 1930)

EX-BASKETBALL PLAYER

Pearl Avenue runs past the high-school lot,
Bends with the trolley tracks, and stops, cut off
Before it has a chance to go two blocks,
At Colonel McComsky Plaza. Berth's Garage
Is on the corner facing west, and there,   5
Most days, you'll find Flick Webb, who helps Berth out.

Flick stands tall among the idiot pumps—
Five on a side, the old bubble-head style,
Their rubber elbows hanging loose and low.
One's nostrils are two S's, and his eyes   10
An E and O. And one is squat, without
A head at all—more of a football type.

Once Flick played for the high-school team, The Wizards.
He was good: in fact, the best. In '46
He bucked three hundred ninety points,   15
A country record still. The ball loved Flick.
I saw him rack up thirty-eight of forty
In one home game. His hands were like wild birds.

He never learned a trade, he just sells gas,
Checks oil, and changes flats. Once in a while,   20
As a gag, he dribbles an inner tube,
But most of us remember anyway.
His hands are fine and nervous on the lug wrench.
It makes no difference to the lug wrench, though.

Off work, he hangs around Mae's Luncheonette.   25
Grease-grey and kind of coiled, he plays pinball,
Sips lemon cokes, and smokes those thin cigars;
Flick seldom speaks to Mae, just sits and nods
Beyond her face towards bright applauding tiers
Of Necco Wafers, Nibs, and Juju Beads.   30

                                                        1958
                                          John Updike (b. 1932)

Ex-Basketball Player: Three of Updike's novels—*Rabbit, Run* (1960), *Rabbit Redux* (1971), and
Rabbit Is Rich (1981)—also describe the life and times of an ex-basketball player.

POEM FOR HALFWHITE COLLEGE STUDENTS

Who are you, listening to me, who are you
listening to yourself? Are you white or
black, or does that have anything to do
with it? Can you pop your fingers to no
music, except those wild monkies go on   5
in your head, can you jerk, to no melody,
except finger poppers get it together
when you turn from starchecking to checking
yourself. How do you sound, your words, are they
yours? The ghost you see in the mirror, is it really   10
you, can you swear you are not an imitation greyboy,
can you look right next to you in that chair, and swear,
that the sister you have your hand on is not really
so full of Elizabeth Taylor, Richard Burton is
coming out of her ears. You may even have to be Richard   15
with a white shirt and face, and four million negroes
think you cute, you may have to be Elizabeth Taylor, old lady,
if you want to sit up in your crazy spot dreaming about dresses,
and the sway of certain porters' hips. Check yourself, learn who it is
speaking, when you make some ultrasophisticated point,
    check yourself,   20
when you find yourself gesturing like Steve McQueen, check
    it out, ask
in your black heart who it is you are, and is that image black or white.
you might be surprised right out the window, whistling dixie on the
    way in.

1969
Imamu Amiri Baraka (b. 1934)

I HAVE NOT LINGERED IN EUROPEAN MONASTERIES

I have not lingered in European monasteries
and discovered among the tall grasses tombs of knights
who fell as beautifully as their ballads tell;

I have not parted the grasses
or purposefully left them thatched.   5

I have not released my mind to wander and wait
in those great distances
between the snowy mountains and the fishermen,
like a moon,
or a shell beneath the moving water.   10

I have not held my breath
so that I might hear the breathing of God,
or tamed my heartbeat with an exercise,
or starved for visions.
Although I have watched him often   15
I have not become the heron,

leaving my body on the shore,
and I have not become the luminous trout,
leaving my body in the air.

I have not worshipped wounds and relics,   20
or combs of iron,
or bodies wrapped and burnt in scrolls.

I have not been unhappy for ten thousand years.
During the day I laugh and during the night I sleep.
My favourite cooks prepare my meals,   25
my body cleans and repairs itself,
and all my work goes well.

1968
Leonard Cohen (b. 1934)

PROGRESSIVE INSANITIES OF A PIONEER

1

He stood, a point
on a sheet of green paper
proclaiming himself the centre,

with no walls, no borders
anywhere; the sky no height   5
above him, totally un-

enclosed
and shouted:

Let me out!

2

He dug the soil in rows,   10
imposed himself with shovels.
He asserted
into the furrows, I
am not random.

The ground   15
replied with aphorisms:

a tree-sprout, a nameless
weed, words
he couldn't understand.

3

The house pitched   20
the plot staked
in the middle of nowhere.

At night the mind
inside, in the middle
of nowhere.   25

The idea of an animal
patters across the roof.

In the darkness the fields
defend themselves with fences
in vain: 30
    everything
     is getting in.

4

By daylight he resisted.
He said, disgusted

with the swamp's clamourings and the outbursts   35
of rocks,
> This is not order
> but the absence
> of order.

He was wrong, the unanswering   40
forest implied:

> It was
> an ordered absence

5

For many years
he fished for a great vision,   45
dangling the hooks of sown
roots under the surface
of the shallow earth.

It was like
enticing whales with a bent   50
pin. Besides he thought

in that country
only the worms were biting.

6

If he had known unstructured
space is a deluge   55
and stocked his log house-
boat with all the animals
even the wolves,

he might have floated.

But obstinate he   60
stated, The land is solid
and stamped,

watching his foot sink
down through stone
up to the knee.   65

7

Things
refused to name themselves; refused
to let him name them.

The wolves hunted
outside.   70

On his beaches, his clearings,
by the surf of under-
growth breaking
at his feet, he foresaw
disintegration   75
                    and in the end
through eyes
made ragged by his
effort, the tension
between subject and object,   80

the green
vision, the unnamed
whale invaded.

1968

Margaret Atwood (b. 1939)

A KITE FOR MICHAEL & CHRISTOPHER

All through that Sunday afternoon
a kite flew above Sunday,
a tightened drumhead, an armful of blown chaff.

I'd seen it grey and slippy in the making,
I'd tapped it when it dried out white and stiff,   5
I'd tied the bows of newspaper
along its six-foot tail.

A Kite for Michael & Christopher: Compare the following poem, "Cross Country," by Heaney's
friend Michael Longley.

But now it was far up like a small black lark
and now it dragged as if the bellied string
were a wet rope hauled upon   10
to lift a shoal.

My friend says that the human soul
is about the weight of a snipe
yet the soul at anchor there,
the string that sags and ascends   15
weighs like a furrow assumed into the heavens.

Before the kite plunges down into the wood
and this line goes useless
take it in your two hands, boys, and feel
the strumming rooted long-tailed pull of grief.   20
You were born fit for it.
Stand in here in front of me
and take the strain.

1979
Seamus Heaney (b. 1939)

CROSS COUNTRY

From our uncomfortable thicket
We studied the man flying his kite
And the cross-country runners
On their exhausted circuits.

I wanted to touch your breasts
But you pretended not to notice
And welcomed the runners into view
As an insomniac might count sheep.

I said that the man with the kite
Was manipulating them on long
Invisible strings: he loomed
At the centre like a puppet-master.

But you said no they could be his
Children: he was fishing in the sky
And something kept tugging at the line
He was too frightened to pull in.

1975

Michael Longley (b. 1939)

PURE MEMORY/CHRIS DEWDNEY

1

On a B.C. radio show the man asked me, coffee half way up
to his mouth, what are the books you've liked recently?
Christopher Dewdney's A *Palaeozoic Geology of London
Ontario*. Only I didn't say that, I started stumbling on the word
Palaeozoic . . . Paleo . . . Polio . . . and then it happened
on Geology too until it seemed a disease. I sounded like an
idiot. Meanwhile I was watching the man's silent gulps. The
professional silent gulping of coffee an inch or two away from
the microphone. Unconcerned with my sinking "live" all over
the province.

2

I can't remember where I first met him. Somewhere I became
aware of this giggle. Tan hair, tan face, tan shirt and a
giggle-snort as his head staggered back. His arms somewhere.

3

The baby. He shows me the revolving globe in the 4 month
old kid's crib. Only it has been unscrewed and the globe turned
upside down and rescrewed in that way so Africa and Asia all
swivel upside down. This way he says she'll have to come to
terms with the shapes all over again when she grows up.

4

He comes to dinner, steps out of the car and transforms the 10
year old suburban garden into ancient history. Is on his knees
pointing out the age and race and character of rocks and earth.
He loves the Norfolk Pine. I give him a piece of wood 120

million years old from the tar sands and he smokes a bit of it.
Recently he claims the rest of the piece is going white.

5

When he was a kid and his parents had guests and he was
eventually told to get to bed he liked to embarrass them by
running under a table and screaming out Don't hit me Don't
hit me.

6

His most embarrassing moment. A poetry reading in Toronto.
He was sitting in the front row and he realised that he hated
the poetry. He looked around discreetly for the exit but it was a
long way away. Then to the right, quite near him, he saw
another door. As a poem ended he got up and officially walked
to the door quickly opened it went out and closed it behind
him. He found himself in a dark cupboard about 2 feet by 3
feet. It contained nothing. He waited there a while, then he
started to laugh and giggle. He giggled for 5 minutes and he
thinks the audience could probably hear him. When he had
collected himself he opened the door, came out, walked to his
seat and sat down again.

7

Coach House Press, December 1974. I haven't seen him for a
long time. His face is tough. Something has left his face. It is
not that he is thinner but the face has lost something distinct
and it seems like flesh. But he is not thinner. He is busy
working on his new book *Fovea Centralis* and I watch him as
he sits in the empty back room upstairs all alone with a
computer typesetting terminal. Has taught himself to use it and
tries to teach me but I don't understand a word and nod and
ask how he is. I can't get over his face. It is "tight", as if a
stocking were over it and he about to perform a robbery. He
plucks at the keys and talks down into the machine. I am
relieved when he starts giggling at something. I tell him I'm
coming down to London in a week and he says he will show
me his butterflies, he has bought two mounted butterflies for a
very good price. If I don't tell anyone he will let me know
where I could get one. A Chinaman in London Ontario sells

them. I start to laugh. He doesn't. This is serious information, important rare information like the history of rocks—these frail wings of almost powder have their genealogies too.

8

His favourite movie is *Earthquake*. He stands in the middle of his apartment very excited telling me all the details. He shows me his beautiful fossils, the white that is on the 120 million year old wood, a small poster of James Dean hitting his brother in *East of Eden*, and the two very impressive mounted butterflies.

9

On the bus going back to Toronto I have a drawing of him by Bob Fones. Wrapped in brown paper it lies above me on the luggage rack. When the bus swerves I put my arm out into the dark aisle ready to catch him if it falls. A strange drawing of him in his cane chair with a plant to the side of him, reading Frank O'Hara with very oriental eyes. It was done in 1973, before the flesh left his face.

10

His wife's brain haemorrhage. I could not cope with that. He is 23 years old. He does. Africa Asia Australia upside down. Earthquake.

1978
Michael Ondaatje (b. 1943)

APPENDIX

WRITING ABOUT POEMS

The same skills used in reading a poem or in writing other kinds of essays—asking questions, forming a thesis, collecting evidence, and verifying your conclusions—will help you write a clear, cogent, and organized essay about a poem. Except in some matters of format, there are no rules about writing such an essay, but the following suggestions may be useful as you prepare to write.

PURPOSE OF THE ESSAY

The purpose of your essay will determine the kind of preparation necessary. Essays on poems may have many different purposes, and each will require some specific preparation. Some essays involve a detailed explanation (or explication) of the poem to reveal its meaning and artistry. This explication is called a *close reading* and requires a detailed examination of the language, imagery, and structure of the poem. Other essays, in order to explain some aspect of the poem, require *research*. Such research may include investigation of the poem's background, its biographical implications, its historical context, and its textual, publishing, or critical history.

Any poem, of course, can serve as the subject of a variety of essays, each with a different purpose. An essay on A. E. Housman's "To an Athlete Dying Young" (p. 87), for example, might examine Housman's use of imagery in the poem; another, how he came to write it. Other essays might discuss Housman's choice of vocabulary, the various drafts of the poem, how the poem's subject matter (or tone or imagery) is typical or untypical of Housman's poetry as a whole, or how the theme of the poem fits into the themes developed in *A Shropshire Lad*, the volume of poems from which it comes. An essay might review the changing critical attitudes toward Housman's poetry, using "To an Athlete Dying Young" as an example; or it might examine the poem as an instance of the elegy, comparing Housman's poem to other earlier or more recent examples. An essay might be devoted to considering the biographical implications of the poem or to an explanation of how Housman, a noted scholar-teacher of Greek and Latin literature, drew on classical poetry for the imagery, structure, or allusions in the poem. Such an essay might reveal how "To an Athlete Dying Young" is part of a wider social or literary context—the Victorian response to Greek literature, history, and art, for instance.

Fundamental to any of these purposes is a careful and intensive reading of the poem in question. Here is a method for starting:

1. Read the poem over several times aloud, experimenting with intonation, emphasis, and tone.
2. Ask the questions that occur to you as you read, focusing those questions by asking the organizing questions suggested earlier in this book. Consider what questions require going outside the poem for information and what questions might need more extensive research.
3. Take notes. Jot down questions and your tentative answers.
4. Organize your notes in response to the topic or assigned purpose of your essay.

For an explication or analysis of the poem—a close reading—you will need to consider the inter-relatedness of all parts of the poem. The language, imagery, allusions, and structure of the poem must be shown to support whatever interpretation you are presenting in your essay. You may wish to use evidence from outside the poem—the statements of other critics, for example—but your primary task in a close reading is a convincing presentation of your own reading of the poem. For a discussion of the poem that involves research, you must begin with your own understanding of the poem and then find, evaluate, and use sources that aid in filling in the background of the poem. Each of these kinds of essays is discussed in this appendix.

Your instructor may wish you to follow a particular style manual or research-paper guide in preparing your paper. If so, follow it *exactly*. Most guides agree on the following points of form and style:

1. The title of your essay should not be enclosed in quotation marks or underlined, but its major words should be capitalized:

Death as Victory

2. The title of a poem, whether used as a part of your own title or elsewhere in your essay, should be enclosed in quotation marks:

Death as Victory in Housman's "To an Athlete Dying Young"

But the title of a book-length poem or a collection of poems should be underlined (italicized):

A Comparison of "To an Athlete Dying Young" with Other
Poems in Housman's A *Shropshire Lad*

3. Each page of your essay should be numbered and identified with your name
or short title: *Bourdette—2* or *Housman's "Athlete"—2*.

4. Quoted passages of more than two lines in length should be indented as
in the following example:

> George Barker, in "To My Mother" and Dylan Thomas, in "A Refusal
> to Mourn the Death, by Fire, of a Child in London" respond in quite
> similar ways to the endurance of the human spirit in the face of de-
> struction. Describing the bombing of London during World War II,
> Barker says of his mother:

> > She will not glance up at the bomber, or condescend
> > To drop her gin and scuttle to a cellar,
> > But lean on the mahogany table like a mountain
> > Whom only faith can move. . . .

> Thomas, too, reveals a similar refusal to minimize the greatness of the
> human spirit:

> > I shall not murder
> > The mankind of her going with a grave truth
> > Nor blaspheme down the stations of the breath
> > With any further
> > Elegy of innocence and youth.

5. Poetry should be quoted *exactly* as arranged by the poet. Be especially careful about capitalization, punctuation, and line lengths:

> The time you won your town the race
> We chaired you through the market-place;
> Man and boy stood cheering by,
> And home we brought you shoulder-high.
> > —A. E. Housman, "To an Athlete Dying Young"

rather than, for example:

> The time you won your town the race we chaired
> you through the market-place; Man and boy stood
> cheering by, and home we brought you shoulder-high.

6. If you are quoting poetry within your own sentence structure, the lines
should be put in quotation marks and the end of the printed line of poetry
should be indicated with a spaced slash [/]:

In "To My Mother," George Barker describes his indomitable mother as one who "will not glance up at a bomber, or condescend / To drop her gin and scuttle to a cellar."

7. Unless your instructor specifically asks for it, detailed summary or line-by-line paraphrase of the poem is usually unnecessary in an essay. The substance of the poem will be clear to the reader if you develop the thesis of your essay in sufficient detail.

8. Sample notes and bibliography entries are given on pages 448–450. Your instructor can recommend one of the several standard manuals or guides that contain further guidelines for outlining, writing, footnoting, providing correct bibliographies, and citing poetry. Your own college or department may have its own style guide that you will be required to follow in preparing your essay.

THE CLOSE READING: EXPLICATION AND ANALYSIS

Developing a Thesis

Whether you are developing your own topic or responding to an assigned topic, you need to make that topic manageable and clear both to yourself and your readers. Essential to this is the development of a *thesis*—a precise statement, preferably expressed in a sentence, of the point you wish to make about the poem.

Just as the question "What does the poem mean?" can be made answerable by turning that question into smaller and more manageable questions, so a general topic or assignment can be developed and a thesis arrived at by turning the assignment into a series of questions. Consider, for example, this possible assignment:

> Explain the theme, or thesis, of Housman's "To an Athlete Dying Young," demonstrating with specific details how that theme is developed throughout the poem.

For this, as for any other topic, you need to consider what the assignment requires, to arrive at a statement or thesis about Housman's theme, and then to provide sufficient evidence that substantiates your thesis. To say, for example, that the poem is about a boy who has died young is too general a statement and does not provide a thesis about the central idea or purpose of the poem. Finally, you need to find evidence in the poem that illustrates and proves your thesis about the theme of Housman's poem.

To begin, you might ask questions like these:

The Close Reading

1. The title of the poem indicates that the poem is addressed to an athlete who has died young. What expectations does the title create? What does the poet (or speaker) say to or about this athlete?
2. The expectation set up by the title and topic of the poem (the death of a youth) may suggest that the poem will be sad or depressing. Is this expectation supported by the details of the poem? What details, if any, alter this expectation?
3. What evidence is there to indicate the poet's (or speaker's) attitude toward the death? How does this attitude help reveal the poem's theme?

After several readings of the poem and with notes of questions and possible answers, you are ready to state a hypothesis, or *working thesis*. Given the title of the poem, you may decide that its theme is a rather surprising one: The early death of the young man is not the occasion for a lament (as it is in some other poems on the same general subject) but one that is described as a triumph. You have arrived at your working thesis by a careful reading of the poem; it is now time to collect and organize the evidence that will support your thesis about the theme.

Collecting Evidence

Collecting evidence includes finding and relating to your thesis the images, allusions, words, details of structure, tone, and nuances of meaning that support the thesis. It is very useful to make a list of that evidence before you begin to write.

Once the evidence has been assembled, you are ready to verify your conclusions; you have, of course, been testing these conclusions in the process of collecting evidence by asking questions like these: Does this comparison mean what I think it means? Is there any evidence to support a reading quite different from mine? Have I left out any significant evidence in arriving at my conclusions? Have I considered the context of the lines I have used as evidence? What are the opposing arguments a reader might make to my argument? What evidence have I supplied to defend my thesis?

Organizing the Essay

Once you have verified your conclusions, you are ready to write your essay, which can be broadly outlined as a presentation of

Thesis
Evidence
Conclusion

More specifically, your outline might follow this more detailed organization:

Thesis: Begin with a statement about the poem and poet under discussion
or an immediate statement of your thesis, with a possible brief statement of the
context within which the thesis will be discussed. For example, you might
explain your initial expectations about the poem (as in the sample essay below),
state what other readers have said about the poem that supports or contradicts
what you intend to say, or make comparisons with the author's other poems or
parallels with poems on the same subject by other poets.

Evidence: Present your evidence in the paragraphs that follow your thesis
paragraph. Organize your material so that each succeeding paragraph relates
clearly to your thesis. You may wish to present your examples chronologically
(stanza by stanza, for instance), by relating and explaining the connections of
key lines, images, or allusions, by discussing comparisons or contrasts, or by
taking one line or phrase of the poem and demonstrating how that one line
provides the key to the theme of the poem.

Any necessary counter-evidence: As you present the evidence that supports
your thesis, you may need to consider presenting any evidence that might appear to contradict your conclusions. Do not be afraid to admit that other readings are possible (if you think they might be) or to give alternative readings of
the evidence. If you have read carefully, you will be prepared to state the more
logical or appropriate reading.

Conclusion: Draw together the various strands of your argument, and restate your thesis in such a way as to avoid needless repetition while at the same
time clinching your argument.

To sum up, the following points are necessary to remember when plan-
ning and writing an essay:

1. Know the exact purpose of your essay.
2. Consider the preparation your purpose involves:
   a. terms to be understood
   b. kinds of evidence required
3. Arrive at a working thesis by turning the assignment into smaller and more
   precise questions.
4. Be able to state your thesis in a single sentence.
5. Assemble your evidence by taking notes and organizing them.
6. Consider the issues that your thesis involves and decide how you will treat
   them. (For example, do you need to explain some paradox(es) in the poem?
   Do you need to explain a central image for your thesis to be clear? Do you
   need to prove some relationship between the poem and the poet's life? Are
   there allusions you need to explain so that your thesis and evidence make
   sense?)
7. Organize your essay carefully. Begin with your thesis paragraph, followed
   by paragraphs of evidence (and counter-evidence if necessary), and your

conclusion, as in the following essay, a sample close reading of A. E. Housman's "To an Athlete Dying Young":

Death as Victory

title

first sentence
identifies poem
and author and
states thesis

A. E. Housman's "To an Athlete Dying Young" is a poem that finds a kind of consoling triumph in what would usually be considered a great tragedy—the death of a young and active person. In fact, when I began this poem, especially after reading Randall Jarrell's "The Death of the Ball Turret Gunner" and Jon Silkin's poem about the death of his young son in a mental institution, I expected Housman's poem about death to be equally sad and depressing. I imagined how I would feel if one of my friends on the football or track team were to die suddenly right after a game. But the death in Housman's poem is not treated as sad or as a terrible defeat, but as a victory. How does Housman do it?

writer's approach,
expectations, and
experience with
the poem

concise restatement
of thesis

attention to setting,
time and verb
tense, situation,
and speaker

The poem opens with a scene set in the past. We don't know when, exactly, except that it was the time the athlete won a race for his hometown. The speaker, who seems to be one of the athlete's fellow townsmen, is addressing the athlete directly.

beginning of a
systematic move
through the poem,
with frequent
reference to its text
and exact
quotation

The second stanza is written in the present. "Today," the day of the athlete's funeral, he is being brought "home" as in the very first stanza, but now it is a final home. The reader has to gather this from the title and the rest of the poem, as well as from the comparison of the first and second stanzas. Otherwise, we wouldn't know that the athlete is dead at all. The athlete is brought home along "the road all runners come." This is the road of death that all runners, and everybody else, must eventually travel.

attention to literal
vs. figurative
meanings

But there could be a literal meaning here, too. The first stanza talks about a kind of athletic competition between towns. Wouldn't it be likely that the race was held on the road connecting the two towns and that perhaps the cemetery is on the same road? The athlete is brought home "shoulder-high," but now in funeral procession rather than as in stanza 1, in triumph, carried on the shoulders of his fans. The "threshold" where he is set down can be taken in the strict sense of the threshold of a house (the grave or tomb is talked of here and later in the poem as if it were a house with a small doorway, threshold, sill, and "low lintel"). Figuratively, the threshold is that of his new state of being—the threshold of death. This "town" is the cemetery, where the graves are talked of as if they were houses, surely a "stiller town" than that of those who are still alive; the athlete is now a "townsman" of this stiller town. But at the same time, he is still a townsman of those who are alive, and they are "stiller" now, at his burial, than they were in the first stanza, when they cheered him through the market-place.

discussion of how various elements in the poem contribute to its theme

Everything in the second stanza applies neatly both to the previous situation of the athlete and to his present one. All this supports the theme of the poem, which suggests that the athlete's death is not the end of his glory. By cleverly dying ("Smart lad, to slip betimes away") before his glory fades, he has managed to keep that glory alive. Somehow, he's made something that is impermanent (fame and glory) permanent and found immortality by dying.

generalizations backed up with examples

attention to poem's allusions and images

The argument about the athlete's cleverness in dying young begins in the third stanza. Each of the last five stanzas gives a kind of reason why the early death of the athlete is not a sad thing, but a triumphant one. For example, in stanza 3, the speaker tells the athlete (and us) that the laurel, a plant used to make prize crowns for athletic heroes in ancient times, withers even faster than the rose, a symbol of beauty. Athletic prowess is ordinarily even more fleeting than beauty. But as the succeeding stanzas remind us, the athlete has slipped away before his record is broken and before his name and reputation are forgotten.

conclusion that returns to implications of theme with final statement of thesis

The poem ends with a picture of the dead, flocking around the athlete with his crown of laurel still unwithered. Silkin's son dies and there seems to be no consolation; nothing at all remains of Jarrell's dead flier except bitterness. For Housman's athlete, however, the laurel of victory and youth will always remain unwithered, since he has escaped the changing world of the living, where fame and beauty fade, by cleverly dying young.

THE RESEARCH ESSAY

Like the essay involving a close reading, the research essay requires a thesis, evidence, and conclusion. The analytical essay on the theme of Housman's "To an Athlete Dying Young" did not use or necessarily require outside sources to substantiate the thesis; however, some topics and assignments will require research. Such investigation will involve examination of original texts, critical books and essays, biographical and historical studies, and other background material. In researching a poem, you will want to keep accurate notes on your reading, quoting exactly and recording precisely the sources of your information. In preparing to do research on a poem or poet, it is useful to know some of the kinds of materials that will help you develop your evidence.

Sources

1. *Standard or variorum editions*   Such editions contain authoritative texts of the poet's work, often with explanatory notes and commentary, dates of composition and publication, variant readings and textual notes. A *variorum* edition will contain the commentary of various critics on the poems and/or all the variant readings of the manuscripts and published texts of the poems. Some variorum editions will summarize all the scholarship on the poems. Standard or variorum editions are available for most poets before the twentieth century. For more recent poets, "complete" or "collected" editions, usually without notes or commentary, are reliable sources for texts. You can discover the most authoritative edition of a poet's work by checking recent bibliographies devoted to the poet or by consulting the footnotes or bibliography of a recent critical study.

2. *Bibliographies*   A bibliography will provide a listing of the poet's books and the criticism of the poet's work. An *annotated* bibliography will give a description of the contents of individual volumes of the poet's work and a description and/or evaluation of the critical books and articles on the poet and individual poems. Bibliographies in book form can be located by consulting the card catalog of your library under the author's name or under "bibliographies." Useful bibliographies are also often listed in standard editions of the poet's work and in the bibliographies of critical studies.

3. *Recent criticism*   Criticism too recent to be listed in bibliographies can be found in weekly or monthly periodicals that carry reviews (*The Atlantic, The New York, Saturday Review,* for example), in critical journals devoted to literature and criticism (*Modern Philology, English Journal, Journal of Aesthetics and Art Criticism*), and in journals devoted to the study of a single figure or historical period (*Shakespeare Quarterly, Victorian Literature, Keats–Shelley Journal*). *The American Poetry Review* is an excellent source of criticism and comment on contemporary poetry. Recent criticism can also be located by looking under the subject or author in the *Reader's Guide to Periodical Literature, Essays and General Literature Index, International Index to Periodicals, British Humanities Index, MLA International Bibliographies,* and *The Year's Work in English Studies.* Richard D. Altick

and Andrew Wright's A *Selective Bibliography for the Study of English and American Literature*, 6th edition (New York: Macmillan, 1979), is especially useful for its listing of journals that carry yearly or specialized bibliographies.

4. *Biography*   Short biographies of poets appear in the *Dictionary of National Biography* (English authors and notables; published 1885–1900, with regular supplements since), *The Dictionary of American Biography* (1922–76), *The Penguin Companion to English Literature* (1971), *The Penguin Companion to American Literature* (1971), and *Contemporary Poets*, 3rd edition (1980). You may also wish to consult book-length biographies of individual poets, some of which also contain bibliographies. Although biographies provide useful, even essential contexts for reaeing the poet's work, every biography has its own strengths and weaknesses: some may be biography mixed with critical, interpretive readings; some may be psychological in emphasis; some may be prejudiced against or biased toward the poet's life and works. As in reading criticism, it is important to recognize the particular emphasis of the biography in question.

5. *Autobiography, letters, criticism*   The poet's own account of his or her life and works, editions of the poet's correspondence, and the poet's own critical books and essays contain information about individual poems, the poet's critical attitudes, and the events that shaped the poet's career. Some critical statements are essential background reading for study of the poet's work: Sidney's "An Apology for Poetry," Wordsworth's "Preface" to the *Lyrical Ballads*, Keats's letters, Shelley's "A Defence of Poetry," for example. Many modern and contemporary poets have also written provocative and useful books of criticism, among them W. H. Auden, T. S. Eliot, Seamus Heaney, Randall Jarrell, Denise Levertov, Robert Lowell, Michael McClure, Howard Nemerov, Ezra Pound, John Crowe Ransom, Adrienne Rich, Wallace Stevens, Yvor Winters, and William Butler Yeats.

6. *Concordances*   A concordance is an alphabetical index of the words in a book or the works of an author, with their immediate context of sentence or line. Concordances are available for most of the major earlier poets (Chaucer, Shakespeare, Spenser, Keats, for example) and for many modern poets (Stevens, Years, for example). A concordance is especially useful for finding a phrase or for studies of the imagery and nuances of meaning in a poet's poetic vocabulary.

7. *Background studies*   Studies of the political, social, religious, intellectual, and artistic climiate within which the poet worked are essential for understanding the attitudes, topics, and allusions in the poetry (see Chapters Six and Seven). A selective bibliography follows this appendix.

Collecting Evidence and Taking Notes

Preliminary work in preparing the research essay will involve the same basics for writing outlined above: asking questions, forming a thesis, collecting evi-

443

The Research Essay

dence, and verifying conclusions. For the research essay, you will be spending time *collecting evidence* through research in areas suggested by your topic. This will include taking notes from the sources you consult and preparing a bibliography of these sources.

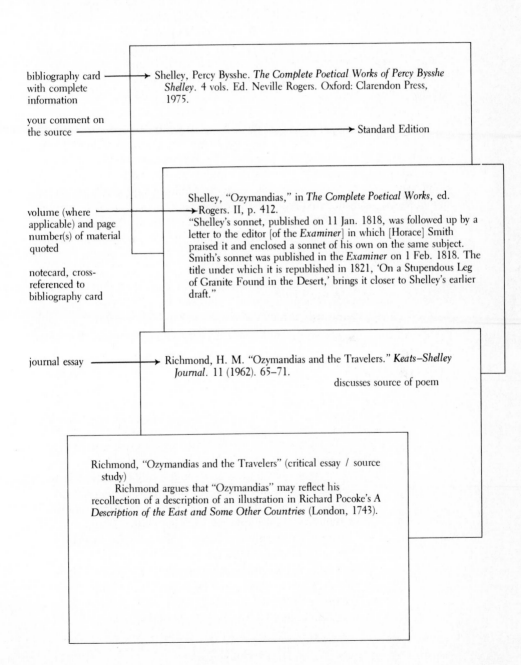

bibliography card with complete information → Shelley, Percy Bysshe. *The Complete Poetical Works of Percy Bysshe Shelley*. 4 vols. Ed. Neville Rogers. Oxford: Clarendon Press, 1975.

your comment on the source → Standard Edition

volume (where applicable) and page number(s) of material quoted

notecard, cross-referenced to bibliography card

Shelley, "Ozymandias," in *The Complete Poetical Works*, ed. →Rogers. II, p. 412.
"Shelley's sonnet, published on 11 Jan. 1818, was followed up by a letter to the editor [of the *Examiner*] in which [Horace] Smith praised it and enclosed a sonnet of his own on the same subject. Smith's sonnet was published in the *Examiner* on 1 Feb. 1818. The title under which it is republished in 1821, 'On a Stupendous Leg of Granite Found in the Desert,' brings it closer to Shelley's earlier draft."

journal essay → Richmond, H. M. "Ozymandias and the Travelers." *Keats–Shelley Journal*. 11 (1962). 65–71.

discusses source of poem

Richmond, "Ozymandias and the Travelers" (critical essay / source study)
    Richmond argues that "Ozymandias" may reflect his recollection of a description of an illustration in Richard Pocoke's *A Description of the East and Some Other Countries* (London, 1743).

Suppose, for example, after reading Shelley's "Ozymandias" and Horace Smith's lesser-known companion poem (p. 376), certain questions occur to you: Why did Shelley and his friend write those poems at that particular time? How did the subject of Ozymandias propose itself? Is Ozymandias a real or fictional figure? Investigation will take you into the texts of the poems, into matters of biography, into details of history (both ancient and nineteenth-century), and into critical commentary on Shelley's poem.

Each researcher has an individual way of taking and organizing notes. Whatever method you use, you should keep an accurate and complete record of the source of your material. One common method is to list each source on a separate bibliography card, and each note, keyed to the bibliography card, on a separate notecard, as in the examples on page 443.

Once your note-taking is completed, you can easily arrange the notecards in the order you plan to use them in your essay. These cards and the bibliography cards are the sources of your *footnotes* or *endnotes* in the completed essay. Each note includes a superscript number at the end of the quoted or paraphrased passage, as in the sample essay that follows, and a citation of the source. Notes are numbered sequentially throughout the essay. In the sample essay the notes appear at the end, followed by the bibliography. This format is common and your instructor may ask you to use it, although bottom-of-the-page footnotes are equally correct.

The bibliography for a research essay includes, in alphabetical order, all the works cited or referred to in the notes, and other sources consulted but not quoted or paraphrased. It may be called "Bibliography," "Selected Bibliography," or "Works Consulted." Study the entries in the bibliography at the end of the following sample essay, noticing how they differ in format from the notes.

Writing "Ozymandias"

Critics have discussed whether Percy Bysshe Shelley's "Ozymandias" (published 1818) is "the finest sonnet he ever wrote: harsh, dramatic, and deeply expressive of his eternal hatred of tyranny"[1] or untypical of his poetry in being "passionless, objective and calm."[2] Some serious studies of Shelley's poetry even ignore the poem entirely or mention it only in passing as they discuss Shelley's longer and more ambitious poems. Whatever conclusions a reader comes to about the merits of the poem, a look at how "Ozymandias" came to be written not only gives a glimpse of Shelley's world in 1817, but illustrates the argument that he would make four years later in his "A

superscript numbers refer to endnotes following essay

thesis

Defence of Poetry" that a poem "is the great instrument of moral good."[3] "Ozymandias" shows how Shelley took what he described in the "Defence" as "a catalogue of detached facts" and made those facts into a poem that teaches a lesson about human nature.[4]

general historical/personal context in which poem was written

In 1817, Shelley was about to leave England, never to return. George III, who had reigned during the American Revolution, was still king of England, but what we think of as the modern world was coming into existence. The first locomotive, capable of speeds up to six miles an hour, had been constructed three years before; political as well as technological reform was in the air. Shelley had spent part of the year in writing political pamphlets urging greater freedom from the tyranny of individuals and institutions. In "A Proposal for Putting Reform to the Vote Throughout the Kingdom," he advocated a way to find out if the people of England wanted reform in Parliament, and in "An Address to the People on the Death of the Princess Charlotte," Shelley regretted the unexpected death of the young princess, but described the execution of three weavers on November 7, 1817, as an even greater tragedy—the death of liberty in England.[5] Mary Wollstonecraft Godwin Shelley, the poet's wife, was about to publish one of the first and most famous science-fiction novels, *Frankenstein, or the Modern Prometheus*, a look into the future at the consequences of man's technological and scientific pride and his tyranny over another; Shelley himself was looking at various fragments of facts from the past that also served as lessons about individual pride and the arrogance of tyranny.

specific context

One of the bits and pieces from which Shelley made his poem "Ozymandias" was talk about antiquities—about ancient wonders and the observations of travelers. This discussion was carried on in the public press as well as in Shelley's own circle of friends. Just the year before, the British Museum had acquired the fragments from the Greek Parthenon, now called the Elgin Marbles after the English diplomat Thomas Bruce, Earl Elgin, who had recovered (or purloined) these fragments from Greece. It was these monumental fragments that had prompted John Keats to write "On Seeing the Elgin Marbles for the First Time."

Just after "Ozymandias" was written, Shelley's mind

was still on the past and what it might teach. Early in
1818, Keats, Leigh Hunt—Shelley's friend who would be
present at his cremation after Shelley drowned in Italy—
and Shelley took part in a competition to see who could
write the best poem on one symbol of the enduring past,
the Nile. Shelley's effort, one critic has said, "betray[s]
embarrassment."[6] Yet, like the poem on the statue of
Ozymandias, the theme of his poem on the Nile is clear:
mankind's claim to power and knowledge is at the mercy
of the greater forces of nature and time:

Sonnet: To the Nile

Month after month the gathered rains descend
  Drenching yon secret Aethiopian dells;
  And from the desert's ice-girt pinnacles,
  Where Frost and Heat in strange embraces blend
On Atlas, fields of moist snow half depend;
  Girt there with blasts and meteors, Tempest dwells
  By Nile's aerial urn, with rapid spells
  Urging those waters to their mighty end.
O'er Egypt's land of Memory floods are level,
  And they are thine, O Nile!— and well thou knowest
  That soul-sustaining airs and blasts of evil,
And fruits and poisons, spring where'er thou flowest.
  Beware, O Man! for knowledge must to thee
  Like the great flood to Egypt ever be.[7]

During the previous year, interest in antiquities had
been stimulated (if it needed any stimulation in Shelley's
group of friends) by some new acquisitions by the British
Museum. In late 1817, the Museum acquired Egyptian

statuary and fragments, including the Rosetta Stone—
which would provide the key to Egyptian hieroglyphics—
and a huge statue of Ramses II, one of the greatest of all
the Egyptian pharaohs.[8] Of Ramses II, a modern
historian has said:

An egoist and a monomaniac, this pharaoh was so
fond of building that almost half the ruins found in Egypt
today originated in his reign. . . . He built himself
a vast funerary temple, known as the Ramaseum,
and erected colossal statues of himself all over the

country . . . [but] a mere hundred years after his death his name was anathema, and his dynasty died out on the demise of his successor.[9]

The inscription on one of those statutes that Ramses II erected to himself had been translated by a Greek traveler who turned Ramses' Egyptian name—*User-ma-Ra*—into Osymandyas.[10]

Shelley and his friend Horace Smith apparently visited the exhibition of Eygptian statuary at the British Museum and were reading a historical account of Ramses in the writings of the Greek historian Diodorus Siculus.[11] Both Shelley and Smith wrote poems on the inscription and the statue, and their interest, particularly Shelley's, may have been further "primed by contemporary enthusiasm for ruins and for engravings of them."[12] H. M. Richmond, in his article "Ozymandias and the Travelers" claims that Shelley's sonnet reflects the poet's recollection of a description and illustration in Richard Pocoke's A *Description of the East and Some Other Countries*, published in 1743.[13]

A draft of Shelley's poem begins,

> There stands by Nile a single pedestal,
> On which two trunkless legs of crumbling stone
> Quiver through sultry mist; beneath the sand
> Half sunk a shattered visage lies, whose frown
> And wrinkled lips impatient of command
> Betray some sculptor's art whose[14]

Shelley scrapped that draft and began again. Both Smith and Shelley's final versions incorporated the inscription on the statue as reported by Diodorus Siculus:

> King of Kings Osymandyas I am. If any want to know how great I am and where I lie, let them outdo my deeds if they can.[15]

Both Shelley and Smith give the lines an ironic twist. The greatness claimed by the inscription, the powerfulness and tyranny implied, is commented on by the destruction that time and nature have produced on the statue. Smith's lines read:

> "I am great Ozymandias," saith the stone,
> The King of kings; this mighty city shows
> The wonder of my hand." The city's gone!
> Naught but the leg remaining to disclose
> The sight of that forgotten Babylon.[16]

Shelley's more famous lines are:

> "My name is Ozymandias, King of Kings.
> Look on my Works, ye Mighty, and despair!"
> Nothing beside remains. Round the decay
> Of that colossal Wreck, boundless and bare
> The lone and level sands stretch far away.

The quotation from Diodorus in Shelley's "Ozymandias" is, according to one of Shelley's biographers, "a sign of Shelley's growing interest in things Greek, which emerges more clearly in *Prince Athanase*, a poem begun in December, 1817."[17]

restatement of thesis with re-emphasis

Just as certainly, "Ozymandias" reveals Shelley's ability to bring together a variety of information in order to write a poem that exemplifies a moral truth. Details drawn from "a Pharaoh, a committee of historians and explorers, and . . . Horace Smith" helped Shelley write the poem.[18] In writing "Ozymandias," however, Shelley welded those facts into a sonnet expressing his statement in "A Defence of Poetry" that "the abolition of personal slavery is the basis of the highest political hope that it can enter into the mind of man to conceive."[19] The poem about the destruction of the emblem of the power and tyranny of Ramses II—Ozymandias—is just one of Shelley's expressions of that highest political hope.

Notes

[1] Richard Holmes, *Shelley: The Pursuit* (New York: E. P. Dutton, & Co., Inc., 1975), p. 410.

[2] Desmond King-Hele, *Shelley: His Thought and Work*, 2nd edition (Madison, N.J.: Fairleigh Dickinson Press, 1971), p. 94.

[3] Percy Bysshe Shelley, "A Defence of Poetry" in *Shelley's Critical Prose*, ed. Bruce R. McElderry, Jr., (Lincoln: University of Nebraska Press, 1967), p. 13.

explanatory
footnote

[4] In "A Defence of Poetry," Shelley argues that "A poem is the image of life expressed in its eternal truth. There is this difference between a story and a poem, that a story is a catalogue of detached facts, which have no other bond of connexion than time, place, circumstance, cause and effect; the other [the poem] is the creation of actions according to the unchangeable form of human nature, as existing in the mind of the Creator, which is itself the image of all other minds" p. 10.

[5] William Bradley Otis and Morris H. Needleman, A *Survey-History of English Literature* (New York: Barnes & Noble, Inc., 1938), p. 475.

citation of work
referred to in   ⟶   [6] Holmes, p. 410.
earlier note

[7] The text of "Sonnet: To the Nile" is from *The Complete Poetical Works of Percy Bysshe Shelley*, ed. George E. Woodberry (Boston: Houghton Mifflin Company, 1901), p. 67.

[8] Holmes, p. 410.

[9] Ivar Lissner, *The Living Past*, trans. J. Maxwell Brownjohn (New York: G. P. Putnam's Sons, 1957), p. 67.

[10] Guy Davenport, "Ozymandias," in his *The Geography of the Imagination* (San Francisco: North Point Press, 1981), p. 279.

[11] Percy Bysshe Shelley, *The Complete Poetical Works of Percy Bysshe Shelley*, ed. Neville Rogers (Oxford:

same source and
page number as   ⟶   Clarendon Press, 1975), II, 412.
previous note   [12] Rogers, II, 412.

[13] H. M. Richmond, "Ozymandias and the Travelers," *Keats–Shelley Journal*, 11, (1972), 65–71.

[14] *The Complete Poetical Works of Percy Bysshe Shelley*, ed. Neville Rogers, II, 320.

[15] Davenport, p. 280. Rogers, in his edition of *The Complete Poetical Works of Percy Bysshe Shelley*, provides the Greek inscription quoted by Diodorus Siculus, II, 412.

[16] Davenport provides the complete text of Smith's poem, p. 280. In annotating Shelley's "Ozymandias," Neville Rogers comments that "Shelley's sonnet, published on 11 Jan. 1818, was followed up by a letter to the editor [of the *Examiner*] in which Smith praised it and enclosed a sonnet of his own on the same subject." *The Complete Poetical Works of Percy Bysshe Shelley*, II, 412.

[17] King-Hele, p. 94.

[18] Davenport, p. 281.

[19] Shelley, "A Defence of Poetry," p. 22.

Bibliography

Abrams, M. H., Gen. ed. *The Norton Anthology of English Literature*. Third Edition. Vol II. New York: W. W. Norton, 1962.

Davenport, Guy. "Ozymandias," In *The Geography of the Imagination*. San Francisco: North Point Press, 1981. 278–281.

Holmes, Richard. *Shelley: The Pursuit*. New York: E. P. Dutton, 1975.

King-Hele, Desmond. *Shelley: His Thought and Work*. 2nd ed. Teaneck, Rutherford, Madison, New Jersey: Fairleigh Dickinson Press, 1971.

Lissner, Ivar. *The Living Past*. Translated by J. Maxwell Brownjohn. New York: G. P. Putnam's Sons, 1957.

Otis, William Bradley and Morris H. Needleman. *A Survey-History of English Literature*. New York: Barnes & Noble, 1938.

Richmond. H. M. "Ozymandias and the Travelers." *Keats–Shelley Journal*, 11, (1962), 65–71.

Shelley, Mary Wollstonecraft. *Frankenstein, or the Modern Prometheus* (*the 1818 Text*). Ed. James Rieger. Indianapolis: Bobbs Merrill, 1974.

Shelley, Percy Bysshe, *The Complete Poetical Works of Percy Bysshe Shelley*. Ed. George E. Woodberry. Boston: Houghton Mifflin 1901.

———. *The Complete Poetical Works of Percy Bysshe Shelley*. 4 vols. Ed. Neville Rogers. Oxford: Clarendon Press, 1975.

———. *Shelley's Critical Prose*. Ed. Bruce R. Mc-Elderry, Jr. Lincoln, Nebraska: University of Nebraska Press, 1967.

works used but not quoted in essay

a line indicates the same author as the preceding entry.

GLOSSARY

The page number(s) following each entry refer to its discussion in the text, which is often fuller than that given here.

accentual meter A kind of meter where the rhythm is determined by recurring accents or stresses. 222

alexandrine A six-foot iambic line; an iambic hexameter. 232, 260

allegory A poem or other literary work in which the characters, events, and settings represent something else; the parables of the New Testament are allegories; examples in this book include Christina Rossetti's "Up-Hill."49

alliteration The repetition of the beginning sounds of words and syllables: "*The decent docent doesn't doze.*" 216

allusion A reference to biblical, literary, historical, or mythological events or persons. 41

amphibrach, amphibrachic foot A three-syllable foot with the stress on the middle syllable: *bǎllóoniňg, mǔséuǐn.* 221

amphimacer, amphimacric foot A three-syllable foot with stresses on the first and last syllables: *Húrrў hóme!* 221

anapest, anapestic foot A three-syllable foot with the stress coming on the last syllable: *cǎvǎliér.* 221

apostrophe Words spoken to an absent person or to an inanimate object. 106

assonance Syllables that are alike in their vowel sounds: *dEcEnt/ tEAchEs.* 219

ballad stanza A quatrain rhyming *abcb*. Usually the unrhymed lines are tetrameters and the rhymed lines trimeters. 257

blank verse Unrhymed iambic pentameter. 269

caesura A break or pause within a line of poetry. 218

carpe diem Latin for "seize the day"; a *carpe diem* poem or theme invites the person to whom it is addressed to act now while youth or opportunity lasts. Examples in this book include Andrew Marvell's "To His Coy Mistress" and Robert Herrick's "To the Virgins, to Make Much of Time." 84, 285

Chaucerian stanza See *rhyme royal*.

chorus A repeated line or group of lines in a song (in a poem, the chorus is called a *refrain*). 274

clerihew A humorous poem composed of two irregular couplets making some comment about the biography of a famous person. 262

conceit An elaborate or unusual metaphor; two of the most famous conceits are John Donne's comparisons of lovers to beaten gold and drafting compasses in "A Valediction: Forbidding Mourning." 290

concrete poem A kind of shaped poem that approaches graphic art in the pictorial representation of meaning. 249

confessional poetry Poems that candidly reveal a great deal about their authors. 54

consonance Syllables that are alike except for their vowel sounds: *pick/peck, doze/does*. 219

couplet A pair of lines that rhyme. 251

created symbol A symbol without traditional associations; one created by the poet for a specific context. Two examples in this book are Blake's "Tyger" and the rook in Coleridge's "This Lime-Tree Bower My Prison." Contrast *traditional symbol*. 26

dactyl, dactylic foot A three-syllable foot with the stress coming on the first syllable: *ágĕnčy*. 221

diction Vocabulary and choice of words. 67

didactic poetry Poetry that teaches. Alexander Pope's "An Essay on Criticism" is an example. 230, 251

dimeter A line with two metrical feet. 222, 240, 251

double dactyl A poem in two quatrains. All lines except the fourth and last (two syllables shorter than the others) are composed of two dactyls. The first is a nonsense line, the second a double-dactyl name (*Lúdwĭg văn Beéthŏvĕn, Beńjămiň Haŕrĭsŏn*). Only the fourth and last lines need rhyme. There must be a single-word double dactyl (*ĭdĭŏsýncřašy*) somewhere. 263

double rhyme A rhyme that includes two syllables: *turtle/fertile*. See *feminine rhyme*, 237.

dramatic monologue A poem spoken by a single fictional *persona*, revealing character or a special view of experience. 48

elegy Usually, a poem written to commemorate someone who is dead, though the term often includes other serious or meditative poems. 118

ellipsis Words that have been left out. 40

end rhyme Rhyme words that occur at the ends of lines. 233

end stopped line A line in which both the grammatical unit and the sense close at the end of the line. Contrast *enjambment*. 252

English sonnet A fourteen-line poem in iambic pentameter, having the rhyme scheme *ababcdcdefefgg*. Also called the Shakespearean sonnet, because it was used (though not invented) by Shakespeare. 266

enjambment In enjambed or run-on lines, the grammatical unit and the sense do not stop at the end of the line, but continue into the next line. 229, 252

epic A long narrative poem describing heroic actions and characters. 98

epigram A brief, witty poem, often using satire. An example in this book is Alexander Pope's couplet "Engraved on the Collar of a Dog Which I Gave to His Royal Highness." 234

epigraph A quotation at the beginning of a poem or other work that relates in some way to its subject. 9

eye rhyme A kind of near rhyme where words look as if they ought to rhyme but do not: *laughter/daughter; care/are.* 238

feminine rhyme Rhymes of more than one syllable. Only the first rhyming syllable is stressed: *turtle/fertile; intellectual/henpecked you all.* 237

figurative language Language in which *images* and comparisons such as *metaphor* and *simile* are frequent. 11

fixed form An arrangement of lines by meter or rhyme fixed by tradition, such as the sonnet, limerick, villanelle, and so on. 251

folk ballads Anonymous songs passed on by word of mouth. Folk ballads are composed in ballad-stanza form and are sometimes as old as the thirteenth century. 258

foot A repeating unit of stressed and unstressed syllables in a line of poetry. 219

form The arrangement or groupings of a poem's lines. 247

found poem An unintentional or accidental poem discovered in a non-poetic context, such as the directions on a child's toy (see Donald Justice's "Order in the Streets") or a textbook or conversation (see Exercise E, Chapter One). 5, 17

free verse Verse without regular accentual or syllabic meter, but often with other kinds of rhythms, such as those of repeated word, phrase, or sentence patterns or some other auditory or visual cadence. 225

haiku A three-line poem in syllabic meter, of Japanese invention, containing five, seven, and five syllables respectively in its three lines. 223

heptameter A line with seven metrical feet. 222

heroic couplets Iambic pentameter couplets are sometimes called heroic couplets because of their use for heroic or epic subjects during the seventeenth and eighteenth centuries. 251

hexameter A line with six metrical feet. When the meter is iambic, such a line is also called an alexandrine. 222, 232

hypermetric Describes a metrical line that contains more syllables than a line of that type ordinarily would; for example, an iambic pentameter line with eleven instead of ten syllables.

iamb, iambic foot A two-syllable foot consisting of an unstressed syllable followed by a stressed syllable: *ăwàit.* 220

image A word picture. 41

In Memoriam Stanza Quatrains rhyming *abba, cddc, effe,* and so on. Alfred, Lord Tennyson used this stanza form in his long poem *In Memoriam A. H. H.* (1850), commemorating the death of his friend Arthur Henry Hallam. 256

internal rhyme Rhyme words occurring within a line instead of at the end of subsequent lines. 233

irony of situation A difference between what might be expected and what actually occurs in a situation. See also *verbal irony.* 39

Italian sonnet A fourteen-line poem in iambic pentameter, having the rhyme scheme *abbaabba* in the first eight lines and any one of a variety of rhyme schemes in the last six lines. Introduced into English poetry in the sixteenth century, the form was modeled on poems by the Italian poet Petrarch; it is also called the Petrarchan sonnet. 263

limerick A five-line comic poem in anapestic trimeter and dimeter, rhyming *aabba.* 261

literal language Language in which words are taken to be exactly what they mean. See *figurative language.* 11

lyric A poem expressing personal emotion rather than telling a story or narrative. 133

masculine rhyme Single-syllable rhymes that always occur on a final stressed syllable: *ate/straight/debate.* 237

metaphor The comparison of two things without the use of *like* or *as.* 9

meter A regularly occurring pattern of stressed and unstressed syllables. A full description of meter gives both the kind of rhythm or poetic foot and the number of such feet in a line. 219

metonymy The representation of something by one of its parts ("Give us a hand!") or by something closely associated with it ("The Pentagon announced today . . ."). 22

mnemonic device A device that assists the memory, as in the rhyme "Thirty Days Hath September," which helps many to recall the number of days in each month. 234

monometer A line with one metrical foot. 222

near rhyme Word endings that are similar, but not quite identical in sound: *speak/take.* Also called *slant rhyme.* 238

occasional poem Any poem, light or serious, profound or silly, written in response to a single event. 156

octameter A line with eight metrical feet. 251

octave The first eight lines of a sonnet. 264

ode A long, usually serious, poem with an involved stanzaic pattern, though without any conventionally fixed form. 88

onomatopoeia The use of words whose sounds imitate what they describe: *Bang! Pop!* 229

open form An arrangement of lines in a poem that is not fixed by tradition. Contrast *fixed form.* 282

ottava rima An eight-line stanza rhyming *ababacbcc.* 261

paradox A statement or idea that is seemingly self-contradictory, yet true. 64

paraphrase A restatement of lines of poetry in different words. 79

parody A humorous imitation. An example in this book is Howard Moss's parody of Shakespeare's "Shall I Compare Thee to a Summer's Day?" 192

pastoral A poem which uses the persona of a rustic or country person, usually with shepherds or shepherdesses as characters and an idyllic rural landscape as setting. 133, 262

pentameter A line with five metrical feet. 222, 240, 251

periphrasis The use of a longer word or phrase in place of a shorter or plainer expression. 147

persona A fictional speaker; literally, a mask. 42

personification The treatment of an inanimate object or an abstract concept as if it were a living thing. 22

Petrarchan sonnet See *Italian sonnet.*

prose poem A poem printed as a prose paragraph with line lengths determined only by the number of letters and spaces rather than by the number of stresses or syllables. An example in this book is James Schuyler's "Milk." 321

pun A play on words; two or more meanings of a word used at the same time. 39

pyrrhic, pyrrhic foot A two-syllable foot, never occurring by itself, consisting of two unstressed syllables. The third foot in the following line is a pyrrhic: "Clóse bŏ|sŏm-friénd| ŏf the| mătúr|ĭng sún." 220

quatrain A group of four lines, usually rhymed. 256

refrain A repeated line or group of lines in a poem (in songs, called a *chorus*). 274

Renaissance A period of great artistic and literary development that began in Italy about 1450 and spread to northern Europe and England during the following century. 137

rhymes Words or syllables that are alike except for their beginning sounds: *doze/toes, does/was.* 219

rhyme royal Also called the Chaucerian stanza, a seven-line stanza rhyming *ababbcc.* 260

rhyme scheme The pattern of rhymes in a poem, indicated, for illustration, by small italic letters: *abab.* 235.

Romantic poets In England, English poets writing at the beginning of the nineteenth century, including Wordsworth, Coleridge, Byron, Keats, and Shelley. 107

run-on See *enjambment.*

satire Poetry or prose that ridicules foolish or vicious behavior. Alexander Pope's long poem "The Rape of the Lock" is a good example.

scan, scansion To scan a poem is to determine its metrical pattern. The scansion includes the rhythm or type of poetic foot, the number of feet per line, and the rhyme scheme of the poem. 239

sestet The last six lines of a sonnet; also, any six-line stanza. 264

sestina An unrhymed poem of six six-line stanzas, followed by a concluding three-line stanza or envoy. The last word in each line of the first stanza is repeated in subsequent stanzas in a complicated pattern. An example in this book is Donald Justice's "Sestina on Six Words of Weldon Kees." 403, 413

Shakespearean sonnet See *English sonnet.*

shaped poem A poem whose pattern of lines pictures what the lines describe. 248

simile A comparison using *like* or *as.* 11

slant rhyme See *near rhyme.*

soliloquy A speech of an actor talking as if to himself but so the audience can hear. 56

sonnet A fourteen-line poem in iambic pentameter. 236, 263

sonnet sequence A series of sonnets on similar themes and sometimes addressed to the same person. 266

Spenserian sonnet A fourteen-line poem in iambic pentameter with the rhyme scheme *ababbcbccdcdee,* invented by Edmund Spenser. 268

Spenserian stanza A nine-line stanza rhyming *ababbcbcc.* The last line is an alexandrine. 260

spondee, spondaic foot A two-syllable foot consisting of two stressed syllables: *Loók oút!* 220

stanza A group of lines forming one unit or division of a poem. 9

stream of consciousness A train of associations in the mind of a speaker or thinker. 80

stresses Syllables that get more time and breath force spent on them than other syllables. 219

structure The organization of the units of a poem; what connects or relates each part to every other part. 234

syllabic meter A kind of meter where rhythm is determined by the number of syllables in a line rather than the number of accents or stresses. 223

symbol A word or image that is meant literally but that also stands for something else, as the Cross symbolizes Christianity and the Star of David symbolizes Judaism. 25

syntax The arrangement of words within sentences. 40

tercet A three-line stanza. When all three lines have the same rhyme, the stanza is called a *triplet.* 252, 253

terza rima Groups of tercets rhyming *aba bcb cdc ded,* and so on. The central line in each tercet supplies the outer rhyme for the next group of three lines. 253

tetrameter A line with four metrical feet. 222, 240, 251

theme The thesis, major idea, or central point of a poem or other piece of writing. 246

tone The poet's or speaker's attitude (sarcastic, innocent, playful, etc.) as revealed in speech by intonation and pitch, in poems by choice of words. 49

traditional symbol A symbol whose associations are public and based on historical, literary, or other traditional references, such as the biblical phrases that associate the innocent with *lambs* who are tended by a *Good Shepherd*. Contrast *created symbol*. 25

trimeter A line with three metrical feet. 222, 240

triplet A three-line stanza with the same rhymes in all three lines, 252, 253

triple rhyme Feminine rhyme that involves three syllables: intel*lectual*/hen*pecked you all*; *tenderly*/*slenderly*. 237

trochee, trochaic foot A two-syllable foot consisting of a stressed syllable followed by an unstressed syllable: *seăsŏn*. 220

verbal irony Words that convey a meaning opposite to their literal sense. See also *irony of situation*. 75

villanelle A French verse form using a recurring rhyme scheme in tercets and the repetition of whole lines; Dylan Thomas's "Do Not Go Gentle into That Good Night" is an example in this book. 259

SELECTED BIBLIOGRAPHY

REFERENCE

Abrams, M. H. *A Glossary of Literary Terms*. 4th ed. New York: Holt, Rinehart & Winston, 1981.

Altieri, Charles F. *Modern Poetry: A Bibliography* [Goldentree Bibliography Series]. Arlington Heights, Ill.: Harlan Davidson, 1981.

Brewer's Dictionary of Phrase and Fable. Centenary Edition. Rev. Ivor H. Evans. New York: Harper & Row, 1970.

Bush, Douglas. *English Poetry: The Main Currents from Chaucer to the Present*. London: Methuen, 1952; rpt. New York, Oxford University Press, 1963.

Dictionary of Literary Biography. Volume 5: *American Poets Since World War II*. 2 pts. ed. Donald J. Greiner. Detroit: Gale Research, 1980.

Graves, Robert. *The Greek Myths*. 2 vols. Baltimore: Penguin Books, 1955.

Hart, James D., ed. *Oxford Companion to American Literature*. 4th ed. New York: Oxford University Press, 1965.

Herzberg, Max J., et al. *The Reader's Encyclopedia of American Literature*. New York: Thomas Y. Crowell, 1962.

Holman, C. Hugh, ed. *A Handbook to Literature*. 4th ed. New York: Odyssey Press, 1980.

Harvey, Sir Paul, ed. *Oxford Companion to English Literature*. 4th ed. Rev. Dorothy Engle. Oxford: Clarendon Press, 1967.

Oxford Dictionary of Quotations. 3rd ed. Oxford: Oxford University Press, 1973.

Preminger, Alex, Frank J. Warnke, and O. B. Hardison, Jr. eds. *Princeton Encyclopedia of Poetry and Poetics*. Enlarged Edition. Princeton: Princeton University Press, 1974.

Rose, H. J. *A Handbook of Greek Mythology*. New York: E. P. Dutton, 1959.

Smith, William James, ed. *Granger's Index to Poetry*. 6th ed. New York: Columbia University Press, 1973 [with supplement covering 1970–1977 (1978)].

Vinson, James D., ed. *Contemporary Poets*. 3rd ed. New York: St. Martin's Press, 1980.

POETRY AND POETICS

Abrams, M. H. *The Mirror and the Lamp: Romantic Theory and the Critical Tradition.* New York: Oxford University Press, 1953.

Allen, Donald and Warren Tallman, eds. *The Poetics of the New American Poetry.* New York: Grove Press, 1973.

Berg, Stephen and Robert Mezey. *Naked Poetry: Recent American Poetry in Open Forms.* Indianapolis: Bobbs-Merrill, 1969.

————. *The New Naked Poetry: Recent American Poetry in Open Forms.* Indianapolis: Bobbs-Merrill, 1976.

Bloom, Harold. *The Anxiety of Influence: A Theory of Poetry.* New York: Oxford University Press, 1973.

Brooks, Cleanth. *The Well Wrought Urn: Studies in the Structure of Poetry.* 1947, Rev. ed. New York: Harcourt Brace Jovanovich. 1968.

Buchanan, Scott Milross. *Poetry and Mathematics. With a New Introduction.* Philadelphia: J. B. Lippincott, 1962.

Bush, Douglas. *Mythology and the Renaissance Tradition in English Poetry.* 1932. Rev. and rpt. New York: W. W. Norton, 1963.

————. *Mythology and the Romantic Tradition in English Poetry.* 1937. Rpt. New York: W. W. Norton, 1969.

————. *Science and English Poetry: A Historical Sketch 1590–1950.* New York: Oxford University Press, 1950.

Engle, Paul and Joseph Langland, eds. *Poet's Choice.* New York: Dell Publishing Co., 1962.

Fussell, Paul. *Poetic Meter & Poetic Form.* Rev. ed. New York: Random House, 1979.

Gibbens, Reginald, ed. *The Poet's Work: 29 Masters of 20th Century Poetry.* Boston: Houghton Mifflin, 1979.

Gibson, Walker. *Poems in the Making.* Boston: Houghton Mifflin, 1963.

Heaney, Seamus. *Preoccupations: Selected Prose 1968–1978.* New York: Farrar, Straus & Giroux, 1980.

Hillyer, Robert. *In Pursuit of Poetry.* New York: McGraw-Hill, 1960.

Holland, Norman N. *Poems in Persons: An Introduction to the Psychoanalysis of Literature.* New York: W. W. Norton, 1973.

Howard, Richard. *Alone with America: Essays on the Art of Poetry in the United States Since 1950.* New York: Atheneum, 1969.

Jarrell, Randall. *Poetry and the Age.* New York: Alfred A. Knopf, 1953.

Jump, John D., gen. ed. *The Critical Idiom.* London: Methuen, various dates. Titles in this series include no. 4, *The Conceit* by K. K. Ruthven; no. 8, *Metre, Rhyme and Free Verse* by G. S. Fraser; no. 16, *Symbolism* by Charles Chadwick; no. 25, *Metaphor* by Terence Hawkes; no. 26, *The Sonnet* by John Fuller.

Kehl, D. G. *Poetry and the Visual Arts.* Belmont, Cal.: Wadsworth, 1975.

Koch, Kenneth. *Rose, Where Did You Get That Red?: Teaching Great Poetry to Children.* New York: Vintage Books, 1974.

Nemerov, Howard. *Figures of Thought: Speculations on the Meaning of Poetry & Other Essays.* Boston: David R. Godine, 1978.

Selected Bibliography

Middlebrook, Diane Wood. *Worlds into Words: Understanding Modern Poems.* New York: W. W. Norton, 1978.

Pound, Ezra. *The ABC of Reading.* New York: New Directions, 1960.

Richards, I. A. *Practical Criticism: A Study of Literary Judgment.* New York: Harcourt Brace Jovanovich, 1956.

Rosenthal, M. L. *Poetry and the Common Life.* New York: Oxford University Press, 1974.

Saintsbury, George. *Historical Manual of English Prosody.* 1910; rpt. New York: Schocken Books, 1966.

Shapiro, Karl. *Prose Keys to Modern Poetry.* New York: Harper & Row, 1962.

Smith, Barbara Herrnstein. *Poetic Closure: A Study of How Poems End.* Chicago: University of Chicago Press, 1968.

Sutherland, James. *A Preface to Eighteenth-Century Poetry.* New York: Oxford University Press, 1948.

Turner, Alberta T., ed. *Fifty Contemporary Poets: The Creative Process.* New York & London: Longmans, 1977.

GENERAL BACKGROUND

Bronowski, J. *The Ascent of Man.* Boston: Little, Brown and Company, 1973.

Brooks, Cleanth and William K. Wimsatt. *Literary Criticism: A Short History.* New York: Vintage, 1957.

Buckley, J. H. *The Triumph of Time: A Study of the Victorian Concepts of Time, History, Progress, and Decadence.* Cambridge, MA: Belknap Press, 1966.

―――. *The Victorian Temper: A Study in Literary Culture.* Cambridge, MA: Harvard University Press, 1969.

Davenport, Guy. *The Geography of the Imagination.* San Francisco: North Point Press, 1981.

Eiseley, Loren. *Darwin's Century: Evolution and the Men Who Discovered It.* New York: Doubleday, 1958.

Ellman, Richard and Charles Feidelson, eds. *The Modern Tradition: Backgrounds of Modern Literature.* New York: Oxford University Press, 1965.

Fussell, Paul. *The Great War and Modern Memory.* New York and London: Oxford University Press, 1975.

Greene, Donald. *The Age of Exuberance: Backgrounds to Eighteenth-Century Literature, 1660–1785.* New York: Random House, 1970.

Houghton, W. E. *The Victorian Frame of Mind.* New Haven: Yale University Press, 1957.

Lovejoy, Arthur. *The Great Chain of Being: A Study of the History of an Idea.* Cambridge, MA: Harvard University Press, 1936.

Mulder, John R. *The Temple of the Mind: Education and Literary Taste in Seventeenth-Century England.* New York: Pegasus, 1969.

Nicolson, Marjorie Hope. *Newton Demands the Muse: Newton's "Opticks" and the Eighteenth-Century Poets*. Princeton: Princeton University Press, 1946.

Pritchard, William H. *Lives of the Modern Poets*. New York: Oxford University Press, 1980.

Thompson, William Irwin. *The Imagination of an Insurrection, Dublin, Easter, 1916: A Study of an Ideological Movement*. New York: Oxford University Press, 1967.

Tillyard, E. M. W. *The Elizabethan World Picture*. New York: Macmillan, 1944.

Willey, Basil. *The Eighteenth-Century Background: Studies on the Idea of Nature in the Thought of the Period*. New York: Columbia University Press, 1941.

————. *The Seventeenth-Century Background: Studies in the Thought of the Age in Relation to Poetry and Religion*. New York: Columbia University Press, 1942.

COPYRIGHTS AND ACKNOWLEDGMENTS

JOHN ASHBERY for "The Instruction Manual." Reprinted by permission of the author and Georges Borchardt, Inc. Copyright © 1956 by John Ashbery.

ATHENEUM PUBLISHERS, INC. for "Zenith: Walker Creek" from *A Voice in the Mountains.* Copyright © 1977 by Peter Davison (New York: Atheneum, 1977). Reprinted with the permission of Atheneum Publishers. "Zenith: Walker Creek" was first published in *The New Yorker.* For "Historical Reflections" from *Jiggery-Pokery: A Compendium of Double Dactyls,* edited by Anthony Hecht and John Hollander. Copyright © 1966 by Anthony Hecht and John Hollander (New York: Atheneum, 1966). Reprinted with the permission of Atheneum Publishers. For "Hobbes, 1651" from *Movie-Going and Other Poems.* Copyright © 1962 by John Hollander (New York: Atheneum, 1962). Reprinted with the permission of Atheneum Publishers. For "The Victor Dog" from *Braving the Elements.* Copyright © 1972 by James Merrill (New York: Atheneum, 1972). Reprinted with the permission of Atheneum Publishers. For "For the Anniversary of My Death" from *The Lice.* Copyright © 1967 by W. S. Merwin (New York: Atheneum, 1967). Reprinted with the permission of Atheneum Publishers. For "Shall I Compare Thee to a Summer's Day?" (copyright 1957 by Howard Moss) from *A Swim off the Rocks.* Copyright © 1976 by Howard Moss (New York: Atheneum, 1976). Reprinted with the permission of Atheneum Publishers. For "Keeping Things Whole" from *Reasons for Moving.* Copyright © 1968 by Mark Strand (New York: Atheneum, 1968). Reprinted with the permission of Atheneum Publishers.

ROBERT BLY for "After Drinking All Night with a Friend . . ." and for "Waking from Sleep." Reprinted from *Silence in the Snowy Fields,* Wesleyan University Press, 1962. Copyright © 1962 by Robert Bly and reprinted with his permission.

BROADSIDE/CRUMMELL PRESS for "Haiku" by Etheridge Knight. Reprinted by permission of Broadside /Crummell Press, Highland Park, Michigan.

CURTIS BROWN, LTD. for "Loose Woman" by X. J. Kennedy. Reprinted by permission of Curtis Brown, Ltd. Copyright © 1964, 1967, 1968, 1969 by X. J. Kennedy.

JONATHAN CAPE LTD. for "Naming of Parts" from *A Map of Verona* by Henry Reed. Reprinted by permission of the author and Jonathan Cape Ltd.

CHATTO AND WINDUS LTD. for "Dulce et Decorum Est" and "Futility" frm *The Collected Poems of Wilfred Owen,* edited by C. Day Lewis. Copyright © 1963 by Chatto and Windus Ltd. Reprinted by permission of The Owen Estate and Chatto and Windus Ltd. Reprinted also by permission of New Directions Publishing Corporation. For "Break of Day in the Trenches" from *Collected Poems* by Isaac Ro-

SUZANNE GROSS for "The Emerald Tree Boa"; reprinted by permission of the author.

HAMISH HAMILTON LIMITED for an excerpt from *The Reason Why* by Cecil Woodham-Smith. Reprinted by permission of The Trustees of the C. B. Woodham-Smith Settlement. Reprinted also by permission of Constable and Company Ltd., Publishers.

HARCOURT BRACE JOVANOVICH, INC. for "Plato Told." Copyright 1944 by E. E. Cummings; renewed 1972 by Nancy T. Andrews. Reprinted from *Complete Poems 1913–1962* by E. E. Cmmings by permission of Harcourt Brace Jovanovich, Inc. For "l(a." © 1958 by E. E. Cummings. Reprinted from *Complete Poems 1913–1962* by E. E. Cummings by permission of Harcourt Brace Jovanovich, Inc. For "The Greedy the People." © 1960 by E. E. Cummings. Reprinted from *Complete Poems 1913–1962* by E. E. Cummings by permission of Harcourt Brace Jovanovich, Inc. For "The Love Song of J. Alfred Prufrock" and "Journey of the Magi" from *Collected Poems 1909–1962* by T. S. Eliot, copyright 1936 by Harcourt Brace Jovanovich, Inc.; copyright © 1963, 1964 by T. S. Eliot. Reprinted by permission of Harcourt Brace Jovanovich, Inc. Reprinted also by permission of Faber and Faber Ltd. For "After the Surprising Conversions" from *Lord Weary's Castle*, copyright 1946, 1974 by Robert Lowell. Reprinted by permission of Harcourt Brace Jovanovich, Inc. For "Chicago" and "Limited" from *Chicago Poems* by Carl Sandburg, copyright 1916 by Holt, Rinehart and Winston, Inc.; copyright 1944 by Carl Sandburg. Reprinted by permission of Harcourt Brace Javanovich, Inc. For "Junk," © 1961 by Richard Wilbur. Reprinted from *Advice to a Prophet and Other Poems* by permission of Harcourt Brace Jovanovich, Inc. For "The Death of a Toad," copyright 1950, 1978 by Richard Wilbur. Reprinted from *Ceremony and Other Poems* by permission of Harcourt Brace Jovanovich, Inc. For "Love Calls Us to the Things of This World" from *Things of This World*, © 1956 by Richard Wilbur. Reprinted by permission of Harcourt Brace Jovanovich, Inc.

HARPER & ROW, PUBLISHERS, INC. for "We Real Cool" from *The World of Gwendolyn Brooks* by Gwendolyn Brooks. Copyright © 1959 by Gwendolyn Brooks. Reprinted by permission of Harper & Row, Publishers, Inc. For "Incident" from *On These I Stand* by Countee Cullen. Copyright 1925 by Harper & Row, Publishers, Inc.; renewed 1953 by Ida M. Cullen. Reprinted by permission of Harper & Row, Publishers, Inc. For "Metaphors" from *The Collected Poems* by Sylvia Plath. Copyright © 1960 by Ted Hughes. Reprinted by permission of Harper & Row, Publishers, Inc. For "Tulips" from *The Collected Poems* by Sylvia Plath. Copyright © 1962 by Ted Hughes. Originally appeared in *The New Yorker*. Reprinted by permission of Harper & Row, Publishers, Inc.

HARVARD UNIVERSITY PRESS for Robert M. Durling's translation of "Una candida cerva" from *Petrarch's Lyric Poems*, © 1976 by Robert M. Durling. Reprinted by permission of Harvard University Press.

SEAMUS HEANEY for "A Kite for Michael & Christopher." Reprinted by permission of the author.

HOLT, RINEHART AND WINSTON, PUBLISHERS for "The Golf Links Lie So Near the Mill" from *Portraits and Protests* by Sarah N. Cleghorn. All rights reserved. Reprinted by permission of Holt, Rinehart and Winston, Publishers. For "The Aim Was Song," "Desert Places," "Design," "Mending Wall," "Nothing Gold Can Stay," "The Silken Tent," "The Span of Life," "Stopping by Woods on a Snowy Evening" from *The Poetry of Robert Frost*, edited by Edward Connery Lathem. Copyright 1923, 1930, 1939, © 1969 by Holt, Rinehart and Winston. Copyright 1936, 1942, 1951, © 1958 by Robert Frost. Copyright © 1964, 1967,

McClelland and Stewart Limited, Toronto. For "Israelis" from *Collected Poems of Irving Layton* by Irving Layton. Reprinted by permission of the Canadian publishers, McClelland and Stewart Limited, Toronto.

MICHAEL McCLURE for an excerpt from "Hymn to St. Geryon, I"; reprinted by permission of the author.

MACMILLAN PUBLISHING CO., INC. for "Poetry," reprinted with permission of Macmillan Publishing Co., Inc. from *Collected Poems* by Marianne Moore. Copyright 1935 by Marianne Moore, renewed 1963 by Marianne Moore and T. S. Eliot. For "Easter 1916," reprinted with permission of Macmillan Publishing Co., Inc. from *Collected Poems* by William Butler Yeats. Reprinted also by permission of Michael and Anne Yeats and Macmillan London Limited. Copyright 1924 by Macmillan Publishing Co., Inc., renewed 1952 by Bertha Georgie Yeats. For "Leda and the Swan," reprinted with permission of Macmillan Publishing Co., Inc. from *Collected Poems* by William Butler Yeats. Reprinted also by permission of Michael and Anne Yeats and Macmillan London Limited. Copyright 1928 by Macmillan Publishing Co., Inc., renewed 1956 by Bertha Georgie Yeats. For "Sailing to Byzantium," reprinted with permission of Macmillan Publishing Co., Inc. from *Collected Poems* by William Butler Yeats. Reprinted also by permission of Michael and Anne Yeats and Macmillan London Limited. Copyright 1928 by Macmillan Publishing Co., Inc., renewed 1956 by Bertha Georgie Yeats.

THE MARVELL PRESS for "Church Going" by Philip Larkin, reprinted from *The Less Deceived* by permission of The Marvell Press, England.

NORMA MILLAY (ELLIS) for "Oh, Oh, You Will Be Sorry for That Word!" from *Collected Poems* by Edna St. Vincent Millay, Harper & Row. Copyright 1923, 1951 by Edna St. Vincent Millay and Norma Millay Ellis.

NEW DIRECTIONS PUBLISHING CORPORATION for "Marriage" from *The Happy Birthday of Death* by Gregory Corso. Copyright © 1960 by New Directions. For "Constantly Risking Absurdity" from *A Coney Island of the Mind* by Lawrence Ferlinghetti. Copyright © 1958 by Lawrence Ferlinghetti. For "Merritt Parkway" from *Jacob's Ladder* by Denise Levertov. Copyright © 1961 by Denise Levertov Goodman. For "O Taste and See" from *O Taste and See* by Denise Levertov. Copyright © 1964 by Denise Levertov Goodman. For "A Pact," "The River-Merchant's Wife: A Letter," "The Garden," "In a Station of the Metro" from *Personae* by Ezra Pound. Copyright 1926 by Ezra Pound. For "The Heavy Bear" from *Selected Poems: Summer Knowledge* by Delmore Schwartz. Copyright 1938 by New Directions. For "Some Good Things to Be Said for the Iron Age" from *Regarding Wave* by Gary Snyder. Copyright © 1970 by Gary Snyder. For "Do Not Go Gentle into That Good Night," "Fern Hill," "A Refusal to Mourn the Death, by Fire, of a Child in London" from *Poems of Dylan Thomas* by Dylan Thomas. Copyright 1945 by the Trustees for the Copyrights of Dylan Thomas, copyright 1952 by Dylan Thomas, copyright 1938 by New Directions. Reprinted also by permission of David Higham Associates Ltd. For "The Dance" from *Collected Later Poems* by William Carlos Williams. Copyright 1944, 1950 by William Carlos Williams. For "The Red Wheelbarrow," "This Is Just to Say" from *Collected Earlier Poems* by William Carlos Williams. Copyright 1938 by New Directions Publishing Corporation. All of the above reprinted by permission of New Directions Publishing Corporation.

THE NEW YORKER for "The Eel Grounds" by Aaron Fischer in The New Yorker, © 1979, reprinted by permission. For "Those Were the Days" by Philip Levine in The New Yorker, © 1981, reprinted by permission. For "A Blessing" by Mekeel McBride in The New Yorker, © 1981, reprinted by permission.

JOHN FREDERICK NIMS for "Love Poem" from *The Iron Pastoral;* reprinted by permission of the author.

W. W. NORTON & COMPANY, INC. for "Corsons Inlet," reprinted from *Collected Poems, 1951–1971,* by A. R. Ammons, by permission of W. W. Norton & Company, Inc. Copyright © 1972 by A. R. Ammons. For "October Spring," "On the Beagle," "Ten Definitions of Lifetime," reprinted from *Open Doorways* by Philip Appleman, by permission of W. W. Norton & Company, Inc. Copyright © 1976 by W. W. Norton & Company, Inc. For "Pure Memory/Chris Dewdney," reprinted from *There's a Trick with a Knife I'm Learning to Do, Poems 1963–1978* by Michael Ondaatje, by permission of W. W. Norton & Company, Inc. Reprinted also by permission of Ellen Levine Literary Agency, Inc. Copyright © 1979 by Michael Ondaatje. First published in Canada by McClelland and Stewart, Ltd. For "From a Survivor," "Living in Sin," "A Valediction Forbidding Mourning," reprinted from *Poems, Selected and New, 1950–1974* by Adrienne Rich, by permission of W. W. Norton & Company, Inc. Copyright © 1975, 1973, 1971, 1969, 1966 by W. W. Norton & Company, Inc. Copyright © 1967, 1963, 1962, 1961, 1960, 1959, 1958, 1957, 1956, 1955, 1954, 1953, 1952, 1951 by Adrienne Rich. For "Easter, 1968," reprinted from *Selected Poems of May Sarton,* edited by Serena Sue Hilsinger and Lois Brynes, by permission of W. W. Norton & Company, Inc. Copyright © 1978 by May Sarton.

HAROLD OBER ASSOCIATES INCORPORATED for "Theme for English B" by Langston Hughes. Reprinted by permission of Harold Ober Associates Incorporated. Copyright © 1949 by Langston Hughes. Renewed 1977.

OXFORD UNIVERSITY PRESS, NEW YORK for "The Groundhog" from *Collected Poems 1930–1976* by Richard Eberhart. Copyright © 1960, 1976 by Richard Eberhart. Reprinted by permission of Oxford University Press, Inc. Reprinted also by permission of Chatto and Windus Ltd.

OXFORD UNIVERSITY PRESS, OXFORD for "The Picture of J. T. in a Prospect of Stone" from *A Peopled Landscape* by Charles Tomlinson (1963). © Oxford University Press 1963. Reprinted by permission of Oxford University Press.

THE PETER PAUPER PRESS for haiku by Basho and Buson from *Japanese Haiku Series I,* translated by Peter Beilenson, © 1955–56 by The Peter Pauper Press.

RANDOM HOUSE, INC. For "In Memory of W. B. Yeats," "Moon Landing," "Musée des Beaux Arts." Copyright 1940, © 1969 and renewed 1968 by W. H. Auden. Reprinted from *W. H. Auden: Collected Poems,* edited by Edward Mendelson, by permission of Random House, Inc. For "Kent State, May 4, 1970." Copyright © 1970 by Paul Goodman. Reprinted from *Collected Poems* by Paul Goodman, edited by Taylor Stoehr, by permission of Random House, Inc. For "Little Lyric," "Could Be." Copyright 1942, 1948 by Alfred A. Knopf, Inc. and renewed 1970 by Arna Bontemps and George Houston Bass. Reprinted from *Selected Poems of Langston Hughes,* by permission of Random House, Inc. For "Why I Am Not a Painter." Copyright © 1958 by Maureen Granville-Smith, Administratrix of the Estate of Frank O'Hara. Reprinted from *The Collected Poems of Frank O'Hara,* edited by Donald Allen, by permission of Alfred A. Knopf, Inc. For "Bells for John Whiteside's Daughter." Copyright 1924, 1927 by Alfred A. Knopf, Inc. and renewed 1952, 1955 by John Crowe Ransom. Reprinted from *Selected Poems, Third Edition, Revised and Enlarged* by John Crowe Ransom, by permission of Alfred A. Knopf, Inc. For "Buick." Copyright 1941 by Karl Shapiro. Reprinted from *Collected Poems: 1940–1978* by Karl Shapiro, by permission of Random House, Inc. For "April Inventory." Copyright © 1957 by W. D. Snodgrass. Reprinted from *Heart's Needle* by W. D. Snodgrass, by permission of Random House, Inc.

INDEX
OF AUTHORS, TITLES,
AND FIRST LINES

When more than one page number follows a title, the italicized number indicates the page where the poem appears.

A

Abbey, Edward 93
About suffering they were never wrong 94
Accidental poems
    Justice, Donald, *Order in the Streets* 5
    Whewell, William, *And Hence No Force, However Great* 17
"A cold coming we had of it 140
Adam 220
A decrepit old gas man named Peter 262
After Drinking All Night with a Friend, We Go Out in a Boat at Dawn to See Who Can Write the Best Poem 324, 345
After the Surprising Conversions 60, 407
After we had burned on the water a while 170
Ah yet, when all is thought and said 207
Aim Was Song, The 388
A little lowly Hermitage it was 261
All My Pretty Ones 55

All through that Sunday afternoon 427
All Watched Over by Machines of Loving Grace 202, 204
AMMONS, A. R.
    Corsons Inlet 107
An Answer to Another Persuading a Lady to Marriage 192, 194, 197
Apology for Wolves, An 42
An axe angles 216
And hence no force, however great 17
ANONYMOUS
    Barbara Allan 258
    A decrepit old gas man named Peter 262
    "For the tenth time, dull Daphnis," said Chloe 262
    Lord Randall 353
    On the Antiquity of Microbes 220
    Western Wind 51
An unduly elected body of our elders 178
A peels an apple, while B kneels to God 281
A poor widwe somdeel stape in age 180
APPLEMAN, PHILIP
    October Spring 63
    On the Beagle 209
    Ten Definitions of Lifetime 37
April Inventory 54, 414
Are God and Nature then at strife 204
A ringing tire iron 216